D1173908

# Nonverbal Communication in Advertising

*Edited by*

## Sidney Hecker
Young and Rubicam, Inc.
New York

## David W. Stewart
University of Southern California
Los Angeles

**Lexington Books**
*D.C. Heath and Company/Lexington, Massachusetts/Toronto*

*Library of Congress Cataloging-in-Publication Data*

Nonverbal communication in advertising.

   Bibliography: p.
   1. Advertising—Psychological aspects. 2. Nonverbal communication (Psychology) I. Hecker,
Sid. II. Stewart, David W.
HF5822.N66    1988    659.1′01′9    87-17143
ISBN 0-669-14172-0

Published simultaneously in Canada
Printed in the United States of America
Casebound International Standard Book Number: 0-669-14172-0
Library of Congress Catalog Card Number: 86-45734

The paper used in this publication meets the minimum requirements of American National
Standard for Information Sciences—Permanence of Paper for Printed Library Materials,
ANSI Z39.48-1984.

88 89 90 91 92 8 7 6 5 4 3 2 1

# Contents

**Part VI Conclusion 253**

# Preface and Acknowledgments

The collection of papers in this book is the outcome of a conference on nonverbal communication in advertising held at Young and Rubicam, New York, in May of 1986. The participants in the conference represented the leaders in research on advertising, particularly the nonverbal aspects of advertising communication. The conference included both academic researchers and practitioners and researchers from the advertising industry. Thus the conference provided a unique forum for the exchange of ideas on a topic that has received far less attention than it deserves.

The conference was jointly sponsored by the Division of Consumer Psychology of the American Psychological Association, the Marketing Science Institute, and Young and Rubicam. The generous financial support of both the Marketing Science Institute and Young and Rubicam made possible a far stronger conference than would have otherwise been possible. We wish to acknowledge this support and express our gratitude to both organizations for their support. The School of Business Administration at the University of Southern California contributed resources to support the compilation and editing of this volume during the 1986–87 academic year. We gratefully acknowledge this contribution.

Many individuals contributed to the success of the conference. Most notable among these individuals were John Farley, Executive Director, and Diane Schmalensee, Director of Research Operations, at the Marketing Science Institute. Their support and encouragement made the task of putting together the conference far easier than would have otherwise been the case. Susan Gianinno, Margaret Mark, Stephanie Kugelman, Sandy Mitchell, and Howard Leonard, all of Young and Rubicam, contributed ideas that helped to make the event stimulating and informative. The logistics of the conference were deftly handled by Frank Mangini and David Berman of Young and Rubicam. Without these individuals the conference might well have been an exercise in chaos rather than a smooth flow of presentations and discussion. We would also like to acknowledge the assistance of Caroline McCarley of Lexington Books for assistance in bringing the papers together in a printed volume.

We would, of course, be remiss if we did not also thank the participants in the conference. While the names of a small number of the seventy-five participants appear on chapters within this volume, other individuals contributed to the conference and to this volume through their discussion and insights at the conference. The contributions of these individuals are reflected indirectly in the quality of the papers assembled in this volume. To all of these individuals, both those who have contributed chapters and those who have contributed in other, less formal ways, we extend our thanks.

An edited volume is the result of considerable effort by all of its contributors, but the ultimate responsibility for the quality of the publication rests with the editors. The contribution of this volume to furthering the understanding of the influence of advertising rests with the contributors. The editors assume all responsibility for errors, omissions, and problems.

# Part I
# Introduction

# 1
# Nonverbal Communication: Advertising's Forgotten Elements

*Sidney Hecker*
*David W. Stewart*

**M**uch of the extant research on advertising and its influence on consumers focuses on the verbal elements of the advertising message. Advertising professionals have long been aware that other, nonverbal elements of the message are at least as important as the verbal message, but until very recently these elements have received scant attention from advertising researchers. The decade of the 1980s has seen an important shift in advertising research, however. The dominance of verbal measures of advertising response has given way to a more balanced perspective that includes a concern for affective and behavioral responses to advertising stimuli, as well as verbal or cognitive responses. It is inevitable that such a shift in emphasis should also produce a greater interest in the nonverbal elements of the advertising stimulus.

Changes in technology are also fostering an interest in nonverbal communication. According to a recent publication of a survey research organization (*The Roper Pulse*, 1987), the current challenge for advertisers is to make their message seen in order to overcome commercial "zapping" by viewers. Visual recall is becoming increasingly important, and corporate symbols and advertising will need to be stronger and eye-catching to capture consumer attention. Nonverbal communication will not only become a means for drawing attention to a verbal message, but it will also become the message itself in many instances.

Nonverbal communication is ubiquitous. It occurs simultaneously with much of verbal communication through body language, gestures, and facial expressions. It occurs in the absence of verbal communication through symbols, social and physical cues, and the structure of the environment itself. Advertising, as well as other forms of persuasive communication ranging from political oratory to religious homilies, has made extensive use of nonverbal communication. The use of imagery, visual associations, drawings and paintings, models, visual memory devices, product and corporate symbols, and music are pervasive in advertising, and all are forms of nonverbal communication. Studies of nonverbal communication in interpersonal situations suggest that a half or more of the variability of response can be attributed to nonverbal factors (Imada and Hakal 1977, McGovern 1977, Young and Beier 1977, Edinger and Patterson 1983). The importance of nonverbal communication is obvious.

The study of nonverbal communication has a rich tradition in the social sciences. Specialized journals are devoted to consideration of the topic, including *Environmental Psychology and Nonverbal Behavior* and *The Journal of Nonverbal Behavior*. Several books have appeared in recent years that deal with the general topic of nonverbal communication. Among these are Hinde (1972), Siegman and Feldstein (1978), Rapoport (1982), Sheikh (1983), Key (1982), and Druckman, Rozelle, and Baxter (1982). Several theories of nonverbal exchange have also been proposed (see, for example, Patterson 1982, Firestone 1977, and Wiener, Devoe, Rubinow, and Geller 1972). These books and theories, while rich sources of information, tend to deal with more basic issues related to the influence of nonverbal communication without dealing with specific applications of this research. Discussions of nonverbal communication in mass media, and especially in advertising, are rare (but see Alesandrini and Sheikh [1983] for a notable exception). Nevertheless, there is a large and growing body of literature in the behavioral and social sciences that directly examines the nature and influence of nonverbal communication. This research has been carried out in such diverse disciplines as anthropology, linguistics, sociology, and social psychology. Such research offers a useful foundation for an examination of nonverbal communication in advertising.

Given the work in other fields and the strength of the influence of nonverbal communication on behavior, it is surprising that so little research has focused on this aspect of advertising. Theories of advertising are necessarily incomplete without an explicit consideration of nonverbal factors. The design of advertising research without a consideration of nonverbal variables risks confounding and loss of internal validity. Advertising creative directors and production executives grapple with the problem of making the best use of nonverbal communication. There is a clear need for a better understanding of nonverbal communication in advertising.

The collection of papers in this book represents a first attempt at a systematic examination of the nonverbal components of advertising. There are both theoretical perspectives and empirical findings among the chapters. Some authors suggest the need for radical new research paradigms for examining nonverbal communication, while others attempt to capture the effect of nonverbal elements in commmunication within more traditional information-processing models and cognitive theory. Still others suggest a need to rediscover and apply the earlier work on unconscious processes pioneered by motivation researchers in the 1950s. Regardless of the approach used, all of the authors share a view that nonverbal communication is at once important and extraordinarily complex. This complexity makes even a definition of nonverbal communication difficult. Indeed, none of the authors offers a definition, preferring instead to define by example.

Examples of nonverbal elements in advertising provide insight into the reason that a definition is difficult and illustrate the enormous range of nonverbal communications. Among the elements that are discussed by one or more of the authors are pictures and illustrations, music, symbols, gestures, "affective" stimuli, grammatical structure of the verbal message, and implied, rather than explicit, conclusions.

These elements are but a small sample of the set of factors that might have been considered. Some are closely linked to verbal communication, while others are distinctly nonverbal. All share a common characteristic, however. They are capable of influencing behavior, affect, or cognition without providing the receiver with an explicit verbal message. The information content is not contained in the meaning of a set of words. In the chapters to follow, various authors provide their own illustrations of nonverbal communication and its influence.

The book is organized into six general sections. Part I consists of the current chapter, which is designed to introduce the topic of nonverbal communication and to provide a general road map for the reader to follow. Part II contains chapters that provide overviews of the area and theoretical perspectives on nonverbal communication. Part III examines the issues associated with measuring response to nonverbal communication. Part IV considers nonverbal dimensions of language, and Part V includes chapters that examine specific nonverbal elements, including music and the use of surrealism. Following these sections of the book is a concluding chapter that attempts to bring together the common themes in all of the papers and to draw some tentative conclusions about nonverbal communication.

Part II contains five chapters. In the first of these, Julie Edell provides a useful and quite comprehensive overview of the area. In this chapter she suggests that nonverbal elements may have their impact in two different ways: (1) they may provide information, and (2) they may change the way information is processed. She then reviews various dependent measures that may be affected by nonverbal elements—attention, cognitive response, beliefs, attitudes about the product, attitudes about the advertisement, and recall. Four theoretical perspectives for explaining the impact of nonverbal communication are reviewed: (1) classical conditioning, (2) nonverbal elaboration, (3) distraction, and (4) mood induction. The chapter concludes with a discussion of the circumstances under which each of these theories may apply.

Ernest Dichter, the founder of motivation research, takes a psychoanalytic view of nonverbal communication in his chapter, which is devoted to a consideration of how to best employ nonverbal cues for influencing viewers of commercials. He concludes that the use of subconscious symbols and nearly invisible gestures works more effectively than overt cues when attempting to persuade consumers. Dr. Dichter offers a number of interesting and intriguing examples of the analysis and use of nonverbal communications based on his long career as marketing consultant and researcher.

James Shanteau introduces the literature on impression formation, which includes an explicit consideration of nonverbal information. He considers the important question of how visual and verbal information are integrated to form global judgments of preference and/or liking for an advertised product. Empirical evidence is offered that suggests that the salience of verbal information is dependent, at least in part, on pictorial information. A theoretical model of impression formation is presented in the chapter. This model, in contrast to others, suggests that a single model of information-processing applies to both semantic and imagerial information, and gives preeminence to nonverbal information in the establishment of impressions.

William Baker and Richard Lutz offer a model of advertising effectiveness, the accessibility–relevance model, that explicitly incorporates nonverbal elements of the advertising stimulus. In contrast to the impression-formation literature, the accessibility–relevance model builds on more traditional approaches to consumer information processing. The model is composed of three elements—a cognitive structure concerning the brand, attitude toward the ad, and brand name familiarity. The authors hypothesize that persuasion is a function of involvement both at the time of exposure to the ad and at the time of purchase. They further hypothesize that the process of attitude change is influenced by advertising message involvement and brand response involvement. The Availability–Valence Hypothesis is contrasted with the Elaboration Likelihood Model and the Principle of Higher-Level Dominance, which represent competing views of attitude change. The authors also offer an empirical test of the model.

Don Lowry, in "Nonverbal Communication: A New Perspective," suggests that different types of people respond differently to nonverbal communications. He offers a simple person typology and discusses the types of nonverbal stimuli most likely to influence each type of person.

The problem of measuring nonverbal responses, especially emotional responses, is considered by Morris Holbrook and Rajeev Batra, in the opening chapter of Part III. These two authors suggest that nonverbal elements elicit different kinds of responses from those elicited by verbal communications, and propose a measure, the Standardized Emotional Profile, for capturing affective responses.

The development of nonverbal dependent measures of affective response are also considered by Esther Thorson and Tom Page, who suggest that the consumer's level of product involvement interacts with the presence of stimuli that evoke affect. In contrast to Shanteau, these authors assume a dual information-processing system, one for episodic processing and one for semantic processing. They suggest that emotional responses to advertising are laid down in both systems, and consider the implications of this hypothesis for measures of attitude toward the ad, brand attitude, and intention to purchase.

The relationship between nonverbal communication and affective response is considered by Andy Mitchell. He offers an empirical study in which he attempts to disentangle the influence of mood created prior to an advertising message from mood created by the ad itself, a difficult but critical methodological problem. He considers the impact of nonverbal cues on mood induction and suggests that positive mood alters the character of information processing.

In the opening chapter of Part IV, Larry Percy suggests that there are nonverbal elements in language itself. He considers the meaning of grammatical structure and syntax, and presents the results of an empirical study that illustrates what creative directors in advertising agencies have known intuitively for some time: How you say something has an impact on the consumer that is at least as important as what is said. Active declarative statements in advertisements appear to be the easiest for consumers to process. This conclusion suggests that the structural characteristics of the language are important determinants of information processing.

Involvement is a central concern of the chapter by Alan Sawyer. The interaction of involvement and an implied but unspoken conclusion versus an explicit conclusion is reviewed in the chapter, and some empirical evidence is brought to bear on the issue. Sawyer suggests that in low-involvement situations, which are typical of much of the processing of advertising, an explicit conclusion is more effective. On the other hand, an implied but unstated conclusion appears to be more effective in producing a change of attitude in high-involvement situations.

A somewhat different perspective on the nonverbal aspects of language is provided by Verne Padgett and Tim Brock, who consider the problem of how consumers interpret unintelligible messages. It is not uncommon that consumers are exposed to messages that they do not fully understand, either because they failed to pay close attention to an advertisement or because they are unfamiliar with the words or product used in the ad. The process by which meaning is assigned to messages that are not understood, and the cues used for assigning such meaning, are the focus of the paper.

In Part V the influence of specific nonverbal stimuli is considered—music and surrealism. Music is the topic of the chapter by Patricia Stout and John Leckenby, who offer a content analysis of fifty television commercials and suggest a coding system for capturing the richness and complexity of music. Carole Macklin offers an empirical study of the influence of music in children's advertising, and uses the results to illustrate both some important generalizations about the influence of music and the problems associated with determining the impact of nonverbal stimuli. Lynn Kahle and Pamela Homer offer a social adaptation view of the use of surrealism in advertising, and suggest that the use of surrealism is particularly useful for suspending beliefs and appealing to fantasy and core values.

In the final chapter, which makes up Part VI of the book, an effort is made to draw some tentative conclusions about nonverbal communication from the chapters included in the book and other literature on the topic. The wide array of theories, perspectives, methodological approaches, and nonverbal stimuli considered by the contributing authors makes generalization difficult. Nevertheless, some common themes do appear to emerge. Perhaps more important, the diversity of the chapters in this volume suggests the need for much more research. A research agenda emerges from this collection, and that agenda is discussed in the concluding chapter. A second goal of this concluding chapter is to place the contributions in the book within the broader context of research on nonverbal communication. There are important similarities between the work presented here and work in other disciplines, such as psychology, sociology, and ethnography. It is our hope that pursuit of a research agenda on nonverbal communication in advertising might be facilitated by an introduction to this more general literature.

# Part II
# Theoretical Perspectives

# 2

# Nonverbal Effects in Ads: A Review and Synthesis

*Julie A. Edell*

There has been much discussion over the last several years concerning the impact of ads labelled as emotional, feeling, image, or noninformational advertisements. These ads share a common factor: Generally they contain numerous nonverbal elements (NVEs). NVEs of advertisements include colors, sound effects, music, and pictures. In order to understand how noninformational ads have their impact, we need to develop a better understanding of the effects of the NVEs they contain.

The purposes of this chapter are (1) to review what we have learned about the effects of NVEs in advertising, (2) to examine the various theoretical mechanisms suggested to explain these effects, and (3) to propose a framework that will predict the mechanism and outcome variables through which an NVE will have its effect. Rather than trying to support a particular mechanism of how NVEs of advertising have an effect, my goal in this chapter is to examine various mechanisms and to specify when each is most likely to operate and the differential advertising outcomes that would result.

As early as 1977, consumer researchers began publishing work that examined the role of NVEs in advertising. Since that time, numerous studies have been presented that show that the inclusion of an NVE within an ad changes the outcome of the ad. Yet, the nature of these changes and the various outcomes that are or are not affected vary greatly from study to study. Why is it that we have not been able to generalize the findings from one study to the next? Is it that different types of NVEs (music versus pictures) operate in fundamentally different ways? Is it that even a particular type of NVE (music) may vary so dramatically that no single theoretical mechanism can be expected to explain how it would operate? Let us consider music for a moment. In one experiment, the addition of music to an ad may be an unfamiliar melody played by an orchestra as background to the spoken words. In another study, the music manipulation may be the singing of a hit record; while in the third the entire audio track of the commercial is sung rather than spoken. These three manipulations of music may result in different processes being affected and therefore different outcomes.

Even a single NVE added to an ad may operate differently depending on the task that the consumer is given (or initiates). If the viewers assume a choice task is imminent, they may make inferences about what the NVE could be saying about the product. Yet, given the same ad with the same NVE in a different environment, the viewer may simply focus on the NVE and not even know what product category is being advertised. It appears that the effects of NVEs within ads are much more complex than researchers initially believed. In this complex environment, it is necessary for researchers to have a framework that articulates the critical constructs that may interact with the NVEs and specifies the theoretical mechanisms by which NVEs may have their effects.

## Theoretical Mechanisms

Almost all of the studies that have examined the impact of NVEs in ads have suggested a theoretical mechanism by which the NVEs have their effect. Several different mechanisms have been proposed in the literature, but a comprehensive comparison of these mechanisms has not yet appeared. Additionally, several mechanisms that have been used to explain other phenomena in advertising seem to be candidates for also explaining some of the findings concerning NVEs. In this section of the chapter, I will review four proposed mechanisms and the studies that have been conducted which suggest these mechanisms to explain their findings: information processing, classical conditioning, distraction, and mood induction. The next section will suggest a framework that details when each of these mechanisms would most likely be operating. The final section outlines the measures one might use to differentiate among mechanisms.

### Information Processing

The first proposed mechanism for how NVEs of ads have their effect is an information-processing mechanism. Basically, this mechanism suggests that NVEs have their effects in the same ways as verbal elements do. It is proposed that there is nothing different about the psychological mechanism by which the consumer processes an NVE. Rather, what is different about NVEs is the information they contain. Advertisers have long known that some information is communicated more effectively when it is conveyed nonverbally rather than in words (Hecker 1984; Runyon 1984). Nonverbal means are often suggested as a method for attracting a particular target audience (Fitch 1985), for communicating feelings (Zajonc 1980), for designating the source of the information, and for showing information about the brand's attributes and benefits (Runyon 1984).

A clear demonstration of how important it is to consider what information is being communicated by the NVE of an ad was provided by Mitchell and Olson (1981). In their study they designed four ads, three of which contained only a picture (a sunset, a kitten, or an abstract painting), the brand name (J, L, or R) and the product category (facial tissue). The fourth contained the line "Brand I Facial Tissues Are Soft" instead of a picture. Subjects were shown all of the ads several times (two, four, six, or eight times) and were instructed to learn the brand names. Among the dependent measures collected were belief-strength scores for fifteen attribute levels. Mitchell and Olson found that for 73 percent of the attribute-belief levels, subjects formed significantly different beliefs for each brand. For example, the brand with the ad containing the picture of the kitten was rated as being significantly higher on the very-soft attribute level than either the brand advertised with the explicit claim of softness or the brand with the ad containing the abstract painting. Subjects even inferred that the brand with the abstract painting would be more likely to come in attractive colors.

This study shows that when asked to form beliefs about a brand, subjects take whatever data they have been given and make inferences about what those data could mean for that brand. This implies that NVEs are no more alike than are sentences. We would not expect two sentences, even two sentences that were exactly the same length, to necessarily communicate the same thing. It is as unrealistic for us to expect two NVEs to have the same effect. At a minimum we must understand what the NVE can communicate about the brand before we can explore whether the mechanisms by which NVEs are processed are the same as or different from the mechanisms used to process verbal elements.

Differences in the messages communicated by NVEs are only one way that the verbal elements and NVEs of an ad may differ. Much of the current interest in NVEs was sparked by research conducted in psychology showing that pictorial stimuli frequently were remembered better than were their verbal equivalents (for example, Shepard 1967). Bower (1972) proposed three conceptual explanations for picture superiority effects in a paired associate learning context: cue redundancy, association strength, and stimulus differentiation.

The cue redundancy explanation is based on the notion that, in addition to the message, a picture contains many incidental pieces of information that can be processed, providing multiple pathways in memory for connecting the NVEs of an ad with the brand name. A second explanation for why picture pairs are more readily remembered than are word pairs is that pictures can often show the relationship between the objects. Thus the association between these objects is more meaningfully and less effortfully made, resulting in a stronger and more memorable association. The third explanation of picture superiority given by Bower (1972) was that pictorial stimuli are more distinctive. This allows the memory code for the pair of items to be more easily distinguishable from other memory codes, and thus the corresponding item is more easily recalled, given the cue. Each of these explanations is consistent with the notion that it is the properties of the NVE that vary, not the cognitive mechanism by which the NVE is processed.

Several studies have empirically tested some of these ideas in an advertising context. One of the first studies to explore the role of pictures in advertising (Lutz and Lutz 1977) used recall of the brand name with product category as a cue as its dependent measure. In this study, subjects were shown ads from the Yellow Pages, with a picture included or excluded. In one group of ads, the brand name and the product category were integrated together in a single picture (interactive imagery), while in the second group the picture showed both the brand name and the product category but they were not integrated into a single image (noninteractive imagery). Ability to recall brand names given the product category was superior for the ads containing a picture only in the interactive imagery condition. This finding supported Bower's (1972) explanation that it is the strength of association between objects that gives pictures their superior ability to be recalled.

In a follow-up study, Childers and Houston (1984) explored a number of related factors to get a much more detailed look at pictorial effects on memory. They varied (1) whether the stimulus was the brand name and product category presented verbally, or whether an interactive picture was included; (2) whether additional information about the brand was available in the ad (Superman Fence Co.) or not (Gateway Fence Co.); (3) whether the stimuli were black-and-white or color; and (4) whether subjects were instructed to focus on the ads' appearance (sensory processing) or the ads' information (semantic processing). The recall task of giving the brand name that matched each product category was administered immediately after viewing the twenty ads and again after two days. Main effects of color and information content were insignificant in both the immediate- and delayed-recall analyses, providing no support for two of the explanations given by Bower (1972). Even when the verbal conditions were enhanced by distinctive and redundant information, the ability of subjects to recall the brand name was not enhanced. Childers and Houston did find that pictorial stimuli resulted in more brand names being recalled in the immediate recall task only when sensory processing had taken place. This result provides additional support for Bower's (1972) association hypothesis and is consistent with the findings of Lutz and Lutz (1977) that it is the strength of the association between items shown pictorially that enhances their recall. However, in the delayed-recall task, pictorial stimuli were recalled at a higher rate regardless of the processing instructions. This finding suggests that the superiority of recall of pictures cannot be completely explained by informational differences. This leaves open the possibility that even recall differences between verbal elements and NVEs are partially caused by different cognitive mechanisms used in their processing.

A second area of research that is consistent with an information-processing explanation of how NVEs of ads have their effect has also been carried out. This area examines attitudes formed as a result of NVEs. Kisielius and Sternthal (1984) also tested Bower's (1972) hypothesis of cue redundancy. They suggested that pictorial elements of ads contain more cues. These additional cues then stimulate the subject to activate more stored information in memory. This results in that information becoming available to be used to evaluate the verbal elements of the ad. Additionally, Kisielius and Sternthal proposed that since the information activated from memory would be less positive than the information contained within the ads, the resulting attitude formed about the advertised brand will be less positive. To test their "availability–valence" hypothesis, Kisielius and Sternthal conducted four studies using an ad for a fictitious shampoo. The ad was fourteen pages, each page containing a verbal message and a line drawing of a person using the product. They found that verbal information alone resulted in a more positive brand attitude than (1) verbal information accompanied by a picture, (2) verbal information accompanied by instructions to image, or (3) verbal information in the presence of other information about favorable alternatives. These findings are all consistent with the availability-valence hypothesis, but since the brand-attitude measures were the only data collected, one is unable to determine whether there were other mechanisms contributing to these effects.

Further support for the cue redundancy explanation of why NVEs show different effects was provided by a study in the social cognition area. Lynn, Shavitt, and Ostrom (1985) reported a study in which they examined four competing models of the role of pictures on the organization and recall of information about an unknown person. Their study led them to conclude that pictures enhanced person memory by fostering more elaboration of stimulus information at encoding. They found that the content of the elaboration was based on material from subjects' idiosyncratic knowledge. Their data provide no insights into whether or not these idiosyncratic associations resulted in less positive evaluation of the stimulus person as predicted by Kisielius and Sternthal (1984), as only recall data were collected.

Clearly, the studies discussed above indicate that an NVE can and often does contain more and different information than do words. This additional or different information can be processed using the same mechanisms used to process verbal information. Whether or not NVEs have differential effects over and above these informationally based effects will be discussed below.

*Classical Conditioning*

Under the classical conditioning mechanism, an NVE of an ad has an effect by transferring the affect generated in response to the NVE to the brand. Thus, the NVE of the ad acts as the unconditioned stimulus (US), and the brand becomes the conditioned stimulus (CS), eventually eliciting the same response (conditioned response, CR) as the NVE. Classical conditioning has been put forth as an explanation of how NVEs in ads have their effect on brand attitudes, behavioral intentions, and choice (Gorn 1982; Mitchell and Olson 1981). The findings of these studies will be presented, and then a discussion of classical conditioning will follow.

The Mitchell and Olson (1981) study was presented above. In addition to the findings concerning beliefs, they also found that the attribute beliefs formed about brands did not explain all of the differences in brand attitudes ($A_B$), due to the different picture conditions. It was only after removing both the effect of beliefs and attitude toward the ad ($A_{Ad}$)that the main effect of picture type on $A_B$ was no longer significant. Mitchell and Olson explained these findings by suggesting that the affect associated with the picture is transferred to the ad and then to the brand.

The classical conditioning mechanism is also suggested by the evidence of a second study by Mitchell (1986). In this study, four different picture conditions (no picture, a positively evaluated picture of a sunrise, a neutrally evaluated picture of an abstract design, and a negatively evaluated picture of a wildcat) were paired with fifty words of copy for four different product categories (toothpaste, ballpoint pen, cola, and deodorant). In this study, differences in $A_B$ and $A_{Ad}$ were found for both product category and picture type, but there were no differences in the attribute beliefs that were formed within a product category due to picture type. No process-tracing methods were used in this study, so we are unable to determine if the subjects were critically evaluating the pictures within the ads or if they automatically liked (or disliked) them and therefore their $A_{Ad}$ and $A_B$ were also more positive (or negative).

Gorn (1982) conducted two studies examining the effects of music on choice. In the first study, subjects were shown a slide of either a blue pen or a beige pen. Accompanying the slide was either positively evaluated or negatively evaluated music. Seventy-nine percent of the subjects seeing the pen paired with positive music selected it, while only 30 percent of those hearing the disliked music selected the pen with which it had been paired. Gorn discusses these results from both an information-processing and a classical conditioning viewpoint and concluded that both are plausible. In the second study, Gorn examined the extent to which the findings of the first study would hold when people knew a product choice was imminent. He found that when subjects were in the decision-making condition, 71 percent chose the pen advertised with information rather than the one paired only with positively evaluated music. However, for those subjects who did not know prior to seeing the ads that they would be making a brand selection, significantly fewer (37 percent) chose the pen advertised with information. Gorn concluded that when a consumer is not in a decision-making mode, classical conditioning of affect from an NVE to the brand is a more viable explanation of the NVE effect than is information processing.

While the results of these studies are consistent with a classical conditioning explanation, they do not ensure that this mechanism is operating. Several conditions would increase the likelihood of witnessing a conditioned response. Most demonstrations of classical conditioning of affect in psychology have paired the CS and US repeatedly with the CS being presented prior to the US rather than simultaneously. Further, because conditioning is not permanent, the relationship must be reinforced at least intermittently or extinction will set in (Bierley, McSweeney, and Vannieuwkerk 1985; Edell and Burke 1984). These conditions have not existed in the current studies of nonverbal advertising. This does not mean that classical conditioning cannot be a mechanism by which affect can be transferred from the NVE to the brand. Bierley, McSweeney, and Vannieuwkerk (1985) convincingly demonstrated that classical conditioning, using music as the US, can alter preferences for arbitrary stimuli (colored geometric shapes). But, as Allen and Madden (1985) suggested in their study attempting to replicate Gorn's (1982) findings, we must investigate other mechanisms and design experiments to test among theoretical positions rather than simply assume that classical conditioning is operating.

## Distraction

Distraction has been suggested by several researchers as a theoretical mechanism by which NVEs can have their effect. A distraction explanation has often been found to be most consistent with the data, especially when the stimuli used in the study closely resembled typical advertisements.

Early work on the role of visuals in advertising was conducted by Rossiter and Percy (1978). They looked at the effects of varying the relative size of the picture and copy in print ads and the abstractness of the copy, controlling for visual-imaging ability and intelligence. They found that when the picture was dominant, subjects rated the brand more positively than when the picture was smaller, and this difference was greater when the copy was concrete. Rossiter and Percy also found that individuals who possessed high visual-imaging ability were so preoccupied with the visual elements of the ad that they paid less attention to the copy, especially when it was long, supporting a distraction hypothesis.

Edell and Staelin (1983) examined the role of pictures in print ads. In their study, the type of information (objective, subjective, or characterization) communicated by ads was crossed with the way the information was communicated (structure). The message was communicated in one of three ways: by a picture only (unframed picture), by a paragraph only (verbal), or by both the paragraph and the picture (verbally framed picture). A number of different processing and outcome measures were collected. Eye movement data showed no differences due to structure in the total amount of time spent viewing an ad nor differences in the time spent on the manipulated portion. In interpreting these results, it is important to note that subjects viewed these ads in a forced exposure setting, but that they decided how long to spend viewing each one.

A second process-tracing measure collected was a concurrent verbal protocol. These data showed differences in the number of brand-evaluative thoughts (support and counterargument) between ads with the unframed picture and ads with the verbal or verbally framed picture. Only 20 percent of the subjects seeing the unframed picture gave any brand-evaluative thought on any of the attributes they had indicated were important. This compares with 83 percent and 89 percent giving at least one brand-evaluative thought in the verbally framed picture and verbal conditions, respectively. A third measure collected which added insight into how subjects had processed the ads was the response time to true–false statements about information contained in the ad. When the subject had seen either the verbal or the verbally framed ad, he or she was able to respond to the statements more quickly than when he or she had seen the unframed pictorial version of the ad. Unaided recall of brand information was also much higher for those brands for which the subject had seen the verbal (2.95) or verbally framed picture (2.85) than the unframed picture (.93).

These data provide a fairly consistent pattern, which shows that when subjects encountered the ad containing the unframed picture, they engaged in a different task than the one they performed when seeing the verbal and verbally framed ads. Yet they spent equal amounts of time viewing each of the ads. This suggests that for the unframed pictures, subjects were distracted from their assigned task of forming brand evaluations and engaged in a different task that involved thinking more about the picture and less about how it related to the brand.

What effect did these processing differences have on attribute beliefs and $A_B$? In the Edell and Staelin (1983) study, the structure of the information interacted with the content. In the unframed picture condition, all of the types of content resulted in similar beliefs and $A_B$, since the content of the ad was not really processed. In the verbal and verbally framed conditions, objective information resulted in more positive beliefs and $A_B$ than when the information was characterization, which in turn was more positive than when the information was subjective.

A third advertising study of the effects of NVEs has findings which were explained by a distraction mechanism. Park and Young (1984) examined the effects of the presence or absence of music in television commercials and the consumers' level and type of involvement (cognitive, affective, and low). Subjects were shown an original commercial for shampoo which either contained or did not contain the music "Tide Is High" as a background. After completing the brand-attitude and ad-attitude scales, subjects were asked to write down any and all thoughts they had during the commercial and then to rate the favorableness of each thought on a seven-point scale. The time taken to complete the thought listing and rating task was also collected. Recall of the product attributes was elicited, and subjects were asked to indicate the amount of attention they had paid to the brand's functional attributes. Belief measures on each of these attributes were then collected.

The written thoughts were classified as: (1) counterarguments, (2) source derogations, (3) support arguments, (4) thoughts relevant to the process of image identification and matching, (5) low-involvement manifestation statements, and (6) others. Several different combinations of these categories were analyzed. None of these categories of cognitive responses showed significant differences due to the music manipulation. Similarly, no main effect of music was found on $A_{Ad}$ or $A_B$.

Several interesting interactions of music and structure were significant. Park and Young (1984) found that when subjects were instructed to engage in cognitive processing, the music in the ad made it more difficult to concentrate on the product information. This was reflected in a measure of attention to the performance claims and in the amount of time it took subjects to write down the same number of thoughts about the brand. Cognitive responses were highly predictive of $A_B$ for subjects in the cognitive involvement condition when the ad contained no music, but were insignificant if the commercial contained music. These data show that music interfered with subjects' motivation or ability to cognitively encode the message of the ad.

A fourth study that uses a distraction explanation for the effects of NVEs is from the social cognition literature. Chaiken and Eagly (1983) examined the interaction of communicator likability and communication modality in two experiments. Their manipulation of modality, while not intended to be an exploration of NVEs, has many parallels. In their first study, a likable or unlikable communicator delivered a message regarding a change to a trimester schedule (fees or grants). The message was delivered either in written form, orally, or via videotape. The modality factor was fully crossed with the pre-exposure manipulation of the communicator's likability. We can think of the modality manipulation as being similar to conditions where one receives the message verbally only, verbally with the speaker's voice as an additional NVE, or verbally with both the speaker's voice and physical appearance as nonverbal cues. One caution that should be noted about this analogy is that in the written condition, subjects were able to set the pace for processing the ad, while in the audio and video conditions it is set by the communicator. This difference may impact the number and type of cognitive responses elicited by the communication. Chaiken and Eagly had subjects give their agreement with the position advocated in the speech; summarize the arguments made in the speech; list their thoughts and ideas about the speaker and his speech; rate the communicator on twelve scales; and indicate how distracted they were from the content of the speech; how difficult it was to understand the speech; the relative amount of time they had spent thinking about the arguments; and how effortful and pleasant the task was.

The thoughts listed were coded as to their valence (positive, neutral, or negative) and as message-oriented or communicator-oriented. In both studies, they found that subjects seeing the videotaped message gave more communicator-oriented thoughts than those hearing the audio message, who in turn gave more than those reading the written message. There were no significant effects on the number of message-oriented thoughts. Examining the negative and positive thoughts, there were differences between studies one and two. In the second study, when subjects received the message with the nonverbal cues about the communicator present, they gave more positive thoughts when the communicator was likable and more negative thoughts when he was unlikable. In study one, only negative thoughts increased as the nonverbal communicator cues became more salient. Subjects seeing the videotaped message also reported that they felt significantly more distracted from the content of the speech and spent more time thinking about the communicator's personal characteristics than subjects in the modalities with fewer NVEs.

As in the Park and Young (1984) study, Chaiken and Eagly found differences in the predictions of agreement with the message scores across conditions. For subjects in the written condition, the only significant predictor of opinion was positive-minus-negative message-oriented thoughts. Within the video and audio conditions, the only significant predictors were communicator attractiveness and positive-minus-negative communicator-oriented thoughts.

From these four studies, several factors can be suggested that indicate when distraction may explain how NVEs of ads have their effects. In each of these studies where results consistent with a distraction explanation were obtained, subjects had been instructed to evaluate the subject of the communication. The NVEs did not have an effect in the Park and Young (1984) study when subjects were instructed to process the ad emotionally or in a very low involvement context. In the cases where pictorial information had an effect, the picture was salient either through its size or by increasing its salience with additional information. Even the music used in Park and Young's (1984) study may have been quite salient, as subjects rated it as being a piece with which they were very familiar. Hence, saliency appears to be a necessary condition for a NVE to have a distracting effect.

## Mood Induction

Only recently has a mood induction explanation been put forth in the advertising literature (Allen and Madden 1985; Gardner 1985). However, as early as 1972, mood induction was given as the explanation for why adding guitar music to sung or spoken folk-song lyrics resulted in a more positive attitude toward the position advocated in the song (Galizio and Hendrick 1972). Galizio and Hendrick measured subjects' moods and found that when the folk songs were accompanied by a guitar, the subjects felt significantly more loving, warm, kindly, satisfied, serious, sad, elated, aroused, and contented than when there was no accompaniment. The authors suggested that the musical accompaniment generated relatively greater positive affective arousal, which created compliance tendencies for the position advocated within the song.

Since this study by Galizio and Hendrick (1972), much more has been learned about the effects of moods. Research has shown that mood states exert an important influence on behavior, judgment, and recall of information. Since Gardner (1985) presented a comprehenesive review of this literature, only selected findings will be discussed here. For example, Isen, Clark, Shalker, and Karp (1978) found that inducing a good mood by giving people a gift resulted in subjects expressing greater satisfaction with products they owned. Johnson and Tversky (1983) conducted four experiments investigating the effects of mood states on people's perception of risk. They found that a negative mood increased subjects' estimates of the frequency of a negative event (for example, street crime, chronic depression, stroke) regardless of how similar the mood-induction story was to the type of event. Both a depressing story and a crime story had the same effect on estimates of the frequency of all types of negative events occurring. Likewise, a positive story decreased the estimate of twenty of the twenty-one different types of negative events occurring. Johnson and Tversky concluded that the mood induced by these brief stories had large and pervasive impacts not only on similar events, but on a wide range of unrelated events as well.

The application of these findings to explain how NVEs of ads might have an effect on brand attitudes and buying behavior seems straightforward. In many advertisements, NVEs are used to increase affective arousal or to convey feelings and emotions. If an NVE is successful in creating an affective reaction, mood, or feeling state, then this mood could influence other evaluations, including the evaluation of the information, the ad, and the brand. Mood research indicates that affective reactions influence cognitive activity and the valence of the activated thoughts. This is highly consistent with the position taken by Zajonc (1980), who stated the following:

> It is a fact, of course, that all sorts of judgments are faster and more efficient for pictures than for words, and this may be so just because pictures are able to evoke an affective reaction more directly and faster than words. An affective reaction aroused early in the encoding process—earlier than it is possible for the interoceptive and motor memories to become effective—might facilitate a complex cognitive encoding sequence by an initial categorization along affective lines, which, as we have seen, requires minimal stimulus information. Such facilitation through early affective sorting that relies not only on discriminada but preferanda as well may also induce a constructive process that can more readily recruit stored content by searching for congruent affective tags. (Pp. 168–169)

Thus, the NVEs of an ad, if they induce affective reactions, may influence what gets activated from memory, increasing the likelihood that valence-congruent thoughts are activated. For example, if a picture creates positive feelings, more positive thoughts from memory will be activated and used to process the incoming information about the brand, which could result in more positive beliefs about the brand's attributes, a more positive evaluation of the ad itself, and thus a more positive brand attitude than if the picture had not been present.

## When Will the Mechanisms Operate?

What are the important factors in determining when each of these respective mechanisms might operate? Advertising researchers have recognized that it is necessary to examine both the audience's involvement with an ad and the focus of that involvement (Gardner, Mitchell, and Russo 1985; Greenwald and Leavitt 1984; Mitchell 1983) in order to understand the persuasion process. Differences in both of these factors affect the content and organization of the memory structure for the ad and the brand. Hence these factors may be useful in structuring our thinking about when each of the theoretical mechanisms by which NVEs are hypothesized to have their effect may operate.

Additionally, it is important to consider what the NVE of the ad communicates. If the NVE is primarily an additional source of information, it may be processed quite differently than if it only arouses an affective reaction. Thus the affective/

informational nature of the NVE will also be important in understanding when the various theoretical mechanisms will operate. Focus of processing, involvement, and the affective/informational nature of the NVE will now each be considered in further detail.

## Focus of Processing

A consumer may have many different foci when processing an ad. Marketers had assumed for many years that consumers were primarily actively searching for brand-attribute information when exposed to an ad. We now realize that for some consumers, on some occasions, ads may be viewed as a source of entertainment. Alternatively, the consumer may take on the role of ad critic, evaluating not the brand but the ad itself. In this discussion, I will make a distinction only between having or not having the evaluation of the brand as the focus of processing.

Which mechanisms would require the consumer to be engaged in a brand-evaluative strategy in order to see the hypothesized effects? The distraction mechanism of how NVEs of ads operate indicates that subjects have as their goal the evaluation of the brand. However, they become distracted from this task by the salient NVE, on which they then focus their limited processing resources.

The mood-induction and information-processing mechanisms would be able to explain the effect of NVEs for both brand-evaluation and non-brand-evaluation processing foci. For example, under the mood-induction explanation, if the consumer was viewing the ad as an ad critic, then if the NVE generates a negative affective reaction, it would cause him or her to evaluate the ad more critically. Likewise, the consumer could have either a brand or nonbrand focus and the information-processing mechanism could still explain the effect of the NVEs. Imagine a situation where the consumer is evaluating the ad. The picture in the ad contains a lot of information about the brand. Upon seeing the picture, the consumer activates his or her "good ad" node in memory. One aspect of that structure is that a good ad contains much product information. Since this ad meets that criterion, it is evaluated as a good ad.

Finally, classical conditioning of affect is unlikely to occur when the brand is the focus of processing. Gorn's (1982) second study failed to show a conditioning effect when subjects were in a decision-making mode, which may be thought of as similar to a brand-processing focus.

## Audience Involvement

Audience involvement, as it has been used in the advertising literature, combines two important aspects of the persuasion process: amount of attention and level of processing (Greenwald and Leavitt 1984). Greenwald and Leavitt specify four levels of audience involvement: preattention, focal attention, comprehension, and elaboration. Preattentive analysis functions to monitor background stimulation for important events. It will not enter into the discussion of how NVEs have their effects. Under focal attention, both perceptual and semantic processing occur, and a sensory trace of the stimulus is formed in memory. Comprehension results in a propositional trace of the ad being stored in memory, usually in an unevaluated form, since the knowledge needed to evaluate the incoming information is not activated. If the fourth level, elaboration, is operating, the audience member is actively supporting or disagreeing with the information in the message. Elaboration allows the message content to be integrated with existing propositional knowledge in memory.

The level of audience involvement provides us with another factor that allows for predictions about when each of the theoretical mechanisms may be operating. Classical conditioning does not require that the subject even comprehend the content of the ad. The reaction to the US is automatic, and repeated exposure to the ad is all that is required for the affect associated with the NVE to be transferred to the brand. Consumers are less likely to attend to the ad after they have seen it repeatedly, supporting the notion that classical conditioning would most likely be operating when attention to the stimulus is focal.

When the consumer is processing an ad at less than full involvement, this increases the chance that distraction may occur. At lower attention levels (less than elaborative involvement), it may be less effortful to simply think about the NVEs in the ad than to evaluate the incoming information. This may occur when the consumer is either unable to elaborate on the content of the ad or not sufficiently motivated to put forth the effort to do so.

A mood induction would most likely occur when the consumers' involvement level is high. A mood induction effects the valence of the thoughts that get activated and are then used to elaboratively process the stimulus information. This type of processing would require an elaboration level of involvement. Similarly, with the information-processing mechanism, the subject is actively evaluating the information in the NVEs of the ad with criteria stored in memory. This requires elaboration involvement.

### Affect and Information

A third aspect that seems critical in our ability to determine the various impacts of NVEs is whether the NVE communicates information and/or causes affective responses. While certainly the stimulus itself has something to do with determining this, it is also a function of the individual. Affect and information are not end points of a continuum, but describe two types of responses a consumer may have to NVEs of ads. Consumers might have neither of these responses or both of them, and the degree to which they experience either one may vary greatly. The dichotomy used here is clearly a simplification.

Classical conditioning and mood-induction explanations both require that the recipient of the communication have an affective reaction to the NVE for the NVE to have an effect. An information-processing explanation requires that the consumer receive brand information via the NVE. The distraction mechanism of how NVEs have an effect is less clear-cut. If the consumer reacts affectively to a NVE of the ad, then he or she may begin to think of other occasions where this reaction has occurred and thus be distracted from evaluating the brand. It is also feasible that distraction could take place without the NVE eliciting an affective reaction. For example, the NVE of the ad might contain an item that reminds the consumer that his or her favorite store has that item on sale. The consumer has been distracted away from thinking about the brand being advertised and thinks instead about the item incidentally shown in the NVE, without having an affective reaction to the item.

Combining these three factors—focus of processing, audience involvement, and affective/informational content—it is possible to make some predictions as to the relative occurrence of the four theoretical mechanisms. These predictions are summarized in figure 2–1.

## Identification of the Mechanisms

It is also useful to think about how we might identify which mechanism is operating by examining multiple measures of the ads' effects. Most of the mechanisms described above hypothesize effects on some outcomes but not on others. By taking multiple measures and contrasting the effects of a verbal-only version of the message with one that adds a properly structured NVE, one may be able to verify if a particular mechanism is operating (table 2–1).

Classical conditioning requires that the NVE elicit an affective response. By comparing multiple dependent measures of the effects of a verbal-only product message to a message that adds an NVE known to elicit a particular affective

| | Nonverbal Element's Effect | |
|---|---|---|
| | Informative | Affective |
| **Non-brand focus** | | |
| Focal attention | No effect | Classical conditioning |
| Comprehension or elaboration | Information processing | Mood induction |
| **Brand focus** | | |
| Comprehension | Distraction | Distraction |
| Elaboration | Information processing | Mood induction |

**Figure 2–1. Conditions under Which Various Mechanisms Should Apply**

**Table 2-1**
**Summary of Hypotheses**
*Predicted differences in dependent variables between the verbal-only and verbal-plus-nonverbal ad conditions (effects listed for combined ad condition).*

| Mechanism | Response to NVE | Dependent Variables | | | |
| | | Brand CR | Beliefs | Recall of Brand Info | $A_B$ |
|---|---|---|---|---|---|
| Classical conditioning | affective | same | same | same | different (like the affect associated with NVE) |
| Information processing | informative | more | different (related to CR) | more, faster | different (related to differences in beliefs) |
| Distraction | affective or informative | fewer | different (related to CR) | fewer, slower | different (related to differences in beliefs) |
| Mood induction | affective | different (valenced like NVE) | different (related to CR) | same | different (related to differences in beliefs) |

response, one should be able to determine if classical conditioning can explain all of the effects or not. If only classical conditioning is operating, then one should see no difference in the number or type of cognitive responses, the beliefs formed about the brand's attributes, or the number of or speed with which items are recalled about the brand between the two forms of the ad. The brand attitudes, however, should be different, with the $A_B$ in the condition seeing the ad containing the NVE being more like the affect associated with the NVE.

Under the information-processing mechanism, an ad containing an informational NVE, when contrasted with one lacking the NVE, will show differences on many dependent measures. The ad with the NVE added should result in more cognitive responses related to the NVE. The beliefs and $A_B$ may also differ between the two ads, but the beliefs and $A_B$ should be consistent with the cognitive responses. Those seeing the ad containing the NVE should also have greater and faster recall of the information than those seeing the verbal-only information.

The distraction hypothesis also predicts many differences on these dependent measures. The NVE here could be either informational or affective. The ad containing the NVE should result in fewer cognitive responses about the attributes of the brand and brand-attribute beliefs and an $A_B$ consistent with those cognitive responses. The ability to recall information presented verbally should be less and the speed of this recall slower for the nonverbal group.

The mood-induction mechanism requires an NVE which elicits an affective response and provides no product information. The nonverbal condition should result in more cognitive responses which are valence-consistent with the affect elicited by the NVE. These differences in cognitive responses should be reflected in differences in brand-attribute beliefs and in $A_B$. Recall of ad information, however, should not vary between the two groups.

## Conclusion

In reviewing the studies that have examined the impact of NVEs in advertising situations, one is able to find evidence consistent with each of the information-processing, classical conditioning, distraction, and mood-induction explanations. In many of these studies, the researcher has selected that mechanism that best fits the results and has presented it as if it were the only way NVEs could have an effect. Yet in examining the literature and in thinking about the underlying theoretical mechanisms, it is difficult to conclude that NVEs work in only one way. This chapter has presented four ways that NVEs could have an effect, has considered how to identify that effect using multiple dependent measures, and has given the conditions under which the mechanism is most likely to be operational. There are a number of issues, however, that this chapter has not addressed:

1. There may be other mechanisms that we have not yet identified that also underlie the processing of NVEs in advertising.

2. Several different mechanisms may be operating together. For example, an NVE may contain both information and affect. It is certainly feasible that the affective elements create a mood, and that mood influences the processing of the information contained within the NVE as well as the verbal components. If this is the case, it may be very difficult to separate the effects.

3. Very little of the research on NVEs in advertising has been conducted in naturalistic viewing environments. In these environments we may see other mechanisms functioning. The attention-getting power of the ad may be the critical variable that explains much of the difference between verbal and nonverbal executions in the real world.

A goal of this chapter has been to bring together the literature on NVEs in ads and to articulate the specifics of each of the theoretical mechanisms, making it less effortful for others to critically examine the evidence and decide what are the most pressing research issues for this field. Additionally, by specifying the outcomes of each of the mechanisms over multiple measures, I hope to encourage researchers to collect the data which will give us more insights into the theoretical constructs underlying the effects of NVEs of ads.

In summary, this chapter has presented four theoretical mechanisms that are feasible explanations of how NVEs of ads may have an impact. Research that has been conducted examining the roles of NVEs has been related to each of these theoretical mechanisms. A framework was developed and presented which allows one to make predictions about the conditions under which each mechanism is likely to be operational. Finally, a methodology is presented for differentiating among the various mechanisms by examining multiple measures of both the process and outcomes of NVEs within ads.

# 3
# Testing Nonverbal Communications

*Ernest Dichter*

Nonverbal communication starts with birth. Most of us learn fairly early how to interpret and understand gestures, facial expressions, and body language. A mother gets very angry at her child but cannot really hide her amusement and smile. The baby will smile back and disarm, disbelieving the verbally expressed anger. Offer a new born baby your finger and it will grasp it.

The young priest learns to listen to confessions. His teacher is the older father-confessor. When it is over, the young priest asks how he has done. The older man tells him, "Very well, except for the fact that whenever the young lady mentioned her escapades you fell silent, and as I watched you, I saw your eyes and pupils opening wide. Luckily, the young lady could not see you, but your silence gave you away."

When the physician examines you, you listen eagerly to his words of reassurance but you also watch his face. If he frowns in a concerned fashion, the message that he conveys is in contrast to his calming words.

In selling, advertising, public and private speaking, and teaching, we use nonverbal signals almost automatically. Some of them are used as accents for verbal statements, such as a friendly smile when we extend our hand in greeting. Others are unplanned and can give us away, revealing our real feelings. Still others can be used to hide our true emotions and to cover them up with what we consider an appropriate accompaniment of nonverbal body and facial language. The communications experts pay attention to the speech, the copy, and the text of the message, but often forget the importance of the correct nonverbal communication.

Actors can learn to convey feelings. They can tell the audience they are hungry by translating this need into a language that the audience will understand. They point to their mouth, making movements with it that indicate the usual gestures accompanying eating. In almost all cultures, this form of expressing one's self will be easily understood, although no sound may have been uttered. It is a nonverbal form of communication.

The main and crucial difference between verbal and nonverbal communication is that the audible language does not need any additional form of translation if the language itself is known. In the nonverbal form, interpretation is required. The dialogue partner has to fill in the meaning of the gesture. The other person will most likely nod to indicate his understanding.

This need for interpretation is both an advantage and a delayed and most cumbersome form of contact. However, because it requires filling in and completing the meaning, it necessitates "re-creating" the original intention of the communicator. The audible or inaudible form of recognition and understanding is often a sort of "Aha, I get you," a nod, or a smile. Nonverbal communication, therefore, because of the extra effort required, becomes more memorable and more effective.

Advertisers are continually struggling to find the most effective form of communication. Yet, in too many instances, they have left out the nonverbal forms of "talking to" and influencing the consumer.

Nonverbal communication can increase or decrease the impact of advertising. With the climbing costs of any form of advertising, it has become imperative that each message does its job as well and as economically as possible.

In my own research, I have found that too many messages are losing a good part of their effectiveness, as through a sieve, due to these errors of coordination. We are told verbally how soothing and relaxing a remedy is, but the accompanying music or background resembles warring jungle tribes.

A bank commercial demonstrates to us how most customers are being squashed by a giant thumb, while trying to convince us that their bank makes their clients grow under their care. How do you tell this story nonverbally? Simple. A giant thumb first crushes the client. Then, the client is fertilized from a huge box and, to make the illustration at least agriculturally correct, he is drenched by an equally giant watering can. Now, lo and behold, he seems to be growing in size. Message: Bank with us and we make you grow. Unfortunately, our study showed that the much more dramatic crushing scene stayed in the viewers' minds. What the nonverbal message should have stressed was: Bank with us and you will grow. Paying more attention to the nonverbal part of the message is the lesson. The dramatic crushing scene was a waste of money and valuable time and left the wrong impression by conveying a negative story.

Unfortunately, most copy research concentrates on the spoken word and, at best, the accompanying music and cartoonlike illustrations.

## Unmistakable Signals

It was to be her place. They had a few drinks. She did not want to form it into words; he did not want to suggest it too boldly. She kept on talking, more-or-less accurately, about her biographical ups and downs. She accompanied her narrative, subconsciously, with a striptease concentrating on her earlobes and earrings. First the left ear and then the right one. Then, a long pause. It was an overture. A nonverbal communication which both understood. It could have been in any country and in any basic language.

"Your in-laws don't like me," explained the street vendor to the rest of the family, the moment they had moved far enough out of hearing range. His explanation was simple and irrefutable: "I watched them wipe their hands after they clasped my lonely hand with both of theirs, overflowing with warmth." Their handkerchief removed any possible remnant of misinterpreted feelings of brotherhood.

Children, and patients who are often comparable to children, trust facial statements, such as wrinkles around the mouth, wide-opened eyes, signaling fear and surprise, pleasure, or anxiety in an interchangeable form, more than the dramatically proclaimed prose of the physician.

Historians tell us that Hitler would have never come to power had we had the truth-revealing tools of nonverbal orchestration that should have gone with his monologues and mostly solo performances. In these often masterfully played one-man shows, the dialogue between the orator and the audience would have been the give-away nonverbal message.

## Imaging and Nonverbal Communication

Most market research today relies on answers to verbal questions alone. Motivational research goes deeper. It does not rely on the often erroneous self-analysis of the respondent's reasons for his actions as given by himself. Motivational research achieves this by formulating first hypotheses and avoiding direct questions. Instead the respondent is asked to tell in detail all the events that accompanied his buying or other decisions. He or she is encouraged to associate freely in a stream-of-consciousness fashion.

Motivational research is not as mysterious as it sounds. It is the same procedure most physicians use if they want to arrive at a proper diagnosis of an ailment. They do not rely on the description of the pain or the reasons given by the patient for his pains. By asking the patient to describe when he noticed the pain, what he did when it occurred, how long it lasted, and so on, the physician can deduce the possible real explanation of the disease. This is facilitated by his assumptions and hunches as to what could have caused the pain. In other words, his explanation is also based on his knowledge, previous experiences, and training. He can also prove or disprove his hunches by additional special tests and examinations. In motivational research we go deeper than verbal statements.

Most of us have images of products. These images can be described by reactions of the five senses and additional images taken from our culture. For instance, a product like coffee can be associated with warmth, intimacy, being masculine, arousing affinity with melodies, tactile experiences, and olfactory ones. In addition, it can be surrounded by images of outdoors or indoors, be related to other fertile products in our culture, such as flowers and landscapes, and also certain activities, dreams and symbols.

Brand names and logos can have masculine or feminine associations. Most of the time, those ending with an "a" or open-design soft vowels suggest femininity. The opposite is true when "o" or consonants are being used.

Even when comparing the roles that the names of countries play in history, we arrive at often far-fetched comparisons. Russia is Mother Russia. Germany is called the Fatherland. One is the mother to be protected, and the other is a stern, commanding, and demanding father.

When showing respondents different names and illustrations and asking them whether they prefer one design or name over another, we are reverting to the shallow level of confusing superficial verbal attitudes with real motivations. Thus, our nonverbal research approach asks the respondent to circumscribe the aura and flora of a psychological nature which surrounds a product or name.

## Testing Nonverbal Communication

In order to determine whether our nonverbal advertising message, packaging, or even brand logo communicates properly in addition to the verbal copy, we have to first establish a frame, an image, or a concept as it exists in the mind of the customer.

The methods which we use consist of various approaches; most of them seek to understand the total image of the product. One of these methods is psychodrama. We encourage the participant to play the role of the product. He or she is the telephone, the toaster, the glass of milk, or coffee. It is role playing, but applied to so-called lifeless products and not to people. We examined the role of motorcycles. Our assignment was to identify with a motorcycle. Very few people mentioned the noise, the feeling of mastery, and the gleeful disturbance of the bourgeois neighborhood. Instead, we were given very rational explanations: It permitted you to weave through heavy traffic, it saved gas, and so on. When we used our nonverbal approach and, for example, suggested a noiseless motorcycle, the importance of the heavy symbol of power and noise became quite clear. We also found such motivations as feeling closer to nature in contrast to the more enclosed feeling of being in a car. The more direct transmission of and connection between the body and the machine were also important. Such findings helped us in developing better marketing approaches through the use of nonverbal imagery.

Similar techniques, which we have used for a typewriter company, were involved in asking people to imagine being a typewriter or a computer keyboard. This approach revealed that many people portray themselves, when playing the keyboard, as being typed on passively rather than actively typing. The practical application resulted in the suggestion to make the shape of the keys more feminine, more receiving.

We asked people to portray a product as if they were dancers or mimes. We have done this, for example, with a telephone for AT&T, with a coffee lightener, Cremora, for Borden, and with relationships such as between mother and baby or between dog owners and dog food.

With the help of a mobile video camera, we have also studied buying behavior in stores. For instance, we found that most people judge the quality and comfort of shoes by trying them on with their hands, and the quality of soap by sliding the hand over the surface of the cake (but this is now often prevented by the packaging.)

These techniques are not as far-fetched as the more sober researcher may think. This approach provides many ways to creatively understand the image the product carries. The tests help to illustrate the experience of a product almost three-dimensionally. Tactile feelings between the material and the user can often lead to new product ideas. The whole phychology of tools in various trades can be better understood when we try to get closer to the soul of the product. For example, hammers made of aluminum, although possibly just as practical as those made of steel, suffer from a contradiction between two nonverbal concepts.

Comparable to an artist, a sculptor, a painter, or a poet, we can see whether or not the advertising message permits the re-creation of the original meaning and life of the product or service we want to sell. While our approach is new, it resembles the artistic process most artists use when they try to capture in their artwork, including even music, the "soul" of the product or situation.

We have symbols and directions in an almost atavistic fashion built in our conscious and subconscious minds. Angels float on wings and are in heaven. Devils, on the other hand, dwell in cracks and sulfur-fuming crevices in the depth of the mysterious entrails of the earth.

Warmth hovers above the cold below. In a study on kitchen appliances, we discovered a basic marketing mistake. The operating buttons for cold were placed on the top of the appliance and for hot at the bottom. Constant complaints were the result of these irrational mental associations. They did not correspond with the rational verbal instructions.

The meaning of colors and shades in relation to the product is also a significant nonverbal factor. One of our techniques, which has proven enlightening, is to ask an audience to select from colors ranging from pale to blazing red the color that goes best with their feeling about the product. We had further tried to penetrate behind the total image by offering the respondents possible insights that go beyond the obvious associations. Detergents would normally be related to cleanliness. In our case studies, consumers have attributed mysterious forces going to work and attacking the dirt inside the washing machine.

This procedure is similar to what a good cartoonist tries to convey by building into his drawings contradictory statements. Cartoonists represent a challenge to the viewer's intelligence. In a recent political cartoon, a summit meeting between Ronald Reagan and Kurt Waldheim takes place on the surface of a balloon. As the balloon deflates during the talk, Waldheim exclaims, "Will you now believe me that I never was a Nazi!", and says good-bye with a Nazi salute.

What we are measuring, therefore, is the interaction between the imaging about a product or service, its relationship to the image created by advertisements, and the suspicion of what the real story is. We help the art director and copywriter to translate our image into storyboards for television and print, as well as packaging. The art director, for example, will know that coffee is an intimate, more masculine, olfactory product, in which color plays an important role. Therefore, coffee should always be shown in intimate surroundings such as a close group gathered in the prairie. We translated the imagery for tea and found that tea was too feminine, had no odor or smoke, and was advertised almost as a medical product. In a marketing plan we composed, we deemphasized the curative powers of tea and changed its gender by associating it with macho men, athletics, and soldiers. Sales increased considerably. Marlboro cigarettes were similarly changed from feminine brands to tattooed symbols of freedom and the "roaming" Marlboro Man, to become the most universally successful cigarette brand.

In a special experiment we tried to relate abstract designs and their meaning. Some of the findings are shown in figure 3–1.

We next asked respondents to use the same approaches in arousing the aura and flora triggered by print or television advertising, as well as by the packaging, the logo of the product, and so on. By comparing the two images, we sought to determine whether or not image congruence had been achieved. We found that a soft drink arouses images of relaxation, softness, quietness, and reward. However, the present advertising, such as for Pepsi Cola, presents a shrieking, noisy, supposedly youthful scene in its commercials. The question arises whether or not the two images really relate to each other.

Our technique then is primarily nonverbal. It can be used on a one-on-one basis or in focus groups. For each one of the five senses, we provide test stimuli in various orders. For the tactile aura, we have used swatches of fabric from rough (burlap) to silk, asking respondents to select the one degree of roughness to fineness that fits their image of the product and advertising. In the olfactory group, we have used perfumes and various scents in a similar fashion.

In other techniques, we elicit answers to questions such as "What sounds, landscapes, feelings, or moods come to mind when you think of milk, bread, or a new home?" We have also tried scenes from nature to measure mood factors by asking for comparisons between a product and an ocean scene, a glacier, pastoral paintings or photographs, storms and intimate home scenes. Such scenes are easily projected via a video cassette player. We have also experimented with cartoons that have condensed the main thought behind a product and political cartoons such as the ones of the MacNeil/Lehrer Newshour by Ranan Lurie on PBS.

The image, described as the nonverbal "soul of the product or service," is analyzed by many different techniques. The effort that goes into creating an image has to be comparable to the skill utilized in translating the verbal message. Copy research thus expands into research covering the relationship between the deeper message and the meaning of the product ascertained by the nonverbal message and the verbal story transmitted to the various target groups. Nonverbal testing of communications reveals that almost any background, landscape, clothing, and music nonchalantly used in a nonverbal and symbolic form can increase or diminish advertising effectiveness. Even the visible or just suggested upward direction of the overall trend in an ad can have considerable influence. Selling an optimistic idea,

We presented respondents with ten configurations and ten words and asked them to match each word with the figure that feels most appropriate for that word.

_____prayer
_____force
_____disappointment
_____resilience
_____contentment
_____heartbreak
_____hope
_____balance
_____nevertheless
_____bitter laughter

This experiment was designed to underscore the following facts:

Meanings do not arise only from logical thought and from learned past associations. We do not relate to the world only on a logical level, nor only in terms of what we have previously learned. New and different and unusual patterns of movement, line, and form convey symbolic meanings to us which we feel emotionally.

In commercial life, in packaging and advertising for instance, the effectiveness of the presentation often depends upon the right feel of the design and pattern. This meaning that arises in emotion can reinforce or negate the verbal message.

The interesting fact is that these emotionally received meanings are not purely subjective—the same pattern tends to convey the same meaning to any viewer.

Strong confirmation of this is found in the fact that there was wide agreement among our 326 respondents in matching the words and figures presented here. Here is an exact breakdown of the most frequently chosen combinations in terms of percentages of respondents:

| Figures | Words | Percentage |
|---|---|---|
| 1 | Hope | 92% |
| 2 | Bitter Laughter | 86% |
| 3 | Force | 54% |
| 4 | Nevertheless | 48% |
| 5 | Resilience | 74% |
| 6 | Prayer | 88% |
| 7 | Disappointment | 41% |
| 8 | Heartbreak | 56% |
| 9 | Contentment | 68% |
| 10 | Balance | 46% |

**Figure 3-1. The Meaning of Meaningless Patterns**

such as cheaper prices, when the underlying sense of direction graphically expresses the opposite can rob the advertisement's subconscious message of a great deal of its power of persuasion.

## Instinctual Insights

While verbal language, with some exceptions, is basically a human skill, nonverbal expressions can also be mastered by subhuman groups. In most cases, they have a purpose anchored in biological factors. Many of the nonverbal expressions such as defense, aggression, and self-centeredness, are important in survival.

Almost any ad or commercial, packaging, or other sales medium involves messages which are understood almost instinctively by the recipient, the customer, or the buyer. Showing a man with a black eyepatch wearing a Hathaway shirt tells us, in a somewhat circuitous fashion, that this shirt would make us more outstanding, more sophisticated-looking. The idea borrows heavily from experiences starting in our childhood. Whenever we had a bandage or had to put a leg or arm in a cast, we attracted attention, usually from a loving parent. What the ad says is, "Wear our brand and you will become more distinguished."

We can add prestige to margarine by showing an imperial crown being put on top of it. Esso's tiger was developed by us as a symbol of power, more universal and direct than any reference to technical octane values. When we show a person expressing positive wonderment about the taste of a dish, we are trying to convey "good taste," or so the adman thinks.

Different products and different services require different nonverbal languages. A before-and-after headache remedy makes use first of defense gestures, combined with self-centered expressions of pain, and afterwards with the facial or other statements telling us about relief. Crossing our arms is a protective defensive gesture. Hitting the table with the fist an aggressive one. Unfortunately, the producers of advertisements of any form have heretofore neglected in copy testing to pay enough attention to the background, the body language, and the symbolism of their messages. They have been too much concerned with the "intellectual" verbal copy, rather than the silent copy which uses the whole world of objects, sounds of a nonverbal nature, background music, clothing, and mood syntax.

In a study for AT&T, we found that even the inconspicuous black phone can take on meaning. It has a soul, as most products have. We let out our anger by slamming the phone down, we express intimacy with the dialogue partner by cradling the phone, or increase the psychological distance by keeping the mouth or earpiece away from us. *Nonverbal* as being discussed in this chapter does not include specifically all forms of nonverbal communication such as clothing, background furniture, music, objects used and shown. We discuss these aspects, but are more interested in body-related gestures, facial expressions, postures, the use of hands, arms, legs, and other expressive possibilities. We do include such borderline expressions as objects used as signals, also expletive language such as sighs, hard breathing, blowing off steam, clapping one's hands, tapping with fingers on a surface, scratching, and many others. For the sake of simplicity, we call nonverbal any form of signal that permits interpretation on the part of the "sender" and on the part of the recipient, the addressee, whether present or not. In the remainder of this chapter I will try to use our rich research experience to set guidelines and warnings for good and poor nonverbal communication.

# What are the Criteria for Good Nonverbal Communication?

## 1. Re-creation

Most communications can be divided into those that are best symbolized by a complete circle and those that leave a section of the circle open. Good communication is the one that invites the respondent to fill in the missing part of the circle. Only when re-creation of the conscious or subconscious intention of the signal is possible does true communication in the psychological sense take place. Such communication is characterized by a feeling of recognition, of "Aha," and of understanding on a deeper level than just logical grammar.

Only humans and some higher apes are capable of this "Aha," "I see," nod of internal insight, the real basis of learning. It precedes the verbal learning. The child is capable of it long before he or she can pronounce or form meaningful words or sentences. One of the basic pleasures of any communication, whether literary or commercial, is the opportunity it offers the partner to complete the circle, to create the full meaning. It explains the original meaning of the word *re-creation*. Some experiments have shown that even when we simultaneously watch a sportscaster and the game itself on television the sportscaster's interpretations, his verbal and particularly nonverbal expressions, such as his face and body language, add to the immediacy and excitement.

## 2. Making Use of Subconscious Nonverbal Signals

Lieutenant Columbo would have a much tougher time solving crimes without the help of many of the silent signals that give the criminal away. By standing compulsively in front of the pot with the palm tree, the villain tells him that the keys to the car and the crime may be hidden there. Freudian slips do only not exist in audible forms but also in movements intended to hide and that instead reveal our fear or shame. We blush when we want to cover up our embarrassment. It is intended as a cover-up but instead we often achieve the opposite effect, much to our distress. What was once a logical physiological response on the part of a chameleon that blended its skin color with that of the background has now become a visually loud alarm informing the bystanders of the clumsy attempt to hide. Instead of defending the perpetrator, it becomes an indisputable lie detector. We may smile and utter friendly words, but our clenched fist, though hidden under the shield of the other hand, tells the real fury. Even a short individual has the power to state his disdain by lifting his head so that his gaze appears to look down on the taller person. If he covers his own eyes by letting the lids droop down and at the same time turns his head sideways, no amount of honey dripping from his lips will disguise his true feelings of disgust.

Nonverbal and often subconscious expressions by various parts of our body are closer to the true motivations. Trying to translate our reasons for buying and voting, or even admitting an attitude in customary verbal language as an answer to questionnaires, even in-depth interviews, does not penetrate to the real depth compared to involuntary movements, facial expressions, or reactions. It is unfortunate that the understanding of silent statements and their interpretations is seldom taught in the study of psychology. We are more likely to find some basis for it in acting schools or in descriptions by good observers and novelists.

### 3. Body Language

It is possible to study the map and significance of various parts of our body and our use of it to provide statements. We have an image of our own body that sneaks into our "direct" language pattern. The gesture which we use to point to a headache may be related to the real location of its source or often to our imagined source of the pain or annoyance. We may have an infection which causes a fever. The root of it may be between the toes, or invisible in the bladder, the liver, or other parts of the body. The observable result of the imbalance is a headache. We rub the assumed responsible spot, calming it, sometimes pounding it, or acting as if we could extract it by some secret maneuvers. At other times we cannot localize the pain. We have the flu. "I hurt all over" is our response to the solicitous inquiry. It is only the well-trained physician who knows better and treats the true origin of the problem.

Advertisers, copywriters, and art directors concern themselves very much with the verbal content of their messages. Most copy research, as the name itself indicates, tests people's reactions to the words, the meanings, and the verbal connotations involved in print, or radio and television advertising. Our research has shown repeatedly that it is often the "ad behind the ad," the interpretation of the respondent, that is critical. These interpretations frequently are based more on nonverbal cues than the verbal message. In analyzing the way people judge the sincerity of a politician, we discovered that many people concentrated on the last few seconds of the speaker when he thought he was off camera. They felt he then let his guard down, wiped off his phony smile or concerned look, and reverted to his real beliefs. It does make sense therefore for the producer of the sales message just as for the trained actor to pay considerably more attention to these important aspects of the truly "hidden persuasion."

### 4. Nonverbal Actions Speak Louder than Words

We have been asked recently to contribute ideas on how to help in getting people to smoke less or drink less alcohol. Our tests have invariably shown that no amount of verbal admonition really works if in the accompanying miniseries or other report or news item people smoke or drink. Their nonverbal statement talks more audibly and powerfully than any spoken death warning. It tells the viewer that smoking or drinking is OK. The hero does it. Almost anyone coming home from work reaches for a cigarette or utters the famous words in the story, "I could use a drink." What we react to, then, are these dramatically portrayed actions, whether they are accompanied by spoken sentences or not.

We cannot really test the success of a commercial or social admonition such as not to smoke by the copy alone. All we can measure is the response patterns that were noticed and provable. Whether the product then was bought or the demand made in the message was actually carried through depends on many more factors than the advertising message or admonition itself. But at least we have made sure that the message was the best possible, composed and constructed to produce positive responses. Introducing nonverbal elements makes the testing more complex and at the same time more reliable.

## 5. Testing the Importance of Nonverbal Forms of Communications

An advanced form of copy testing should include a systematic analysis of reactions to the many elements of the unspoken, often symbolic contributions to the effectiveness of the commercial or ad. We have pointed out in previous articles on copy testing that asking people, in whatever forms, whether they like a commercial or not or whether it would make them buy the product is misleading. Instead we have introduced and tested techniques that permit the measurement of response patterns such as degrees of identification or emotional responses and finally rehearsal of purchase. None of these approaches permit the inadmissible pattern of playing the role of an advertising critic. Under normal circumstances, only 10 to 15 percent of our reactions to any literary content (using this term in its broadest sense) involve critical responses. When we watch movies or plays, we don't mumble to ourselves that the acting or the plot is bad. The moment we do that, we have failed to become involved in the play. Thus when we used mechanical devices such as green and red buttons to be pushed whenever we like or dislike a spot, as in the Stanton–Lazarfeld program analyzer, we are using a universe of only 10 percent of all possible reactions.

Motivational copy research, which we call the measurement of response patterns, takes into consideration the fact that there are multiple patterns of response involved in reactions to advertisements. Our categories for responses are emotional involvement, integration, an understanding of the total psychological sequence and plot, and finally the rehearsal of purchase or action intended. Each one of these categories is ascertained not by critical questions but by those that reveal to us the degrees of each response. We ask with whom did you identify in the ad or commercial; who got you emotionally excited, left you neutral; and many other questions, introducing degrees on a scale until we finally ask what were your action responses, if any, that you could discover within yourself. A relatively simple approach that we have used with success is to screen out spoken messages and ask people to react to the various stimuli which accompany the copy.

We have also used a type of projective test comparable to the Rorschach test. In this test, ink blots without any specific meanings are shown, and test subjects are asked to tell a story. It is the prototype of a projective test. The ink blots are created by making a blot on a piece of paper and then folding it so that a symmetrical figure emerges. The respondent is asked to interpret this in-itself-meaningless illustration and to describe what he sees or really what he projects into it.

Some people concentrate on the small protruding elements of the blot picture, others try to interpret the total impression left. Differences are registered according to whether or not the holes left within the blot are used for interpretion or whether they are neglected and seen as holes. In some of the tables, color is also used. Subjects sometimes react primarily to the color spots, others leave them out. These various reactions "projected" into the ink-blot tables and figures permit psychological interpretations. In our tests applied to commercial and similar messages we cannot go into all these clinical details. We can however separate people into those types that are influenced by different aspects of the background, the music, the noises, and the mood created, and those who concentrate only on the foreground; those who notice details, and those who see only the total picture and gestalt. By comparing the verbal and nonverbal elements of the message, we measure the bow, the bridge between the respondent and the total message, rather than only paying attention to the reactions of the respondents to the foreground and verbal aspects of the message.

We can distinguish various reactions and relationships between verbal and nonverbal details of a message:

a.  Accentuation of verbal by nonverbal messages
b.  Contradictory relations between both
c.  Superfluous signals added nonverbally
d.  Interruptive functions
e.  Artificial or stereotype

We have also experimented with tests where the roles of nonverbal and verbal signals have been reversed. Respondents are shown or asked to listen to verbal statements and then enticed to develop or imagine the scene, the music, the clothing, the background that would go best with these stories. In a sense, then, what we test is the relationship in the respondent's mind between the images, the nonverbal completion of the sales message that will create a more satisfying and convincing total opus. By analyzing the various test results into a comprehensive chart, we can deliver to the writer and producer a blueprint for the effect he wanted to create. The questions we ask our respondents are designed to elicit one or more of the roles played by the nonverbal message.

## 6. Specific Experiments

We have successfully used experiments for various purposes. Covering up the background in a print ad, and if necessary also the illustration, we ask respondents to design and describe the illustration, background, and so on that would accompany the message. Similarly we may eliminate the music, the background, gestures, or the objects that are not directly related to the product and ask our respondents to complete and develop the full message. A second and related method that we have used is to ask the respondents to match various possible messages with a list of nonverbal stimuli such as music, background, and so on. A third approach is to separate the verbal and nonverbal aspects of advertisements and ask respondents to describe on a rating scale whether or not the various nonverbal elements have accentuated the verbal content, have proven to be contradictory, or are superfluous, interruptive, or artificial. In other words, rather than asking people to criticize the relationship between verbal and nonverbal stimuli, we solicit from them descriptions of directly observed feelings within themselves. We can then assign degrees and ratings to the various functions listed before or, if needed, add new ones.

If we chart these functions on a graph, we recieve a clear-cut profile of these relationships and have the possibility of improving the interrelationships between the two groups of messages, if needed. While we have our own criteria, such as the desirability of enhancing the impact of the message, we can deliver to the producer of the messages an analysis of his attempts or make recommendations on how the two aspects can be enhanced according to his intentions. Just as in "direct" copy research, we can pretest the weight and effectiveness of additional relevant elements of the persuasion techniques applied.

## 7. Some Findings

In many commercials, the actors who have tasted a cereal and want to convey to us how good it tastes make the mistake of turning to the viewer and winking at him as if he were a conspirator. We have found that what happens psychologically is that the protagonists, the sales people on the screen, suddenly change their roles, thus breaking the illusion and inviting us to be part of the action. It is comparable to a movie actor suddenly abandoning his part and talking to the theatre audience directly. A similar mistake occurs when a couple playfully acts out the role of the fragrance of a perfume, a shampoo, a cosmetic, or for that matter any other product, then change to a more serious mood with a kiss designed to accentuate the erotic or similar effect the product has had on them.

It would go beyond the frame of this analysis to cover all the possible good and bad interrelationships between verbal and nonverbal messages. In a number of commercials, children fight with each other, although in a friendly fashion, stealing the food item from the other. The intention is, of course, to illustrate the desirability of the product. The nonverbal message, however, which we found comes through, is the fight itself as a negative stimulus and lesson. In many shampoo ads, the woman caresses her hair in an exaggerated fashion. In a study on modern shampoos we found that working women react to this as a wasteful use of time. "We could never afford to spend that much time washing our hair." The viewers compared their behavior with the nonverbal actions shown in the ad or the commercial and did not "get" the praise of the shampoo brand intended. It is very important, therefore, that the producer of the messages pay attention to the type of background material. We have found it can often overshadow the story itself. Elegant and expensive furniture or clothing is often better remembered than the attempt to sell a fashion item. Tests can discover such competition within the message. But the more we learn about the importance of the relationship between the two languages, the better we can avoid these mistakes right from the start.

The important conclusion is that backgrounds, gestures, music, clothes, and the many other aspects of the sideshows that can be offered by nonverbal clues must contribute to an invitation to the viewer or reader to complete the circle of re-creation of the originator of the message. Pure illustration of an already fairly clear message is therefore not only a waste of space, time, and money, but also disturbing. It robs the respondent of participation and thus of a registration of the message in a more permanent manner.

## Summary

We don't pay enough attention to the testing of nonverbal messages in advertising. Copy research concentrates to a large extent on the verbal aspect of the message. This chapter describes methods that have proven effective in measuring the relationship between the verbal and nonverbal aspects of the total communication. By covering up the nonverbal aspects of an ad and asking people to complete the gestalt of the total communication, and reversing this procedure, we can find out whether accentuation, contradiction, and superfluous effects are being created. These tests indicate which interrelations are helpful in the sales results of advertising and whether the wrong message is being conveyed. A number of findings of such tests of the relationship between verbal and nonverbal correlations have been reported.

The main point for copy testing is that making the respondent a pseudo-advertising expert has to be avoided. Instead of asking whether a respondent likes or dislikes commercials and parts of them, the method recommended is one of measuring response patterns directly.

# 4

# Consumer Impression Formation: The Integration of Visual and Verbal Information

*James Shanteau*

The purpose of this chapter is to describe the application of Consumer Integration Theory (CIT) to the formation of advertising impressions based on visual and verbal information. The chapter is organized into nine sections: (1) presentation of general background, (2) overview of the information-integration approach to impression formation, (3) review of some relevant impression-formation studies, (4) description of the processing assumptions of CIT, (5) formal development of the CIT model, (6) examination of predictions from CIT, (7) consideration of advertising implications, (8) discussion of future research directions, and (9) concluding comments.

## Background

The basic question is: How does visual information combine with verbal information in the formation of advertising images? Although there have been a number of consumer research analyses of this question (Alesandrini 1983; Edell and Staelin 1983; Gardner and Houston 1986; Lutz and Lutz 1977; Mitchell 1983; Mitchell and Olson 1981; Percy and Rossiter 1983; Rossiter and Percy 1983), the present chapter addresses the problem from a different perspective. The approach taken here draws from the extensive literature on impression formation (Anderson 1981; Asch 1946; Cook 1984).

Visual and other types of nonverbal stimuli have long been of interest in the study of impression formation (Birdwhistell 1970; Lampel and Anderson 1968; Washburn and Hakel 1973; Weitz 1974). This interest has led to investigations of how verbal and visual information combine in forming impressions (for example,

This chapter was prepared while the author was a visiting professor of marketing at the Johnson Graduate School of Management at Cornell University. The author's research described here was supported in part by the National Science Foundation (Grant BMS-20504), the Army Research Institute (Contract MDA 903-80-C-0209), and Kansas State University (BGR Grant). The author wishes to acknowledge the helpful comments of Gary Gaeth on both the theory and the manuscript. Additional insights and comments were provided by Norman Anderson, Jay Russo, David Stewart, and Dick Wittink.

Archer and Akert 1984; Arvey and Campion 1984; Brien, 1979; Shanteau and Nagy 1984). Despite its relevance, this literature has yet to be summarized and brought to the attention of advertising researchers.

Compared to typical analyses in advertising, the approach taken in impression-formation studies has three notable differences. First, the emphasis is on impressions rather than on memory or knowledge. The importance of this distinction has been demonstrated in studies comparing impressions and memory. Differences have been observed between what is remembered from a set of stimuli and the impression formed from that stimuli. Anderson and Hubert (1963), for instance, found primacy or first-impression effects for impressions, but observed a tendency towards recency for memory recall (also see Riskey 1979).

Based on such results, Anderson (1981, p. 256) argued that impressions "have a life of their own, independent of the particular experiences out of which they were formed. . . . Once the meaning has been extracted, the (stimulus) word is a verbal husk, no longer needed, that may be stored in a verbal memory or simply forgotten" (p. 250). Thus, memory for stimulus material has proved to be largely irrelevant in analyses of impression formation (Crano 1977).

Recently, advertising researchers have come to appreciate this distinciton between impression and memory. As pointed out by Lichtenstein and Srull (1985, p. 122), "consumers who have an objective of forming an evaluation of a product at the time of information acquisition will form an evaluation that is stored and accessed independently of the original information." Beattie and Mitchell (1985, p. 153) conclude that "a direct link between recall and persuasion will occur only under highly restrictive conditions." These arguments (also see Tsal 1985a, b) suggest that there are important limitations to the use of recall measures, such as the Starch index (1966), for evaluating advertising effectiveness. Instead, it is advertising impressions, and the decisions based on those impressions, that are the focus of this chapter.

Second, impression-formation studies emphasize affective response measures. In part, this reflects a desire to measure judgments on a dimension that is natural for subjects. It is also a recognition of the importance of affect in a variety of domains (Zajonc and Markus 1985). As a result of the emphasis on affect, the literature on impression formation has maintained a degree of focus often missing in consumer research (Jacoby 1978).

In comparison, analyses of advertising have incorporated a bewildering array of response measures. These include measures of memory (Childers and Houston 1984), immediate and delayed recall (Gardner and Houston 1986; Hutchinson and Moore 1984), attitudinal components (Mitchell and Olson 1981), beliefs and intentions (Percy and Rossiter 1983), quality and satisfaction (Tsal 1985a), semantic-differential scales (Holbrook and Moore 1981), and paired-associate learning (Lutz and Lutz 1977). In an elaborate analysis of verbal–visual effects, Edell and Staelin (1983) used the following dependent variables: process-tracing techniques, eye movements, reaction times, measures of knowledge and interest, believability, ratings of importance, and memory recall, plus measures of attitudes, beliefs, and intentions. Given this diversity of response measures, it is not surprising to find little consistency across studies.

The final distinction concerns the conceptual framework used to investigate visual and verbal information. Following Paivio's (1971) cognitive psychology analysis, most advertising researchers have adopted a "dual coding" perspective, based on separate semantic and imaginal coding systems. Much of the research has revolved around determining which system is influenced by what kind of information and under what conditions. Therefore, a conceptual distinction is drawn between the information contained in words and pictures.

In contrast, impression-formation researchers have taken the view that there is little or no fundamental difference between verbal and visual information. Words and pictures (as well as other types of nonverbal stimuli) are simply treated as information sources to be integrated in forming an impression. Some investigators have even argued that there is no distinction between verbal and nonverbal communications (for example, Birdwhistell 1970). Others adopt the view that pictures may influence how words are interpreted in forming an impression (for example, Lampel and Anderson 1968). Either way, verbal and visual stimuli are not treated as conceptually distinct in impression formation.

Therefore, impression formation provides an alternative perspective to that typically taken in advertising research. The purpose of this chapter is to explore the potential applications of this perspective.

## Information Integration

The emphasis here will be on research conducted within the framework of the information integration approach to impression formation (Anderson 1981, 1982). This approach has been applied to topics ranging from jury judgments (Kaplan and Kemmerick 1974) and risky decision making (Shanteau 1974, 1975) to judgments by children (Butzin and Anderson 1973) and decisions made by expert auditors (Ettenson, Krogstad, and Shanteau 1984) and soil judges (Gaeth and Shanteau 1984). There have also been several applications in the consumer behavior area (Lynch 1985; Shanteau and Troutman 1975; Shanteau, Troutman, and Ptacek 1977).

Information integration has two advantages over other frameworks for investigating visual–verbal combination: First, it provides a cohesive theoretical approach to human judgment and decison making (Shanteau 1985). In contrast, advertising research on visual–verbal effects often lacks a connection to broader theories and issues. The absence of an adequate theoretical base is, of course, a common criticism of research on consumer behavior (Foxall 1980; Jacoby 1978; Shanteau 1983).

The premise behind information integration is that human judgment results from the evaluation and combination of information extracted from judged stimuli. The goal is to derive a quantitative description (the "cognitive algebra") of the process used to arrive at the final judgment. This quantitative description then reflects the subjects' information-integration strategy.

A second advantage is that most information-integration studies have been conducted within a common research paradigm. This paradigm includes an emphasis on (1) testing various models of the integration process, (2) deriving estimates of the model parameters, and (3) performing analyses at the individual subject level. These steps are accomplished using functional measurement procedures (Anderson 1981, 1982). The approach differs from others in that the integration rule (that is, model form) is *not* assumed *a priori* but rather is derived from the pattern of data. Thus, the approach is sensitive to changes or shifts in processing strategy.

The research paradigm leads to an emphasis on methodological controls, careful experimental designs, tests of individual models of behavior, and an integrative approach to theory construction (Shanteau 1985). Because of the cohesiveness of information-integration studies, it is possible to make comparisons, discover parallels, and see extensions that would be difficult in a less coordinated research domain.

## Studies of Visual-Verbal Integration

The studies reviewed in this section reflect different approaches to manipulating verbal and visual information in impression formation. These studies illustrate how the relative influence of verbal and visual information depends on various mediating variables. In particular, five types of variables are considered: word–picture interactions, situational effects, past experience, individual differences, and words as substitutes for pictures. In each case, empirical results are described along with some implications for visual–verbal processing.

### Word–Picture Interaction

One of the earliest investigations of visual stimuli in impression formation was reported by Lampel and Anderson (1968). Female college students evaluated the datability of males described by a photograph and two personality-trait adjectives. As shown in figure 4–1, the results revealed that for more attractive photographs, the influence of personality traits increased. Thus, the importance of verbal trait information increased as the visual attractiveness increased (also see Nagy 1975).

Analysis of the data pattern revealed support for a weighted averaging model, where the weight given to the verbal adjectives depends on the scale value (high or low) of the photograph. Apparently, when visual information is crucial to the judgment, as in dating, the influence of verbal information depends on the relative value of the visual information (Shanteau and Nagy 1976, 1979).

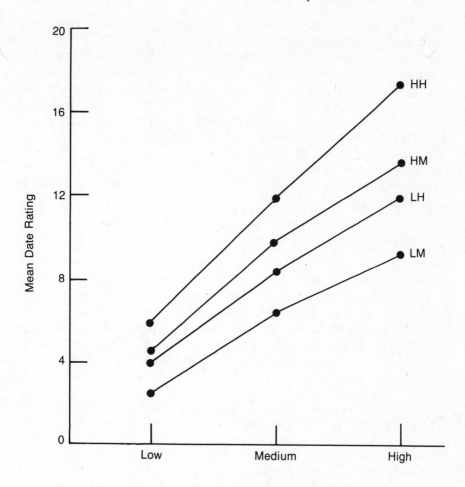

Source: adapted from Lampel and Anderson (1968).

Note: Diverging pattern of lines is expected from a differential-weight averaging model: as photos become more attractive, adjectives have greater weight.

**Figure 4–1. Plot of Mean Attractiveness of Dates Described by Trait Adjectives and Photographs.**

*Situational Effects*

In a consumer behavior study, Shanteau and Ptacek (1978; also see Shanteau and Ptacek 1983) analyzed the influence of usage situation and purchase motivation on product preferences. Consumers were presented with supermarket displays with real brands selected to exemplify various attribute combinations. With paper towels, for instance, nine actual products were selected on the basis of (1) thickness/manufacturer and (2) color/visual pattern (see figure 4–2). For a difficult job situation, thickness/manufacturer was found to dominate; that is, consumers largely ignored color/visual pattern. For a kitchen decor situation, on the other hand, the color/visual pattern of paper towels dominated and thickness/manufacturer was largely ignored.

These results were interpreted as supporting a generalized averaging model for product attributes. Although averaging was able to describe the data pattern in most cases, the parameters (for example, attribute weights) were found to depend on the consumption situation. That is, visual appearance was important in some contexts and not others.

## Past Experience

Nagy (1981) examined the role of relevant (verbal) and irrelevant (visual) factors in personnel selection. Job applicants were described in terms of both job-relevant information (recommendations and years of experience) and job-irrelevant information (sex, age, and physical attractiveness). The relevant information was imbedded in realistic job application forms, with photographs attached to illustrate the irrelevant information. Using professional personnel selectors and business students as subjects, Nagy found strong reliance on job-relevant information for both types of subjects. Job-irrelevant information, however, was used more by students than by professionals.

The pattern of results for both students and professionals revealed that information was averaged to make a hiring recommendation. Moreover, Gaeth (1984) found that with special training, students could learn to reduce the use of the irrelevant visual information. Thus, past experience and training of the subject determined whether the impression was based on only verbal information or both verbal and visual information. This suggests that experienced consumers may use visual information differently than novices. How knowledgeable consumers process visual information is an interesting but as yet unresolved question.

## Individual Differences

Brien (1979) examined the influence of three factors on the selection of a hospital by expectant parents: (1) hospital policies and procedures, (2) staff (for example, nurses) characteristics, and (3) physical appearance of the hospital. Three groups of parents varying in knowledge/awareness of childbirth were used as subjects. Before childbirth, physical appearance was most important to naive, unaware parents; it was least important to two groups of more knowledgeable, aware parents. After childbirth, all parents were similar in deemphasizing appearance. Thus, those parents who knew most about childbirth were least likely to use visual appearance in selecting a hospital.

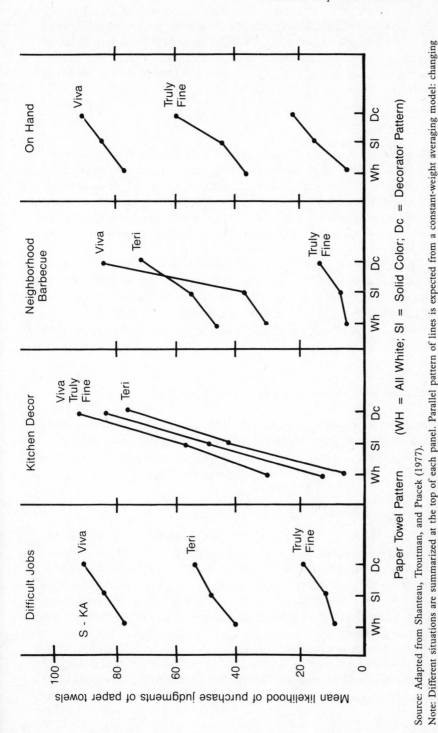

Source: Adapted from Shanteau, Troutman, and Ptacek (1977).

Note: Different situations are summarized at the top of each panel. Parallel pattern of lines is expected from a constant-weight averaging model: changing slope across panels corresponds to shifts in attribute weight values.

**Figure 4-2. Plot of Mean Likelihood-of-purchase Ratings for Paper Towels Selected according to Attributes of Thickness/Manufacturer and Color/Visual Pattern.**

Using an averaging model framework, Brien obtained parameter estimates of impact values (weight times scale value) for the three groups. These values illustrated the importance of individual differences in the evaluation of physical appearance. Moreover, the source of these differences was localized in the knowledge/awareness of the subjects.

### Words as Substitutes for Pictures

Brien, Haverfield, and Shanteau (1983) asked expectant parents to rank various attributes for their importance in selecting an obstetrician; included in the verbal list of attributes was "physical appearance." Each husband and wife responded separately. Out of 20 attributes, wives gave physical appearance an average ranking of 18.0 and husbands gave a ranking of 18.5. Only the physician's age and sex were ranked as less important. (Incidentally, both husbands and wives ranked "sincere concern for the patient" to be number one.)

In this study, self-explicated parameters were used (Anderson 1982). Such parameter estimates have been found in many settings to produce orderings similar to averaging model–derived parameters. These estimates revealed that when visual information was presented in a verbal list, it was unimportant. That is, inherently visual information, such as physical appearance, is apparently discounted when it is described verbally.

## Assumptions of Consumer Integration Theory

There are two major processing assumptions behind CIT. The first is that visual information is processed before verbal information. The second is that all information, whether visual or verbal, is combined by a serial averaging process. Justification for each of these assumptions will be provided in this section.

### Primacy of Visual Information

The initial step in CIT is the processing of visual information. The view is that visual material, when available, is processed first, and that this sets the stage for later processing of verbal information. This means that visual information dominates initial impressions. This does not imply, however, that the final impression is similarly dominated by pictures. Since additional information may be incorporated into the impression, the final impact of a picture depends on how much more (besides the picture) is processed.

There are three sources of evidence to support the assumption of visual priority. First, analyses of eye movements indicate that when viewing an ad, "people respond to people first" (Ohlsten, as quoted in Gwynne and Panati 1977). As part of a study for an advertising agency, eye movements of 250 housewives were unobtrusively recorded while they watched television commercials. "A person in a commercial commanded instant visual attention," according to Ohlsten. Only later did the consumers look at the product label and verbal slogans (Gwynne and Panati 1977). Although eye movements are not conclusive evidence of order of processing, these results are consistent with the assumption that visual information is examined first.

Second, Edell and Staelin (1983, p. 48) proposed a processing model for advertising in which the first step is to "look at layout of ad." Using print ads, they employed a variety of responses, including process-tracing techniques, to measure subjects' reactions. They found that different processing strategies were used depending on the relation between picture and text. All processing, however, began with the analysis of pictorial information. Although part of the evidence depends on memory-recall measures (which as noted above are not necessarily reflective of impression formation), unpublished evidence indicates that pictures are processed first in evaluating an ad (Edell, personnel communication, 1986).

Third, several studies comparing pictures with word descriptions (as opposed to combining pictures and words) suggest verbal primacy. Based on various sources of evidence, Holbrook and Moore (1981) argue that words are processed sequentially and pictures are processed simultaneously. Accordingly, they predict and find evidence of wholistic, interactive processing of pictorial representations and piecemeal, linear processing of verbal representations (also see Domzal and Unger 1985 and Kisielius and Sternthal 1984). While such evidence is circumstantial, it is consistent with the visual-primacy assumption of CIT.

## Serial Averaging

In contrast to the largely indirect evidence on visual primacy, the evidence on the serial averaging assumption is substantial and direct. Although any number of relevant studies could be cited, including several described previously, three papers incorporating varied methodologies will be presented here.

Troutman (1977) asked husbands and wives to make judgments of car seats and pediatricians, where each option was described by one or two attributes. The results at both the individual and aggregate levels supported an averaging model (see Troutman and Shanteau 1976). Other model forms, such as adding, were incapable of describing the observed results. After making judgments separately, Troutman also had husbands and wives make joint judgments. These combined judgments then consisted of two elements: (1) each spouses' initial evaluation, plus (2) the subsequent interaction of husband and wife. These joint judgments were also consistent with an averaging model. Thus, the model was supported for both individual spouse and couple judgments.

Gentry and Shanteau (1977) compared a serial averaging model (see equation 1 below) with a Bayesian opinion-change model (Green 1962). Consumers were asked to state both prior and posterior purchase intentions of shoe purchases. Several versions of the Bayesian model were constructed with varying numbers of parameters.

Although the modified Bayesian models did an adequate job of describing consumers' judgments, the serial averaging model was superior in every case. The study concluded that the averaging framework provided a better account that than the Bayesian approach.

Wong (1973) examined the interaction of source credibility and message content on impression formation. Two pieces of information were provided, each attributed to a source of varying credibility. The results for each source separately supported the combination rule implied by averaging. Moreover, when the information from the two sources was combined, the data patterns followed the predictions of an averaging model. Specifically, the importance (credibility) attached to one source was found to interact with the relative importance of the other source: as one weight went up, the other went down. Further, the form of the interaction was as predicted by an averaging model.

## Consumer Integration Theory

Consumer Integration Theory is proposed as a description of how visual and verbal information is combined to form an impression. The model is based on the two assumptions of visual primacy and serial averaging. These assumptions lead to the five-step CIT model outlined in table 4–1. The five steps are (1) first reactions to visual stimuli, (2) first reactions to verbal stimuli, (3) initial impressions based on a combination of visual and verbal first reactions, (4) further processing to extract attribute values, and (5) updating of impressions as additional attributes are extracted. Each of these steps will now be considered in more detail.

1. The first reaction to visual stimuli reflects the more-or-less automatic processing of pictorial displays. Following Holbrook and Moore (1981), pictures are assumed to be processed in an immediate, wholistic fashion.

**Table 4–1**
**Five Steps of CIT Model**

| Process | Model |
|---------|-------|
| Visual first reaction | $I_0 = w_0 s_0$ |
| Verbal first reaction | $w_1 s_1$ |
| Initial impression | $I_1 = c_1 s_1 + (1 - c_1) I_0$ <br> where $c_1 = w_1 / (w_0 + w_1)$ |
| Extract attributes | $w_j , s_j$ <br> for $j = 1 , n$ |
| Updated impression | $I_j = c_j s_j + (1 - c_j) I_{j-1}$ <br> for $j = 1 , n$ |

2. The first reaction to verbal stimuli reflects the initial processing of textual material. Most likely, this is based on headlines or other brief attention-getting material.

3. The initial impression is formed from an average of the visual and verbal first reactions. This is what constitutes the traditional "first impression."

4. Subsequent processing (if any) involves the analysis and extraction of additional attribute information. This reflects evaluation of both external and internal (for example, memory) information sources.

5. The overall impression is based on an updated multi-attribute judgment. The updating process is described by an ongoing serial averaging process.

*Proportional-Change Model*

CIT used a version of averaging called the proportional-change model. Originally proposed to account for attitude change (Anderson and Hovland 1957), this model describes how old impressions are updated by new information to form revised impressions. Thus, it leads to a dynamic integration process in which new information is continually "folded into" the prevailing impression.

The proportional change model can be written as

$$I_j = c_j s_j + (1 - c_j) I_{j-1}, \tag{1}$$

where the I's represent the impressions before and after receipt of the j-th piece of information. The information is represented by its scale value, s, and the change parameter, c. Equation 1 is an averaging model since the two terms, c and $(1-c)$, sum to one.

Change parameters are related to traditional attribute weights by the following expression:

$$C_j = w_j / (w_0 + w_1 + w_2 + \ldots + w_j). \tag{2}$$

The c's can thus be viewed as relative (normalized) weight values.

An important feature of the CIT model is the incorporation of a dynamic decision process. As opposed to static or one-time views of judgment, the dynamic perspective stresses the evolution of impressions over time. As consumers gather and process more information, their impression of an option gradually evolves. This is reflected both in the five steps of table 4–1 and in the proportional-change model in equation 1.

## Analysis of CIT Predictions

There are numerous predictions which can be derived from the CIT model. Although the details are laid out elsewhere (Shanteau 1987b), comments about two general classes of predictions are appropriate here. The first concerns order effects. The existence of order effects in judgment and decision making is well established (Anderson 1981; Slovic and Lichtenstein 1971). With *primacy*, early information dominates (for example, Anderson and Barrios 1961; Hendrick and Constantini 1970; Stewart 1965); with *recency*, later information dominates (for example, Shanteau 1972; Stewart 1965; Weiss and Anderson 1969).

Most previous analyses of order effects have concentrated on such questions as: Does early or late information have more impact? The results are often inconsistent and contradictory. As noted by Anderson (1981, p. 153), there is a "welter of conflicting results on order effects. . . . Seemingly similar experiments find primacy, recency, neither, or even both, with little visible pattern." Thus, studies of stimulus-order effects have yet to produce consistent patterns of results.

In comparison, the present analysis focuses on the relative importance of early and late processes. The research question shifts from which piece of information is most important to which process is most important. This emphasis on process-order effects has several implications. One is that the early steps of CIT are likely to dominate when subjects engage in initial (shallow?) processing, as is frequently the case in display advertising. Given that visual information is immediately available, it should not be surprising to find it closely connected with primacy. Alternately, the latter steps of CIT are more likely to dominate when subjects engage in deeper processing, as might be the case in a carefully read print ad. Accordingly, recency should be expected with such processing.

The second general comment concerns the relation between CIT and involvement (Krugman 1965). Level of involvement describes both the general level of interest of the consumer and the consumer's motivation to acquire information (Assael 1987). High involvement is reflected by consumer interest in obtaining information; low involvement, in contrast, is characterized by lack of interest (Engel, Blackwell, and Miniard 1986). The five-step CIT model in table 4–1 corresponds to high-involvement consumer information processing. It is not necessary to assume, however, that consumers always go through all five steps. Rather, processing may well stop after the initial impression.

This suggests a connection between the processing steps of the CIT model and level of involvement. In particular, the initial steps may correspond to low involvement. If this characterization is correct, then the first-impression weight provides a measure of level of involvement. When involvement is low, weight should fall almost entirely on the first impression. When involvement is high, the weight should shift to the later processes, and hence the first-impression weight will decrease. Moreover, CIT suggests that there may be a relation between order effects and involvement. That is, low involvement is connected to primacy and high involvement to recency.

A similar argument appears in the Elaboration Likelihood Model (ELM) of Petty and Cacioppo (1983). They propose two routes to persuasion—central and peripheral. Under low-involvement (peripheral) conditions, "attitudes will be formed and changed without any extensive cognitive work" (p. 10). In contrast, the high-involvement (central) route "occurs when a person is both motivated and able to think about the merits of the advocacy presented" (p. 21). Thus, the peripheral route may have some correspondence to the initial impression of CIT, and the central route may reflect more complete processing. It may be worth exploring other similarities between the present approach and that advocated by Petty and Cacioppo.

## Advertising Implications

The present approach leads to several implications about the effects of visual information in advertising. First and foremost, CIT is predicated on pictorial materials having a primary role in the initial impressions to ads. Further, if there is little or no subsequent processing, then visual information will dominate the final impression as well. If, on the other hand, there is subsequent processing, then visual material provides a starting point which is gradually eclipsed by later text information. Either way, CIT predicts that visual information provides the starting point in the consumer's impression of an ad.

Second, CIT implies that the relative importance of visual and verbal information in an ad is a function of the extent of subsequent processing. When consumers carefully analyze the content of an ad, the text, not the picture, is likely to dominate. More intense analysis is reflected by increasing emphasis on the latter steps in the CIT model. This can be measured through the change (or weight) parameters of the serial averaging model.

Third, involvement with an ad is likely to play a major role in determining whether visual or verbal material is most influential. Under low involvement, visual information is important because it is processed first and there is little subsequent processing of verbal information. Under high involvement, there is more processing of text material and hence pictures should have less influence. The CIT framework is useful because it provides a parameter, the initial-impression weight, that reflects the importance of early processing. Although many factors may influence the initial weight parameter, it can provide a starting place for developing an empirical measure of level of involvement.

Finally, experience of consumers should influence the relative impact of visual and verbal information. More experienced consumers presumably are likely to look beyond a picture and to evaluate text. Less experienced consumers, in comparison, are likely to stay with their impressions formed from visual material. Although the effect of experience is starting to receive some attention in the consumer behavior literature (for example, Alba and Hutchinson 1987; Cole, Gaeth, and Singh 1986), it has been the focus of considerable research in studies of decision making (for example, Shanteau 1984). Experienced decision makers have been found to be psychologically different from novices in ways such as problem recognition (DeGroot 1965) and decision strategy (Shanteau 1987a). Perhaps similar differences will be observed in analyses of experienced consumers.

## Additional Comments

### Future Research Directions

There are at least two directions in which further research would seem fruitful. First, it would be valuable to replicate some of the basic impression-formation studies using persuasive material typical of advertising. For instance, it would be interesting to investigate the interaction between visual attractiveness and extent of verbal processing (observed by Lampel and Anderson 1968) using advertising materials. If this finding is replicated, then it suggests that more attractive pictures would produce greater processing of text materials. Of course, it is possible that some of the impression-formation results will not replicate using persuasive stimuli (Cialdini, Petty and Cacioppo 1981). If so, it would be worthwhile exploring the reasons for the differences.

Second, it may be beneficial to make use of the explicit models and parameters provided by the CIT framework. Although there have been many attempts to analyze how verbal and visual information is combined, most of these efforts have not involved explicit models with estimable parameters. In contrast, the present approach provides both a framework for evaluating process models and a set of techniques for estimating model parameters (Shanteau 1985). The CIT approach, therefore, could help shift research on verbal–visual processing away from loose qualitative descriptions toward more precise quantitative analyses.

### Compensatory versus Noncompensatory Models

In consumer research and elsewhere, a distinction is often drawn between compensatory and noncompensatory models. This distinction is felt to be important because it delineates the type of trade-offs possible in processing communications such as ads. Wright (1975, p. 60) states that "compensatory strategies picture a person averaging (or adding) data so that positive and negative data have a balancing impact on his overall product impression." Thus, Wright classifies averaging as compensatory. On the other hand, "noncompensatory strategies assume a consumer combines data such that the presence (absence) of one attribute may not compensate at all for the absence (presence) of others" (Wright, p. 61, all parentheses are in the original). Examples of noncompensatory models include elimination-by-aspects, lexicographic, conjunctive, and disjunctive rules.

Despite Wright's classification, weighted averaging actually satisfies the properties of both compensatory and noncompensatory models. Anderson (1972) has shown, for instance, that averaging models can mimic conjunctive and disjunctive strategies, depending on the system for assigning weights. Further, if weights are a function of scale values (as shown in figure 4–1 for the Lampel and Anderson study), then the model exhibits noncompensatory properties. When the weights are constant (as shown in figure 4–2 for the Shanteau and Ptacek study), then the model is compensatory. Thus, averaging models can have both compensatory or noncompensatory properties. This is important in advertising because it means that one model, averaging, may be able to describe what previously was assumed to be two qualitatively different processing strategies. Accordingly, the distinction between compensatory and noncompensatory may need to be reexamined in the case of averaging.

### Hierarchical Judgment

Louviere and Gaeth (1987) proposed a method for describing multi-attribute judgments with large numbers of attributes. In their *hierarchical information integration* approach, Louviere and Gaeth group attributes into logical or functional categories. These categories are combined in turn into an overall judgment. By concatenating the judgment models from each category, a single judgment equation can be derived. Among other consequences, Louviere and Gaeth show that it is possible for the overall process to be nonadditive, even though each of the within-category processes is additive; this can happen, for instance, when there is an interaction between categories, but no interaction within categories.

In consumer behavior, important decisions frequently require consideration of numerous attributes in a hierarchical fashion. In selecting a hospital, for example, a consumer may make judgments about convenience, size, cost, physical facilities, and so on. Each of these judgments would likely be based on several attributes. The overall evaluation, therefore, would reflect the combination of these judgments. CIT might be expanded to incorpoate such judgments by incorporating additional hierarchical layers of processing.

## Conclusion

Consumer Integration Theory is offered as a precise description of how verbal and visual information is combined in advertising. Starting with research on impression formation, CIT was developed around the twin assumptions of visual primacy and serial averaging. The approach is able to account for many diverse findings in impression formation generally and visual–verbal effects in advertising specifically. In addition, it leads to testable predictions about order effects, involvement, consumer experience, and various interactions. Further research is needed both to examine these predictions and to explore additional elaborations of the model.

# 5
# The Relevance–Accessibility Model of Advertising Effectiveness

*William E. Baker*
*Richard J. Lutz*

Advertising effects research has identified numerous ways in which advertising can influence brand choice. Using a general situational contingency approach, the Relevance–Accessibility Model (RAM) attempts to explain when different advertising effects will be most effective (and most ineffective) in influencing brand-choice behavior. The RAM represents an assimilation of recent research in cognitive and social psychology, behavioral learning theory, and advertising theory, including research on (1) how consumers process advertising information, (2) how information is stored in and accessed from memory, and (3) how people use information to facilitate judgments.

When the focus of research moves from advertising effects to advertising effectiveness, the appropriate perspective views advertising as but one possible source of information that consumers may or may not use to evaluate brands. Critical to this perspective is the need to distinguish clearly between the *advertising exposure occasion* (for example, home, car, advertising pretest), where current advertising effects research has focused predominantly, to the *brand response occasion* (for example, in-store brand choice), where advertising effectiveness is truly determined. The RAM is based on the view that the primary goal of advertising is not to change brand attitudes at the advertising exposure occasion, but to influence brand choice by communicating *relevant* information that is easily retrieved, that is, *accessible*, and used at the brand response occasion to discriminate among brand alternatives. Thus, the primary goal of advertising is to give a brand a "relative advantage" over its competitors.

According to the RAM, breakdowns in advertising effectiveness occur for two general reasons: (1) when advertising information is not accessed (that is, not retrieved) at the brand response occasion or (2) when accessed advertising information is perceived as irrelevant to the brand choice process. To be optimally effective, then, advertising messages must (1) contain the type of information that consumers are most likely to use to discriminate brands at the brand response occasion and (2) maximize the accessibility of that information at the brand response occasion.

A central proposition of the RAM is that perceived informational relevance is a function of consumer decision-making involvement (DMI) at the brand response occasion. At different levels of DMI, qualitatively different types of information are sought by consumers (pure affect, heuristic quality cues, or relative usage benefits) to discriminate brand alternatives.

Unlike *tactical* research (for example, benefit segmentation, conjoint analysis) designed to determine specific advertising message content, the RAM operates at the *strategic* level to identify the molar level of information that advertising should communicate in any given situation. Thus, the model makes predictions about the conditions under which pure affect (for example, feeling ads), heuristic cues (for example, highly credible spokespeople), or brand attributes (for example, usage benefits) is the most effective type of information to convey through advertising.

Major implications for the design and evaluation of advertising that follow from the RAM perspective include: (1) a need to focus on expected DMI as a critical input to advertising message strategy formulation and advertising pretest methodologies; (2) a systematic approach for deciding whether to pursue affective, heuristic, or attribute-based advertising; (3) the importance of determining the qualitative type of information that consumers are expected to use at the BRO before proceeding with techniques (for example, conjoint analysis) designed to identify the most important specific information to include in advertising messages (that is, identifying strategy before deciding on tactics); and (4) a systematic approach for choosing the most appropriate measure(s) of advertising effectiveness.

The purpose of this chapter is to outline some of the basic aspects of the RAM. Since a complete presentation of the model is precluded by space constraints, the focus will be on the two fundamental constructs that distinguish the RAM from its predecessors, that is, the *brand response occasion* and the *advertising exposure occasion*. The goal, then, is to develop these two "building block" constructs as fully as possible and thus lay the foundation for subsequent model conceptualization and empirical testing.

## Background

Prior to developing a contingency theory of advertising effectiveness, it is important to review briefly what is currently known about the ways in which advertising can work. That is, one cannot reasonably predict which advertising strategy is most likely to succeed (or fail) in a given situation unless the ways in which advertising potentially *can* operate in that situation have been identified. After the likelihoods of these effects occurring in that situation are assessed, predictions regarding the effectiveness of various strategies can be made.

Traditionally, conceptualizations of advertising effects have assumed brand evaluation to be mediated by the effortful analysis of performance-related information and, ultimately, the formation of performance-related beliefs about the brand (Lavidge and Steiner 1961; McGuire 1978). These effects have often been conceptualized as working through a construct called brand-attribute Cognitive Structure (Lutz 1975, 1977; Lutz and Swasy 1977; Toy 1982).

In recent years this traditional view has been amended to reflect the evaluative implications of advertising information that is *unrelated* to specific aspects of brand performance (Zajonc 1968; Gorn 1982; Mitchell and Olson 1981) and evaluation processes that do *not* require the effortful processing of advertising content (Krugman 1965; Nord and Peter 1982; Petty and Cacioppo 1981).

### Three Constructs through Which Advertising Effects Can Operate

The following discussion focuses on the empirical bases for three advertising-generated constructs capable of directly mediating brand judgment: Cognitive Structure, Attitude toward the Ad, and Brand-Name Familiarity.

**Cognitive Structure.** Cognitive Structure (CS) is an informational construct in the sense that any brand-related affect (that is, liking) generated through the CS construct is derived from a series of performance-related beliefs. More specifically, advertising-generated CS refers to the bundle of utilitarian and hedonic beliefs associated with any given brand.

Theoretically, the notion that specific brand beliefs mediate global brand evaluation grew from the work of Rosenberg (1956) and Fishbein (1963, 1967). Their multi-attribute summation models provide the mechanism by which brand beliefs are converted into brand attitudes. Early use of these models centered on the impact of utilitarian beliefs (for example, performance qualities). Academic recognition in marketing of the importance of hedonic beliefs (for example, self-image enhancement) is more recent (Hirschmann and Holbrook 1982) and has its roots in socio-cultural (Levy 1959, 1964) and Freudian (Dichter 1968) perspectives.

CS-based mediation is also consistent with the information-processing perspective of the 1970s (Anderson 1974; Bettman 1979). As a result, a plethora of empirical research centering around the concept of brand-attribute CS dominated persuasion research throughout the decade (See Wilkie and Pessemier 1973; Ryan and Bonfield 1975; Miniard and Cohen 1979).

**Attitude toward the Ad.** The executional elements of advertising are capable of evoking purely affective and evaluative reactions that are wholly or partially independent of belief formation (Wells, McConville, and Leavitt 1971; Schlinger 1979; Lutz 1985; Baker 1985). An ambiguous pleasant or unpleasant feeling or the elicitation of a specific mood such as sensuousness or joy exemplify affective reactions. Evaluative reactions include assessments of advertisement credibility and believability. Evidence suggests that attitude toward the ad (AAD), whether based on purely affective or on more evaluative antecedents, is capable of directly mediating consumer brand attitudes and behavior.

Mitchell and Olson (1981) first demonstrated that affective reactions to advertisements significantly mediated brand attitude after the evaluative effects of advertising-generated brand beliefs on brand attitude were removed statistically. Other research has shown significant direct effects of AAD on brand attitude and purchase intention using covariate analysis or structural modelling methodologies (Shimp 1981; Moore and Hutchinson 1983, 1985; Batra and Ray 1985; Baker 1985; MacKenzie, Lutz, and Belch 1986) and the experimental manipulation of advertising-generated affect (Gorn 1982; Kroeber-Riel 1984; McSweeney and Bierly 1985).

**Brand-Name Familiarity.** Zajonc (1968) demonstrated that exposure to a stimulus can enhance the liking of that stimulus *independently* of cognitive evaluations or contextual associations. As stated by Zajonc (1968, p. 1), "mere repeated exposure of the individual to a stimulus object enhances his attitude. . . . By mere exposure is meant a condition making the stimulus accessible to the individual's perception." In a marketing context, it follows that repeated exposure to a brand name (or package) should be able to mediate brand judgments independently of cognitive evaluation or contextual association.

Recent studies in an advertising context (Moore and Hutchinson 1985; Baker 1985; see Baker et al. 1986) support the robust results found in the social psychology literature (see Harrison 1977). In these advertising-related studies, repeated exposures to brand names significantly increased brand attitudes and purchase intentions after other potential advertising effects (for example, CS and AAD effects) were removed statistically. This research suggests that brand name familiarity effects are (1) applicable to advertising, (2) durable over time, and (3) strongest when information pertaining to other constructs is not recalled at the time of brand evaluation.

*Involvement and Accessibility Moderate*
*Constructs' Mediational Potential*

In the past few years, the effects of cognitive structure, attitude toward the ad, and brand-name familiarity have been studied in tandem. The thrust of this work is to identify factors that specify when each construct is most likely to dominate advertising-based evaluations. These efforts represent attempts to move from the study of advertising effects (that is, studying how advertising can work) to the study of advertising effectiveness (that is, determining the factors that influence when a given advertising effect does work).

**Involvement.** A large body of research relating consumer involvement to advertising effects has accumulated (see Krugman 1965, 1971; Robertson 1976; Park and Young

Young 1986; Gardner 1985; MacKenzie, Lutz, and Belch 1986). The dominant involvement-based perspective is the Elaboration Likelihood Model (ELM) (Petty and Cacioppo 1981). The ELM rests on the proposition that consumer involvement at the time of message reception determines the type of information that is encoded and subsequently used to evaluate the brand. The ELM identifies two general persuasion routes. When consumers are highly involved at the time of message reception, the *central route* is operative and brand evaluations are derived from the effortful interpretation of message arguments. When consumers are not involved, the peripheral route is operative and brand evaluation is a function of peripheral persuasion cues such as source credibility.

The most important general result of the involvement research stream is that involvement influences the type of advertising effect that is most effective in a given situation. Attribute information is most effective when involvement is high. Executional information (for example, source credibility) is most effective when involvement is low.

Within the RAM perspective, the key problem with this research is that involvement has been studied only at the advertising exposure occasion (that is, consumer motivation to process advertisements), and not at the brand response occasion. The RAM advocates that involvement must be studied at *both* occasions.

**Information Accessibility.** The proposition that information accessibility at the time of brand evaluation is a prerequisite to the use of that information derives from a long-standing assertion in the psychology literature (Tversky and Kahneman 1973; Reyes, Thompson, and Bower 1978) and has recently been proposed in a marketing context as the availability-valence hypothesis (AVH) (Kisielius and Sternthal 1984). The AVH states that brand evaluation is a direct function of the valence (that is, evaluative implications) of information that is accessed into working memory at the time of brand response.

Two direct implications of the AVH concerning the mediational ability of advertising-related constructs are: (1) the ability of any given construct to mediate brand judgment is a function of the accessibility of construct-related information at the time of evaluation; thus if attribute beliefs are accessed, then CS contributes to the brand evaluation; if evaluative reactions to advertisments are accessed, the AAD contributes to the evaluation, and so on, and (2) the mediating effects of construct-related processes are additive in nature, implying that different constructs can impact *simultaneously* on brand judgments.

Baker (1985) tested these implications by measuring both the accessibility and mediational strength of CS, AAD, and BNF across levels of repetition and delay. Results generally supported the first implication of the AVH; the mediational potential of different constructs was a function of their accessibility. However, results contradicted the AVH's second implication. Direct effects of constructs were *not* apparently additive. When cognitive structure mediation was strong, attitude toward the ad and brand-name familiarity mediation were inhibited, *regardless* of their accessibility.

When the effect of attitude toward the ad was strong, the direct effect of brand-name familiarity was inhibited regardless of its strength.

The major implication of this research is that the AVH is incomplete in the sense that information that is accessed at the brand response occasion may not necessarily influence brand judgment. That is, Baker's results are consistent with the idea that AAD information may have been accessed during the judgment process, but subsequently discounted as irrelevant relative to attribute information. Thus, accessibility may be a necessary but not *sufficient* condition for the mediational potential of any given advertising information. The RAM adopts this position.

**The Principle of Higher Level Dominance.** The Principle of Higher Level Dominance (PHLD) incorporates effects of both involvement and accessibility (Greenwald and Leavitt 1984). It proposes that consumer involvement with an advertising message determines the level of processing that the message receives and, hence, the level of information that is encoded during message reception. When involvement is very low, pure affect is encoded; when involvement is low, heuristic quality cues are encoded; and when involvement is high, detailed attribute information is encoded.

The PHLD asserts that consumer involvement at the time of advertising message exposure affects the perceived relevance of different types of advertising information for processing. As involvement increases, the ability of lower-level information to mediate brand evaluation is inhibited because it is perceived as less relevant during message exposure and as a result receives less processing. The lack of processing makes this information less accessible relative to the higher-level information that is the focus of consumer attention.

The RAM also asserts that consumer involvement influences the perceived relevance of information, but it proposes that advertising effectiveness is determined by both consumer involvement at the time of message processing (by determining the type of information that is encoded) and consumer involvement at the time of brand choice (by determining the type of information that is sought by consumers to discriminate brand alternatives). Thus the RAM extends the propositions of the PHLD to incorporate the brand response occasion.

## Advertising Effectiveness Research Requires a Change in Research Perspective

The Availability-Valence Hypothesis, Elaboration Likelihood Model, and the Principle of Higher Level Dominance all represent moves away from advertising effects research towards advertising effectiveness research because they identify factors that determine the type of advertising effect that can be expected to operate in a given situation. They overlook, however, some changes in perspective that are needed when one moves to the study of advertising effectiveness. The Relevance-

Accessibility Model (RAM) is built upon three major premises that prior research has wholly or partially ignored.

### Advertising Effects Occur at the Brand Response Occasion

A commonality among the AVH, PHLD, and ELM is that they study advertising effects at the advertising exposure occasion. That is, they all assume that the relevance, accessibility, and evaluative implications of advertising information are determined at the point of advertising reception. The RAM makes no such assumption.

According to the RAM, advertising effectiveness must be studied in the context of the brand response occasion (BRO) (that is, where and when brand choices are made), not the advertising exposure occasion (AEO) (that is, where and when advertisement presentation occurs). The RAM assumes that brand choices are made in the context of the BRO, not the AEO. The two are clearly distinct in time and space; therefore, their roles in determining advertising effectiveness must be considered separately.

Once the focus of research shifts to the BRO, two major barriers to advertising effectiveness emerge that are not readily apparent when research centers on the AEO. First, advertising must provide information perceived as *relevant* relative to other informational sources that may be consulted at the BRO (for example, usage experiences, package information). Second, advertising-generated information must be highly *accessible* (that is, easily retrieved) relative to any competing sources of information.

### An Extended Accessibility Perspective

With one major exception, the RAM asserts that brand evaluation is typically a function of the valence of raw information (that is, pure affect, heuristic quality cues, relative performance information) that is accessed into working memory at the BRO. The exception occurs when consumers have strong, highly accessible brand preferences. Prior preferences are expected to drive brand response when the consumer believes (1) there is no new information pertinent to the brand choice (for example, there have been no changes in the characteristics of brand alternatives), (2) there are no new brands to consider, and (3) there is no change in evaluation context (for example, buying a wine for a gift as opposed to personal consumption) (Lingle and Ostrom 1979; Carlston 1980; Lichtenstein and Srull 1985; Biehal and Chakravarti 1986). In all other scenarios, raw information is expected to drive brand response.

This perspective is similar to the availability-valence hypothesis with two exceptions. First, the RAM identifies factors at both the AEO (for example, advertising-message involvement, message repetition, message design factors) and the BRO (decision-making involvement, memory cues, and so on) that influence information accessibility. The AVH discusses only factors at the AEO. Second, the RAM supposes that information accessibility is a necessary but not sufficient condition for information usage at the brand response occasion. The RAM proposes that consumers can access, but then discount, information as irrelevant to the choice task. The AVH assumes that all accessed information affects the choice process.

The RAM employs the network model of memory (Anderson and Bower 1980) and spreading activation theory (Anderson 1983; Bower 1981; Pirolli and Anderson 1985) to frame how (1) factors at the AEO influence the structural accessibility of advertising information (that is, accessibility as a function of how efficiently advertising information is stored in brand memory) and (2) factors at the BRO influence the process whereby stored information enters working memory (that is, accessibility as a function of retrieval cues and deliberate consumer information search through brand memory).

### The Concept of Relative Advantage

According to the RAM, the goal of advertising is to contribute to the brand judgment process by giving a brand a "relative advantage" over competing alternatives at the BRO, and *not* (necessarily) to generate favorable brand attitudes at the AEO.

**Brand Response Potential as the Key Dependent Variable.** The summary force toward or away from the brand, *brand response potential* is an internal construct embodying the motivational properties of salient cognitive and affective brand information recalled during the BRO. It is perhaps best construed as an approach-avoidance tendency, an immediate precursor to overt behavior. The motivational properties of brand associates are those properties which provide information regarding the ability of the brand to satisfy the behavioral goals present during a particular BRO (for example, behavioral goals may range from wanting to buy the best brand in a particular product class, a satisfactory brand, or any available brand).

Brand response potential subsumes choice-related constructs including brand preference and purchase intention. Within the RAM, brand preference is defined as the explicit, context-dependent assessment of a brand's relative advantage over one or more other brands. Brand preference is a function of the choice-related motivational properties of brand information that is accessed and utilized at the BRO to discriminate brands. Brand preference embodies the consequences of brand response potential because it explicitly reflects the notion of relative advantage; the brand with the highest brand response potential at the BRO is by definition the most preferred brand.

Choice is a behavioral expression of preference at the BRO, but a preference is not necessarily explicitly formed or sufficiently encoded into memory at the BRO that it will be accessed and utilized at subsequent BROs (see Fazio 1986). Thus, choice is a behavioral reflection of preference, but that preference may be limited to one BRO only.

### Predicting Relative Advantage

First, as already emphasized, relative advantage must be predicted by focusing on expected consumer behavior at the BRO, not consumer perceptions of advertising at the AEO. Second, attitudinal reactions towards brands at the BRO are insufficient to predict relative advantage. The specific information that consumers are expected to use at the BRO to discriminate brands must be identified (for example, specific performance dimensions like automobile styling or heuristic cues like manufacturer reputation). Third, brands must be compared explicitly on the basis of the information that is expected to be used to discriminate them.

If advertising information is both (1) perceived to be relevant and (2) accessible, then it is likely to influence assessments of relative advantage and brand response potential. If it is either irrelevant or inaccessible, then it is not likely to contribute to the brand response process.

## Advertising Effects at the Brand Response Occasion

### Three Distinct "Levels of Information" Mediate Brand Response Potential

The RAM advocates a "levels of information" approach to studying consumer activity at the BRO and provides a methodology for identifying the level of information expected to mediate brand response potential at any given BRO. The information level perspective specifically identifies the type of information that consumers are expected to use at the BRO to make their brand choices.

**"Levels" Identification.** Given the predominance of advertising message strategies that emphasize the use of affective (that is, feeling) and heuristic (for example, credible spokespeople) appeals, it is clear that astute advertisers have known for decades that consumers do not always employ specific performance-related information at the BRO.

A significant amount of recent research has established consumers' use of *heuristic quality cues* to form brand attitudes and purchase intentions. Heuristic cues such as source credibility (Sternthal, Dholakia, and Leavitt 1978; Chaiken 1980; Petty, Cacioppo, and Schumann 1983); brand-name prestige (Wheatley, Walton, and Chiu 1982; Raju 1977), price (Monroe 1973; Gardner 1971), and the deliberate evaluation of advertising execution elements (Gardner 1985; Park and Young 1986; Lutz 1985) mediate brand evaluation when consumers do not have the motivation, opportunity, or ability to discriminate brands on the basis of attribute performance beliefs.

After Mitchell and Olson (1981) demonstrated the ability of attitude toward the ad to directly mediate brand attitudes, a stream of research emerged to investigate the role of advertising-generated *affective states* on brand attitudes and choice, particularly via affective classical conditioning (Gorn 1982; Nord and Peter 1980; Kroeber-Riel 1984; McSweeney and Bierly 1984) and the brand-name familiarity construct (Baker et al. 1986; Obermiller 1985; Moore and Hutchinson 1985). The ability of affective mood states to bias the encoding, interpretation, and retrieval of message information is also garnering increasing research attention (see Gardner 1985).

The RAM proposes that pure affect, heuristic quality cues, and attribute beliefs constitute three qualitatively different levels of information (cf. Greenwald and Leavitt 1984). Each successive level provides increasingly direct, concrete evidence regarding a brand's utility relative to competing alternatives. *Pure affect* is the lowest level; it provides vague, nondescript brand information. The natural reinforcing properties of affect, however, can be sufficient to change brand choice behavior (Batra and Ray 1985; Kroeber-Riel 1984; Nord and Peter 1980). *Heuristic quality cues* are at an intermediate level, providing descriptive information that may be used to make global absolute influences about a brand's performance (for example, credible source). *Relative attribute information* is the highest level of information; it provides specific performance information that allows direct comparisons among competing brand alternatives.

**Summary.** The RAM takes the perspective that advertising effectiveness should be studied in the context of "levels of information." Three levels of information can mediate brand response potential: *"relative" benefits*, that is, relative utility across one or more performance dimensions; *heuristic cues*, that is, reassuring attribute surrogates such as trustworthy spokespeople; and *pure affect*, that is, the feelings generated by the ad.

## Three Persuasion Routes Correspond to the Three Levels of Information

In the last several years, theoretical and empirical evidence regarding persuasion routes involving different levels of information has proliferated in the marketing literature (for example, Krugman 1965; Batra and Ray 1982; Gorn 1982; Petty, Cacioppo, and Schumann 1983; MacKenzie, Lutz, and Belch 1986). This research typically has focused on only two routes, but a careful analysis of the research suggests three routes. Studies by Batra and Ray (1983, 1985) and Gorn (1982) have centered on distinguishing between effects of pure affect and relative performance information. Other work (MacKenzie, Lutz, and Belch 1986; Petty, Cacioppo, and Schumann 1983) has distinguished between effects of relative performance information and heuristic quality cues. Combined, the independent effects of all three levels of information discussed above have been studied. The principle of higher-level dominance (Greenwald and Leavitt 1984) postulates that three qualitatively different levels of advertising message involvement lead to the encoding of three qualitatively different types of information roughly corresponding to the three levels of information identified above. The PHLD explicitly asserts that the perceived relevance of advertising message information at the advertising exposure occasion is the primary determinant of the level of processing that the messages receive, and, hence, the type of information that is encoded and used at the AEO to form brand attitudes. *If involvement at the AEO in part determines the type of information that consumers prefer to encode and use to form brand perceptions at the AEO, it logically follows that involvement at the BRO should affect the type of information that is sought to discriminate brand alternatives.* Thus, the principle of higher-level dominance also implies the existence of three persuasion routes.

*Decision-Making Involvement Activates*
*One of Three Brand Response Routes*

Decision-making involvement is defined as a motivational construct embodying the degree of cognitive effort expended by the consumer to implement a brand response process. Within the context of the RAM, a *brand response process* is defined as the judgmental process that culminates in the evoking of a brand response potential. It involves four interdependent stages: (1) invoking a preferred brand response route, (2) accessing brand associates, (3) selecting a specific brand response rule, and (4) implementing the brand response rule.

Both the Elaboration Likelihood Model and the Principle of Higher Level Dominance identify involvement as the critical mechanism that switches the focus from one level of information to another. Likewise, decision-making involvement is the "switching mechanism" of the RAM.

A key proposition of the RAM is that qualitatively different brand response routes are invoked by consumers along the decision-making involvement continuum. Brand response routes are defined primarily on the basis of the level of information used in the brand response process, but also by the deliberateness by which brand associates are accessed from memory and the *minimum* cognitive effort required to implement the evaluation. Therefore, brand response routes are defined as generic brand response processes that invoke qualitatively similar brand information, deliberateness of information acquisition, and cognitive operations.

**Level of Information.** The RAM assumes that as decision-making involvement increases, increasingly complex representations of the product class and specific competing brands in memory become activated as potential sources of input into the brand response process (see Fiske 1982). At the low end of the DMI continuum, consumers are expected to seek simple affective responses to discriminate brands. In the middle of the DMI continuum, heuristic quality cues are expected to be sought; and at the high end of the DMI continuum, consumers seek relative attribute information to make their brand choices.

**Information Acquisition.** As decision-making involvement increases, the information acquisition process becomes increasingly deliberate. Deliberateness is the degree to which consumers control the accessing of brand associates into working memory. As deliberateness increases, the acquisition process becomes more a function of motivated consumer search and less a function of external activating cues and automatic processing.

A direct implication of increasing deliberateness is that the choice to input a given piece of information into the brand response process becomes increasingly a function of relative importance rather than relative salience (that is, order of retrieval). Thus, at the low end of the DMI continuum, brand associates must be accessed effortlessly if they are to contribute to brand judgment. In the middle of the DMI continuuum, information search stops after the first piece of information perceived to be a reliable brand discriminator is accessed. At the high end of the DMI continuum, consumers are likely to thoroughly search brand-memory networks for the most important brand associates before choosing a subset to include in the judgment process.

**Minimum Cognitive Effort.** As DMI increases, qualitatively different brand response rules characterized by increasing complexity are implemented. At the low end of the DMI continuum, the automatic reinforcing properties of accessed information typically determine brand response potential. In the middle of the DMI continuum, simple inferences drawn from accessed brand associates drive brand response potential. At the high end of the DMI continuum, multiple cognitive operations performed on accessed brand associates characterize brand response potential formation.

**Predicting Decision-making Involvement.** Decision-making involvement can be predicted if its antecedents are identified and measured. The purpose of this discussion is to identify antecedents of DMI at a general level, not to generate an exhaustive taxonomy (see Muhlbacher 1985; Kapferer and Laurent 1985 for more specific antecedents). The RAM views decision-making involvement to be a direct function of perceived risk. This perspective is consistent with research that ties decision-making involvement to perceived product class differentiation (for example, Robertson 1976; Batra and Ray 1983).

Assuming that DMI is a product of perceived risk, it follows that DMI has two general antecedents. The first antecedent is the perceived probability of making a poor brand choice. The second antecedent is the perceived consequences of making a poor choice. When buyers perceive both a high probability and serious consequences of a poor choice, DMI can be expected to be high. When buyers perceive a high probability but only minor consequences of a poor choice decision, then DMI can be expected to be low. When buyers perceive both a low probability and trivial consequences of a poor choice, DMI can be expected to be very low.

*Specification of Three Brand Response Routes*

Descriptions of each of RAM's three brand response routes follow. Each description includes the route's motivational antecedents, the level of information that is used to mediate relative advantage formation, the deliberateness by which information to be used in the brand response process is accessed, the cognitive requirements to implement the brand response process, and the specific construct-related processes that are most likely to be operational within the route.

**Consumer Mindlessness.** The "mindlessness" route is expected to be invoked at the extreme low end of the DMI continuum. Relative-advantage mediation and brand-response potential formation are expected to be a function of the intrinsic reinforcing qualities of brand-associated affect. In behavioristic terms, positive affect is expected to motivate approach behavior, while negative affect is expected to motivate avoidance behavior (Nord and Peter 1982; Ross and Ross 1975). Any intervening processes that may occur between the time of affect retrieval and actual brand choice are considered artifactual, as affect is the true cause of behavior (Skinner 1974).

Deliberate effort is not required either to retrieve brand-associated affect (Posner and Snyder 1975; Bargh 1984) or to transform the affect into a behavioral response (Zajonc and Marcus 1982), because affect is presumed to be accessed automatically and, consequently, generate a brand response potential automatically.

To be effective when mindlessness is operating, it is sufficient for advertising to associate positive feelings to the brand (for example, "Reach out and touch someone!"). Given the absence of deliberate cognitive effort, the advertising-generated feelings must be automatically accessed at the brand response occasion in order to impact on the brand response process. This implies that the generated affect must be strong (Dutta and Kanungo 1972), heavily repeated (Nord and Peter 1980), and/or externally cued at the brand response occasion. The advertising-based construct processes best suited to operate through this route are affect transfer (Gorn 1982) and the exposure effect (Baker et al. 1986).

Advertising-generated affective input may be ambiguous affect (for example, good–bad feelings) or may take a more specific form as in mood responses (see Gardner 1985). Since mood responses are more specific, they may possess more motivational properties in some brand response occasion contexts than does ambiguous affect (for example, in the case of perfume, associating sexual arousal to a brand may lead to a stronger brand response potential than association to an ambiguous positive feeling).

**Consumer Satisficing.** The "satisficing" route is expected to be used in the middle of the DMI continuum. When consumers satisfice they are expected to seek information reassuring them that they are making a good choice. Price (Monroe 1973), brand name prestige (Wheatley, Walton, and Chiu 1978), the number of brand benefits (Alba and Marmorstein 1987), and source credibility (Petty, Cacioppo, and Schumann 1983) are all examples of heuristic quality cues that can mediate brand response potential when consumers are not motivated to use more specific information such as relative usage benefits. It also follows that knowledge of simple attribute possession (for example, knowledge that Bayer is gentle to the stomach, not whether it is gentler to the stomach than other aspirins) can evoke a strong brand response potential when consumers are satisficing.

Satisficing is also defined by deliberate, but biased, information acquisition. That is, consumers deliberately seek specific information to make their judgments, but use the first information perceived to be a reliable brand discriminator because there is insufficient motivation to thoroughly search brand response schemas (see Taylor and Fiske 1978). Thus, the *relative* accessibility of heuristic cues and absolute brand-attribute possession is expected to become critical to its use at the brand response occasion. Factors that influence the structural accessibility of information in brand memory networks (for example, message repetition, cognitive elaboration) or which bias the information acquisition process play a large role in determining which heuristic quality cue or attribute discriminates brands. Two major factors that bias the information acquisition process are external cuing (Anderson 1983; Bargh 1984) and automatically accessed affect (see Bower and Gordon 1982; Clark and Isen 1982).

Deliberate cognitive effort is required to select and implement the brand response rule. In other words, deliberate effort is required to comprehend the evaluative meaning of accessed information and to generate the inferences leading to the brand evaluation. For example, if brands are discriminated on the basis of brand name prestige, then one or more brands must be comprehended on the basis of prestige, and evaluative inference based on prestige must be generated deliberately.

To be effective under satisficing, advertising messages need only emphasize heuristic quality cues (for example, Bayer is recommended by doctors two to one or simple attribute possession (for example, Bayer works fast). Given the low motivation to search brand response schemas for the best heuristic cues or the most important attributes, it is also imperative that advertising-generated brand associates are accessed *prior* to other acceptable heuristic cues. This proposition is consistent with research on the effects of relative information accessibility (that is, order of retrieval of information) in psychology (Taylor and Fiske 1978; Hogue 1984) and the research on information prominence and problem framing in marketing (Gardner 1983; Wright and Rip 1980). The construct-related processes corresponding to the functioning of this route are AAD-based inference-making (MacKenzie, Lutz, and Belch 1985), source credibility effects (Petty, Cacioppo, and Schumann 1983), and the BNF-based frequency effect (Baker et al. 1986).

**Consumer Optimizing.** The "optimizing" route is expected to be used when buyers perceive both a high probability and serious consequences of a poor choice. When consumers optimize, brand response potential is derived via the systematic integration of relative attribute beliefs on utilitarian (for example, Camaros are faster than Firebirds) and/or hedonic (Camaros symbolize an adventurous spirit more than Firebirds) performance dimensions. Information acquisition is deliberate and thorough relative to the other brand response routes (that is, perceived informational importance drives information usage rather than order of retrieval). Consumers are motivated to exhaustively search brand response schemas and the external environment (for example, point of purchase information) for pertinent relative benefit information.

Significant cognitive effort is required to implement the optimizing route. Unlike mindlessness or satisficing, the brand response process requires explicit inter-brand comparisons and is typically multidimensional in nature. Brand response potential is the output of systematic compensatory or noncompensatory strategies that require consumers to disaggregate brand performance into its most important dimensions. Considerable deliberate effort is generally required to form relative attribute beliefs and to assimilate these beliefs into an overall brand evaluation (Bettman 1979; Lutz and Swasy 1977; Toy 1982).

To be effective when consumers are optimizing, advertising must generate relative performance beliefs (for example, Bayer provides faster pain relief than Excedrin). Unlike the other response routes, message cogency is more important than message accessibility. That is, it is more important that advertising cogently communicate information on a brand's most influential performance dimensions than maximize the accessibility of message information relative to other informational sources. The construct operating through this route is brand attribute cognitive structure.

### Nonmotivational Antecedents of the Invoked Brand Response Route

Decision-making involvement is the primary construct in the RAM. It determines the level of information that consumers seek to discriminate brands and how that information is accessed and used. Hence it determines the type of information which advertisements must contain in order to be effective. The RAM does not assume, however, that DMI is the only factor that determines the operative brand response route at any given brand response occasion. Several factors can moderate DMI effects.

**Information Availability.** Before information can become accessible, it must be available. As information becomes available, particularly in a form that facilitates its input into the brand response process, its usage in brand response processes increases. A DMI-invoked brand response route cannot become operative unless the level of information corresponding to that route is available either in memory or at the brand response occasion.

**Consumer Ability and Opportunity.** The operative brand response route corresponds to the uppermost limit allowed by the level of consumer motivation, ability, and opportunity at the brand response occasion (Petty and Cacioppo 1981; Batra and Ray 1986). It follows that consumers must have the ability and opportunity to implement the motivationally preferred brand response route. If the ability and opportunity are not present, then consumer cognitive activity becomes limited and the DMI-invoked route cannot be implemented (Alba and Hutchinson 1986; Wright 1973, 1980).

**Consumer Experience.** Extensive experience with specific brand response rules decreases the cognitive effort required to access (Anderson and Pirroli 1983) and implement these rules (see Alba and Hutchinson 1986). Conversely, a lack of practice increases the cognitive effort required to implement a given brand response rule. For example, a value-based brand response rule arguably requires the explicit consideration of multiple dimensions: price and one or more attribute dimensions. Thus it should be expected typically to require a level of consumer DMI corresponding to the optimizing route. If, however, estimations of the quality of brand alternatives are well learned, and consumers have practiced combining price and quality estimates into value estimates, then the level of cognitive effort may correspond to a lower point on the DMI continuum, and the value-based brand response rule may thus be invoked easily at a level of DMI that corresponds more closely to the satisficing route.

**Tie-breaking.** Perhaps the strongest moderator of DMI-invoked persuasion route follows directly from the literature on lexicographic choice processes (Tversky 1972; Bettman 1979). In a lexicographic choice process, consumers attempt to discriminate brand alternatives on the basis of the performance dimension perceived to be most important. If discrimination is not possible because brand alternatives "tie" on that dimension, then consumers must move to the next most important dimension to discriminate brand alternatives.

It follows that if the implementation of a brand response process fails to generate a relative advantage, then another brand response route may be invoked to discriminate brands. For example, if consumers are motivated to optimize but brands are perceived as similar across attribute dimensions, then a heuristic quality cue within the satisficing route may become the effective discriminator. Likewise, if heuristic cues are unable to discriminate brands, then the mindlessness route may be used to discriminate the brands.

More specifically, if DMI remains the same after an unsuccessful brand response process, then the consumer is expected to reinvoke the same brand response route (for example, new benefit dimensions, heuristic cues, or sources of affect can be accessed to attempt to differentiate brands). If DMI remains the same, but implementation of another brand response process within the same route is not possible (for example, availability, ability, opportunity constraints come into play), or if DMI decreases, then the consumer is expected to invoke a brand response route corresponding to a lower level of DMI (for example, consumers move from satisficing to mindlessness). If DMI increases after the unsuccessful brand response process implementation, then the consumer can be expected to switch to a brand response route corresponding to a higher level of DMI (for example, consumers move from satisficing to optimizing). Finally, if no brand response route can effectively discriminate brands, then the consumer is expected to behave randomly.

## Advertising Effects at the Advertising Exposure Occasion

### Advertising Message Involvement

According to the RAM, advertising-generated brand associates must be accessible at the brand response occasion for advertising to be effective. The RAM identifies advertising message involvement as an AEO-based construct fundamental to advertising effectiveness because it is the primary determinant of the type of advertising information that is encoded at the time of advertising exposure.

Advertising message involvement (AMI) is defined as a motivational construct embodying the amount of cognitive effort directed by the consumer at processing the contents of an advertising message. The RAM proposes that different levels of processing along the AMI continuum lead to the encoding of different levels of information. At the high end of the AMI continuum, consumer cognitive activity is expected to lead to the encoding of relative benefit information. In the middle of the AMI continuum, absolute brand information is typically encoded. At the extreme low end of the AMI continuum, consumer encoding is generally limited to simple affective associates.

### Predicting AMI

In the most general terms, message-directed arousal at the advertising exposure occasion is the primary antecedent of AMI (Kroeber-Riel 1979; Cohen 1982). Arousal is generated by a complex interaction of external (for example, the qualities of the advertising message and internal (for example, product class interest) factors. Advertising strategists can directly influence the former but have limited control over the latter.

Evidence suggests that message stimuli perceived as relevant (Toy 1982; Brock and Albert 1978; Greenwald and Leavitt 1984), novel (Berlyne 1970), or intensely affective (Kroeber-Riel 1979; Dutta and Kanungo 1972) at the advertising exposure occasion receive greater attention and more intense processing than other message stimuli. This results in greater accessibility over other message stimuli.

Internally-based antecedents of AMI include factors such as general product class interest (Muhlbacher 1985), competing goals at the time of advertising message reception (Kapferer and Laurent 1985), consumers' need for additional information

(Burnkrant and Sawyer 1983), and anticipated decision-making involvement (Petty and Cacioppo 1981).

## The Consequences of AMI on Message Processing

The RAM conceptualization of information encoding at the advertising exposure occasion is consistent with Alba and Hasher's (1983) prototypical schema theory of information encoding, Fiske's (1982) proposition that evaluative schemas change with involvement, Alba and Hutchinson's (1986) distinction between analytic and non-analytic processing, and recent theoretical and empirical evidence in advertising on the effects of AMI on levels of processing effects on information encoding (Greenwald and Leavitt 1984; Batra and Ray 1985; Park and Young 1986; Gardner 1985).

**Level of Processing.** Level of processing refers to the extent to which a brand memory network is activated and utilized to encode meaningful brand associates from the message stimulus. The level of processing is a direct function of AMI when the inhibiting effects of factors such as consumer processing ability and opportunity are not present. The AMI-determined level of processing is postulated to set off a chain of cognitive activity that typically leads to the encoding of different levels of information along the AMI continuum.

The RAM postulates that as AMI increases, increasingly complex representations of the product-class concept as well as specific brand concepts in memory are activated. At the extreme low end of the AMI continuum, brand response schema activation is haphazard and is limited to the external activation of message-based concepts (for example, a picture of the brand may ignite the brand concept node) and the automatic activation of these concepts' habitual brand associates (for example, feelings about the brand) (Posner and Snyder 1975; Zajonc 1980). In the middle of the AMI continuum, elements of the brand memory network are deliberately activated to facilitate complete message comprehension, interpretation, and integration with respect to current *brand knowledge*. At the extreme high end of the AMI continuum, highly controlled activation of multiple brand memory networks facilitates comprehension, interpretation, and integration with respect to current *product class knowledge*.

Thus, consumers' levels of processing determine the nature and extent of prior knowledge that is used to interpret and evaluate message arguments. The output of this process is the deliberate (or nondeliberate) generation of abstractions that house the interpreted meaning of the message in the brand memory network (see Alba and Hasher 1983).

A message abstraction is defined here as a self-generated semantic proposition derived from the content of an advertising stimulus that acts as an interpretational summary of one or more advertising message elements. It may or may not resemble the intended meaning of the advertising stimulus, depending on the information's compatibility with existing consumer beliefs and values. Since abstractions are interpretational summaries of message content, they are stored in memory more efficiently than the message stimulus itself.

The RAM argues that the type of abstraction generated at the AEO is dependent on the level of processing that the message receives. Affective abstractions refer to self-generated semantic propositions containing affect, mood, or emotion. They are expected typically to be evoked *automatically* at the low end of the AMI continuum where message processing does not involve explicit schema activation and as a result is limited to simple automatic reactions to advertising messages. The valence of affective reactions is dependent on the valence of the affect associated to activated message concepts (for example, beautiful sunsets automatically evoke positive feelings; disaster sites automatically evoke negative feelings).

Absolute brand abstractions are self-generated semantic propositions that describe the brand but are incapable of directly facilitating the relative comparison of competing brand alternatives (for example, Camaros are fast). Absolute brand abstractions typically are evoked in the middle of the AMI continuum where message information is interpreted solely within the context of information in the brand memory network. The valence of the abstraction is dependent on the consistency of the message information with activated information in the *brand* memory network.

Relative brand abstractions are self-generated semantic propositions that describe the brand and are capable of facilitating the relative comparison of competing brand alternatives during a particular brand response occasion (for example, Bayer relieves pain better then Excedrin). Relative abstractions are evoked at the high end of the AMI continuum where consumers are motivated to interpret brand information in the context of entire *product-class* memory networks.

**Level of Information Sought for Processing.** The RAM, like other recent theoretical accounts (Greenwald and Leavitt 1984; Mitchell 1981; Batra and Ray 1985) and empirical research (Petty, Cacioppo, and Schumann 1983; Park and Young 1986; Gardner 1985), asserts that AMI not only determines the overall level of processing that a message receives but also the level of message information that consumers perceive to be *worth* processing.

For example, if AMI is at the extreme high end of the continuum, correspondingly higher levels of information become the focus of processing (for example, relative usage information) and lower levels of information (for example, highly affective stimuli, heuristic quality cues) either play indirect roles (see MacKenzie, Lutz, and Belch 1986) or are ignored completely (Petty and Cacioppo 1981; Greenwald and Leavitt 1984).

*Consequences of AMI on the Level of Information*
*Encoded at the AEO*

If AMI influences the level of message processing and the level of information that is attended, it follows that qualitatively different advertising-generated brand associates are structurally more accessible along the advertising message involvement continuum. The RAM identifies three levels of AMI that correspond in intensity to the three levels of DMI discussed earlier. These three levels correspond closely to three of the four levels of AMI recently postulated by Greenwald and Leavitt (1984).

**Very Low AMI.** Consumers are not motivated to actively comprehend, interpret, or integrate message content into their brand or product-class memory networks. As a result, neither absolute nor relative abstractions typically are generated during message exposure. Instead, consumers react passively to the message, generating few coherence (inferences which tie together the different propositions of a message and allow complete comprehension), simplifying (inferences which summarize the meaning of the message in an easily retrievable form), or integrative (inferences which relate message information to prior knowledge and allow generation of a relative attribute beliefs) cognitive responses (Alba and Hutchinson 1986).

The level of processing typically associated with very low AMI is termed *sensory identification*. Sensory identification processing is limited to the recognition (that is, external activation) of advertising message stimuli and the automatic activation of their habitual associates (Posner and Snyder 1975). Only advertising elements that are comprehended automatically (for example, affective reaction to a beautiful sunset) and encoded without effort (for example, intense affective reactions can create strong memory traces without deliberate rehearsal or elaboration) are likely to be sufficiently encoded at the advertising exposure occasion such that they are accessible at subsequent brand response occasions.

Automatic activation is limited to those message elements that can leave strong, efficiently stored memory traces in the absence of significant consumer processing. Simple visual imagery, particularly intense affect, meets these requirements better than other brand associate types (Bower 1981; Bargh 1984; Zajonc 1980). The RAM predicts that simple affective reactions are likely to be the only level of information to be encoded sufficiently when AMI is very low. This is consistent with other perspectives on very low involvement message processing (Batra and Ray 1983, 1985; Kroeber-Riel 1984; Gorn 1982).

**Low AMI.** When AMI is low, consumers are motivated to comprehend and relate message information to the brand memory network, but are not motivated to relate message information to the product-class memory network. Processing is focused on message information that facilitates the generation of absolute abstractions. Neither peripheral information such as affect-evoking executional elements nor the comprehension or interpretation of message implications relative to competitive brands are the focus of message processing.

Low AMI is characterized by *comprehension* level processing. Messages are interpreted in the context of activated portions of the brand memory network. Those portions of the network that are necessary to comprehend and interpret the message at a relative level are not deliberately activated. That is, memory networks are activated to interpret the ad at an absolute level (for example, the car is fast, the source is an expert, the style is sporty, and so on, not to determine if the advertised car is faster or sportier than its competition). Since abstractions are absolute in nature, the most accessible type of information to result from this processing is expected to be absolute brand associates (for example, heuristic quality cues and attribute possession beliefs). Message content elements that are not interpreted or summarized via absolute abstractions are less likely to be as accessible structurally because they are not the focus of attention or of abstraction generation.

**High AMI.** When AMI is high, consumers are motivated to comprehend and relate message information to the product-class memory network. Processing is focused on specific information that allows interpretation of the brand at a relative level. Relative performance information that can be used to compare brands is sought for processing, while other information is not processed. If no information in the ad is perceived to be pertinent to interbrand comparisons, then processing is likely to be limited (Brock and Albert 1978; Toy 1982).

High AMI is characterized by *integration* level processing. Activation is directed effortfully to areas of the brand response schema that allow the comparison of message stimulus information with concepts and events relating to competing brand alternatives (for example, comparing message information on Camaros with knowledge about Firebirds to assess the relative speed of Camaros). Integration level processing typically leads to the generation of relative abstractions. Thus, the most accessible advertising-generated brand associates are typically relative in nature.

Since message information is related explicitly to existing knowledge, highly credible message arguments must be made. Depending on the content of activated concepts, relative abstractions may or may not carry the meaning intended by the advertiser. As a result, the associates encoded during message exposure may bear little resemblance to the actual propositions in the message (Wright 1980; Petty and Cacioppo 1979, 1981).

### Moderators of AMI Effects on Brand Associate Accessibility

While AMI is considered the primary determinant of the accessibility of different types of information, many other factors affect the accessibility of advertising-generated brand associates. Moderators of AMI effects include consumer processing ability, opportunity, and expertise; message design features; ad execution management; advertising repetition schedules; and external cuing at the brand response occasion.

The RAM asserts that proper management of the above factors is necessary but not sufficient to maximize the accessibility of advertising-generated brand associates relative to competing information sources at the brand response occasion.

That is, it is unlikely that these factors typically will compensate for a lack of consumer motivation to process the message at the required level, particularly in nonintrusive media such as magazines.

**Consumer Opportunity and Ability.** Consumer processing opportunity and ability can inhibit implementation of the preferred level of processing (Wright 1980; Petty and Cacioppo 1981; Batra and Ray 1986). If the ability or opportunity is not present to encode brand associates at the motivated level of processing, then the operative level of processing is limited to the uppermost level permitted by ability and opportunity factors.

**Consumer Expertise.** The highly efficient and interconnected brand and product-class memory networks of experts decrease the effort required to activate and utilize these memory networks (Alba and Hutchinson 1986). At encoding, comprehension and elaboration are easier and faster. It is also likely that fewer facts need to be encoded effortfully (that is, most information is already integrated into memory structures), so more processing capacity can be allocated to the task of integrating new information into the network.

**Message Design Factors.** Brand associate accessibility is a function of message content efficiency, vividness, and associational explicitness. Efficiently communicated messages (for example, visual or concrete verbal information) increase the storage efficiency of the message content. Vivid stimuli (for example, visual demonstrations) increase the interconnectedness of message content. Explicit association of message content to the brand name and within message repetition of a key message proposition can increase the trace strength of the message content with the brand concept. Message construction can also encourage (for example, via open-ended questions) or facilitate (for example, via comparative advertising) abstraction generation.

**Advertising Execution Involvement.** Advertising execution involvement is a motivational construct embodying the degree of cognitive effort directed by the consumer at processing the executional properties of an advertising stimulus without regard to their brand relatedness. An ad execution abstraction is any self-generated semantic or episodic proposition evoked by the advertising stimulus that is not directly related to the brand concept. Advertising Execution Involvement (AEI) directs consumers' attention away from the message and thus weakens the structural accessibility of message-related information. That is, AEI inhibits the accessibility of brand information by decreasing the amount of processing that the message receives.

**Message Repetition and Delay.** Brand associate accessibility is in part a function of the frequency of exposure of the advertising stimulus. If message exposure facilitates the practice of a given brand associate, then increasing levels of message exposure increases accessibility by increasing the strength of the associate's memory trace (Anderson and Pirroli 1983; Baker 1985). Brand associate accessibility is also a function of the time lag between the last activation of the associate because trace strength weakens with time (Anderson 1983; Sawyer and Ward 1981). Decreasing the time lag between the most recent activation and the onset of the brand response process increases the accessibility of the brand associate by limiting the decay of the associate's memory trace.

**External Cuing.** Relatively poor structural accessibility can be compensated for by the effective use of memory cues at the brand response occasion.

## Maximizing Advertising's Contribution to the Brand Response Process

The key proposition of the RAM is that an advertising message strategy that maximizes the *accessibility* of *relevant* brand associates has a higher probability of contributing to the brand response process than do alternate message strategies. The optimal message strategy is one that anticipates the level of DMI that is expected to characterize the consumer at the BRO and then includes pertinent information in the ad that is encoded at the AEO. The "matching" of involvement levels at the AEO and BRO is thus the fulcrum that advertising must use to gain leverage in the market. Figure 5–1 depicts this matching process diagramatically.

*Message Content Must Correspond to the
DMI-Invoked Brand Response*

To develop maximally effective advertising, advertisers must identify the brand response route that the target market is expected to use at the BRO. This can be accomplished by predicting DMI through the analysis of its antecedents. If DMI is expected to be very low and consumers are expected to engage in "mindlessness," then the *sole* goal of advertising should be to communicate *affect*, perhaps through a message designed to facilitate affective classical conditioning. If DMI is expected to be low and consumers are expected to satisfice, then advertising should communicate information on a satisficing heuristic, perhaps an expert endorser, or absolute information on an important attribute (for example, fast pain relief). Finally, if DMI is expected to be high and, thus, lead to optimizing, then advertising should communicate relative attribute information via credible, cogent arguments.

The unique contribution of the RAM, then, is in its emphasis on identifying the qualitative level of information that is expected to discriminate brand alternatives at the point of purchase. The RAM proposes a need for "molar" message segmentation on the basis of expected decision-making involvement *prior* to the specification

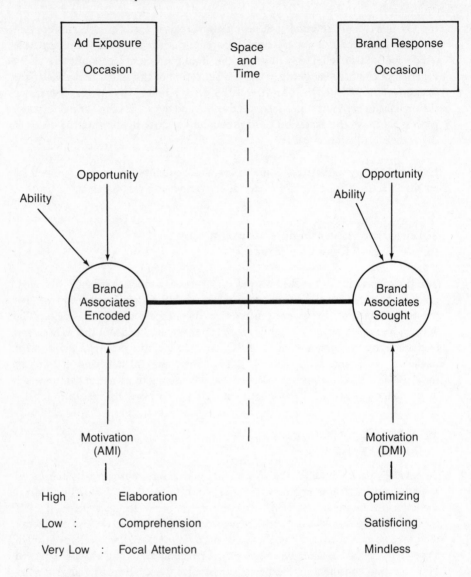

**Figure 5-1. Diagrammatic Depiction of the Relevance-Accessibility Model**

of specific message content. If DMI-based segmentation is ignored, the RAM argues that advertising is likely to communicate at an irrelevant informational level (for example, advertising emphasizes relative performance when consumers are motivated to seek only heuristic cues).

Beyond developing advertising messages that communicate information at the informational level that corresponds to the route expected to be invoked at the DMI, it is also important that the information "within" the expected route is highly appropriate. That is, if consumers are optimizing, the most important usage benefits must be communicated in the advertising message. If consumers are satisficing, the most powerful, most reassuring heuristic cues must be used; and if consumers invoke "mindlessness," stimuli should be chosen that evoke the strongest, most positive affective reactions. Thus, once the expected route has been identified, standard research procedures (focus groups, conjoint analysis, MDS, benefit segmentation, and so on) can be used to determine the best information to use within that route.

*Maximizing the Accessibility of Maximally*
*Relevant Advertising Information*

Assuming that the most relevant informational level is identified correctly, advertising effectiveness is maximized when the *accessibility* of advertising information relative to other information sources (for example, usage experiences, point-of-purchase displays) is maximized. Maximizing the *accessibility* of any given advertising-based brand associate requires the explicit manipulation of both motivational and nonmotivational accessibility antecedents.

**AMI–DMI Correspondence.** The likelihood that advertising will contribute to the brand response process is an inverse function of the discrepancy between AMI and DMI. Advertising-generated brand associates become increasingly relevant as the correspondence between AMI and DMI increases, because the qualitative level of information sought at the brand response occasion increasingly corresponds to the level of information encoded at the advertising exposure occasion. And, advertising-generated brand associates become increasingly accessible as the discrepancy between AMI and DMI decreases because internal memory search is directed at finding brand associates relevant to the operative brand response route. When AMI and DMI are very low, affective reactions can be encoded efficiently at the AEO and are sought at the BRO. When AMI and DMI are both low, heuristic cues can be encoded efficiently at the AEO and are sought at the BRO. When AMI and DMI are both high, relative usage benefits can be efficiently encoded at the AEO and are sought at the BRO (see figure).

**Nonmotivational Keys to Accessibility.** Even with AMI–DMI correspondence, the nonmotivational antecedents of accessibility must be managed properly to maximize the accessibility of advertising information at the BRO. Important considerations include message design management, ad execution management, repetition schedules, and external cuing at the brand response occasion.

## Summary

*Five Steps to Advertising Effectiveness*

First, advertising messages must be *relevant* (that is, information must be in the qualitative form that consumers are expected to use at the brand response occasion). Second, advertising message information must be relatively *more appropriate* than competing sources of information (that is, discuss the most important attributes, most reassuring heuristic cues, most intensely affective stimuli). Third, the message must generate *positively valenced* brand associates (that is, messages must be credible and lead to positive attribute beliefs, heuristic cue values, or positive affective associations). Fourth, advertising information must be *available* (that is, advertisements must be processed at a level that leads to the efficient encoding of the message information in the proper qualitative form). Fifth, advertising-generated brand associates must be *highly accessible* relative to competing sources of information (for example, usage experiences, package information) at the brand response occasion. A breakdown at any of these steps is likely to lead to a breakdown in advertising effectiveness.

*Measures of Advertising Effectiveness*

The RAM has two major implications for measuring advertising effectiveness. First, measures of advertising effectiveness must focus on what buyers think or feel about the brand, not what they thought, felt, or can recall about the advertisement. When consumers are optimizing, effectiveness measures must tap consumer beliefs about the brand's usage benefits relative to competitors. When consumers are satisficing, effectiveness measures must determine if advertising-communicated heuristic cues are highly salient in memory. When consumers are "mindless," effectiveness measures must determine the extent to which consumers *feel* more positively about the brand.

Second, if purchase intention or simulated choice measures are taken in a pretest situation, it is critical that the *expected level of DMI* at the time of brand choice is simulated during the pretest. Otherwise, pretest results are likely to be derived at an irrelevant informational level; that is, artificially high DMI created by the pretest environment could cause consumers to discriminate brands on the basis of performance dimensions, when in "real life" they discriminate them on the basis of simple affective responses.

# 6
# Nonverbal Communication: A New Perspective

*Donald Lowry*

Nonverbal communication represents the most fundamental of human instincts. As such, it is a powerful tool for developing intrinsic trust in media communications. Nonverbal messages communicate to core, and as a result, they cross cultures, contexts, and systems. Language is learned, and words have preconceived definitions. When language is introduced into communication, incongruent messages can result. Obviously this is all common sense. Why then is it difficult for advertising researchers to focus on nonverbal communication as the fundamental persuasive and catalytic tool for connective media advertising?

Communication Companies International (CCI) thinks that one of the reasons is the difficulty in differentiating or even isolating nonverbal messages. We believe we have an understanding of human communications that will facilitate this type of research and evolve it into the most useful information an advertiser can have. Our understanding allows us to develop a congruency between language and behavior or symbolism in such a way as to create media messages targeted to the core or intrinsic trust of the consumer.

The key to our understanding is that there are types of people/consumers that have very different ways of perceiving things and making judgments about what they hear and see. In other words, we differentially affiliate to communication, verbal and nonverbal. These affiliations segment into four fundamental groups to whom words, actions, symbols, music, and other sensory stimuli all have a differential hierarchical appeal.

Briefly, let's look at the characteristics of these four groups as they are manifested by core values and intrinsic trust systems. A deeper understanding of the groups can be found in tables 6-1 and 6-2 and figures 6-1 to 6-4 where the common denominator in motivating these differential characteristics is seen to be the pursuit of self-esteem.

Our four groups have been segmented through the use of color and are based on a derivation of the Jungian perspective on psychological type.

Starting with the *Orange* or spontaneous group, above all they must be free to act. Action or "doing" carries its own reward. They do things for the joy of doing. They choose to be impulsive, to act upon the idea of the moment. This is the

**Table 6-1**
**Intrinsic Value Matrix**

| PERSONAL STYLE | BLUE | GREEN | BROWN | ORANGE |
|---|---|---|---|---|
| **core need** | self-actualization | competency | social belonging | freedom |
| **overall mood** | enthusiasm | cool, calm, collected | concerned | excitable |
| **trust** | imagination | logic, consistency | authority | chance |
| **pride themselves for** | empathy | competence | dependability | impact |
| **in management** | the catalyst | the visionary | the traditionalist | the troubleshooter |
| **perception** | significance | categorical | discrepancy | harmonics |
| **supports, fosters** | growth | invention | institutions | recreation |
| **virtue** | loyalty | strength, determination | generosity | courage |
| **stressed by** | feeling artificial | inadequate | rejection | restrictions rigidity |
| **strives for, seeks** | love | insight | jurisdiction | freedom |
| **at work** | a catalyst, harmonizing | pragmatic | procedural | varied |
| **esteemed by** | helping people | finding insights | being of service | being resourceful |
| **wants to be appreciated for** | unique contributions | ideas | accuracy, thoroughness | cleverness |

free spirit, who takes pride in freedom beyond all else. The words and phrases that best characterize them are: — Urge or whim — Impulse is to really live — Take off for "somewhere else" — Action for itself — Thrive when outcomes not known — Test the limits! — Great in a crisis — Needs variations — Loves tools — Feeling of pride only in freedom — Action cannot be postponed — Precision — Endurance — Boldness — Exciting, lighthearted, and full of fun — Charming, witty — Charged with adventure — Tries new foods and vacation spots — Enjoys randomness — Only temporarily defeated — Waiting is psychological death — Do it now — Joy in doing — Performance — Performing arts — Construction work — Love to wander — Today is today — Fraternal — Spontaneous relationships — Clutter is acceptable — Specific goals unimportant — Process oriented — No desire for closure, completion, or finishing — Generosity, sharing.

The core of the *Orange* group is symbolized in the flight of an eagle, in the sensation of hang gliding, in the action and risk of driving a motorcycle, in

**Table 6-2**
**Intrinsic Value Matrix**

| PERSONAL STYLE | BLUE | GREEN | BROWN | ORANGE |
|---|---|---|---|---|
| **intrinsic intelligence** | with people | with strategy | with material | with senses |
| **when disturbed** | becomes hysterical | becomes complusive | becomes complaining | becomes punitive |
| **searching for** | roles | problems | security | stimulation |
| **dislikes** | hyprocrisy | injustice | disobedience | ineptness clumsiness |
| **thinks** | dogmatically | agnostically | pessimistic-ally | opportunistic-ally |
| **fantasizes being** | a messiah | a wizard genious | an aristocrate | a virtuoso |
| **loves** | integrity, honesty | justice | obedience | grace, elegance |
| **causes guilt** | letting someone down | lacking will power | greed | cowardice |
| **irritated by** | being treated impersonally | illogical thinking | violating rules and regulations | being told how to do things |
| **mood in relationships** | meaningful | aloof, objective | serious responsible | sensuous, exiciting |
| **rewarded by** | acceptance of who they are | affirming their wisdom | appreciating their service | being given freedom |
| **nurtures** | vision of a better world | technological insights | helpfulness | competitivness |

skillfulness in handling a tool, and in the freedom of the outdoors. Our second group is the *Brown* or responsible group, who, above all, must belong. No matter what social unit is involved, they must earn this place of belonging by being useful, by fulfilling responsibilities, by being of service, giving to and caring for others instead of receiving from them. The words and phrases that best characterize them are: — Must belong — Useful — Belonging must be earned — No freeloader — Caretaker — Work ethic — Parental attitude — Compelled to be bound and obligated — Desires hierarchy — Should be rules — General theme of pessimism — Store up — Membership — Socializers — Conservation — Tradition — Fundamentals — Foundations — Be Prepared — Responsible — Care for others — Promoter — Home and family — Dutiful — Sense of history — Hates wasting time — "Shoulds" and "oughts" — Right and wrong — Must be appreciated (often is not) — Establishes and maintains institutions — Teacher, banker, accountant, officialdom — Saves — Perpetuates heritage — Questions change — Standards — Steadfast — Dependable, reliable — Backbone of institutions and society — Punctual — Schedules — Predictable.

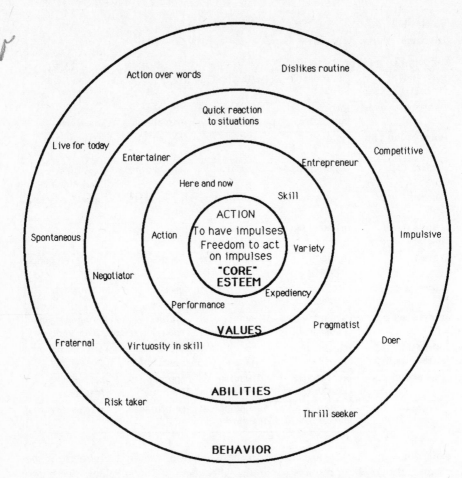

**Figure 6–1. Consumer Profile: Orange Consumer**

The core of the *Brown* group is symbolized in the patriotism of the American flag, in the structure of groups and organizations, in the security of banks and savings books, in the responsibility of parenting, in the caring of nursing and teaching, and in the pride of lineage and aristocracy. Our third group is the *Blue* or feeling group, who, above all, must be authentic. They must find their real self, their unique identity, and live their lives as an expression of it. For them, integrity means the unity of inner self with outer expression. Life is a dream, in which they must find meaning. The words and phrases that best characterize them are: — Becoming — Search for self — Purpose in life is to have a purpose in life! — Hungers for self-actualization — To become real — Hunger for unity and uniqueness — To be in harmony with inner self — To have a life of significance — Making a difference in the world — Sensitive to subtleties — Gestures and metaphoric behavior —

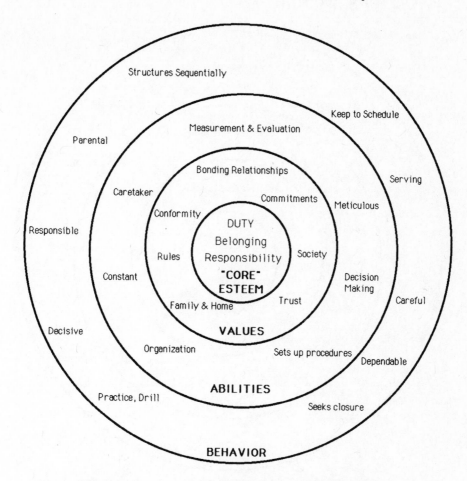

**Figure 6-2. Consumer Profile: Brown Consumer**

Enthusiastic anticipation — Devoted to relationships — Influence upon minds — Writes and speaks with poetic flair — Authenticity — Cultivate potential in others — Can assume varying identities — Powers of empathy — Often withholds self-knowledge from others — Spiritual — Has difficulty placing limits on time and energy — Works towards vision of perfection — Passionate pursuit of creative effort — Can be an intellectual butterfly — Tastes all the abundance of life — Romanticize their experiences — Interested in people-watching — Future oriented — Sees possibilities in people — Bearer of Truth — Eternal commitment to Love.

The core of the *Blue* group is symbolized in the vision of peace, in the romance of love ballads, in the drama of stage and screen, in the importance of people, and in the warmth of a hug or a handshake. Our final group is the *Green* or inquisitive group, who, above all, must be competent. They want to understand and

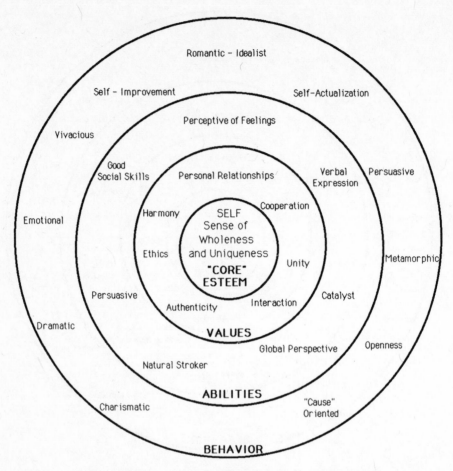

**Figure 6–3. Consumer Profile: Blue Consumer**

control the realities of life. This control represents the power to acquire abilities. The words and phrases that best characterize them are: — Power or control over Nature — Capabilities, abilities, capacities, skills — Loves intelligence — Stores wisdom — Critical of own capabilities — Must be competent — Urgency — Obsessed to learn — Compulsion to improve — Precision, exactitude — Militant ability — Must understand objects and events — "Should-be-able-to's" — Perfectionist — Individualist, may appear arrogant — Constant self-doubt — Believes things are obvious to all — Precise language — Learning is a 24-hour preoccupation — Knowledge is play — Must improve continually — Play is work — Develops models, explores ideas, builds systems — Often too abstract for others — Past gives direction to future — Hates errors in logic — Speculates on others' motivations — Often oblivious to others' emotions — Thinks through relationships carefully — Societal

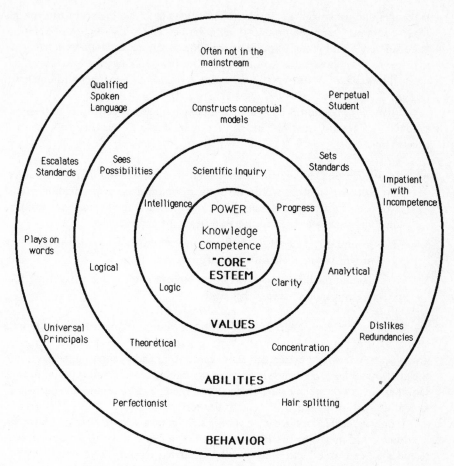

**Figure 6-4. Consumer Profile: Green Consumer**

rules have little force — Relatively disinterested in wealth — Qualified language patterns.

The core of the *Green* group is symbolized in the vision of genius, in the challenge of science, in the complexity of models and systems, in the perfectionism of symmetry, and in the mystery of the pyramids.

CCI feels that without this information, nonverbal or metacommunicated messages can be delivered alongside verbal messages that may or may not be congruent or persuasive. Furthermore, and more dangerously, the entire communications package may be mistargeted, and, as a result, mistrusted.

Imagine, for example, the paradox of a Blue actor delivering the benefit statements of a Green or high-tech product to a Brown target audience. The result has to be a confused message even though all the normal demographic and psychographic parameters are in place. The actor cannot *not* metacommunicate his Blue or intrinsic core; the product cannot *not* be perceived as high tech; and the target audience cannot *not* impulse or trust messages that do not communicate to their core. Therefore, understanding this information allows for a predictability in the development of universally appealing messages or for direct and impactful targeting.

When we as communicators are failing to persuade the consumer to trust our products, we are not trusting our own intuitive ability to integrate this information. Why?

- We as communicators misunderstand that we are operating in a "communications culture." In other words, all of us in the business of persuading people have been educated within that culture and therefore tend to create communication that appeals to the culture instead of the consumer.

- We as communicators are influencing the advertising message to what we perceive will work, even with primary research input.

- We as communicators tend to create an atmosphere for our advertising that speaks to cultural or learned behavior.

There is a tendency for those of us in the communication business to be a specific type of person. Certainly this type of person, who is identified in the Green group, is the one who is concerned about integration and integrating messages and the one who holds the greatest intuitive potential for reaching all types of people. However, we can get stuck in an our-own-worst-enemy syndrome and find our esteem and pride tied up in our own communication culture.

If only we understood what a charging stallion means to the Orange consumer, a helping hand means to the Brown consumer, a pause to smell a flower means to the Blue consumer, and what a truly integrated message means to us!

Through the use of CCI's prolfiling techniques, any conventional advertising research can be dramatically dimensionalized. Any one piece of information can evolve from a blur into four distinct images. Furthermore, any one piece of information can all of a sudden take on new meaning at a nonverbal or metacommunicative level.

# Part III
# Measuring Response to Nonverbal Communication

# 7
# Toward a Standardized Emotional Profile (SEP) Useful in Measuring Responses to the Nonverbal Components of Advertising

*Morris B. Holbrook*
*Rajeev Batra*

A s indicated by the chapters in this book on advertising and consumer psychology, researchers have increasingly begun to turn their attention toward such nonverbal components of print ads and television commercials as visual imagery (for example, Mitchell and Olson 1981; Rossiter and Percy 1980) and music (for example, Gorn 1982; Hecker 1984). This shift in our focus on the independent variables embodied by advertising content will inevitably produce accompanying changes in our emphasis on various dependent variables of interest. For example, nonverbal components of advertising content may exert their effects less on measures of recall (for example, Starch or Burke scores) and more on various kinds of emotional response (Zielske 1982). Yet the role of emotion in advertising remains a relatively nascent and still poorly understood area of investigation (Holbrook and O'Shaughnessy 1984).

Recent attempts to study emotional responses to advertising have included work on attitude-toward-the-ad (Batra 1984; Batra and Ray 1986; Gardner 1985; Holbrook 1978; Lutz, MacKenzie, and Belch 1983; MacKenzie, Lutz, and Belch 1986; Mitchell and Olson 1981; Moore and Hutchinson 1983; Park and Young 1986; Shimp 1981; Shimp and Yokum 1982), investigations of single affective dimensions such as warmth (Aaker, Stayman, and Hagerty 1986), explorations of self-contained instruments borrowed from psychologists such as Plutchik (1980) to test their applicability in the context of television commercials (Holbrook and Westwood 1986), and the use of omnibus studies to reduce large numbers of ad hoc scales down to a manageable number of underlying factors (Schlinger 1979; Wells 1964; Wells, Leavitt, and McConville 1971). It seems fair to say that, for all their virtues, none

The authors gratefully acknowledge the support of N.W. Ayer, which provided partial funding for the study reported here.

of these studies has yet taken a really comprehensive view of the work on emotions in the social sciences as the basis for constructing a battery suitable for application to the case of advertising. The purpose of the present investigation, therefore, is to construct such an instrument. Specifically, we seek to create a standardized emotional profile (SEP) containing a modest number of multi-item indices that can be used to assess emotional responses to print ads or television commercials (especially the latter). Such a set of scales should be especially useful to those wishing to explore the effects attributable to the nonverbal components of advertising.

## Background

Innumerable social scientists, philosophers, and marketing or consumer researchers have approached the classification of emotions from a number of different viewpoints. As summarized by Holbrook (1986), these approaches to constructing emotional typologies have included (1) listing, (2) logical division, (3) data reduction, and (4) theory development and testing. Advocates of these various perspectives have created a bewildering variety of analytic frameworks from which to choose. These competing schemes include a plethora of names, terms, and other emotion-related vocabulary. The resulting linguistic options appear to converge in some areas and to diverge in others. Thus, questions concerning their unique significations and common meanings remain a fascinating issue.

Accordingly, we took as our first task the major chore of constructing an interpretable representation of the previous diverse work on emotional classification. Toward this end, we began by constructing a huge matrix. Down the left side of this matrix, we listed every type of emotion that we could find clearly delineated in the literature. Across the top, we listed the major authors on the subject of emotion.

Most authors have dealt with only a few of the various types of emotion. It followed that most cells of the matrix remained blank. In the remaining cells—for which given authors have addressed particular emotions—we listed the three or four words, phrases, or scales most centrally used by the author of interest to represent the emotion in question.

Obviously, this selection involved the exercise of considerable judgment on our part. In general, we agreed quickly and harmoniously on the three or four items to choose for each cell. Where agreement proved more elusive, we discussed the relevant issues until reaching a consensus, sometimes resolving the debate by adding or combining categories to complicate or simplify the emerging picture (cf. Lincoln and Guba 1985).

The resulting 29″-by-26″ or 754-celled matrix, with each row containing several annotated entries, is too large to present here. However, we can indicate the nature of our review and synthesis by listing the names of each emerging type of emotion, providing references to the authors concerned with each, and citing the key terms or scales used by each author. This review and synthesis appears in table 7–1 which is based on the following 26 sources (list alphabetically):

## Table 7-1
## Review and Synthesis of Emotional Types Developed in the Literature

| Emotional Type | Author | CATEGORY/Items |
|---|---|---|
| JOY | Arnold | DELIGHT, JOY |
| | Block | PLEASANT, contentment, love, elation |
| | Davitz | ACTIVATION, COMFORT, happiness, gaiety, enjoyment |
| | de Rivera | JOY, delight, enjoyment, ecstasy |
| | Ekman | HAPPINESS |
| | Frijda | PLEASANTNESS |
| | Izard | ENJOYMENT, delighted, happy, joyful |
| | Mehrabian | PLEASURE, happy, pleased, satisfied |
| | Nowlis | ELATION, elated, overjoyed, pleased |
| | Osgood | joy, glee, worried laughter |
| | Plutchik | JOY, delighted, joyful, happy |
| | Solomon | CONTENTMENT, EUPHORIA, JOY |
| | Tomkins | ENJOYMENT, JOY |
| SURPRISE | de Rivera | WONDER, amazement, astonishment, surprise |
| | Ekman | SURPRISE |
| | Frijda | CONTROL, surprise, amazement |
| | Izard | SURPRISE, surprised, amazed, astonished |
| | Osgood | dismay, bewilderment, surprise, amazement, awe |
| | Plutchik | SURPRISE, puzzled, confused, surprised |
| | Pribram | novelty, unfamiliarity, arousal (endorphin level) |
| | Tomkins | SURPRISE, AWE, STARTLE |
| SADNESS | Arnold | SORROW, SADNESS, REJECTION |
| | Block | grief |
| | Davitz | DISCOMFORT, depression, grief, sadness |
| | de Rivera | SORROW, distress, despair, grief |
| | Ekman | SADNESS |
| | Frijda | UNPLEASANTNESS |
| | Izard | DISTRESS, downhearted, sad, discouraged |
| | Mehrabian | DISPLEASURE, melancholic, despairing, bored |
| | Nowlis | SADNESS, regretful, sad, sorry |
| | Osgood | acute sorrow, pity, dreamy sadness; despair, boredom, adoration |
| | Panksepp | PANIC/SOCIAL LOSS, loneliness, grief, separation, distress |
| | Plutchik | SADNESS, sad, depressed, unhappy |
| | Solomon | DESPAIR, GRIEF, SADNESS, SORROW |
| | Tomkins | DISTRESS, ANGUISH |
| ANGER | Arnold | ANGER |
| | Block | anger |
| | Davitz | MOVING AGAINST, hate, anger |
| | de Rivera | ANGER, anger, annoyance, irritation, rage |
| | Ekman | ANGER |
| | Izard | ANGER, enraged, angry, mad |
| | Nowlis | AGGRESSION, defiant, rebellious, angry |
| | Osgood | sullen anger, rage, stubbornness |
| | Panksepp | RAGE, IRRITATION, FRUSTRATION, indignation, hate, anger |
| | Plutchik | ANGER, angry, annoyed, irritated |
| | Schlinger | ALIENATION, irritation |
| | Solomon | ANGER, INDIGNATION, RAGE |
| | Tomkins | ANGER, RAGE |
| | Wells | IRRITATION, irritation |

*Table 7-1 continued*

| Emotional Type | Author | CATEGORY/Items |
|---|---|---|
| DISGUST | Arnold | AVERSION |
| | de Rivera | REJECTION, aversion, disgust, loathing |
| | Ekman | DISGUST |
| | Frijda | (OUT OF) CONTROL, disgust, loathing |
| | Izard | DISGUST, distaste, disgust, revulsion |
| | McHugo | DISGUSTED, SCORNFUL, disgusted, scornful, angry |
| | Osgood | annoyance, disgust, contempt, scorn, loathing |
| | Plutchik | DISGUST, disgusted, revolted, displeased |
| | Tomkins | DISGUST |
| CONTEMPT | Davitz | MOVING AGAINST, contempt |
| | de Rivera | CONTEMPT, scorn, pity, contempt |
| | Izard | CONTEMPT, contemptuous, scornful, disdainful |
| | Solomon | CONTEMPT, INDIFFERENCE, PITY |
| | Tomkins | CONTEMPT |
| | Wells | IRRITATION, terrible, stupid, ridiculous |
| | Wright | SOURCE DEROGATION |
| FEAR | Arnold | FEAR |
| | Block | UNPLEASANT, worry |
| | Davitz | INADEQUACY, fear, panic, depression |
| | de Rivera | FEAR, ANXIETY, HORROR, DREAD |
| | Ekman | FEAR |
| | Izard | FEAR, scared, fearful, afraid |
| | McHugo | FEARFUL, ANXIOUS, sad, fearful, anxious |
| | Nowlis | ANXIETY, clutched-up, fearful, jittery |
| | Osgood | fear, horror; physical pain, dread, anxiety |
| | Panksepp | FEAR, PAIN, anxiety, alarm, foreboding, uncomfortable restraint |
| | Plutchik | FEAR, timid, scared, afraid |
| | Solomon | ANGST, ANXIETY, DREAD, FEAR, TERROR, TIMIDITY |
| | Tomkins | FEAR, TERROR |
| SHAME | Block | humiliation |
| | Davitz | INCOMPETENCE, shame |
| | de Rivera | SHAME, humiliation, inferiority, weakness |
| | Izard | SHAME, SHYNESS, sheepish, bashful, shy |
| | Solomon | EMBARRASSMENT, SELF-CONTEMPT, SELF-HATRED, SHAME |
| GUILT | Block | guilt |
| | Davitz | DISSATISFACTION, remorse, guilt |
| | de Rivera | GUILT, repentence, regret, remorse |
| | Izard | GUILT, repentent, guilty, blameworthy |
| | Solomon | ANGUISH, GUILT, PENITENCE, REGRET, REMORSE |
| AFFECTION | Aaker | WARM, appealing, gentle, well-done |
| | Block | INTERPERSONAL RELATEDNESS, love, sympathy, nostalgia |
| | Davitz | MOVING TOWARD, love, affection, passion |
| | de Rivera | LOVE, ESTEEM, ACCEPTANCE |
| | Nowlis | SOCIAL AFFECTION, affectionate, forgiving, kindly |
| | Plutchik | ACCEPTANCE, accepting, receptive, affectionate |
| | Schlinger | EMPATHY, personal, intimate |
| | Solomon | FRIENDSHIP, LOVE, RESPECT |

*Table 7–1 (continued)*

| Emotional Type | Author | CATEGORY/Items |
|---|---|---|
| ACTIVATION | Block | ACTIVATION, INTENSITY |
| | Frijda | ACTIVATION |
| | Mehrabian | AROUSAL, stimulated, excited, aroused |
| | Nowlis | VIGOR, ACTIVATION, active, energetic, vigorous |
| | Wells | VIGOR, vigorous, exciting, energetic, enthusiastic, exhilerated |
| HYPERACTIVATION | Davitz | HYPERACTIVATION, anger, panic, passion |
| | Schlinger | CONFUSION, distracting, effortful, complex |
| HYPOACTIVATION | Block | LOW INTENSITY, bordeom |
| | Davitz | HYPOACTIVATION, MOVING AWAY, boredom, depression, apathy |
| | de Rivera | DEPRESSION, boredom, apathy, helplessness |
| | Mehrabian | LOW AROUSAL, sluggish, dull, sleepy |
| | Nowlis | FATIGUE, drowsy, dull, sleepy |
| | Solomon | DEPRESSION |
| COMPETENCE | Arnold | DARING |
| | Davitz | ENHANCEMENT, confidence, inspiration, determination |
| | de Rivera | CONFIDENCE, ambition, courage, determination |
| | Mehrabian | HIGH DOMINANCE, influential, in control, dominant |
| HELPLESSNESS | Mehrabian | LOW DOMINANCE, controlled, awed, guided |
| SURGENCY | Aaker | ENTERTAINING, clever, imaginative, amusing |
| | McHugo | AMUSED, WARMHEARTED, amused, warmhearted |
| | Nowlis | SURGENCY, carefree, playful, witty |
| | Schlinger | ENTERTAINMENT, pleasurable, enjoyable, entertaining, fun to watch, funny, enthusiastic |
| | Wells | HUMOR, jolly, merry, playful, humorous, amusing |
| SKEPTICISM | Aaker | DISLIKE, phony |
| | Nowlis | SKEPTICISM, skeptical, suspicious, dubious |
| | Osgood | surprise, distrust; puzzlement, incredulous doubt |
| | Schlinger | ALIENATION, exaggeration, unrealistic |
| | Wright | SOURCE DEROGATION |
| PRIDE | Block | pride |
| | de Rivera | PRIDE, exultation, superiority, vanity |
| | Nowlis | EGOISM, egoistic, self-centered, boastful |
| | Solomon | PRIDE, SELF-LOVE, SELF-RESPECT, VANITY |
| SERENITY | de Rivera | SECURITY, HUMILITY, SERENITY |
| | Nowlis | NONCHALANCE, nonchalant, leisurely, at rest |
| | Osgood | silent laughter, quiet pleasure, complacency |
| | Pribram | COORDINATION, comfort, low stress, low effort (ACTH-pituitary) |
| | Wells | SENSUOUSNESS, tender, gentle, soothing, serene, lovely |
| CONFLICT | Arnold | HATE, DISLIKE |
| | Nowlis | TENSION, resentment, frustration, hate |
| | Solomon | FRUSTRATION, HATE, RESENTMENT, SELF-PITY, SPITE |
| DESIRE | Arnold | WANTING, DESIRE, HOPE |
| | de Rivera | DESIRE, ADMIRATION, craving, jealousy, envy |
| | Panksepp | EXPECTANCY, desire, hope, appetitive behavior |
| | Pribram | ACTIVATION, appetitive behavior (Dopamine) |
| | Solomon | ENVY, HOPE, JEALOUSY |

*Table 7-1 (continued)*

| Emotional Type | Author | CATEGORY/Items |
|---|---|---|
| DUTY | Solomon | DUTY, Moral, responsible, obedient |
| FAITH | Solomon | FAITH, WORSHIP |
| GRATITUDE | Solomon | GRATITUDE |
| INNOCENCE | Solomon | INNOCENCE |
| INVOLVEMENT | Aaker | PERSONAL RELEVANCE, informative, convincing, worth remembering |
| | Krugman | INVOLVEMENT, number of connections |
| | Schlinger | RELEVANT NEWS, useful, gave new idea, learned from it |
| | Wells | PERSONAL RELEVANCE, important, meaningful, valuable |
| DEJA VU | Belch & Lutz | REPETITION, RELATED EVALUATIONS |
| | Schlinger | FAMILIARITY, same old thing, seen before, not novel |
| | Wells | FAMILIARITY, well-known, familiar, copycat, old |
| INTEREST | Belch & Lutz | CURIOSITY, THOUGHTS |
| | Frijda | ATTENTION/REJECTION, interest |
| | Izard | INTEREST, attentive, concentrating, alert |
| | Nowlis | CONCENTRATION, contemplative, clear-thinking, concentrating |
| | Osgood | expectancy, intrigued interest |
| | Panksepp | EXPECTANCY, anticipation |
| | Plutchik | EXPECTANCY, expectant, curious, inquisitive |
| | Pribram | ACTIVATION, readiness (Dopamine) |
| | Tomkins | INTEREST, EXCITEMENT |
| | Wells | UNIQUENESS, novel, original, imaginative, ingenious |
| | Wright | CURIOSITY, THOUGHTS |
| DISTRACTION | Belch & Lutz | NEUTRAL, IRRELEVANT THOUGHTS |

Aaker and Bruzzone (1981); Arnold (1960); Belch and Lutz (1982); Block (1957); Clore and Ortony (1983); Davitz (1969); de Rivera (1977); Ekman et al. (1982); Frijda (1970); Greenwald (1968); Izard (1977); Krugman (1965); McHugo, Smith, and Lanzetta (1982); Mehrabian (1980); Mehrabian and Russell (1974); Nowlis (1965); Osgood (1966); Osgood, Suci, and Tannenbaum (1957); Panksepp (1982); Plutchik (1962, 1980); Pribram (1980); Russell (1980); Schlinger (1979); Solomon (1976); Tomkins (1980); Wells (1964); Wells, Leavitt, and McConville (1971); Wright (1973).

As a compendium of the emotional classification schemes available in the literature, the review and synthesis found in table 7-1 has proven invaluable in our work toward constructing a more compact standardized emotion profile (SEP). In brief, we used the list of terms and scales provided by the table to select a set of three or four items that, in our judgment, best captured the consensus on terminology across authors. Again, we pursued agreement by means of endless discussions of the appropriate vocabulary. These discussions converged on the list of twenty-nine a priori multi-item emotional indices shown in table 7-2.

## Table 7-2
## A Priori Multi-Item Emotional Indices

| INDEX [Multi-Item Alpha] | Items (Multi-Judge Alpha) [Mean Multi-Judge Alpha] |
| --- | --- |
| JOY [.96] | Joyful (.84), Happy (.78), Delighted (.75), Pleased (.70) [.77] |
| SURPRISE [.87] | Surprised (.53), Amazed (.46), Astonished (.36)[11] [.45] |
| SADNESS [.88] | Sad (.69), Distressed (.49), Sorrowful (.61), Dejected (.27) [.52] |
| ANGER [.90] | Angry (.54), Irritated (.58), Enraged (.34), Mad (.49) [.49] |
| DISGUST [.93] | Disgusted (.42), Revolted (.39), Annoyed (.66), Full of loathing (.43) [.47] |
| CONTEMPT [.93] | Scornful (.50), Contemptuous (.50), Disdainful (.53) [.51] |
| FEAR [.87] | Fearful (.52)[11] Afraid (.51)[10], Anxious (.59) [.54] |
| SHAME [.89] | Ashamed (.48), Embarrassed (.42)[11], Humiliated (.36)[11] [.42] |
| GUILT [.86][a] | Guilty (.16)[9], Remorseful (.25)[10], Regretful (.48)[10], Regretful (.62)[10] [.38] |
| AFFECTION [.91] | Loving (.84), Affectionate (.79), Friendly (.73) [.79] |
| ACTIVATION [.89] | Aroused (.59), Active (.69), Excited (.78) [.69] |
| HYPERACTIVATION [.47] | Panicked (.50)[9], Confused (.59)[10], Overstimulated (.37)[11] [.48] |
| HYPOACTIVATION [.73] | Bored (.74), Drowsy (.39), Sluggish (.32) [.48] |
| COMPETENCE [.82] | Confident (.32), In control (.33), Competent (.38)[11] [.34] |
| HELPLESSNESS [.72] | Powerless (.47)[11], Helpless (.38)[11], Dominated (.09)[11] [.31] |
| SURGENCY [.94] | Playful (.85), Entertained (.82), Lighthearted (.78) [.82] |
| SKEPTICISM [.93] | Skeptical (.61), Suspicious (.59), Distrustful (.51) [.57] |
| PRIDE [.57] | Proud (.71)[11], Superior (.22)[11], Worthy (.46)[11] [.46] |
| SERENITY [.89] | Restful (.76), Serene (.72), Comfortable (.56), Soothed (.78) [.71] |
| CONFLICT [.79] | Tense (.58)[11], Frustrated (.36)[11], Conflictful (.48)[10] [.47] |
| DESIRE [.90] | Desirous (.54), Wishful (.65), Full of craving (.71), Hopeful (.55)[11] [.61] |
| DUTY [.69] | Moral (.44), Virtuous (.45), Dutiful (.45)[10] [.44] |
| FAITH [.86] | Reverent (.58), Worshipful (.34)[9], Spiritual (.58)[9] [.50] |
| GRATITUDE [.88] | Grateful (.48)[11], Thankful (.56)[11], Appreciative (.62) [.55] |
| INNOCENCE [.55] | Innocent (.52), Pure (.58)[10], Blameless (−.18)[11] [.31] |
| INVOLVEMENT [.72] | Involved (.60), Informed (.11), Enlightened (.40), Benefited (.27) [.34] |
| DEJA VU [.76] | Unimpressed (.68), Uninformed (.39), Unexcited (.69) [.59] |
| INTEREST [.60] | Attentive (.56), Curious (.64) [.60] |
| DISTRACTION [.75] | Distracted (.30), Preoccupied (.47)[11], Inattentive (.45) [.40] |
| MEAN [.81] | Mean [.52] |

[a]Due to a clerical error, "regretful" (GUILT) was inadvertently substituted on the questionnaire for "interested" (INTEREST). This resulted in a moderately low reliability for the latter index (.60).
[9,10,11]Where indicated, because of zero variance in the relevant item for one or more respondents, the alpha is based on 9, 10, or 11 judges.

Even this list of emotional indices, based on a review and synthesis of the literature, appears too unwieldy for expeditious use in most studies of emotional responses to nonverbal content or other aspects of print ads and television commercials. Accordingly, we undertook an empirical study intended to reduce the preceding set of a priori indices to a more compact battery of scales accounting for most of the variance in emotional responses to advertising content. Specifically, we used the set of a priori indices shown in table 7–2 to measure emotional responses to seventy-two television commercials in order (1) to establish the reliability of the twenty-nine a priori indices themselves, (2) to isolate the key underlying dimensions of emotional responses to television commercials, and (3) to select a more parsimonious battery of scales for purposes of constructing a standardized emotional profile (SEP).

## Method

### Commercials

Test commercials consisted of seventy-two recent or current executions that had appeared on prime-time television. These seventy-two commercials were chosen to provide a judgmental representation of the range of emotions likely to be found in television advertising. Other recent work has pursued the objective of constructing a representative probability sample of prime-time television commercials (Olney, Holbrook, and Batra 1986). Here, by contrast, our purpose was to select the advertisements that would cover the full spectrum of relevant emotions.

The seventy-two television commercials were randomly split into two sets (free of brand repetition within sets), were randomly ordered (within sets), and were randomly assigned to six video tapes (containing twelve commercials each). These six tapes were themselves rotated in order (to avoid fatigue effects) and were shown to twelve judges who coded their assessments of the commercials in the following rating task.

### Rating Task

Judges rated their responses to the seventy-two commercials on one hundred nine seven-position check-mark scales of the following format:

I felt—Bored     VERY :__:__:__:__:__:__:__: NOT AT ALL

The one hundred nine scales represented the twenty-nine a priori emotional indices presented earlier as well as five more global ad-response indices included for purposes of concurrent validation (discussed later). They were randomly ordered, divided into four approximately equal sets, and rotated to avoid order and fatigue biases.

Completion of these ratings posed a major coding task for the judges, typically requiring about eight hours to cover all seventy-two commercials. For this reason, the aforementioned order randomizations and subset rotations appeared particularly important. Moreover, checks of interjudge reliability and internal consistency seemed especially critical (see below).

### Judges

The emotional response ratings were provided by twelve adult female judges recruited from members of the local community *not* associated with the business school where the research was conducted. Mostly, the respondents consisted of people who lived or worked in the neighborhood of the university and responded to recruiting posters displayed in nearby public places. Though they must be viewed as a convenience sample, these respondents appeared suitable for service as judges by virtue of their serious purpose and their lack of close association with the business-school environment.

## Interjudge Reliability and Internal Consistency

**Multi-judge Alpha.** We assessed interjudge reliability in the manner suggested by Holbrook and Lehmann (1980). Specifically, for each of the one hundred nine scales, we viewed judges as items in a twelve-item multi-judge index assessed for reliability (across the seventy-two commercials) by means of coefficient alpha (Cronbach 1951).

**Multi-item Alpha.** Further, at the next level of analysis, each of the twenty-nine *a priori* measures of emotion constituted a multi-item index composed of three or four scales (each of which was itself based on the scores of twelve judges). Hence, we also examined coefficient alpha for the three- and four-item a priori emotional indices as a gauge of their internal consistency.

## Principal Components Analysis

Besides these reliability assessments, our chief analysis for the present purposes consisted of a principal components solution (with rotation via the varimax criterion). In this principle components analysis, the seventy-two commercials served as the relevant units of observation. Each commercial was represented by its scores on the twenty-nine *a priori* emotion indices (where each index was itself based on the sum of three or four scale items and each scale item was in turn based on the aggregated ratings of twelve judges).

The resulting principal components served two purposes. First, their interpretation indicated the nature of the key dimensions underlying emotional responses to television commercials. Second, a consideration of the highest-loaded indices suggested a more parsimonious battery of scales to be used in the construction of a standardized emotional profile (SEP).

## Concurrent Validity of the Emotional Dimensions

Concurrent validity of the principal components as meaningful representations of emotional responses to advertising was assessed, in part, by using factor scores for the seventy-two commercials to predict the aforementioned global ad-response measures that had been randomly embedded within the one hundred nine rating scales for purposes of checking concurrent validity. These five a priori three-item validation indices appear in table 7–3. As before, these validation criteria were assessed for multi-judge and multi-item reliability and were then used as targets to

**Table 7-3**
**Validation Criteria**

| INDEX<br>[*Multi-Item Alpha*] | Items (Multi-Judge Alpha)<br>[*Mean Multi-Judge Alpha*] |
| --- | --- |
| Ad Approval [.97] | Admiring of the ad (.70), Appreciative of the ad (.72), Approving of the ad (.73) [.72] |
| Agreement with claims about brand [.95] | Convinced about the brand (.60), Persuaded about the brand (.51), Agreeing with claims about brand (.63) [.58] |
| Disagreement with claims about brand [.93] | Unconvinced about the brand (.64), Not persuaded about the brand (.62), Disagreeing with claims about brand (.60) [.62] |
| Favorable predis-position to brand [.97] | Immediately favorable toward the brand (.63), Initially inclined toward the brand (.61), Spontaneously predisposed toward the brand (.61) [.61] |
| Unfavorable predis-position to brand [.96] | Immediately unfavorable toward the brand (.56), Immediately inclined against the brand (.64), Spontaneously predisposed against the brand (.58) [.59] |
| Mean [.96] | Mean [.62] |

be predicted by the emotional dimensions represented by the commercials' principal component scores. For this purpose, each validation index was regressed (across commercials) on the relevant set of factor scores.

## Results

*Interjudge Reliability and Internal Consistency*

**Multi-judge Reliabilities for Separate Emotion Items.** The interjudge reliabilities for all items in the emotional indices appear in parentheses in table 7-2, with the mean multi-judge reliability across the items in each index shown in brackets on the right of the table. The overall mean of the bracketed interjudge reliabilities is .52. In general, this suggests fair agreement among judges on the differences among commercials on each separate item used in the overall instrument. However, it represents an extremely severe criterion in that it foregoes the advantages obtained by combining scale items into multi-item indices. For this reason, we place more emphasis on the bracketed multi-item reliabilities shown in the lefthand column of table 7-2.

**Multi-item Reliabilities for the Emotional Indices.** The multi-item emotional indices show excellent internal consistency as assessed by coefficient alpha. These multi-item reliabilities range from .47 to .96, with a mean of .81. In general, therefore, they reach levels commensurate with the commonly accepted cutoffs of .80 for refined instruments and .60 for instruments still under development (Nunnally 1967).

## Principal Components Analysis

Principal components analysis, as is often the case, failed to produce a clear mandate for the number of dimensions to retain in the final solution. The scree plot showed no marked elbows to establish a cutoff. Four factors had eigenvalues greater than 1.0, but no indices loaded strongest on the fourth factor. For this reason and on the basis of interpretability, we chose a three-component solution.

This three-dimensional solution—with eigenvalues of 13.6, 4.9, and 2.8—accounted for 73.3 percent of the variance in the emotional indices. The resulting varimax-rotated loadings (organized in descending order of magnitude for each dimension) appear in table 7–4.

### Table 7–4
### Loadings of Emotional Indices on Three Varimax-Rotated Principal Components

|                  | *Pleasure* | *Arousal* | *Domination* |
| ---------------- | ---------- | --------- | ------------ |
| Duty             | .86        | .05       | .13          |
| Faith            | .82        | .20       | .06          |
| Pride            | .79        | .11       | −.13         |
| Affection        | .79        | .32       | −.33         |
| Innocence        | .77        | .23       | −.18         |
| Gratitude        | .76        | .49       | −.10         |
| Serenity         | .75        | .14       | −.35         |
| Desire           | .66        | .43       | −.20         |
| Joy              | .61        | .56       | −.43         |
| Competence       | .49        | .29       | −.38         |
| Interest         | .16        | .86       | .13          |
| Hypoactivation   | −.32       | −.77      | .05          |
| Activation       | .26        | .76       | −.12         |
| Surprise         | −.12       | .75       | .21          |
| Deja Vu          | −.49       | −.73      | .29          |
| Involvement      | .43        | .73       | −.08         |
| Distraction      | −.37       | −.66      | .24          |
| Surgency         | .34        | .63       | −.45         |
| Contempt         | −.32       | −.62      | .55          |
| Conflict         | −.29       | −.06      | .90          |
| Guilt            | .12        | .02       | .90          |
| Helplessness     | −.14       | .05       | .87          |
| Sadness          | .12        | −.12      | .85          |
| Fear             | −.20       | .17       | .84          |
| Shame            | −.10       | −.33      | .71          |
| Anger            | −.29       | −.41      | .65          |
| Hyperactivation  | −.38       | .45       | .62          |
| Disgust          | −.30       | −.51      | .62          |
| Skepticism       | −.50       | −.44      | .61          |

Interpretation of table 7–4 suggests that the three rotated principal components might best be construed as representing Pleasure, Arousal, and Domination. These dimensions recall the PAD framework developed by Mehrabian and Russell (1974) except that our third component refers to domin*ation* (that is, a feeling of being dominat*ed*) rather than domin*ance* (that is, a feeling of being one who domin*ates*). In this sense, our results parallel the familiar contrasts among Evaluation, Activity, and Potency found by Osgood, Suci, and Tannenbaum (1957).

More specifically, *pleasure* refers intuitively to such feelings as joy, affection, gratitude, and pride (all loaded strongly on the first dimension). *Arousal* reflects interest, activation, surprise, and involvement (all highly correlated with the second dimension). *Domination* involves a sense of helplessness, sadness, fear, and disgust (all closely related to the third dimension). One or two indices appear somewhat arbitrary in their assignments—for example, contempt (negative on arousal) and anger (positive on domination)—but these tend to have high loadings on more than one dimension.

### Concurrent Validity of the Emotional Dimensions

The reliabilities for the five validation indices appear in table 7–3. Mean multi-judge reliability (.62) and mean multi-item reliability (.96) were both quite satisfactory, exceeding the levels obtained for the emotional indices themselves.

Table 7–5 presents the results for OLS regressions of the validation criteria on the three emotional dimensions. All beta weights were significant at $p < .00005$ and were in the same direction (with reversals, of course, for *dis*agreement and *un*favorability). All multiple R's were also significant at $p < .00005$, with a root-mean-squared R of .87. As would be expected with strongly intercorrelated dependent variables (mean intercorrelation = .86), the beta coefficients tended to be not only consistent in direction but also roughly comparable in magnitude. With the exception of unfavorable predisposition to the brand, the other validating measures responded about equally positively to pleasure and arousal, with a somewhat weaker negative response to domination.

### Table 7–5
### Beta Weights and Multiple Correlation Coefficients for Regressions of Validation Criteria on Emotional Dimensions

|  | *Pleasure* | *Arousal* | *Domination* | *R* |
|---|---|---|---|---|
| Approval of ad | .52 | .72 | −.25 | .92 |
| Agreement | .52 | .56 | −.32 | .83 |
| Disagreement | −.47 | −.60 | .34 | .84 |
| Favorable predisposition | .55 | .59 | −.39 | .90 |
| Unfavorable predisposition | −.34 | −.51 | .59 | .85 |

Note: All coefficients and multiple correlations are significant at $p < .00005$.

In general, the OLS regressions strongly support the concurrent validity of the emotional dimensions derived via principal components analysis. Predictive fits were quite strong (root-mean-$R^2$ = .87) and, equally important, all three dimensions consistently made highly significant contributions to the explanation of variance in the validating criteria. Apparently, the three emotional dimensions help explain (concurrently measured) approval of the ad, agreement with its claims, and favorable predisposition toward the brand advertised.

## Conclusions

The results presented in the foregoing analysis offer considerable encouragement for the line of attack pursued in the present study. In general, the emotion indices appear adequately reliable in terms of interjudge reliability (multi-judge alpha) and strongly reliable in terms of internal consistency among items (multi-item alpha). Moreover, the three-dimensional principal components solution makes sense, corresponds intuitively to Mehrabian and Russell's (1974) PAD paradigm, and strongly predicts the five criteria used to assess concurrent validity.

With respect to developing a standardized emotional profile (SEP), the results also point us toward directions for future research. Specifically, we may use the results shown in tables 7–2 and 7–4 to begin our selection of key items to include in the SEP. We suggest proceeding in the following five steps:

1. Eliminate from consideration any indices whose average multi-judge reliability falls below .50 (table 7–2);

2. Eliminate from among the remaining contenders any index whose multi-item reliability falls below .80 (table 7–2); here, an exception will be made for interest (an index that was disadvantaged by the accidental omission of one of its component items, as explained in the footnote to table 7–2);

3. Retain the three remaining indices loaded most strongly on each dimension (table 7–4);

4. For those indices based on four rather than three items, eliminate the item with the lowest multi-judge reliability (table 7–2);

Randomize the order of the remaining items to create a 27-item standardized emotional profile (SEP).

These five steps result in the proposed SEP instrument shown in table 7–6 with the items grouped rather than randomized (as in step 5).

We should emphasize that the proposed SEP aims at a parsimonious representation of emotional responses to advertising. The cost of this parsimony is the omission of some emotional types that may be important under certain circumstances (for example, pride, joy, anger, or disgust). In such situations, the additional emotions of interest should, of course, be included as supplements to the SEP.

**Table 7-6**
**Proposed SEP Instrument**

| Dimension | Indices | Items |
|-----------|---------|-------|
| Pleasure | Faith | Reverent<br>Worshipful<br>Spiritual |
| | Affection | Loving<br>Affectionate<br>Friendly |
| | Gratitude | Grateful<br>Thankful<br>Appreciative |
| Arousal | Interest | Attentive<br>Curious<br>Interested[a] |
| | Activation | Aroused<br>Active<br>Excited |
| | Surgency | Playful<br>Entertained<br>Lighthearted |
| Domination | Sadness | Sad<br>Distressed<br>Sorrowful |
| | Fear | Fearful<br>Afraid<br>Anxious |
| | Skepticism | Skeptical<br>Suspicious<br>Distrustful |

[a]This item was added to complete the Interest index.

Further work on emotional responses to advertising in general and to its nonverbal components in particular should focus on refining and validating our proposed SEP instrument. For example, new data collected using SEP should apply confirmatory factor analysis to test the stability of the pleasure, arousal, and domination dimensions. Also, the reliability and ability of these dimensions to predict our validating criteria should be assessed on new sets of data. Finally, the SEP framework should be tested for its ability to reflect advertising content and to predict independently collected response variables such as attitude-toward-the-ad or -brand and shifts in buying intentions or purchase outcomes.

We hope that, in time, such work will converge on a robust and parsimonious SEP, suitable for general application to the case of print ads and television commercials. We do not intend such as SEP as an all-purpose panacea nor as an obligatory copy-testing device. Rather, as already emphasized, we acknowledge that specific applications may require the inclusion of additional emotional indices drawn elsewhere from our larger list (such as pride or anger). However, we do see the SEP as promising assistance to the new streams of research directed toward the investigation of increasingly subtle aspects of ad content. Thus, for example, we expect the SEP to prove useful in measuring responses to the nonverbal components of advertising.

# 8

# Effects of Product Involvement and Emotional Commercials on Consumers' Recall and Attitudes

*Esther Thorson*
*Thomas J. Page, Jr.*

Product involvement and emotional executions in television commercials play important roles in numerous models of consumer information processing and have received significant attention in recent consumer research. The research on involvement has largely been conducted using artificial advertisements in the print medium, and the generalizability of these results to other media, such as television, is questionable. The research on emotion has generally not related that construct to other constructs, and therefore the effects of interactions between emotion and other variables that can affect consumer information processing have not been widely investigated. Because emotion and involvement appear to be important in determining how consumers process information, the research reported here will experimentally investigate their relationship using actual television commercials.

Design of the research reported here was guided by the model of consumer processing shown in figure 8–1 (Thorson and Friestad, in press). Its primary assumption is the distinction between episodic and semantic memory storage, an idea first articulated by Tulving (1972). Episodic memory is the storage of autobiographical information, that is, personal events experienced by an individual over time. Semantic memory stores general knowledge about the world. All experiences enter the memory system via episodic processing. Semantic information is created by performing mental operations (that is, categorization, judging, evaluation, generalization, and comparison) on the material in episodic store.

Effects of product involvement and emotional executions can be conceptualized in terms of the episodic–semantic processing model. When consumer involvement with a product is low, there is no motivation to store commercial experiences anywhere except in episodic memory. They are experienced over time, an episodic trace of them is laid down, and no further related processing occurs (unless the individual is later cornered by an advertising researcher). However, when consumer

The authors thank Maria Heide for directing the research, Dann Hauser, Nicole Post, and Lisa Wagner for testing the subjects, and Hsi-Hua Yang-Dietz for help in handling the data.

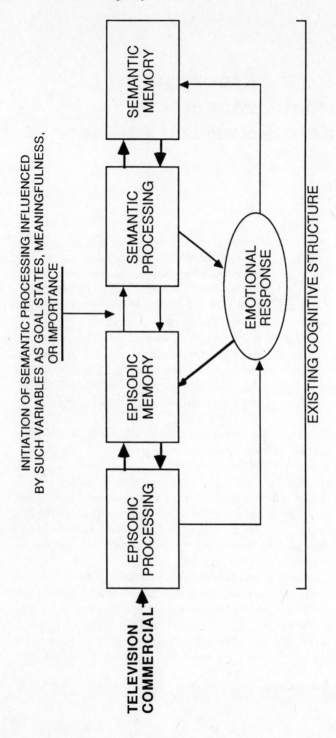

Figure 8-1. Episodic and Semantic Memory Processing of Television Commercials

involvement with a product is high, it is likely that mental operations that create semantic memory traces will occur. The individual may compare incoming brand information with information about other brands already stored in memory, or may counterargue with claims about the advertised brand. Any of these mental acts will create semantic traces. There is evidence (Friestad and Thorson 1985) that creation of both episodic and semantic traces make recall more probable, and that evidence, together with the assumptions about how product involvement influences the memory system, leads to our first hypothesis.

*Hypothesis 1:* Recall of commercials for more highly involving products will be better than for commercials for less involving products.

The model also predicts differences in attitude and intention to purchase as a function of product involvement. When commercials are registered only as episodic traces, associated affect traces may also be laid down, but full formation of attitudes as traditionally defined does not occur. Attitudes, defined in terms of beliefs and associated affects (Kiesler, Collins, and Miller 1969), depend upon the mental operations that create semantic memory. Srull (1983) and Friestad and Thorson (1985) have shown that under conditions in which people are likely to encode commercials only as episodes, when they are later asked to report attitudes, they appear to rely on "computation" of the attitudes from the episodic traces. Their attitudes are not directly influenced by the actual structure of the commercials themselves, but instead on the less detailed and vivid memory traces of the commercials. Because most commercials emphasize positive aspects of brands with executional detail likely to be lost in the episodic trace, attitudes are likely to be less positive. Under conditions in which people are likely to engage in semantic processing of commercials, attitudes are created on-line (Srull 1983). On-line attitudes reflect the strength of commercial executions as originally experienced, and hence they tend to be more positive. Indeed, both Srull (1983) and Friestad and Thorson (1985) demonstrated more positive attitudes toward semantically processed commercials than toward those episodically processed. A more positive attitude toward the message will in turn result in a more positive intention to purchase. This reasoning leads to our second hypothesis.

*Hypothesis 2:* Attitudes toward brand and product category, intention to purchase, and attitude toward purchase will be more positive under high product involvement than under low product involvement.

An emotional commercial is one that emphasizes subjective impressions or feelings rather than factual or objective aspects of the product (Holbrook and O'Shaughnessy 1984). It is important to realize, however, that the emotion lies in the viewer and not in the commercial. In other words, an emotional commercial is one that is capable of creating an emotional response in the viewer. This emotional response is one that involves an interaction between cognitive and physiological mechanisms in the viewer that produces intense feelings (for example, the "lump in the throat"). Thus, the presence of an emotional response during the creation of memory traces is presumed to have two effects. When a commercial produces an emotional response, that response is recorded as part of that commercial's episodic trace. This makes the trace stronger and thereby increases the likelihood that the trace will be recalled at a later time (Thorson and Friestad, in press). Second, the emotional response enhances the probability of semantic processing of the commercial, hence increasing the richness of stored information used to process the commercial. This makes it more likely that the individual will generalize from the commercial to other existing traces. These presumed effects lead to our third hypothesis.

*Hypothesis 3:* Recall of emotional executions will be better than recall of neutral executions.

When emotion is positive, as in most television commercials, attitudes formed either on-line (having semantic memory created during viewing) or later (when only episodic memory has been created during viewing) will be more positive than when no emotion is present. Thus, our fourth hypothesis is as follows:

*Hypothesis 4:* Attitudes toward brand and product class, intention to purchase, and attitude toward the act of purchasing will be more positive for emotional executions.

Note that the model predicts equivalent and additive effects of product involvement and emotional executions. When either involvement or emotion is present, there is greater likelihood of creating semantic memory. Consequently, the presence of either variable predicts equal improvement in memory and attitudes. When both involvement and emotion are present, there are two possible outcomes. Once semantic memory becomes activated, a ceiling effect on recall and attitudes may be reached. This possibility predicts that the High Emotion–High Involvement (HE–HI) condition will not differ from either Low Emotion–High Involvement (LE–HI) or High Emotion–Low Involvement (HE–LI). On the other hand, the presence of both variables may significantly increase the probability of semantic processing over the presence of each variable individually. In this case, the HE–HI condition will show additive effects, or at least a significant increase over either HE–LI or LE–HI. The research conducted here will examine this question.

The final hypothesis concerns processing costs of involvement and emotional executions. To explain this hypothesis, it is first necessary to examine the secondary task procedure and its use as a method of measuring the cognitive effort spent in processing a message.

Measurement of attentional demands of television viewing has proved to be a difficult problem in mass communication research (Reeves, Thorson, and

Schleuder, in press). A method that shows promise as an index of attention is the reaction time secondary task. Subjects are asked to press a button in response to an intermittent secondary stimulus such as a flash or tone, while maintaining attentional engagement with a primary task. The assumption underlying the procedure is that the amount of cognitive effort, or processing capacity, required to perform both tasks simultaneously is more than the individual has available. Thus, if the individual is engaged in the primary task, performance on the secondary task will be poorer than if the secondary task were performed by itself. Performance on the primary task, however, is not hindered by performing the secondary task. Therefore, performance on the secondary task can be used as an indicator of the amount of effort devoted to the primary task. See Kerr (1973) for an excellent discussion of this procedure.

Psychologists have used the secondary task for many years, usually to index the attentional costs of simple primary tasks like digit naming (Wickens 1980). For such primary tasks, increased attention slows reaction time to the secondary task. Recently, however, the secondary task paradigm has been used to index the attentional costs of complex primary tasks such as reading and watching television. Britton and his associates (Britton, Westbrook, and Holdredge 1978; Britton, Holdredge, Curry, and Westbrook 1979; Britton 1980; Britton, Zieglar, and Westbrook 1980; Britton, Glynn, Meyer, and Penland 1982; Britton and Tesser 1982; Britton, Graesser, Glynn, Hamilton, and Penland 1983) varied the difficulty of text passages  along four dimensions: global complexity (for example, easy stories versus difficult texts), grammatical structure (word choice and syntax), semantic content (more versus less meaningful), and the amount of prior knowledge about the texts. Texts that were complex, had difficult syntax and more meaning, and those involving more use of prior knowledge, consistently produced faster RTs, indicating low demands on attentional capacity. Britton, Westbrook and Holdredge (1978) explain this counterintuitive finding by concluding that "simple" material allows the reader to form more associations with existing knowledge which in turn occupy most of the available processing capacity and leave little capacity to perform the secondary task. "Complex" material, on the other hand, inhibits the formation of associations with existing knowledge, causing the primary task to occupy less processing capacity and thereby leave more for the secondary task.

In the television literature, the secondary task has been used to study children's attention to ordered and jumbled versions of a television story (Meadowcroft and Reeves 1985), the comparative attentional cost of watching soap operas by habitual and new viewers (Ibok 1985), the cost of understanding science articles (Shapiro 1985), the cost of processing time-compressed television advertising (Hausknecht and Moore 1985), and the cost of audio and video complexity in television commercials (Thorson, Reeves, and Schleuder 1985). While there has been some variation in results, Meadowcroft and Reeves (1985), Hausknecht and Moore (1985), and Thorson et al. (1985) found results similar to Britton's. More complex media messages yielded faster reaction times to a secondary task.

An assumption of the episodic–semantic model is that there are greater attentional costs when people perform mental tasks that create semantic traces than when they perform only episodic processing. This assumption leads to the prediction that product involvement and emotional executions will affect reaction time to a secondary task. If Britton, Westbrook, and Holdredge's (1978) explanation based on the ability to form associations with the incoming information is generalizable, then one would expect both high involvement and emotional executions to produce slower reaction times. A high level of product involvement should cause the viewer to bring more existing knowledge to bear on the processing of the commercial and thereby make it easier to form associations that occupy processing capacity. An emotional response in the viewer is, by definition, one that involves associations between the viewer's experiences and the incoming information. This leads to our fifth hypothesis.

*Hypothesis 5:* High involvement and the presence of an emotional response will create greater attentional costs and thereby slow reaction time to the secondary task.

The next step is to choose operationalizations of product involvement and emotional executions.

## Product Involvement

It has become clear that involvement is not one but a class of constructs, and there appear to be as many different definitions and operationalizations as there are researchers investigating the constructs. Psychologists developed the foundational concepts for the study of involvement. Sherif and Cantril (1947) discussed "ego involvement," which referred to matters related to one's own self or ego. Later, Sherif and Hovland (1961) referred to "issue involvement" as having personal meaning. In mass media research, Krugman (1965) defined involvement as the bridging connections consumers make between brands and their own experience. Petty and Cacioppo (1979) distinguished issue involvement, where the topic is of personal importance, from response involvement, where situational concerns lead to temporary personal importance. Houston and Rothschild (1977) analogously distinguished enduring and situational involvement.

In 1985, two scales of involvement were introduced. Laurent and Kapferer argued that consumer involvement is most thoroughly characterized with a scale consisting of four factors: perceived importance/risk, probability of negative consequences of purchase, sign (symbols of self or identity), and pleasure. Zaichowsky suggested instead a single-factor test of product involvement that consists of twenty bipolar adjectives such as important–unimportant, useful–useless, and desirable–undesirable. Both scales showed satisfactory internal and external validity, but because Laurent and Kapferer's four factors were highly correlated with each other, especially for the category of convenience goods used in the present study, Zaichowsky's approach seemed preferable. Indeed, if the products chosen here showed differential values on the four-factored scale, it would not have been clear which scale(s) to use in categorizing product involvement.

## Emotion

The concept of emotion in advertising has also been variously defined and operationalized (Holbrook and O'Shaughnessy 1984; Thorson and Friestad, in press). Emotional commercials have been defined as the opposite of those that emphasize factual attributes of products (Preston 1968; McEwen and Leavitt 1976, Lautman and Percy 1984). Emotion has been defined as attitude toward the ad, which is operationalized by having viewers evaluate their attitude toward a commercial in terms of affective pairs like good–bad or like–dislike. (Mitchell and Olson 1981; McKenzie and Lutz 1982; Moore and Hutchinson 1983).

For present purposes, it seemed desirable to index whether subjects experienced feelings during viewing. This approach is consistent with the work of Leckenby and Stout (1984), who categorized emotional commercials by how people talked about their feelings while watching; with Friestad and Thorson (1985), who asked viewers to turn a dial to indicate degree of positive and negative feelings during viewing; and with Aaker, Stayman, and Hagerty (1986), who asked viewers to draw a line to indicate degree of feeling of warmth during viewing. In the present study, pretest subjects watched commercials and then rated them on three bipolar adjective scales: personal–impersonal, warm–cold, and emotional–neutral. While simple, this scale proved in an earlier pretest to be highly correlated with the dial-turning measure of experienced emotions (Friestad and Thorson 1985).

## Method

### Subjects

A total of 79 business-school students (39 males) participated in the product-involvement pretest, 81 business students participated in the pretest of emotional level of commercials, and 67 of the business students tested in the product-involvement pretest participated in the main study. The pretest was performed in the classrooms in the first week of classes. The experiment was performed in the journalism school later in the semester. All students received course-related credits for their participation. Since students were used to determine product involvement and emotional response to the commercials, their use as subjects in the main experiment is consistent with the manipulations of interest.

*Involvement Pretest*

Zaichowsky's (1985) Product Involvement Scale was administered during class time in two business classes. Product categories were chosen on the basis of expectations about their level of involvement for college students and in light of the pool of television commercials available for the study. A total involvement score was calculated for each student for each product. The means of the scores shown in table 8–1 were then used to select commercials to be pretested for emotional impact.

*Emotion Pretest*

The 81 business students in the emotion pretest were shown 27 commercials in two counterbalanced orders. Expert judgment concerning the emotional impact of each commercial was used to insure that the pretest commercials contained both neutral and emotional messages. After each commercial, students responded on a 7-point scale to three bipolar adjective scales: emotional–neutral, personal–

**Table 8–1**

**Mean Pre- and Post-Test Measures of Commercial Emotion and Product Involvement**

| | Pretest | | Manipulation Check | |
|---|---|---|---|---|
| | *Emotion* | *Involvement* | *Emotion* | *Involvement* |
| **HE–HI** | | | | |
| Greeting cards | 5.4 | 101 | 5.3 | 5.1 |
| Camera | 6.2 | 115 | 5.4 | 4.9 |
| Airline | 5.5 | 118 | 5.3 | 5.4 |
| Mean > | 5.7 | 111 | 5.3 | 5.1 |
| **HE–LI** | | | | |
| Dog food | 3.6 | 66 | 3.9 | 3.2 |
| House paint | 4.4 | 81 | 4.3 | 3.5 |
| Bacon | 4.5 | 76 | 4.5 | 4.0 |
| Mean > | 4.2 | 74 | 4.2 | 3.6 |
| **LE–HI** | | | | |
| Ice cream | 3.0 | 102 | 3.6 | 3.8 |
| Bread | 2.8 | 105 | 3.7 | 3.8 |
| Gasoline | 3.0 | 112 | 3.8 | 4.1 |
| Mean > | 2.9 | 106 | 3.7 | 3.9 |
| **LE–LI** | | | | |
| Furniture polish | 1.9 | 67 | 2.9 | 2.8 |
| Chewing tobacco | 2.5 | 32 | 3.1 | 2.3 |
| Room deodorizer | 1.8 | 69 | 3.0 | 3.4 |
| Mean > | 2.1 | 56 | 3.0 | 2.8 |

impersonal, and warm–cold. The three scales were embedded with six others not relevant to the present study. Three high-emotion commercials for high involvement products (HE–HI), three high-emotion commercials for low-involvement products (HE–LI), three low-emotion commercials for high involvement products (LE–HI), and three low-emotion commercials for low-involvement products (LE–LI) were chosen. Subject-derived categorizations were consistent with *a priori* selection of the commercials, lending credence to the operationalization of "emotional." Emotion and product-class involvement scores for each of the twelve commercials are shown in table 8–1. A *t*-test comparing the high and low emotion group means showed the high emotion group to be significantly higher in emotion ($t = 18.25, p < .05$).

## Main Study Design and Procedure

Both product involvement and commercial emotion were varied within subjects in a two-by-two analysis of variance design. Subjects were assigned randomly to one of three counterbalanced orders of the twelve commercials. Two practice commercials preceded each order.

Subjects were instructed that their primary task would be to watch the commercials. At random intervals in each commercial, a tone would sound and they were to press a response key as quickly as possible. Before testing, subjects received eighteen tones to which they responded with a button press. The resulting reaction times provided a baseline of individual speed and a covariate for the reaction-time analysis of variance.

At the close of each commercial, six freeze-frames would appear one at a time. After each, the subject was to indicate verbally to the experimenter whether he/she had just seen the frame in the preceding commercial. Three or four of the frames were targets for each commercial; two or three were foils. The target-to-foil ratio was varied across the twelve commercials.

After viewing all twelve commercials, students were asked to free-recall. They were given sheets with nine lines following the word *message*, and asked to remember as many of the commercials as possible and to write as much information about each as they could, being as specific as possible.

Next, the students were asked to rate their attitudes toward each commercial (identified by brand name and product category) on three bipolar adjective scales: good–bad, dislike–like, and unpleasant–pleasant. These items were intermixed with manipulation check scales for involvement and emotion. The three emotion items were the same scales used in the pretest. The three involvement scales were items from Zaichowsky's Product Involvement Inventory (of concern to me–of no concern to me, involving–uninvolving, and boring–interesting). A third form asked for purchase likelihood (likely–unlikely, seven-point scale) for each of the twelve brands. The fourth form asked subjects to rate a decision to purchase the brand on three seven-point scales: foolish–wise, beneficial–harmful, and bad–good. Fifth, subjects ranked the importance of one product attribute of each product (identified only by category) on two seven-point scales (good–bad, important–unimportant), and the likelihood that each brand had the attribute (very likely–very unlikely, seven-point scale). For purposes of this research, the free-recall protocols were analyzed by two coders only in terms of the number of mentions of brand name and of product category.

## Results

### Manipulation Checks

Table 8–1 shows the mean manipulation check scores for emotion and involvement in each commercial. Although there was some shifting of scores, the high-emotion conditions remained clearly higher ($\overline{X}$ = 4.8) than the low-emotion conditions ($\overline{X}$ = 3.4). A *t*-test of the group means still showed the high emotion group to be significantly higher than the low emotion group ($t$ = 11.58, $p$ < .05).

The manipulation check of product involvement was not identical to the Zaichowsky pretest but rather a subset of the items. A second difference was that the pretest presented subjects only with product categories. The manipulation check, however, involved presenting brand names in the context of a commercial, rather than as product category alone. Given the degree of change involved, the manipulation check demonstrated consistent underlying involvement differences with the mean for high-involving products ($\overline{X}$ = 4.5) significantly higher than for low-involving products ($\overline{X}$ = 3.2, $t$ = 9.70, $p$ < .05). The greatest relative change was seen in the LE–HI group, where involvement was lower than what would have been expected from the pretest. Presumably either identifying products as particular brands or locating them in a low-emotional commercial, or both, led to the drop. This drop should be noted in evaluation of the results.

### Memory

Hypotheses 1 and 3 suggested stronger memory for high-emotion and high-involvement commercials. These hypotheses were tested in terms of product category and brand-name recall. For number of mentions of product category, there was no significant effect of involvement ($F(1,65)$ = .78, $p$ < .05), and a significant effect of emotion in the opposite direction to that hypothesized ($F(1,65)$ = 5.25, $p$ < .03, $\overline{X}$ low = 1.11, and $\overline{X}$ high = .94). The hypothesized effects did, however, occur for number of brand-name mentions, with high involvement producing more frequent brand-name mentions than low ($F(1,65)$ = 8.66, $p$ < .01) and high emotion more brand-name mentions than low ($F(1,65)$ = 3.99, $p$ < .05). The brand name results are shown in figure 8–2.

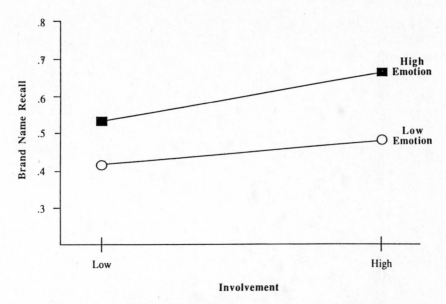

**Figure 8-2. Brand Name Recall as a Function of Emotion and Involvement**

*Attitude*

Figures 8–3 through 8–6 display the attitudinal results. Hypotheses 2 and 4, that higher involvement and the presence of emotion would make attitudes more positive, were supported in each case. There were significant main effects in the predicted direction for both involvement and emotion. None of the interactions were significant.

The implication of the hypotheses was that involvement and emotion would have similar strength of effect. As can be seen in figures 8–3 through 8–6, the presence of high product involvement or emotion did produce similar attitudinal scores. For example, brand attitude under HE–LI ($\overline{X}$ = 10.8) and LE–HI ($\overline{X}$ = 10.3) were nearly equal. This was true for the other three attitudinal measures.

*Reaction Time*

Hypothesis 5 suggested that high involvement and high emotion would produce lengthened reaction times. Results, however, showed no significant effects of either variable on reaction time, although emotion approached significance ($F(1,54)$ = 2.32, $p$ < .13) with the high-emotion reaction time ($\overline{X}$ = 395 msec) longer than the low-emotion reaction time ($\overline{X}$ = 384 msec). Use of the baseline reaction time (that is, no primary task) as a covariate left this result unchanged. A comparison of the mean baseline reaction time to the mean reaction time of each of the four conditions showed

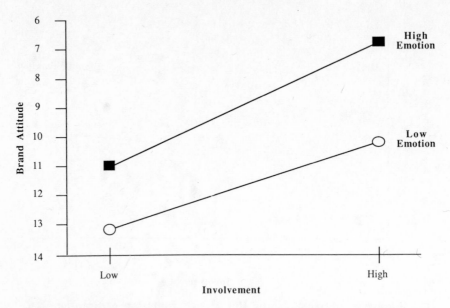

**Figure 8–3. Brand Attitude as a Function of Emotion and Involvement**

that for the HE–HI condition, the reaction times were significantly slower at the .10 level. The difference in reaction time for the other three conditions and the overall average of all four conditions were not significantly different from the baseline.

## Discussion

In this study, the clearest effect of product involvement and commercial emotion was enhancement of attitudinal measures. Strong effects for both involvement and emotion were obtained on brand-name mentions, but no effect was obtained for product category. One possible explanation for the lack of effects on product-category recall may be that the product category is likely to be recalled equally well under conditions of either episodic or semantic processing. Under conditions of episodic processing, subjects would be likely to store the information in its most general form, which would be product category (for example, "I saw a commercial for furniture polish"). When conditions that are likely to cause semantic processing exist, the product category remains an important cue, but now the brand name may also become an important element of the trace. This would occur when the subject has engaged in some sort of mental operation (for example, comparison of brands) that has made the brand name a stronger part of the trace.

The attitude results obtained in this research are largely consistent with the episodic–semantic model of memory discussed earlier. Subjects engaged in episodic

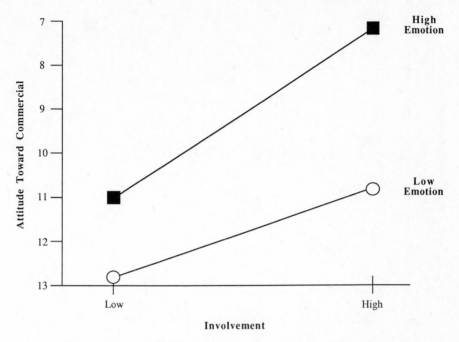

**Figure 8-4. Attitude toward Commercial as a Function of Emotion and Involvement**

processing are not likely to form strong attitudes, but subjects engaged in semantic processing are likely to form strong attitudes as a result of the mental operations engaged in during processing of the commercial. Since the information contained in the commercials is designed to create favorable attitudes, subjects engaged in semantic processing would be expected to exhibit the more favorable attitudes, the result found in the present study.

The attitude and recall results obtained in this research may shed some light on a growing body of research that concludes that there is no relationship between attitudes and recall (Petty, Cacioppo, and Schumann 1983). Attitudes are formed as a result of mental operations on the incoming information, and as such, they, along with a few other very specific pieces of information (for example, brand name), are likely to become very strong elements of the subsequent semantic trace. However, other specifics, such as executional details, may not form very strong elements of the trace. Thus, it may be quite possible to produce strong changes in attitude as a result of semantic processing, and yet recall of the actual commercial itself may be no better than that produced by episodic processing. Part of our future research is aimed at determining just which elements of the commercial trace are affected by semantic processing and which are not.

Reaction times to the secondary task also failed to show significant effects of involvement and emotion, although the emotion effect approached significance,

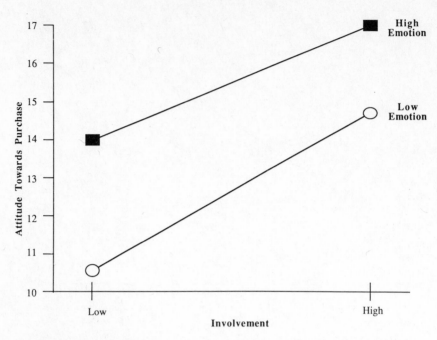

**Figure 8–5. Attitude toward Purchase as a Function of Emotion and Involvement**

with high emotion slower than low emotion. Although the sixty-seven subjects in the study provided sufficient power for the memory and attitude measures, given only four reaction times per commercial per subject, the power to discriminate real differences in reaction times may not be sufficient. In a planned replication study, the number of subjects and reaction times per commercial will be increased to provide sufficient power to detect real differences.

Although the statistical power in this research may have been insufficient to detect differences in reaction times, it may instead be that the secondary task procedure itself is not capable of detecting differences in an individual's internal mental state even though mental state differences may affect other dependent measures. As stated earlier, both emotion and involvement reside in the subject, and even though they may affect attitude, intention, and brand-name recall, they may not affect processing capacity at the level measured by the secondary task. The research discussed earlier concerning the secondary task used manipulations that involved changes in the stimuli (for example, complexity, meaningfulness, and so on) rather than changes in the subject. These changes in the nature of the stimuli may have been so large that changes in the amount of processing capacity were easily detectable. However, in the present research the changes were internal to the subject and, while they were sufficient to produce changes in attitude, intention, and brand-

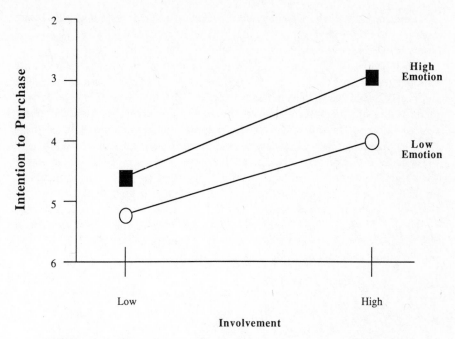

**Figure 8-6. Intention to Purchase as a Function of Emotion and Involvement**

name recall, they may not have been sufficient to produce detectable differences in the secondary task. Future research on the secondary task method should focus on determining just how sensitive the procedure is to different types of manipulations.

It is interesting to compare the attitudinal results in this study to those of Petty, Cacioppo, and Schumann (1983). Using print ads, manipulation of response involvement (high-involvement subjects were told they could choose a brand from within the advertised product category as a gift for participating) and manipulation of a noncontent variable (presence or absence of a celebrity endorser), both the involvement and the noncontent effects were different from those obtained here. Under  low involvement, celebrity endorsers produced more positive attitudes than noncelebrity endorsers. But under high involvement, both endorser types produced the same attitude level, and one no different from the low-involvement noncelebrity condition. In contrast, the results here showed increased positive attitudes as a main effect of both product involvement and emotion (our noncontent variable). Whether these differences resulted from the variations in operationalization of involvement and noncontent variables (emotion versus endorser type) or from differences between the processing of television and print is not clear. The contrast, however, provides an interesting challenge for further research examining the comparative influences of involvement and noncontent variables like emotion.

One limitation of the present study concerns the fact that real commercials were used as stimuli. While this greatly enhances the external (ecological) validity of the study, it increases the risks to internal validity. Using actual commercials means that there is a possibility that variables other than emotion and involvement were manipulated. During the design of the experiment, every attempt was made to reduce this possibility. However, it soon became apparent that in order to find enough commercials that suited our needs, it would not be possible to counterbalance all possible confounding variables. Thus a decision was made to counterbalance those variables that were most likely to have a significant impact on the results, and disregard the rest. Even this proved to be difficult because of the lack of unfamiliar brands with highly emotional appeals. (It would appear that less well-known brands do not use emotional commercials, perhaps because of their high production costs.) While we realize that this is a possible shortcoming of our study, we feel that investigating the effects of real commercials instead of artificial ones does make a useful contribution to understanding how consumers process information.

# 9

# Current Perspectives and Issues Concerning the Explanation of "Feeling" Advertising Effects

*Andrew A. Mitchell*

R ecently there has been considerable interest in understanding the role of affect in human information processing (for example, Zajonc 1981; Zajonc and Markus 1982) and, more specifically of "subjective feeling states" or mood in persuasion (for example, Ray and Batra 1983; Gardner 1985; Srull 1984). In an advertising context, these feeling states could occur for two reasons. First, the media environment may create the feeling state. For instance, if an advertisement is run in a situation comedy, the comedy may produce a positive feeling state in the viewer prior to exposure to the advertisement. Second, the advertisement itself may induce a feeling state in the individual. There are a number of examples of advertisements, termed *feeling* advertisements, that seem to be designed to induce these states.

In this chapter, a number of issues are examined concerning the effects of feeling states in an advertising context. The first issue is whether the effects of feeling states induced prior to the exposure to an advertisement are different from those induced by the advertisement itself. The second issue concerns the explanation of these effects. Can, for instance, these effects be explained by differences in the information encoded during exposure to the advertisement? The third issue is whether the effects of these feeling states are similar to those induced by placing a positively or negatively evaluated photograph in an advertisement.

In the next section, these three issues will be discussed. Then, the results of an experiment designed to examine these issues will be presented. Finally, the implications of the experimental results on the three issues will be discussed.

---

The author would like to thank Christopher August for his assistance in the data collection and analysis. He would also like to acknowledge the numerous conversations that he has held with Alice Isen and Thom Srull on a number of the issues discussed in this paper.

# Theory

## Differences in Media-versus Ad-Based Mood Effects

In a previous study, Srull (1984) examined the effect of a mood induced prior to the presentation of a message which contained information about a hypothetical product. In this study, there were two manipulations. The first was the valence of the induced mood. Here, positive, neutral, and negative moods were induced by having subjects "re-live" a previous life experience that corresponds to that mood. The second was the processing strategy used by the subject during exposure to the advertisement. For this manipulation, subjects were instructed either to read the information in the message and form an evaluation of the advertised brand or to read the information in the message and look for misspelled words and grammatical errors. The results of numerous studies (for example, Hastie and Park 1986; Lichtenstein and Srull 1985; Gardner, Mitchell, and Russo 1977) indicate that this manipulation affects whether or not subjects form an evaluation of an object (for example, a new brand) while they are exposed to information about the object (for example, an advertisement for the brand).

After seeing the advertisement, the subjects were given a filler task that required them to write the names of as many states as they could on a map of the United States. The purpose of this task was to eliminate the effect of the mood manipulation, so the measures of the subjects' evaluations of the advertised product would not be affected by this manipulation. After completing this task, subjects provided their evaluations of the advertised product.

The results of the study, as reported by Srull (1984), indicated that the mood manipulations had an effect only when subjects formed an evaluation of the advertised brand during exposure to the advertisement (on-line or brand processing). Subjects in a positive mood formed more favorable evaluations of the advertised brand than subjects in a neutral mood, who, in turn, formed more favorable evaluations than subjects in a negative mood. When subjects did not form an evaluation of the advertised brand while exposed to the advertisement (impression after or nonbrand processing), the mood manipulation had no effect on the brand evaluations.

Since the moods were induced prior to exposure to the advertisements, this manipulation simulates media-induced moods. It is hypothesized here that one important difference in the effect of media-versus advertising-induced moods *may* occur when subjects do not form an evaluation of the brand during exposure to the advertisement. When the mood is induced by the advertisement, a representation of the mood *may* be associated with the brand in memory (for example, Bower 1981; Clarke and Isen 1982). At a later point, when subjects form an evaluation of the brand, this representation of the mood may become activated and, if it does, it may affect the evaluation that is formed. Consequently, when the mood is induced by the advertisement, positive moods may result in more positive brand evaluations irrespective of whether or not subjects formed an evaluation of the brand during exposure to the advertisement.

## Explanation for the Effects of Moods on Brand Evaluation

A number of studies, including the study by Srull (1984) discussed earlier, find that subjective feeling states affect evaluations and choice. Veitch and Griffith (1978), for instance, found that subjects who heard broadcasts reporting good news evaluated anonymous others more favorably than subjects who heard broadcasts reporting bad news. Isen et al. (1978) found that subjects who received a gift evaluated products that they owned more favorably than subjects who received no gift. Finally, Gorn (1982) found that subjects were more likely to select a pen that they had seen advertised with positively evaluated music than with negatively evaluated music. Although these studies used different manipulations, all of these studies, with the exception of Gorn (1982), interpreted these manipulations as manipulations of subjective feeling states. Gorn (1982) interpreted the results of his study as classical conditioning; however, recently Allen and Madden (1985) have suggested a mood interpretation of the results. This interpretation bears serious consideration, since numerous studies have used music to manipulate mood (for example, Clark and Teasdale 1985).

The issue to be examined here is why these effects occur. A number of different hypotheses have been proposed in the literature to explain these effects (for example, Isen 1984, Mitchell 1986). The first hypothesis is the encoding hypothesis (for example, Bower, Gilligen, and Monteiro 1981). Under this hypothesis, the valence of an individual's feeling state affects the encoding of information in memory. For instance, individuals experiencing positive feeling states encode primarily positive information in memory. The second hypothesis is the retrieval hypothesis (for example, Teasdale and Fogerty 1979). Here the valence of an individual's subjective feeling state affects what information is retrieved from memory. For instance, more positive information is retrieved by individuals in a positive feeling state.

The next hypothesis is a response bias hypothesis. Here subjects in a positive feeling state tend to evaluate everything more positively, independent of what information is recalled from memory. The fourth hypothesis is a classical conditioning hypothesis (for example, Gorn 1982). According to this hypothesis, the pairing of a positively or negatively evaluated stimulus (the unconditioned stimulus), which in the Gorn study was music, with an unknown brand (the conditioned stimulus), will result in the conditioning of the evaluation to the brand (for example, Staats and Staats 1958). If the unconditioned stimulus should also create different subjective feeling states, these different feeling states are simply an epiphenomenon. Finally, the differences in attitude may be due to demand effects. Subjects in studies that manipulate subjective feeling states simply guess the purpose of the experiment and respond in the appropriate way.

*Mediators of the Feeling States*

The final issue that will be examined in this chapter is whether the typical mediators of attitude formation in an advertising context will explain differences in attitudes caused by subjective feeling states. Here the typical mediators of attitude formation are cognitive responses (for example, Greenwald 1968; Wright 1973), attitude toward the advertisement (for example, Lutz 1985; Mitchell and Olson 1981), and beliefs about the advertised brand (for example, Fishbein and Ajzen 1975; Mitchell 1986).

A number of studies indicate that combinations of these variables mediate attitude formation in an advertising context. For instance, in a study reported by Mitchell (1986), the placement of a valenced photograph in an advertisement affected brand attitudes and attitude toward the advertisement, but not the beliefs that were formed about the advertised brand. In order to explain the finding of this study and other studies examining the effect of visual stimuli, a Dual Component Model was proposed. In this model, both attitude toward the advertisement and the beliefs formed about the advertised brand mediate attitude formation.

Based on the hypotheses presented in the previous section, this model may also explain the effects of advertisements that induce subjective feeling states. The effects of these subjective feeling states may operate either through the beliefs that are formed or through attitude toward the advertisement. For instance, according to the encoding hypothesis, the subjective feeling state may affect the beliefs that are formed. Alternatively, the subjective feeling state may have an effect on the evaluation of the advertisement. Advertisements that induce positive feeling states may be evaluated more positively.

## Research Goals

The purpose of this study was to examine the three general issues discussed earlier. The first is whether or not subjective mood states induced during exposure to an advertising message have an effect on brand attitudes when subjects do not form an evaluation of the advertised brand during exposure to the advertisement. The second is to examine some of the hypotheses of why "subjective feeling" states affect evaluations. The third is to examine the effect of "subjective feeling" states on the mediators of attitude formation and change, and whether the Dual Component Model, which was developed to explain the effects of visual stimuli in advertisements, would also explain the effects elements in advertisements that induce subjective feeling states.

## Method

*Design*

In order to achieve the research goals discussed earlier, a two-by-two full factorial design was used. The first factor was whether or not subjects formed an evaluation of the advertised brand during exposure to the advertising message. The manipulations used to achieve these effects were virtually identical to those used by Srull (1984). In one condition (on-line or brand processing), subjects were instructed to form an evaluation of the advertised brand during exposure to the advertising message. In a second condition (impression after or nonbrand processing), subjects were instructed to examine the advertising message for misspellings, awkward sentences, and for portions of the message that were difficult to understand.

The second manipulation was an induction of a positive or neutral mood. Music was used as the mood-induction procedure for three reasons. First, music could be played while subjects were exposed to verbal information about the product without seriously disrupting their processing of this information. Second, since Gorn (1982) also used music in his study, it was hoped that by using music to manipulate mood in this study we might be able to sort out the alternative explanation for his results. Finally, Blaney (1986) has argued that music is one of the best procedures for manipulating mood, since it is least likely to result in cognitive priming.

In order to select the appropriate music for this manipulation, a number of pretests were undertaken. For these pretests, a number of musical tracks that were thought to induce either a positive or neutral mood were selected. In the actual pretests, a number of undergraduates listened to a musical track for one minute and then reported their moods by filling out a series of scales. The scales used to measure their moods were five seven-point bipolar scales anchored by "happy-sad," "pleasant–unpleasant," "serious–carefree," "elated–depressed," and "gloomy-carefree." For a control condition, a number of undergraduates heard no music, but just reported their mood by filling out the scales.

The music that was found to most consistently induce a positive mood was "Sing, Sing, Sing" played by Benny Goodman. The music that was found to consistently have no effect on mood was a repetition of portions of the "Closing" from the album "Glassworks" by Philip Glass. To enhance the neutral effects of this music, sounds of waves were added in the background. The pretest scores from the mood scales were 5.45 for positive mood manipulation, 4.60 for the neutral mood manipulation, and 4.50 for the control condition.

*Subjects*

The subjects were forty-eight undergraduates of both sexes recruited from business classes at the University of Toronto. In the recruitment process, the subjects were asked to volunteer for an advertising study that would last about one half-hour and were told that they would be paid $5.00 for their participation. A sign-up sheet was then passed around and, if they were interested in participating, they were asked to write down their names, phone numbers, and times when it would be convenient for them to participate. At a later point, they were called to schedule a time for them to participate in the study, and at this point they were randomly assigned to conditions.

*Advertising Message*

The advertising message contained the headline "Presenting a Useful Idea for Students—The Denson Work Lamp," and about a hundred words of copy. The copy provide eight pieces of information about the products. These were that it (1) clamps on a variety of surfaces, (2) adjusts to a number of preset positions and angles, (3) has a two-position intensity switch, (4) has a coiled cord, (5) is made of plastic, (6) is available in black or white, (7) accepts standard bulb sizes, and (8) costs $36.95.

The copy was written and pretested to ensure that undergraduates would evaluate the work lamp as slightly positive to avoid ceiling effects from the mood manipulation. After this was assessed, a slide containing the copy was produced.

*Procedure*

After the subjects entered the laboratory, they were seated at desks and were told that they would see an advertisement for a work lamp that a company was planning to introduce in Canada. They were also told that since the product was new, the company had not actually produced any advertisements. Instead, they would see the copy that would appear in the advertisement and would hear the music that would be used in the advertisement while they looked at the copy.

At this point, the subjects were given the appropriate instructions for either the brand or nonbrand processing condition. The appropriate music for the condition was then started and, at the same time, the slide with the advertising message was shown on the screen in front of the subjects. After one minute, both the slide and music were turned off.

The subjects were then given two minutes to write down their thoughts while exposed to the advertisement. After completing this task, they were given an article describing a computer simulation of plant growth that contained a number of misspelled words. The subjects were instructed to read the article and circle all the misspelled words. It took the subjects approximately seven minutes to complete this task, on average. The purpose of this task was to eliminate the effects of the mood manipulation, so all subjects would be in a neutral mood when the recall and attitude measures were taken and thus the results of this study could be compared to the results of Srull (1984).

The same mood scales used to pretest the music were then given to the subjects to assess their mood at this point. After completing these scales, the subjects were given a short filler task that required them to multiply two four-digit numbers.

Finally, the subjects were given a series of questionnaires to measure their attitudes toward the Denson Work Lamp and the advertisement, and the associations that subjects had with both the advertised brand and the advertisement. The attitudes were always measured before the associations, and the order of measuring the attitudes and associations with the advertised brand and the advertisement were counterbalanced.

In order to obtain measures of the associations with the Denson Work Lamp, subjects were asked to think about Denson Work Lamps, and write down everything that came to mind. The experimenter then drew a seven-point bipolar scale anchored by the adjectives "good–bad" on the blackboard and asked the subject to indicate how good or bad they thought it was that a work lamp contained each association by writing the appropriate number next to each association that he or she had written down. The same procedure was used to measure the associations with the advertisement.

After completing the final questionnaire, the subjects were asked to write down what they thought the purpose of the experiment was. Then they were debriefed, paid, and dismissed.

## Dependent Variables

Four different dependent variables were analyzed in this study. The scales and procedures used to measure each of these variables are discussed in this section.

**Brand Attitudes.** The mean of three nine-point scales was used to measure overall attitudes toward the brand ($A_o$). The adjectives anchoring these scales were "good–bad," "like–dislike", and "pleasant–unpleasant." Attitude toward the act of purchasing and using the brand ($A_{act}$) was measured by three nine-point scales anchored by the adjectives "good–bad," "foolish–wise," and "beneficial–harmful." Finally, behavioral intentions (BI) were measured on a nine-point scale anchored by "not at all likely to buy" and "very likely to buy."

**Attitude Toward the Advertisement.** The mean of four five-point scales was used to measure attitude toward the advertisement ($A_{ad}$). The adjectives anchoring these scales were "good–bad," "like–dislike," "irritating–not irritating," and "interesting–uninteresting."

**Predicted Attitude from the Elicited Product Beliefs.** The associations with the Denson Work Lamp that were written down by each subject were first coded by two coders as to whether they were product attribute, product evaluation, advertisement, or advertisement evaluation statements, using the coding scheme below.

| Category | Definition |
|---|---|
| Product Attribute Statement | Any statement that describes the product, mentions a particular characteristic of the product, or mentions how it performs. |
| Product Evaluation Statement | Any statement that gives an overall evaluation of the product. |
| Advertisement Statement | Any statement that describes the advertisement—what the copy said or mentioned of the music that was played. |
| Advertisement Evaluation Statement | Any statement that gives an overall evaluation of the advertisement. |

The coders agreed on 0.88 percent of the statements. Disagreements were settled through discussion.

The evaluations of each product attribute statement were then summed to form a measure of the predicted attitude from the elicited product beliefs.

**Cognitive Responses.** The thoughts that the subjects reported during exposure to the advertisement were coded twice. First they were coded by two coders into product and advertisement thoughts using the coding scheme below.

| | |
|---|---|
| Product Thought | Any statement that describes the product—how it performs, a particular characteristic of the product, or an evaluation of the product. |
| Advertisement Thought | Any statement that describes the advertisment—what the copy said, a description of the advertisement, or an evaluation of the advertisement. |

Next, the product thoughts were coded by two coders into support and counter-arguments using the coding scheme developed by Wright (1973), and the advertisement thoughts were coded into positive and negative advertisement thoughts using the coding scheme given below.

*Positive Statements About the Advertisement*

Any positive evaluative statement about the advertisement or any aspect of the advertisement, such as the copy or the picture used in the advertisement.

*Negative Statement About the Advertisement*

Any negative evaluative statement about the advertisement or any aspect of the advertisement, such as the copy or the picture used in the advertisement.

The agreement between coders for the product and advertisement thoughts, support and counterarguments, and positive and negative advertisement thoughts were 0.85, 0.82, and 0.78, respectively. Disagreements were settled through discussion.

## Results

In this section the experimental results will be examined and discussed. First, however, we will examine three factors that may affect the validity of the results. These are whether the subjects guessed the purpose of the experiment, whether the processing strategy manipulation was successful, and whether the filler task eliminated the effects of the mood manipulation.

## Demand Characteristics

In order to determine whether or not the subjects guessed the purpose of the experiment, we examined their responses to our request for them to write down the purpose of the experiment. Virtually all of these responses essentially repeated the cover story given to them.

## Processing Strategy Manipulation Check

In order to determine whether the processing strategy manipulation was successful, the percentage of product and advertising thoughts that were reported under each condition were analyzed. These percentages are shown in table 9–1. If the manipulation was successful, most of the statements for the brand processing manipulation should be product statements, while most of the statements for the nonbrand processing manipulation should be advertisement statements. The results indicate that this occurred for the nonbrand processing manipulation, where over 85 percent of the statements were advertisement statements. For the brand processing manipulation, the percentage of the statements that were product statements was not quite as high—62 percent. An examination of the advertisement statements with this manipulation indicated that most of these statements were statements concerning the music. Consequently, the nonbrand processing manipulation seems to have been successful; however, the brand processing manipulation seems to have resulted in a fairly substantial number of advertisement statements.

## Mood Manipulation Check

Recall that after the subjects saw the advertisements, they were asked to read a passage and circle the misspelled words in the passage. As mentioned previously, the purpose of this task was to eliminate the effects of the mood manipulation, so that the subjects would be in a neutral mood when the attitude and recall measures were taken. To determine whether this, in fact, occurred, the subjects' responses to the mood scale, which were obtained after they completed this task, were analyzed by a two-way ANOVA. This analysis indicated that both the main effects and the interaction were not significant ($p > 0.22$). The mean score for the positive and neutral mood conditions were 4.23 and 4.54, respectively.

**Table 9–1**
**Percentage of Thoughts**

|  | *Brand Processing* | *Nonbrand Processing* |
| --- | --- | --- |
| Product thoughts | 62 | 14 |
| Advertisement thoughts | 38 | 86 |

*Brand Attitudes*

The effect of the processing strategy and mood manipulations on the overall brand attitudes are shown in figure 9–1. An examination of the means in each cell indicates that the positive mood manipulation produced more positive attitudes than the neutral mood manipulation. A two-way ANOVA indicated that these effects were highly significant ($p < 0.001$).

The brand attitudes for the neutral mood manipulation were slightly higher under Nonbrand Processing than under Brand Processing, while for the positive mood manipulation the means under Brand and Nonbrand Processing were virtually identical. The differences between the Brand and Nonbrand Processing conditions with the neutral mood, however, were not large enough to produce a significant interaction.

Similar effects were found for both attitude toward the act of purchasing and using the brand ($A_{act}$) and behavioral intentions (BI). For $A_{act}$, the mood manipulation was highly significant ($p < 0.01$); however, for behavioral intentions the differences were only marginally significant ($p < 0.08$).

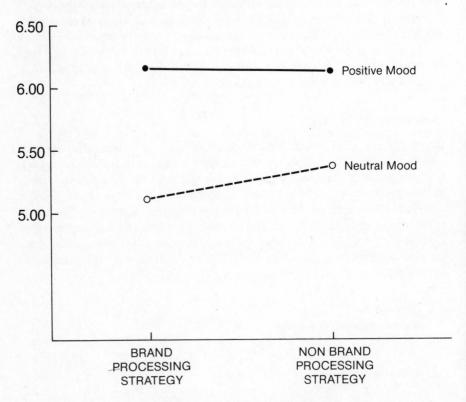

**Figure 9–1. Overall Brand Attitude**

These results, then, indicate that the positive mood manipulation had a strong effect on brand attitudes under both a brand and nonbrand processing strategy. These findings should be contrasted to those found by Srull (1984), where the mood manipulation only had an effect with a brand processing strategy.

## Cognitive Responses

A number of different analyses were undertaken to examine the effect of the mood manipulation on cognitive responses. First, the effect of the mood manipulation on (1) the number of support arguments and (2) the number of counterarguments generated was examined. For both types of statements, the mean number of statements generated under neutral and positive moods were almost the same. For instance, in the positive mood condition, an average of 0.62 support arguments were generated per subject, while in the neutral mood condition 0.50 were generated per subject. Consequently, a two-way ANOVA indicated only a main effect for processing strategy for both variables ($p < 0.02$). Neither the main effect of mood nor the interaction was significant ($p > 0.34$).

Second, the differences in the number of support and counterarguments were examined under the positive and neutral mood manipulations. As expected, these differences were also almost the same between these two conditions. For the positive mood condition, the value was $-0.42$, while for the neutral mood condition it was $-0.37$. A two-way ANOVA indicated that neither the main effects nor the interaction was significant ($p > 0.35$).

Finally, the effects of the mood manipulation on the number of positive and negative advertisement statements were examined. Again, the number of these types of statements was almost identical between the positive and neutral mood conditions. For instance, 0.42 positive advertisement thoughts per subject were found in the neutral mood condition, and 0.46 positive advertisement thoughts per subject were found in the positive mood condition. A two-way ANOVA indicated only a significant main effect due to processing strategy for both of these variables ($p < 0.001$). Neither the main effects of mood nor the interactions were significant ($p > 0.46$). Similar results were found for the differences in the number of positive and negative advertisement statements.

In summary, the mood manipulation seems to have little effect on the various categories of cognitive responses generated.

## Attitude Toward the Advertisement

A two-way ANOVA was used to examine the effect of the mood manipulation and processing strategy on attitude toward the advertisement. If the mood manipulation operates in the same manner as a valenced photograph in an advertisement, then a main effect for the mood manipulation should be found. The results of the ANOVA, however, indicated that neither the mood nor the processing strategy manipulation had a significant effect on this variable ($p > 0.76$). An examination of the cell means indicated that they are virtually identical across cells.

## Product Attribute Evaluations

If the mood manipulation produced an encoding effect, then there should be differences in the valence of the product attribute information recalled from memory. In order to examine this, a two-way ANOVA on the sum of product attribute evaluations was conducted. The results indicated a main effect for mood only ($p < 0.01$). As can be seen in table 9–2, the sum of the product attribute evaluations was more positive when the subjects were in a positive mood during exposure to the advertising message.

Since these differences may be caused by either the amount of information recalled or the evaluation of the information recalled, additional analyses were performed. These analyses indicated that both of these effects occurred. A two-way ANOVA indicated that subjects recalled significantly more product attribute information when they were in a positive mood during exposure to the advertisement ($p < 0.05$). On average, subjects recalled 5.54 product attribute statements in the positive mood condition and 4.92 product attribute statements in the neutral mood condition. The evaluations of this information also tended to be more positive in the positive mood condition (1.20 vs. 0.43), however, these differences were only marginally significant ($p < 0.07$).

## Prediction of Attitudes

In the previous analysis, it was found that the mood manipulation had an effect on the brand attitudes that were formed. It also had an effect on the sum of the product attribute evaluations. No effect, however, was found in attitude toward the advertisement.

In this section, we will examine the effect of these two mediators on brand attitudes in each of the conditions. Before examining these effects, it should be noted that previous research has indicated that with a Brand Processing strategy, both attitude toward the advertisement ($A_{ad}$) and the prediction of attitudes from the product attribute beliefs (SE) that were formed have been found to have a significant effect on brand attitude. However, with a nonbrand processing strategy, only $A_{ad}$ has been found to have a significant effect (for example, Gardner 1985).

**Table 9–2**
**Sum of Product Attribute Evaluations**

|  | Brand Processing | Nonbrand Processing |
| --- | --- | --- |
| Neutral mood | 1.92 | 2.33 |
| Positive mood | 5.25 | 8.08 |

In order to examine the effect of attitude toward the advertisement and the prediction of attitudes based on product attribute beliefs, separate regression analyses were estimated for each cell. The results of the regression analyses are shown in table 9–3. Here it can be seen that the results of the regression analyses for the neutral mood/brand processing cell are similar to those found in previous studies. The coefficients for the $A_{ad}$ and SE variables are both positive and statistically significant, and these two variables explain a little over 50 percent of the variance in brand attitudes.

The results for the neutral mood/nonbrand processing cell is also somewhat similar to previous studies in that $A_{ad}$ has a highly significant positive effect on brand attitudes. The results also indicate that the prediction of attitudes from product attribute beliefs (SE) has a significant effect; however, the sign of the coefficient is negative. An examination of the simple correlation between brand attitudes and SE indicates that it is small, negative ($-0.09$), and not statistically different from zero ($p > 0.39$). This indicates that the effect of SE in the regression equation was a statistical anomaly.

In both positive mood conditions, however, the regression coefficients for both attitude toward the advertisement ($A_{ad}$) and the predicted attitude from the product attribute beliefs (SE) are *not* significantly different from zero. In addition, the percentage of the variance explained is considerably lower. One reason for the insignificant coefficients may have been multicollinearity; however, this did not seem to be the case. The correlations between the two independent variables were small

**Table 9–3**
**Prediction of Attitudes**
*Beta Coefficients (t - statistics)*

|  | $A_{ad}$ | SE | $R^2$ |
|---|---|---|---|
| Brand processing | | | |
| Neutral mood | | | |
| | 0.589** | 0.342*** | 0.52 |
| | (2.546) | (1.886) | |
| Positive mood | | | |
| | 0.329 | 0.310 | 0.15 |
| | (1.025) | (0.966) | |
| Nonbrand processing | | | |
| Neutral mood | | | |
| | 0.945* | $-0.533$** | 0.70 |
| | (4.619) | (2.606) | |
| Positive mood | | | |
| | 0.377 | 0.345 | 0.24 |
| | (1.294) | (1.184) | |

*$p < 0.01$
**$p < 0.05$
***$p < 0.10$

(−0.08 and −0.28). In addition, all of the simple correlations between the predictor variables and brand attitudes were also small and insignificant.

These results indicate that under neutral mood conditions, the mediators of attitude formation are similar to those found in other studies. However, under positive mood conditions, none of the traditional mediators of attitude formation seem to have much effect on brand attitude.

## Explanations

The results of this study shed some light on the validity of the different explanations for mood effects that were discussed earlier. First, it should be noted that two of the explanations, state-dependent learning and the retrieval hypothesis, could not be examined in this study because mood was not manipulated at time of retrieval. A previous study reported by Milberg and Mitchell (1983), which did examine these hypotheses, could not find any evidence for them. In addition, Bower and Mayer (1985) recently reported that they could not replicate state-dependent learning.

The study reported here found that mood had a strong effect on brand attitude formation, but no effect on the number of support or counterarguments generated and no effect on attitude toward the advertisement. Although the encoding hypothesis was found to hold in this study, there seemed to be little relationship between the valence of the information recalled from memory and the attitudes that were formed under the positive mood condition. Under the neutral mood condition, the traditional mediators, as predicted by the Dual Component Model, seemed to affect attitude formation; however, under the positive mood condition, there was little relationship between these mediators and brand attitude formation.

This leaves us with three possible explanations of these effects. These are the response bias, classical conditioning, and the demand effects explanations. According to the response bias explanation, individuals in a positive mood evaluate objects more positively. Since subjects in the positive mood condition formed an evaluation of the advertised brand while they were in a positive mood, this explanation is consistent with this finding. Subjects in the nonbrand processing condition, however, formed their evaluation of the advertised brand when they were no longer in a positive mood, yet under this condition they still formed more favorable attitudes. One possible explanation for this, which would be consistent with the response bias explanation, is that when they formed their attitudes later they activated their knowledge structure for the brand, and this knowledge structure contained a representation of the mood. The activation of this structure recreated the mood which, in turn, affected the evaluation. If this actually occurred, then the response bias explanation would hold in this situation.

The classical conditioning explanation is also somewhat difficult to assess although it does not seem to be appropriate. In the literature, most of the argument surrounding the validity of a conditioning explanation of experimental results using human subjects centers on whether or not the subjects were aware of the contingency (cf., Brewer 1974). If subjects were aware of the contingency, then the results may be due to demand effects, where subjects guess the experimental hypotheses and behave accordingly, or theoretically, awareness may be required to transfer affect from the unconditioned stimulus to the conditioned stimulus. If the latter is true, then a cognitive explanation may provide a better explanation of the results. For instance, if subjects are aware of the contingency, they may have formed different beliefs about conditioned stimulus (cf. Fishbein and Ajzen 1975).

In the study reported here, subjects were told that the music was part of the advertisement for the Denson Work Lamp, and the link between the advertisement and the product was obvious. Consequently, subjects were clearly aware of the contingency.

In addition, the mood manipulation had a strong effect on the beliefs that were formed about the product. This indicates that there were differences in the higher level processes that occurred between the positive and the neutral mood conditions during exposure to the advertisement. The results of the regression analysis, however, indicated that under the positive mood condition, the beliefs that were formed had little effect on attitude formation. One could, therefore, argue that the resulting differences in higher level processes were epiphenomenal and that classical conditioning represents the true explanation of the findings. This, however, seems to push this explanation beyond its intended limits.

A greater problem for the classical conditioning explanation is the finding of no differences in the number of positive and negative statements about the advertisement or in the attitude toward the advertisement between the positive and neutral mood conditions. This suggests that while more positive attitudes were induced with the Benny Goodman music, this music had the same effect as the Philip Glass music on the evaluation of the advertisement. If the advertisement is considered to be the unconditioned stimulus, then a classical conditioning explanation would not be valid, since it would require the advertisement with the Benny Goodman music to be evaluated positively. One could argue that the music was the unconditioned stimulus, however, the effect of the music had to operate through the advertisement in this situation and the evaluation of the music has to be in the context of the advertisement. Since the only difference in the advertisements between the positive and neutral mood conditions was the music; if the advertisements were evaluated equally in both conditions, then the music should also have been evaluated equally.

In summary, both the experimental setting, which created awareness of the linkages between the music, advertisement and product, and the finding of differences in the product attribute beliefs that were formed between the positive and neutral mood conditions, suggest that a cognitive explanation may be more appropriate than a classical conditioning explanation. In addition, the finding of no difference in the evaluation of the advertisement in the positive and neutral mood conditions provides further evidence that the classical conditioning explanation is not appropriate.

Finally, the demand effects explanation also does not seem valid. First, no one specifically mentioned that the Benny Goodman music should create more positive attitudes, when asked to write down the purpose of the study. In fact, most subjects reacted neutrally to the use of this music in the advertisement, so it does not seem likely that they would hypothesize that it should create more positive attitudes. In addition, in a number of studies (for example, Srull 1984; Milberg and Mitchell 1984), differential effects of mood were found depending on whether or not subjects executed a brand or nonbrand processing strategy. It seems highly unlikely that subjects could have generated these differential hypotheses.

Technically, the experimental situation used in the study reported here does not provide a strict test of whether or not classical conditioning can account for the effect of the mood manipulation on brand attitude. For instance, in order to differentiate between a cognitive theory explanation and a conditioning explanation, one needs to demonstrate that subjects were not aware of the contingency (cf. Brewer 1974). Awareness of the contingency may result in demand effects, where subjects guess the experimental hypotheses and behave accordingly, or theoretically awareness may be required to transfer affect from the unconditioned stimulus to the conditioned stimulus.

## Tentative Conclusions

The results of this study indicate a number of tentative conclusions concerning the effects of mood in an advertising context. These conclusions should be considered tentative for a couple of reasons. First, some of these conclusions are based on differences in results between the study reported by Srull (1984) and the study reported here. These two studies, however, used different mood manipulations, so it is possible that the differences in findings may be due to the different mood manipulations. Second, we cannot be certain that the results found in this study can be solely attributed to mood. Currently, our understanding of the effects surrounding different mood manipulations is limited, so it is possible that some of the mood manipulations that currently are used may also be manipulating other psychological constructs which, in turn, may be affecting the results (cf. Rholes, Riskind, and Lane 1987). For this reason, Isen (1984) has suggested the use of converging operations where different mood manipulations are used in similar studies to determine if they produce the same effects.

Given these caveats, then, the following tentative conclusions are proposed. First, moods induced before and during an advertising message have a strong effect on attitude formation; however, if the mood is induced before the message, these effects will occur only if the consumer forms an evaluation of the advertised brand while the consumer is still in the mood. If the mood is induced by the advertised message, these effects will occur whether or not consumers form an evaluation of the advertised brand while they are still in the induced mood.

Second, moods induced before the message will not affect the encoding of information from the advertised message (cf. Srull 1983); however, moods induced during an advertising message will affect the encoding of this information. Third, the encoding effect of moods does not seem to explain mood effects on attitude formation when subjects do not form an evaluation of the advertised brand during exposure to the advertising message.

Fourth, the traditional mediators of attitude formation do not seem to mediate the effects of positive moods induced during exposure to the advertising message. In the reported study, the mood manipulation had no effect on cognitive responses or attitude toward the advertisement. While the mood manipulation did affect the encoding of the product attribute information from the advertisement, the prediction of the overall attitude toward the brand based on this information was not significantly related to brand attitudes. Fifth, the finding that the mood manipulation had an effect on brand attitudes when subjects executed a nonbrand processing strategy indicates that some representation of the mood or the music is associated with the cognitive structure for the brand in long-term memory.

Finally, as discussed in the previous section, the results of this study suggest a response bias explanation of the results. The other hypotheses explaining the effects of mood on brand attitudes were generally discounted. This, of course, does not mean that another explanation, that was not examined in this study could not explain these effects.

# Part IV
# Nonverbal Dimensions of Language

# 10
# Exploring Grammatical Structure and Nonverbal Communication

*Larry Percy*

A s one considers the world of nonverbal communication, one's thoughts turn quite naturally to various visual phenomena: proxemics, kinesics, and various other observable behavior. And while these first thoughts tend to be visual-response oriented, on second thought various linguistic and para-linguistic considerations come to mind: voice stress, pitch, loudness, and so on. But while examples of nonverbal communication abound, *defining* nonverbal communication is quite another matter. In a review by Harper, Wiens, and Matarazzo (1978), a number of definitions ranging from the very broad to the very narrow are presented, while at the same time they acknowledge that not only a definitional but a semantic problem—with terms such as nonverbal communication, nonverbal modality, nonverbal sign, nonverbal act, nonverbal behavior, and so on—pose real problems in this area of research. There really is no consensual definition at present. In this chapter we must add to this consensual confusion by extending the linguistic response in nonverbal communication to considerations of grammatical structure. Specifically, what is it about the grammatical construction of, say, a headline in an advertisement that might occasion alternative responses?

Language can be subtle at times in its effects. Weiner and Mehrabian (1968) have pointed out that the words of a particular communication may transmit information that is complementary, supplementary, or redundant to the information transmitted in other components in the communication. Changes in the form of referent, for example, GM versus General Motors Corporation, are the kinds of variations that receivers of a message respond to as much as they respond to other nonverbal components in communication. As Weiner and Mehrabian go on to point out, careful consideration will show that what appears to be the same thing (that is, the same content) said with different words can be a basis for inferring quite different feelings or attributes from the message.

No one doubts the importance of the words chosen in verbal communication in determining just how effective that communication is likely to be. And while

---

The author wishes to express his appreciation for the efforts of Debra Sellitti and Carol Robbins in contributing to the analytic efforts involved with the study reported in this chapter.

attention may be paid to ensuring that descriptions or attributes within a target message reflect those things most likely to be meaningful to the target receiver, very little, if any, consideration seems to go into possible interactions among those descriptions or attributes. One hopes that there will be a positive, additive relationship among multiple descriptive elements in a communication, but it simply isn't always the case. To the extent that there are incongruities between the verbal elements in a communication, for example, potential dissonance or confusion may result.

## Some Semantic Properties in Processing

It is not unusual to find in the study of semantics the fact that the same words may have different meanings, or that different words may have the same meaning (although when you stop to think about it, no two words are likely to have exactly the same meaning). Of course, we know these words as synonyms and homonyms; and there has certainly been a great deal written about their strong effects in language. For example, when subjects are asked to recall lists of words that contain synonyms, it is not unusual for them to substitute another synonym for that word in playback (cf. Grossman and Eagle 1970; Kausler and Settle 1973). With homonyms, the problem is that when receivers hear or see words with diverse or multiple meanings, they are quite likely to be immediately reminded of the several meanings of the word (Conrad 1974). Associated problems with synonyms and homonyms in advertising have been discussed by Percy (1982).

While it is obvious that different words may have different meanings, as Palmer (1976) points out, their simple meanings are in and of themselves not of much interest. Only when these different meanings are in some way related does one become concerned with their probable impact upon comprehension in communication. One can get a feel for the potential problem here by looking at what linguistics refers to as the Field Theory of Semantics. Palmer reminds us that this theory is really derived largely from de Saussure's (1916) notion of value. De Saussure pointed out that in a chess game, a knight is not a knight because of any inherent quality such as size or shape, but rather for what it can do in the game relative to other pieces on the board. He described this relational aspect in language through a concept of value, arguing, for example, that the word *sheep* in English has a different value from the word *mutton* in French because the English language also contains the noun *mutton*. He further argued that when considering a group of synonyms, if one of them did not exist, its content or meaning would be transferred to the remaining words in the group. As one example of what he means, consider the synonyms "dread," "fear," and "be afraid." This field of fearing is divided among the three verbs (or actually, as we know, many others as well). But if one of these verbs did not exist, its meaning would nevertheless exist among the others.

There are numerous other examples of this phenomenon from many other languages (cf. Hjelmslev 1953; Ullmann 1962; Nida 1964), all of which deal with lists of words referring to items of a particular class dividing up a semantic field (hence the term Field Theory of Semantics). However, in almost every case, the important point to notice is that the words are *incompatible*. We cannot say, for example, that this is a "light dessert" and also of the same product that it is a "heavy dessert," any more than we could describe an animal as both a cat and a dog. Sentences with incompatible terms will thus contradict each other. Often this contradiction is the result of a straightforward understanding of the world around us: dogs are simply not cats, or vice versa; and light desserts are not heavy.

But Palmer (1962) reminds us that this is really not the salient point. What is relevant is that the terms are incompatible, even if there may be no clear distinction in the real world. This, of course, is what concerns us in this chapter. It is not merely the explicit verbal content of words, but their underlying meanings and associations, their nonverbal components, that ultimately drives comprehension.

It is certainly true that in marketing communications one must be very concerned that the attributes used to describe a product are both applicable and compatible so as not to cause any potential dissonance problems in product evaluation. As important as this consideration is to marketers, its importance is almost trivial by comparison to many other areas of communication where, quite literally, one's life may be at risk. While it is difficult to find any examples of where this important issue of semantic compatibility has been examined in the literature, especially beyond the psycholinguistic literature, a fascinating study has been reported by Elwork, Sales, and Alfini (1977), where the effects of semantic and grammatical construction upon how instructions to a jury by a judge will be interpreted was studied. Findings indicated that clearly significant differences in the way a judge's instructions were received and understood resulted from semantic differences in those instructions—even though in every case the instructions were "correct." They were simply misunderstood as a result of various semantic constructions. In fact, in one case there were opposite interpretations of the instructions. Clearly, the question of semantic usage can be a critical variable in effective communication. It shouldn't take too much of a leap to suspect that variations in grammatical structure too will affect message reception and comprehension.

## Grammatical Structure in Processing

The psycholinguistic literature is replete with examples of how grammatical structure facilitates processing of messages. For example, we know that active declarative sentences are significantly more easily processed than active questions, which in turn are easier to process than passive sentences; that negative sentences are yet more difficult to process, and so on (cf. Wason 1965; Slobin 1971; Kanouse 1972). Various verb forms are more or less likely to stimulate deduction versus inductive reasoning (Kanouse 1972); the number of words in a sentence (Wearing 1973), whether they are concrete or abstract (Paivio, Yuille, and Madigan 1968), all influence how well we are likely to process a piece of communication. And when we look at the influence of implied quantifiers, we begin to see how we move from a verbal response to nonverbal communication. Here, the nature of the verb form will elicit a particular implied quantifier when none are explicit. Manifest verbs that tend to have strong inductive generalizing (or inference) power tend to communicate low implicit quantifiers such as *some* or *a few*, while verbs that tend to have low inductive generalizing ability tend to elicit high implicit quantifiers such as *most* or *all* (Abelson and Kanouse 1966). In other words, a sentence like "Our mouthwash destroys germs" would be understood by the receiver to mean "Our mouthwash destroys most or all germs," since the verb *destroy* has low inductive generalizing power. On the other hand, a sentence like "Buy the best" would be understood to mean "Buy some or a few of the best," because the verb *buy* is a manifest verb with high inductive generalizing ability.

From this example, it would seem that response to verbal stimuli can indeed be a function of a nonverbal communication. In order to explore this issue further, we will examine the extent to which the same "thought," as manifested in four distinct grammatical constructions of the same verbal stimuli, might lead to significantly different interpretive responses. Specifically, we will be looking to see the extent to which embedding versus branching clauses (known to affect, for example, memory and comprehension: cf. Goldman-Eister and Cohen 1971; Hamilton and Deese 1971), constructed from essentially the same words, lead to different responses after processing. Since we are dealing with the same words, meant to convey the same thought, simply presented in a grammatically different fashion, any observed difference in the response must be attributed to the grammatical construction alone, basically a response to nonverbal communication.

This chapter will report the results of a preliminary and follow-up study of the communication response to the following four sentence stimuli:

1. It's not just the calories that count, it's the taste.
2. It's the taste that counts, not just the calories.
3. It's the taste, not just the calories, that count.
4. It's not just the calories, it's the taste that counts.

## Study One

In this first study, adult male and female subjects were randomly assigned to one of four experimental cells and asked for the first thoughts that came into their mind on hearing the sentence. Next, they were asked whether or not they felt the sentence implied that taste or calories was more important in a product that was so described.

As table 10–1 indicates, regardless of the sentence heard by the subjects, roughly the same number of words were elicited in response. Each of the words elicited was classified according to Laffal's (1973) concept dictionary. What he provides is a

**Table 10-1**
**Average Number of Words Elicited**

| Sentences | X | n |
|---|---|---|
| 1. It's not just the calories that count, it's the taste. | 2.58 | 36 |
| 2. It's the taste that counts, not just the calories. | 2.61 | 31 |
| 3. It's the taste, not just the calories, that count. | 2.73 | 30 |
| 4. It's not just the calories, it's the taste that counts. | 2.52 | 27 |

collection of words from the English language that have been organized to reflect the "kinds" of content represented in the words. These concepts, or categories of content, are presumed to reflect cognitive–conceptual sets which are evoked whenever a pertinent word is encountered. By classifying the elicitations for each sentence, we are in effect doing a content analysis of the response utilizing the semantic structure of the language used in the response stimulated by the sentence. The null hypothesis would surely be that given a common semantic base, the thoughts generated by those words should be similar. But as the correlations in table 10-2 reveal, the profile (as measured over twenty measured concepts) of the responses, while certainly not unique, is far from common.

Looking further at these classifications, we find that of the twenty concepts utilized by the subjects in response to these sentences, half were common to all sentences; and in fact the bulk of the words used in each case could be categorized by these ten concepts. Significantly,

$$(\chi^2 = 9.74; n = 3)$$

However, sentence four is much *less* likely to elicit words common to those from the other sentences: 83 percent, 79 percent, and 87 percent of the words elicited for the first three sentences reflected a common underlying cognitive base, but only 68 percent of those elicited by the fourth sentence.

This is further underscored when we look at the percentage of subjects offering thoughts that were uniquely classified for a particular stimulus sentence. Table 10-3 reveals that while sentence 4, as expected, has a high percentage of subjects offering thoughts unique from those elicited by the other sentences, receivers of sentence 2 also were significantly more likely to offer unique thoughts. What this suggests is that while the thoughts elicited by the first three sentences tend to be

**Table 10-2**
**Pearson Correlation Matrix of Laffal Concept Profiles**

| | | | | |
|---|---|---|---|---|
| 1. It's not just the calories that count, it's the taste. | 1.000 | | | |
| 2. It's the taste that counts, not just the calories. | 0.740 | 1.000 | | |
| 3. It's the taste, not just the calories, that count. | 0.859 | 0.753 | 1.000 | |
| 4. It's not just the calories, it's the taste that counts. | 0.773 | 0.602 | 0.710 | 1.000 |

**Table 10-3**
**Composition of Thoughts Elicited by Stimulus Sentences**

| | % Common Words* | % Unique Words | % Unique Subjects** |
|---|---|---|---|
| 1. It's not just the calories that count, it's the taste. | 83 | 5 | 14 |
| 2. It's the taste that counts, not just the calories. | 79 | 15 | 39 |
| 3. It's the taste, not just the calories, that count. | 87 | 2 | 7 |
| 4. It's not just the calories, it's the taste that counts. | 68 | 13 | 33 |

$*\chi^2 = 9.74$; significant at .03 probability
$**\chi^2 = 49.84$; significant at .001 probability

largely reflected by the same ten concepts, the remaining thoughts are more likely to be shared between sentences 1 and 3, but not with sentence 2.

What this analysis implies is that although the semantic content of these four sentences is virtually identical, what is communicated by the grammatical structure of the sentence can be significantly different.

Another way of looking at the words elicited by these sentences is their concrete and imaging value. If differences were to occur here, we would have more than the meaning differences implied by the Laffal concepts to deal with; we would have potential learning differences as well. In terms of concreteness, it has been well established that more concrete words are better remembered and tend to be more meaningful and as a result better comprehended (Yuille and Paivio 1969). Would it not be reasonable to assume that if a stimulus elicited more concrete thoughts, it too would enjoy some of these same attributes? In any event, the resulting cognitive response, which reflects its interpretation in memory, certainly does.

Beyond this question of memory and learning, Paivio (1971) has pointed out that both recognition and recall occur more accurately and faster for concrete words. Additionally, a number of other studies have shown that concrete words are more positively associated with comprehension (Begg and Paivio 1969; Paivio 1971; Sheehan 1970). Given this, one should expect better sentence comprehension to follow from more concrete responses. Finally, Rossiter and Percy (1978) found that representation of advertising claims for a hypothetical new beer when concrete generated almost twice the favorable attitude for the product as more abstract ones.

Each of the cognitive elicitations for the four stimulus sentences was checked for concreteness as reported by Toglia and Battig (1978). Their work followed very closely that of Paivio et al. (1968), the only major difference being their usage of *low concrete* as the low-end anchor rather than *high abstract,* consistent with Spreen and Schultz (1966). The specific instruction to subjects given by Toglia and Battig was as follows:

Words differ in the extent to which they refer to the *concrete* objects, persons, places, or things that can be seen, heard, felt, smelled, or tasted, as contrasted with *abstract* concepts that cannot be experienced by our senses. The purpose of this experiment is to rate a list of 480 words with respect to their "concreteness" in terms of sense experience. Any word that refers to objects, materials, or persons should be given a *high concreteness* rating (at the upper end of the numerical scale). Any word that refers to an abstract concept that cannot be experienced by the senses should be given a *low concreteness* rating (at the lower end of the numerical scale). For example, think of the word "carpet," which can be experienced by our senses and therefore should be rated as high concrete; the word "ambiguous" cannot be experienced by the senses as such and therefore should be rated as low concrete (or abstract). Because words tend to make you think of other words as associates, it is important that your ratings *not* be based on this and that you judge only the concreteness of sense experiences as directly aroused by each word.

Approximately 80 percent of the thoughts elicited by the stimulus sentences were classifiable by the Toglia and Battig word norms. And as the data in table 10–4 reveal, there was no significant difference in the types of responses that could not be classified.

Looking at the "concreteness" ratings for all of the responses classified, the 56 percent above the Toglia and Battig mean of 4.4 for sentence 3 (versus 44 percent, 40 percent, and 45 percent for the other sentences) suggests that the sitmulus sentence 3, "It's the taste, not just the calories, that count," tended to elicit more highly concrete thoughts. While only marginally significant (at about the 86 percent significance level), it is interesting that sentence 3 is the only clearly center-embedded sentence.

We shall discuss this issue in more detail below in connection with recall and comprehension, but for the moment we note that there is evidence that suggests right-branching sentences (such as the other stimuli) should be more easily comprehended. This raises the interesting speculation that while a center-embedded sentence may be more difficult to comprehend, it nonetheless generates concrete (albeit indeterminate) responses. Table 10–5 details the percentage of words classified above the mean for the concreteness of the elicited thoughts.

Closely related to the concept of concreteness is that of imagery value in words (Paivio 1971); the two measures have about three-quarters of their variance in common.

## Table 10–4
## Elicitations Not Classified by Toglia and Battig Word Norms

| Word Type | Sentence 1 | Sentence 2 | Sentence 3 | Sentence 4 |
|---|---|---|---|---|
| Nouns | 7 | 7 | 8 | 10 |
| Pronouns | 4 | 4 | 3 | 1 |
| Adjectives | 3 | 2 | 4 | 2 |
| Verbs | 4 | 2 | 3 | 2 |
| Adverbs | 1 | 1 | 0 | 0 |
| Percentage not classified | 20 | 20 | 22 | 22 |

$\chi^2 = 6.37, n = 12$

**Table 10-5**
**High Concrete and High Imagery Elicitations**

| Sentence | High Concrete* | High Imagery** |
|---|---|---|
| 1. It's not just the calories that count, it's the taste. | 44 | 40 |
| 2. It's the taste that counts, not just the calories. | 40 | 37 |
| 3. It's the taste, not just the calories, that count. | 56 | 62 |
| 4. It's not just the calories, it's the taste that counts. | 45 | 45 |

*$\chi^2$ = 5.66; significant at .14 probability
**$\chi^2$ = 15.06; significant at .06 probability

As a result, even though it is not strictly impossible for more abstract words to evoke visual images, unless learned specifically, it is much less likely (Rossiter and Percy 1983). For example, although words like *fantasy* or *dream* are highly abstract, they may exhibit high imagery value.

Unlike concreteness, research on the imagery value of large verbal units such as sentences is sparse. Among the few studies available to us, however, there is a strong suggestion that imagery value enhances communication. Jorgensen and Kintsch (1973) have shown that sentences with higher imagery value tend to be evaluated significantly faster as true or false; and Holyoak (1974) has found them significantly easier to understand than sentences rated low in image value. And as Percy (1982) has suggested, following the work of Williams (1979), who found that high-imagery syllogisms were faster and more accurately solved than the same syllogism made up of low-imagery words, advertising claims which more easily arouse visual imagery of items and relationships should be more easily comprehended. Hence, the sentence stimuli eliciting higher imagery thoughts should be more easily comprehended.

Once again we turn to Toglia and Battig (1978) for imagery norms. The instruction they gave was as follows:

Words differ in their capacity to arouse mental images of things or events. Some words arouse a sensory experience, such as mental pictures or sound, very quickly and easily, whereas other words may do so only with difficulty (i.e., after a long delay) or not at all. The purpose of this experiment is to rate 480 words as to the ease or difficulty with which they arouse a mental image. Any word that in your estimation arouses a mental image (i.e., mental picture, or a sound, or other sensory experience) very quickly and easily should be given a *high imagery* rating (at the upper end of the numerical scale). Any word that arouses a mental image with difficulty or not at all should be given a low imagery rating (at the lower end of the numerical scale). For example, think of the word "buffalo." "Buffalo" would probably arouse an image relatively easily and would be rated as high imagery; "relevant" would probably do so with difficulty and be rated as low imagery. Because words tend to make you think of other words as associates, it is important that your ratings *not* be based on this and that you judge only the ease with which you get a mental image of an object or event in response to each word.

Looking at the imagery word norms for all of the responses classified, the 62 percent above the Toglia and Battig mean of 4.55 for sentence 3 (versus 40 percent, 37 percent, and 45 percent for the other three sentences) again suggests that stimulus sentence 3 tends to elicit more high-imagery thoughts. Here, the difference tends to be much more significant (the 94 percent significance level). The parallel between the concreteness and imagery ratings is consistent with our expectations from the literature.

After the subjects were asked for the first thoughts that were stimulated by the sentences, they were asked whether taste or calories was most important to the product described. The correct inference in each case, of course, was taste; and indeed, the majority of subjects did in fact say taste. However, among the minority saying calories, there was a significant difference between sentence stimuli. As the data in table 10–6 indicates, those exposed to sentence 2, "It's the taste that counts, not just the calories," were significantly more likely to incorrectly infer that calories was the most important consideration in the product.

One explanation of this result might be found in the recency literature, which suggests that words that have been heard (or read) more recently are retrieved more rapidly than words which occurred longer ago. And this coupled with the increasing difficulty of correctly dealing with the negative, right-branching clause ("not just the calories") in processing, could result in subjects being more likely to misattribute calories rather than taste as the dominant product attribute in this grammatical construction.

Also, even though it might be argued that *taste* should be expected to have been more likely to have been correctly processed and remembered simply because it is a more frequently used word than *calories* in the English language (used over one hundred times per million words versus about four times per million for *calories*, according to Thorndike and Lorge, 1944), this issue of word frequency has been shown in a study by Scarbourgh, Cartese, and Scarbourgh (1972) to be confounded by recency effects.

## Study Two

As a result of the differences noted in the first study, a second was undertaken among a balanced design of fifty adult subjects for each of the four stimulus sentences.

**Table 10–6**
**Inference Derived from Stimulus Sentences – 1**

| Sentence | Incorrect Calorie Inference | Correct Taste Inference |
|---|---|---|
| 1. It's not just the calories that count, it's the taste. | 11 | 89 |
| 2. It's the taste that counts, not just the calories. | 23 | 77 |
| 3. It's the taste, not just the calories, that count. | 13 | 87 |
| 4. It's not just the calories, it's the taste that counts. | 15 | 85 |

$\chi^2 = 6.34$; significant at .10 probability

In this study we asked first for subjects to repeat verbatim the sentence they had just heard read to them; then (as in Study One) whether they felt the main point of the sentence was taste or calories; and finally, whether they felt the product described was high, medium, or low in calories.

When looking at the number of subjects able to correctly recall verbatim the sentence they had just heard, we found a reasonably significant variation in the response. As the data in table 10–7 reveal, subjects receiving sentences 1 and 3 were much less likely to correctly recall the sentence than subjects receiving sentence 4, and to a lesser degree sentence 2. One thing in common to the two better-recalled sentences is that the positive clauses are contiguous: "It's the taste that counts." Given the more difficult nature of recalling negative sentences (cf. Gough 1965; Slobin 1966), perhaps this, compounded by the implied object of the main clause in the first sentence and the center-embedded subordinate clause of the third sentence, affected recall.

It is probably useful at this point to consider why, in general, the sentences were not well recalled. To begin with, as already mentioned, each sentence is built around a negative subordinate clause, and negative constructions are more difficult to recall and comprehend. Additionally, there is quite a bit of evidence that self-embedded sentences such as these are among the most difficult to recall (Forster and Ryder 1971; Holmes 1973; Miller and Isand 1964). Interestingly, the type of self-embedded sentence seems to affect recall, which could have an influence on the results reported here. Unfortunately, while Holmes (1973) did find that right-branching sentences (main clause appears first uninterrupted—sentence 2) were more easily recalled than center-embedded sentences (main clause interrupted by subordinate clause—sentence 3), he also found this for left-branching embedded sentences (subordinate clause appears first uninterrupted—sentence 4) as well. However, there seems to be no doubt that as the number of subordinate clauses increases or becomes more difficult (as with sentence 1), sentences become more incomprehensible (Hamilton and Deese 1971).

Looking next at the results of asking whether taste or calories was the main point of the sentence, (table 10–8) again, as in Study One, sentence 2 is most likely to generate the most incorrect inference of calories, albeit not at a statistically significant level.

**Table 10–7**
**Correct Verbatim Recall of Stimulus Sentences**

| Sentences | Correct Recall |
|---|---|
| 1. It's not just the calories that count, it's the taste. | 58 |
| 2. It's the taste that counts, not just the calories. | 66 |
| 3. It's the taste, not just the calories, that count. | 60 |
| 4. It's not just the calories, it's the taste that counts. | 70 |

$\chi^2$ = 6.11; significant at the .11 probability

**Table 10-8**
**Inference Derived from Stimulus Sentences - 2**

| Sentences | Incorrect Calorie Inference | Correct Taste Inference |
|---|---|---|
| 1. It's not just the calories that count, it's the taste. | 18 | 82 |
| 2. It's the taste that counts, not just the calories. | 22 | 78 |
| 3. It's the taste, not just the calories, that count. | 16 | 84 |
| 4. It's not just the calories, it's the taste that counts. | 14 | 86 |

$\chi^2$ = 3.12; significant at .42 probability

Finally, in an effort to determine whether or not the inference drawn about the caloric content of the product described differed by grammatical structure of the sentence, subjects were asked whether they felt the product described was high, medium, or low in calories. Analyzing the extremes of high or low suggests a somewhat significant difference, at about the 92 percent significance level. The most consistent result was shown by receivers of the center-embedded sentence 3, who were more strongly driven to conclude that the product was higher in calories. These results are summarized in table 10-9.

## Summary

The results reported here, while not always highly significant, nevertheless indicate that grammatical structure does indeed function as a nonverbal communication element. Specifically, we have seen where grammatical variations of an advertiser's claim meant to communicate that taste is the critical attribute of their product, not merely lower calories, can significantly influence the likelihood that the message will be correctly communicated.

To begin with, we found that when subjects are asked for their thoughts upon hearing the advertiser's claim, there were significant variations in the response. If receivers of a message produce different cognitive responses as a result of the grammatical structure of that message, clearly we have a potentially dangerous

**Table 10-9**
**Calorie Inference Drawn from Stimulus Sentences**

| Sentences | High in Calories | Low in Calories |
|---|---|---|
| 1. It's not just the calories that count, it's the taste. | 22 | 20 |
| 2. It's the taste that counts, not just the calories. | 32 | 18 |
| 3. It's the taste, not just the calories, that count. | 36 | 10 |
| 4. It's not just the calories, it's the taste that counts. | 38 | 20 |

$\chi^2$ = 6.54; significant at .08 probability

situation, underscoring the need to (1) always test communciations for cognitive response and (2) if even so much as a grammatical change is made in the copy, test again. In the specific case reported here, the two sentences with significantly more unique cognitive responses generated quite different thoughts. The sentence "It's the taste that counts, not just the calories" stimulated more positive types of thoughts, while the sentence "It's not just the calories, it's the taste that counts" was more negatively oriented in the thoughts elicited. Add to this that the type of thoughts (in terms of concreteness and imagery) also differed significantly—for yet another sentence—and we can see that the message communicated by these four grammatical variations of the same basic semantic set are potentially quite different.

We also found that learning, recall, and comprehension all varied, and often significantly, as a function of the grammatical composition of the message. The key point here is not so much that these differences may or may not be large, but that there are differences. In advertising, it is difficult enough to communicate effectively. None of the differences we observed in these tests suggest that the majority of receivers would have problems with the message; but some will. Anything one can do to help ensure better processing helps the overall effectiveness of one's advertising. In advertising, one can never count on significantly affecting large portions of a target market; and as a result, one is grateful for even very small changes in a positive direction. Understanding that the grammatical construction of a message will influence how it is processed adds another checkpoint in maximizing one's communication efforts.

# 11
# Can There be Effective Advertising without Explicit Conclusions? Decide for Yourself

*Alan G. Sawyer*

L et me begin this chapter by describing as best as I can remember several advertisements that have appeared in the last few years. A television commercial for Quik chocolate milk mix shows a boy and girl, each about six years old, talking on the front steps. Their conversation goes something like this: "All Mom and Dad ever say is no, no, no . . . but they never say no to Quik. I wonder why? Is it the milk? I bet they've never tasted it. Otherwise, they'd say no. Still, why don't they say no? They say no to everything else. . . ."

A commercial for Burger King during the notorious "Battle of the Burgers" (see Sawyer and Dickson 1985) begins when a perky young woman comes on the screen and says, "I've got a question. Pay attention, there will be a quiz later. People prefer their hamburgers at home flame-broiled. Now, if McDonald's and Wendy's *fry* their hamburgers and Burger King *flame-broils* theirs . . . where do you think people should go for a hamburger?"

A commercial for IBM shows two men in an office at what seems to be the end of a hard day. The first person (a not-too-intelligent looking, large fellow with a rumpled shirt and askew tie) asks the other person (who appears to be neater, more intelligent, and less frazzled), "Hey, what's that?" Second person: "It's a smart desk—with a personal computer. It helps me do stuff in half the time." First person: "Computer, huh? I don't need that. Besides, computers and me, we don't mix. I rely on Burt. Where are you going?" Second person: "To the game. You want to go?" First person: "No. Actually, I've got quite a bit of work to do." (Second

In addition to the presentation at the AMA/MSI Advertising and Psychology Conference, this research has been presented to and benefited from comments from the marketing faculties at The Ohio State University, University of Wisconsin, University of Florida, University of Washington, and Western Ontario University, as well as participants at the 1984 AMA Doctoral Consortium at Northwestern University. Thanks go to Paul Miniard for helping formulate the idea for this research, Daniel Howard and April Atwood for help in data collection, and Richard Lutz for his comments on a draft. Finally, this chapter is dedicated to David Suchman and, especially, Rahe Corlis, who helped the author begin to discover the potential of open-ended communications.

person picks up his coat and leaves the office and the telephone rings.) First person: "Maybe that's Burt! Burt, is that you? Where are you? At the game!"

A DeBeers commercial opens with the word *DeBeers* at the top of the screen and then, to the accompaniment of soft, romantic music, shows several zooming close-ups of hands caressing each other and beautiful diamonds. A silhouette of young lovers fades back to more hands and diamonds. The commercial ends with an announcer's voice saying, "More profound than words. Diamonds," with the superimposed words, "A diamond is forever."

Finally, a print ad for Michelob beer shows a large picture of a beaded bottle of Michelob with a close-up of the label. At the bottom are the only words other than the label. The slogan reads, "Some things speak for themselves." A companion television commercial simply shows a zooming close-up of a bottle of Michelob being slowly poured into an icy glass to the accompaniment of the increasingly loud sound of the Michelob musical theme. The announcer closes the commercial by declaring the "Some things speak for themselves" slogan.

These examples of recent advertisements vary on several dimensions. However, one thing they share is the fact that, unlike most advertisements, *these ads do not attempt to explicitly draw a conclusion for the audience. Instead, these advertisements leave the conclusion open and leave it to the audience to draw its own conclusion from the message.* For example, I assume that the designers of the Quik commercial hope that the audience goes through a process something like the following: Although the parents say no to many things, as most parents must because of dangers to the children, they do not say no to Quik because Quik is good for kids. It has lots of healthful ingredients. The reason why the kids think that the parents would say no if they had tasted it is that, although Quik is good for the children, it also tastes terrific. The designers of the Burger King ad hope that the audience will reach the syllogistic conclusion that people ought to go to Burger King, and not to Wendy's or McDonald's, because they can get flame-broiled hamburgers only at Burger King. Wendy's and McDonald's fry their hamburgers. The makers of the IBM ad presumably hope that the audience will come to the conclusion that the harried and rumpled office worker would have more time and would not have to depend upon Burt if he, like his counterpart, used a smart desk.[1] I would guess that the DeBeers organization hopes that potential purchasers of diamonds would conclude by themselves that diamonds are a lasting symbol of never-ending love. Finally, Anheuser-Busch executives hope that viewers of the Michelob ads will decide from past experience, prior advertising, or a concurrent personal conclusion that it is the great taste of Michelob and the quality of the brewing process that speak for themselves.

Advertising copywriters have at least two choices. The advertiser can *tell* the person to buy the product because it will do this or that. Or the advertiser can create a situation which shows the benefits of the product without directly telling the person what to do. Without an explicit intention to tell something, this open-ended advertisement places a person in a situation in which the person might be able to accept new ideas without any threat to old ideas. In effect, the open ad tries to benefit from people reaching a conclusion by themselves or *telling themselves* a conclusion without having it supplied by the advertiser.

There is a direct analogy between open-ended (no explicit conclusion) versus close-ended advertising (in which an explicit conclusion to buy the product in question is included) and *non-directive and directive psychotherapy*. Howard D. Hadley described this difference quite well in a 1953 article in *The Journal of Applied Psychology* which was reprinted from *Advertising Agency*:

Non-directive psychotherapy is built around these central concepts:

1. That all individuals have the basic capacity to understand the forces in their lives which cause them unhappiness and pain. Moreover, they also can understand those forces which lead to pleasure and well-being.

2. That all individuals, by personal effort, ultimately can overcome the bad or enhance the good forces in their lives.

3. That this process is made easier, quicker, or more effective in an atmosphere that is friendly, sincere, and understanding.

In non-directive therapy, the therapist does not assume any of the usual responsibilities such as prescribing treatment or even directly defining the cure. Instead, the therapist attempts to set up with the individual a relationship, an atmosphere, in which the person may talk or act without danger of being criticized. It is one of complete acceptance. With this tender environment, the person himself comes to understand and to re-evaluate the forces operating to make him happy or unhappy.

Directive therapy differs in that it usually requires a direct assault upon the individual's maladjustments: the person is tested, analyzed, and then told what is wrong and given a prescription for a cure. It is similar to going to a doctor only to find out you have appendicitis. He puts you in a hospital, removes the diseased organ, and your body then is able to complete the recovery. When dealing with the physical body, the doctor's obligation is often greater than the patient's. When dealing with a person's mind, this method sometimes falls down because the person is reluctant to believe or is unable to accept the diagnosis of the therapist. The therapist can only discover and point out the path, he cannot walk it. Many persons benefit from this advice but many others do not (Hadley, 1953, p. 496).

As will be discussed later, there are many variables that may be important determinants of whether an explicit conclusion is more effective in advertising than a no-conclusion message. At the risk of making an explicit conclusion (to what I hope are involved readers), however, the position of this paper is that *open-ended advertisements and other types of persuasive messages are much more likely to be persuasive when the audience is highly involved in the topic of the message than when the audience is only lowly involved in the topic and content of the message.* In fact, given that extant research reviewed suggests that there are situations in which the inclusion of an explicit conclusion may be more persuasive, I hypothesize that there will be an interaction between the involvement of the audience and whether the persuasive message has an explicit conclusion. This interaction, depicted in figure 11–1, is such that the *explicit conclusion or close-ended message may be more persuasive under conditions of low involvement, but the reverse effect—a superior persuasiveness of the open-ended message—is much more likely under conditions of high involvement.*

This hypothesized interaction is consistent with the empirical results of relevant past research, reviewed below. Moreover, a series of experiments designed

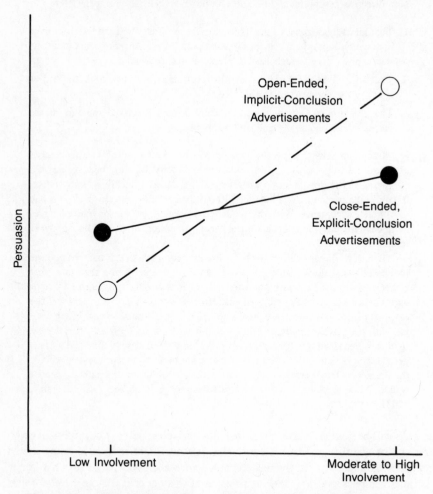

**Figure 11–1. Persuasive Effects of Open-ended vs. Closed-ended Advertising Messages and Level of Consumer Involvement**

to explicitly test this hypothesis and briefly described below provide further empirical support. After a description of this research, there will be a discussion of possible underlying psychological processes which may explain the potentially greater persuasiveness of open-ended messages. Finally, this chapter will conclude with a discussion of marketing situation variables that may influence the effectiveness of open-ended advertisements and how such a communication strategy may be especially effective in highly involving nonadvertising contexts.

## Past Research

The question of whether or not to include an explicit conclusion in a persuasive message is not a new one. This issue has been examined in some classic research by some of the most noted persuasion researchers in psychology and communication. Probably the first "researcher" to study the effects of an explicit conclusion versus no conclusion was Aristotle, who suggested that the best rhetoric is that which uses arguments that are stated sufficiently clearly that the audience can understand them immediately, but the appropriate conclusion is not immediately obvious.

The first communication research to explicitly study this issue was done by Hovland and Mandell (1952). They tested two messages that advocated the devaluation of the American dollar. The message outlined the general economic condition that would make devaluation of a country's currency worthwhile, and then discussed how these conditions existed in the United States. For one group of college student subjects, the conclusion to this syllogistic argument was explicitly stated; the other group saw a message in which this conclusion was absent. The result showed a strong advantage for the explicit statement of the conclusion in terms of gaining opinion change.

Hovland and Mandell's experiment and results were essentially replicated in an experiment by Fine (1957). Fine exposed his college-student subjects to two different messages about the control of biological warfare; these messages differed only in that the explicit-conclusion message contained a final paragraph concluding that biological warfare was not a "super" threat since the United States could defend against it. In the nonexplicit-conclusion message, subjects were urged at the end of the basic message to draw their own conclusions on the basis of the arguments presented in the article, instead of being exposed to the explicit conclusion paragraph. Fine found a small superiority of the explicit-conclusion message in terms of attitudes.

Both the Hovland and Mandell and Fine experiments used relatively complex messages that may have been difficult to comprehend. Low comprehension would particularly penalize an open-ended message, since its success depends on subjects completely comprehending the subtleties of the arguments and cannot simply rely on the processing of a conclusion at the end of the message. It also seems very likely that the student subjects in both experiments were very low in involvement because they cared little about the true answer to the topic of communications; there is little inherently interesting or involving to student subjects about whether currency should be devalued or whether biological warfare is a threat to the United States, especially in the context of an obvious experiment in the classroom.

Thistlethwaite, DeHaan, and Kamenetaky (1955) tried to alleviate the past research problems of differential comprehension of closed and open messages and the low subject involvement. In their attempt to improve on the past research, these researchers used new Air Force recruits as subjects and exposed them to persuasive messages about the wisdom of the United States fighting in the Korean war. It seems that these subjects would be at least moderately involved in this message, given that the subjects were recruited for the Korean war which was ongoing at the time of the research. Thistlethwaite and his colleagues also tried to ascertain the effects of whether or not the message was understood by using a multiple-choice test which measured whether they remembered and understood the conclusion or what would be a logical conclusion from the message. The results showed that, as suspected, the explicit-conclusion message was better comprehended than the no-conclusion message. However, there was no difference in terms of persuasion between the two messages. Furthermore, there was no difference in persuasion when comprehension was statistically controlled.

McGuire (1969) surveyed the extant evidence about conclusion drawing and came to a somewhat pessimistic conclusion about the probable benefits of leaving the message conclusion to the audience:

> It may well be that if the person draws the conclusion for himself he is more per-suaded than if the source draws it for him; the problem is that in the usual com-munication situation the subject is either insufficiently intelligent or insufficiently motivated to draw the conclusion for himself, and therefore misses the point of the message to a serious extent unless the source draws the moral for him. In communication, it appears it is not sufficient to lead the horse to water; one must also push his head underneath to get him to drink (McGuire 1969, p. 209).

However, the Thistlethwaite et al. experimental results suggest that the possi-bility of any advantage for explicit-conclusion messages may be lessened, nullified, or even reversed if subjects comprehend the premise arguments in the message (or the hoped-for conclusions in the implicit-conclusion message) *and* are also motivated to read and understand the message and form a conclusion. Subjects in the latter experiment were much more likely to be involved and motivated to attend to and understand the message than were the subjects in the two previous experiments. Thus, it seems that the results of these experiments are not inconsis-tent with the above hypothesis about the interaction of audience involvement and whether a message includes an explicit conclusion.

There is considerable empirical evidence that advertisements without explicit conclusions can be very effective. For example, Ray and Sawyer (1971) found in *post hoc* analyses of an experiment that manipulated ad repetition and product type that ads that explicitly make a forceful conclusion ("grabber ads") were less likely to improve with six exposures than advertisements much more subtle and indirect in their claims (that is, "non-grabber ads"). Advertisers have for years claimed the benefits of "soft-sell" advertisements. The superiority of soft-sell advertisements has been empirically supported (Silk and Vavra 1974), and many advertising agencies such as Doyle, Dane, and Bernbach extoll the virtues of soft-sell advertising such as the famous Volkswagen commercials.

Research has also demonstrated the potential effectiveness of persuasive messages that require the audience to use its own self-insight (for example, Stotland, Katz, and Patchen 1959). Messages ending with questions instead of statements can also be more persuasive (see Burnkrant and Howard, 1985; Petty, Cacioppo, and Heesaker, 1981; Swasy and Munch 1985).[2] One piece of anecdotal evidence of the power of such a message appeal was reported eleven years ago in *Psychology Today*. Chance (1975) reported the results of a communication program called "Alternatives." This communication campaign appeared on five television stations, twelve radio stations, and in eighteen newspapers over a period of sixty weeks. Some of the ads in this mental health campaign provided the viewer or reader with a solution to the problem, while others left the conclusions to the reader.

> For instance, George and Harriet, an ad with a solution, talked about a quarrelsome couple. It told George that he needed to listen, to try to understand why Harriet nagged. The ad explained, "It's so simple to stop and think—'What am I saying with my words, my actions, my feelings? And what are other people saying with theirs?' " Pills and Booze, an unresolved spot, warned against drug and alcohol abuse as escape routes. It ends with the questions, "How many drinks does it take to get a raise? How many pills does it take to bring back love?"
>
> The best ads turned out to be those that asked questions. Surveys showed that the open-ended spots were more likely to be remembered. And when unresolved ads were used, teenagers were more apt to call a help line (the Crisis and Information Center) about problems such as alcoholism and drug abuse. For example, the best open-ended spot directed at young people averaged 211 calls a week, but the best comparable resolved ad averaged only 156. Many of those calls came from kids who were hanging on by their fingertips, so the numbers represented a great deal more than just statistical significance. . . .
>
> To those who sell mental health—or widgets, for that matter—the implication is that ads should focus on questions, not answers. They should make our brains itch, not anesthetize them. An answer, even a poor one, lets a person push the problem out of his head; those left hanging will keep wrestling with the riddle until they come up with a solution or find someone who can help.
>
> If mental health has been hard to peddle, maybe it's because we've given too much attention to answers and not enough to questions. (Chance, 1975, p. 78).

Finally, I was fascinated to hear the presentation (chapter 3 in this book) by Ernest Dichter, one of the most respected and ubiquitous advertising researchers in the history of advertising. He seems to strongly believe that one of the greatest "sins" in advertising is to tidy up everything and tell the consumer what he or she[3] should believe. Instead Dr. Dichter suggests that often advertisers should consider letting the consumer decide for himself or herself what is important and what should be taken away from an advertisement.

Finally, the central hypothesis of this chapter also seems consistent with the opinions of the authors of two excellent recent advertising and persuasion textbooks. Aaker and Myers (1975) stated:

> Should the conclusions and what an advertiser wants a receiver to take away be spelled out in the message and made explicit or should a receiver be made to draw his or her own conclusions? . . . It is often advantageous to leave something out of a message. The principle of closure suggests that curiosity may be aroused and motivation to inquire further about the brand thus encouraged. If such motivations cannot be reasonably expected, however, it may be risky to assume that a receiver will indeed "draw his own conclusions," and, in this sense, complete messages are more appropriate. In general, research has suggested that stating conclusions is more appropriate when the target segment is less likely to be motivated and capable of determining the appropriate conclusion (Aaker and Myers, 1975, p. 404).

Petty and Cacioppo (1981) reviewed some relevant research and ended their discussion as follows:

> Once a message has been constructed and presented, what is the most effective way to end it? Should the message end by stating the conclusion explicitly, or should the conclusion be left for the audience to draw? Hovland and his colleagues reasoned that drawing a conclusion would increase the likelihood that recipients comprehend and retain the message arguments; but if recipients *could* draw the correct conclusion themselves, then retention and yielding would be enhanced. An example may clarify their reasoning. Consider the case of a professional racquetball player instructing a novice. As she explains the general dynamics of hitting a racquetball, she focuses on the proper position of the ball to the body, the trajectory of the arm, and the desired placement of the ball on the front wall. One purpose of her instruction is to convince the novice that she must snap her wrist when striking the ball. Is the novice more likely to change her swing and snap her wrist if the conclusion is stated explicitly ("thus, you must snap your wrist. . . .") or if she is left to "discover" this conclusion on her own? . . . The answer is that it depends. If the novice is either unmotivated or unable to discover that conclusion, then she can accept it only if the pro ends the instructions by stating the conclusion for her. But if the novice is able to "discover" the conclusion, either during the course of the message or shortly thereafter, then she will be more persuaded than if the conclusion is drawn for her. Observations such as these are the basis for the adages "experience is the best teacher" and "I told you so" (Petty and Cacioppo, 1981, p. 76).

However, despite the appeal of and potential of open-ended advertisements, advertisers have often been reluctant to employ them in the past. Indeed, most advertising textbooks that take a position side more with McGuire's 1969 opinion than those of Aaker and Myers and Petty and Cacioppo. Perhaps an examination of psychological processes that may underlie or mediate the communication effects of messages with or without a conclusion can be both enlightening and persuasive.

## Possible Underlying Processes

The notion that the persuasive communications which depend upon the audience drawing its own conclusions are potentially more persuasive than messages with explicit conclusions is quite appealing in that it is compatible with many popular theories in psychology and communication. These theories include psychological reactance, attribution and self-perception theory, cognitive dissonance theory, behavioral modification theory, cognitive response theory, and the central versus peripheral processing theory, as well as other interesting "micro-theoretical notions" (Ray 1978) from psychology and advertising. *If* attended to and *if* comprehended, a message which does *not* draw an explicit conclusion for the audience and instead leaves that conclusion for the audience to decide should benefit from:

1. less psychological reactance;
2. the attribution and self-perception by members of the audience that they were the (internal) source of the conclusion and the source was not an external one such as the message itself or a specific source (announcer, brand endorser, brand, company) of the advertising message;
3. a perception of less bias on the part of the message and its sponsor;
4. greater liking of the ads due to a perception of uniqueness and respect for the audience;
5. greater cognitive dissonance due to both the possibly greater effort necessary to process the open-ended message and an accordingly greater desire to form a conclusion consistent with the arguments in the message and, if the audience initially disagrees with the likely point of the message, a greater willingness to change their attitude to be consistent with the message;
6. satisfaction of successfully reaching a conclusion (if one was made by the audience);
7. more self-generated thoughts and conclusions;
8. greater processing of the central message arguments;
9. more vivid and personal cognitive responses and conclusions; and
10. greater persistance over time of any immediate communication effects such as changes in attitude or behavior intention.

Brehm (1966; see also Clee and Wicklund 1980) proposed a theory of *psychological reactance* to account for the effects of potential or actual decreases in a person's range of free behaviors. Brehm theorized that threats or actual reductions in persons' freedom to act as they wish will arouse a state of psychological reactance which, in turn, will lead to attempts to regain the eliminated freedoms or to remove the threat of elimination. A person viewing a no-conclusion message might be much less apt to feel pressured to change his mind in the direction desired by the message and hence will be less defensive and open to change. This willingness or lack of resistance to change is in contrast to the effects of the likely greater psychological reactance aroused when the audience is exposed to a hard-sell message which strongly advocates a particular conclusion.

Another likely benefit of an open-ended persuasive message involves the *attribution and self-perception processes* (see Cialdini 1985; Settle and Golden 1974) generated by that message. An open-ended message that, in effect, states that the audience should decide for itself may benefit from an attribution process on the part of the audience that results in the audience attempting to make a conclusion and changing their attitude to be consistent with that conclusion. When subsequently examining their beliefs about the message topic, the audience is less likely to conclude that the source of that belief came from an advertiser, an advertising message, or some other aspect of the advertisement such as an announcer or celebrity endorser, and is instead much more likely to conclude that the source of that belief was an *internal* one (that is, the audience member himself or herself). The self-perception that "I decided that this product was the best" may be a powerful persuasive agent or, at least, removes the potentially powerful negative factor of attributing one's conclusion or belief to an external cause in the total communication and persuasion process.

An open-ended message should also benefit from the audience's *attribution of less bias* in the message and on the part of the source of the message. Since an open-ended message leaves the conclusion to the audience, it is much less likely to be perceived as explicitly trying to influence the audience and/or to distort the facts. Empirical support for this comes from psychological literature that has studied the effects of "overheard" communications in which the audience of the message perceives that the source of the message is unaware that their message was being overheard (Walster and Festinger 1962; Brock and Becker 1965; Mills and Jellison 1967; Mills and Aronson 1965). Recent thought and research by Wright and his colleagues (Wright 1986; Kirmani and Wright 1986) about consumers' attempts to conterargue ads and to decipher the "schemer schema" or persuasion technique is also consistent with the notion of fewer counterarguments to open-ended advertisements, since there are less overt attempts to persuade the audience.

A type of *behavior modification* (Nord and Peter 1980) process may help messages without an explicit conclusion because open-ended messages are likely to be better liked by the audience. Most messages make conclusions. In fact, prototypical explicit conclusion advertisements are hard-sell ads like the famous Ted Bates commercial for Bufferin in which the hammer beats on the line drawing of a head, the B's beat the A's in the race to the stomach, and the announcer forcefully announces "Take Bufferin for faster pain relief." Surveys such as Bauer and Greyser's (1968) study show that two of the largest irritants in advertising are the heavy amount of repetition and hard-sell commercials with insistent conclusions about products that are for such unpleasant problems as body odor, false teeth, and bad breath. It is very likely that consumers prefer advertisements (and products) that do not do these irritating or even obnoxious things. Soft-sell ads are much more likely to be rated favorably by consumers. Certainly the judicious use of humor such as the Federal Express, Wendy's, and Volkswagen campaigns are classic examples of soft-sell advertising.[4] The audience may like implicit conclusion ads because these ads do not threaten the audience's perceived freedom to decide. Another probable pleasing factor related to but distinct from psychological reactance is that these ads are likely perceived as pleasantly unique due to the fact that they do not tell the audience what to do but instead, in effect, say to the audience, "You are intelligent enough to make up your own mind; I leave the decision up to you." Research about the effects of attitude towards the ad (for example, MacKenzie, Lutz, and Belch 1986) and likable, soft-sell ads (Silk and Vavra 1974) emphasize the importance of attitude towards the ad in helping to enhance the persuasiveness of the advertisement.

It is also likely that open-ended ads are more difficult to process. This may result in a negative ad affect. However, some researchers (for example, Cohen 1959; Wicklund, Cooper, and Linder 1967) speculate that *greater effort* such as might be required from a more difficult-to-process message such as an open-ended message would, especially for a message that advocates an attitude counter to the current position of the audience, produce greater *cognitive dissonance* and potentially greater attitude change in the direction advocated by the message. Linder and Worchel (1970) explicitly tested whether messages linking smoking to lung cancer were more effective in terms of persuasion when subjects were required to reach their own conclusion from a series of syllogisms (see McGuire 1960) than from identical messages that contained more conclusions and required less conclusion drawing by the audience. Linder and Worchel found that the more conclusions subjects were asked to draw for themselves (which ranged from six out of seven in the "high-effort" condition to four out of seven in the "moderate-effort" condition to two out of seven in the "low-effort" condition), the greater the attitude change. Moreover, there was an interaction such that the attitude change effect of level of effort as manipulated by the number of conclusions the audience had to draw for themselves was quite large for smokers (who were more likely to initially disagree with, dislike, or be wary of a message that linked smoking to lung cancer), whereas the attitude change as a function of effort was statistically insignificant for nonsmokers. Thus, Linder and Worchel's interaction between initial opinion and level of effort results are consistent with the cognitive dissonance notion that open-ended messages which may require more effort can, due to that greater effort, result in greater attitude change. Since Linder and Worchel's nonexperimentally manipulated variable of *initial* attitude (smoker versus nonsmoker) is likely highly confounded with *involvement*, and *effort* was experimentally manipulated by whether the audience had to make few or several *conclusions*, this interaction result is thus also very consistent with the overall hypothesis of this chapter.

Cognitive dissonance experiments which manipulate effort and find a greater amount of attitude change in high effort conditions for counterattitudinal messages have been analyzed by Chapanis and Chapanis (1964). They preferred an alternative explanation to the one preferred by adherents of the cognitive dissonance model. Instead of greater cognitive dissonance elicited by the greater amount of required effort, Chapanis and Chapanis suggested that a more appropriate explanation would involve the *greater satisfaction* of successful completion of a task. It could very well be that comprehension of open-ended messages does require greater effort, due to the greater need to analyze and pay attention to underlying message arguments since the overall conclusion is not neatly summarized for the audience. Messages without a conclusion take away the "easy" route to reaching a conclusion and force the audience to spend more time and effort. However, there may be some satisfaction in successfully reaching an effortful conclusion (see Linder and Worchel 1970).

Research also offers strong evidence that audience members will spontaneously strive to make inferences and conclusions under certain conditions.[5] Kruglanski's (1980; Kruglanski and Ajzen 1983) *theory of lay epistemology* posits that the perceived cost of committing an inferential error will influence whether a spontaneous inference is formed. An experiment by Kruglanski and Freund (1983) which manipulated the perceived costs (personal importance) of making incorrect inferences found that subjects who were told that their performance would be evaluated (high-cost condition) or not (low costs) made more valid inferences in the former condition. Of course, empirical evidence also has demonstrated that self-generated conclusions or cognitive responses can strongly influence attitudes (for example, Greenwald 1968; Wright 1973, 1980). Consistent with Kruglanski's theory and results, Preston (1977) has reported that advertising audiences are also very likely to "complete" ambiguous advertising statements or claims. Under conditions resembling low involvement, Preston's subjects tended to make false conclusions (or, in Kruglanski's terminology, incorrect inferences) which, if the advertiser could or should be considered as the cause of the incorrect conclusion, would be judged deceptive.

Petty and Cacioppo's *Elaboration Likelihood Model* (1981, 1983), which is quite similar to Kruglanski's theory, suggests that consumers process advertising messages in one of two ways (see also Chaiken 1980 for a similar model). The *central route* is one in which consumers carefully process the information and arguments in a message and then form attitudes based upon their reaction to those pieces of information and arguments. Such careful processing of information is likely to occur only when the audience is highly involved with the topic of communication and/or believes that the communication has personal relevance for the consumer himself or herself. Such careful processing of information is implicitly assumed by most theories of communication and attitude change. However, Petty and Cacioppo proposed that a second route, the *peripheral route*, is common in many advertising situations. The peripheral route occurs when the consumer is low in involvement with the message or message topic and is less likely to pay careful attention to the content of the message and contained information and arguments. Instead, even if the audience pays some minimum amount of attention to the advertisement, subjects are likely to rather incompletely process the advertising and look for cues from which to form a judgment about the message and any discussed topic. Such inferences about the merits of the advocated position may be based on various simple cues in the message situation. Cues which might be peripherally processed and influence the direction and nature of any resulting attitude change might include the trustworthiness and attractiveness of the source (such as an ad spokesperson), the number of arguments (but not their quality; see Alba and Marmorstein 1986), or the apparent extremity of the message's advocated position. When involvement is manipulated so that the message topic is deemed by the audience as either personally relevant or not, Petty and Cacioppo have demonstrated in a series of experiments (for example, Petty, Cacioppo, and Schumann 1983) that simple cues such as an attractive or famous endorser positively influence attitudes under low involvement but do not influence attitudes under high involvement. Instead, high involvement situations induce the audience to pay more attention to and be more apt to utilize the arguments and the quality of those arguments in the message as a determinant of their attitudes and attitude change. The presence or absence of a conclusion in an advertising message may very well be a type of cue that is processed peripherally under low involvement.

Consistent with Petty and Cacioppo's theory and the overall hypothesis of this chapter, consumers under low involvement may less carefully process the underlying arguments and instead completely process only the ending conclusion, and form their attitudes based upon that conclusion. However, more highly involved consumers are more likely to pay more attention to and have their attitudes influenced by the supporting arguments in an implicit conclusion message because (1) the fact that there is no conclusion may motivate the audience to draw a conclusion in order to successfully "complete" the ad (Zeigarnik 1927; Heimbach and Jacoby 1972) and (2) they are more motivated to closely examine the message arguments regardless of whether or not there is a conclusion because the message is personally relevant and important. However, a consumer who is low in involvement and exposed to a close-ended advertisement is more likely to read the conclusion and perhaps form an opinion based upon that conclusion than to carefully examine the supporting message arguments. (However, an opposite prediction from Petty and Cacioppo's model for the low involvement condition would be that the better liked no conclusion message format might be peripherally processed and result in superior persuasiveness of the no conclusion message.)

Open-ended advertising messages that elicit a conclusion from the audience may also benefit from the likelihood that conclusions drawn by the audience are much more likely to be *personal and vivid*. Advertising research has demonstrated that cognitive responses that involve personal "connections" (Krugman 1967), or thoughts (Leavitt, Waddell, and Wells 1970) or are based on personal experiences (Fazio and Zanna 1981) are likely to be more persuasive. Personally generated conclusions or reactions are also likely to be more vivid to that person, and such vividness can result in greater persuasiveness (Kisielius and Sternthal 1984, 1986; Taylor and Thompson 1982). Such personal conclusions are similarly likely to emanate from direct behavioral experience and thus produce attitudes more directly accessible at opportunities to choose a consistent or inconsistent behavior (see Fazio and Zanna 1981).

Messages that force the consumer to spend more time and more effort or simply to expend higher (or deeper) levels of processing are very likely to have measurable positive immediate effects that are also much more likely to persist over time than messages that are not as deeply processed at the time of initial exposure. Due to the above-discussed likelihood that open-ended messages require greater in-depth processing in order for one to reach a conclusion and, in fact, are not likely to be persuasive unless such a successful effort to make a conclusion is expended by the audience, open-ended advertisements' effects are likely to be immediately effective under some conditions as discussed above and, given immediate effects, those effects are very likely to *persist longer over time* than any immediate effects of close-ended advertising messages (Sawyer and Ward 1979; Tyler, Hertel, McCallum, and Ellis 1979).

## New Empirical Results

After reviewing the literature in 1982, I derived the hypothesis set forth in this chapter. Since no extant empirical data existed that explicitly tested this hypothesis, Daniel Howard (now at Southern Methodist University) and I conducted a series of laboratory experiments that attempt to directly test the hypothesized interaction between audience involvement and whether an advertising message includes an explicit conclusion.[6] Ads were designed by a professional artist for two types of products: razors and toothbrushes. These products served as replications in the experimental design. Both the razor ads and the toothbrush ads used an identical format in which there was a headline that encouraged people to read some information given in detail in the body of the advertising text about four competing brands of the product in question; the information was attributed to an independent consumer testing organization. A fictitious product was reported in the detail information to have fared best on three of five attributes, tied for best on a fourth attribute, and tied for second on a fifth attribute. Whether or not the ad in question had a conclusion was manipulated by a closing statement which either encouraged the readers to decide for themselves which product they should buy or concluded *for* them that they should buy or use the fictitious brand because it was the best product for them.

For example, a disposable razor ad began with the headline "Discover the Difference." Underneath the large headline was copy encouraging the audience to read the below results of an independent testing organization. Detailed numerical information was then given about four products on five attributes. The ending conclusion was in moderately large type and stated either "Now That You Know the Difference, Shave With Edge—The Disposable Razor That is Best for You" (explicit conclusion condition) or "Now That You Know the Difference, Decide for Yourself Which Disposable Razor *You* Should Shave With!" (no conclusion condition). The headline and two ending lines for the toothbrush ad read "Get the Facts Before You Buy Your Next Toothbrush" and ended with "Now That *You* Have the Facts, Try the Winner—Hygent" (explicit-conclusion condition) or "Now That *You* Have the Facts, Decide for Yourself Which Toothbrush You Should Buy" (no-conclusion condition).

Involvement was manipulated in a manner identical to the procedure used by Petty, Cacioppo, and Schumann (1983) by telling subjects that they would receive a gift for their participation in the experiment. Subjects were either informed that, as a gift for their participation in the research, they would be allowed to choose a particular brand of disposable razor (high involvement for razor ads and low involvement for toothbrush ads) or that they would be allowed to choose a brand of toothbrush (low involvement for razor ads and high involvement for toothbrush ads). As in Petty, Cacioppo, and Schumann's experiment, high involvement subjects were in addition told that the advertisement and product for the ad in question would soon be test-marketed in medium-sized cities throughout the midwest, including their own city (Columbus, Ohio); low involvement subjects were told that the advertised product in question was being test-marketed elsewhere.

In this empirical research manipulating both message copy (open-ended and close-ended advertisements) and audience involvement, we found more positive ratings of the open-ended ads on such dimensions as "unusual," "truthful," "did not threaten my freedom to decide," and "not high pressure." However, the open-ended ads were more likely than the close-ended ads to be perceived as "had too much information for me to read." Despite that latter perception, the open-ended advertisements under higher involvement conditions were much more effective than close-ended ads. Open-ended advertisements resulted in greater *memory* of the attributes listed in the advertising, more *correct memory* of the attributes, greater *confidence in the accuracy of that memory*, more positive *beliefs*, *attitudes* and *purchase intentions*, and a greater *likelihood of choosing* the advertised brand as a gift for participation in the experiment. Moreover, this latter behavioral effect remained in a one-week subsequent test. This pattern of results provides strong support for the overall hypothesis of an interaction between involvement and message appeal. It also is not inconsistent with much of the above speculation about possible underlying mechanisms of processes that mediate this effect. Clearly, open-ended advertisements that do not contain an explicit conclusion offer excellent potential for advertisers whose situation is appropriate for such advertising. Moreover, the initial results suggest that more research on this topic can produce results that would be both useful to advertising practitioners and exciting and informative to advertising theorists.

## Key Moderating Variables

The thesis of this chapter is that open-ended advertising messages that do not explicitly draw a conclusion for the audience and instead leave the conclusion for the audience to develop on its own can be very effective. These open-ended messages are most likely to be effective under conditions of at least moderate involvement on the part of the audience. However, like most interesting microtheoretical notions in psychology and advertising (Ray 1978), there are several other variables in the marketing and advertising situation that will also interact with or mediate the potential effectiveness of open-ended advertising messages. These other factors can be grouped along the traditional Lasswell (1948) dimensions of *who* says *what* to *whom*, how (in *what medium* with *what schedule*) and with what effect.

### Brand Market Share, Familiarity, and Reputation

First of all, the market position of the product and brand is likely to be an important factor. Hadley (1952) suggested that it was very likely that more *well-known brands with larger market shares* were more likely to benefit from the indirect, implicit-conclusion advertising than smaller share, less familiar brands. As suggested in footnote 1, market leaders such as IBM are likely to benefit more from open-ended advertising than smaller share brands for a variety of reasons. First of all, previous advertising may provide the cues to a "proper" conclusion. For example, the no-conclusion Michelob ad described earlier very likely benefits from past Michelob advertising. Consumers are not unlikely to know that Michelob claims it is worth the extra price, has quality ingredients, and so forth. Thus, the consumer may provide a conclusion already formed in his or her mind based on previous advertising. For the self-perception explanation offered earlier to be valid, the consumer would have to attribute his conclusion to his own decision processes at the time of viewing the open-ended advertisement and *not* decide that the source of that conclusion generated at the time of viewing the open-ended ad was derived from previous explicit conclusion advertising. The commercial by IBM for the "smart desk" may not have had to mention explicitly the IBM brand name to be effective. Given IBM's large market share, it may be sufficient (and more believable) to try to stimulate generic demand for smart desks and computers of all types and brands—a communication objective that is likely to be more achievable and produce fewer counterarguments than an ad that attempts to convince the consumer that he should consider only IBM products. Of course, the largest market share brand is likely to benefit most from generic product advertising. Moreover, Nelson's (1974) economic theory predicts that, independent of the advertising copy, heavier advertising budgets and resulting frequency of media exposure will be (correctly, according to Nelson) used by consumers as a cue to conclude that the highly frequently advertised brands have the highest quality. Thus, a no-conclusion message is likely to receive the "benefit of the doubt" on the part of the consumer and, hence, be more likely to have a favorable conclusion drawn by the audience.

In addition to high market share brands, *very low market share brands* may benefit from open-ended advertising. There may be a type of inverted U-curve effect such that no-conclusion advertisements are most effective for brands high in familiarity, reputation, and market share, least effective for brands with moderate market share, and moderately effective (less effective than for high market share brands) for relatively new, low market share brands. The reason for the relative high persuasiveness for low market share brands involves the credibility needed and gained by unfamiliar brands from open-ended advertisements. As stated above, no-conclusion advertisements are perceived as more trustworthy and credible. Large market share brands are less likely to require credibility. These brands probably already have some credibility. However, new or low share brands lack credibility; these brands also are likely to face a situation in which members of the audience have not formed a positive opinion, and these consumers are very likely to disagree with the position of the advertisement. Given the results in the Linder and Worchel (1970) experiment, it seems likely that open-ended messages will be appropriate for such products which face an audience highly likely to be unfamiliar and disagree with any explicit conclusion that the unfamiliar, low share brand is best.

## Characteristics of the Audience

The particular type of person or market segment that is the audience of a particular advertisement is likely to also be an important determinant of whether an open-ended message is more effective than a close-ended one. The likelihood that people with an initial opinion counter to that advocated in the message might be particularly susceptible to an open-ended message has just been discussed. There may also be other important segmenting variables. For example, a *personality high in need for cognition* (Cacioppo and Petty 1982) may be more likely to be motivated to attempt to form a conclusion when exposed to a no-conclusion message. On the other hand, it may be that these people react very negatively to open-ended messages because they prefer closure. It also seems very likely that an open-ended message will be effective for a *more intelligent or educated audience*. As with refutational advertising messages, more educated or intelligent people are more likely to be able and willing to comprehend an open-ended message and to reach a conclusion (Ray and Sawyer 1973; Sawyer 1973). Cooper and Dinerman (1951) analyzed a movie which used an indirect, no-explicit-conclusion format to help the audience reach the conclusion that intergroup prejudice was stupid and not in anyone's best self-interest. The results of their analysis indicated that the portions of the movie which left the conclusions for the audience to draw for themselves were more effective than were the portions of the movie that explicitly stated the conclusion ("Messages stated in generalized form are not likely to be accepted by any significant portion of an audience"), but that "messages which are not explicitly stated are likely to be entirely lost upon the less intelligent members of the audience" (Cooper and Dinerman 1951, p. 264).

Finally, the *level of involvement* is obviously an important factor in determining the effectiveness of either an open-ended or close-ended communication. However, the effects of involvement may not be as simple as depicted in figure 11–1 and discussed above. Although space does not permit a full discussion of the problems of conceptualizing and operationalizing *involvement* (Greenwald and Leavitt 1984; Burnkrant and Sawyer 1983; Cohen 1983), some discussion is required here. For example, it is likely that the graph in figure 11–1 should be altered so that, at the zero level of involvement, any effects of open-ended or close-ended advertising are either zero or very small and equal. At non-zero but low levels of involvement, it may be that, as hypothesized in this chapter, a close-ended message is more effective than the open-ended message. However, *if* the messages are equally attended to and comprehended, it is likely that the two appeals are equally effective under low involvement (Thistlethwaite et al. 1955). At moderate levels of involvement, open-ended messages are likely to be more persuasive—as discussed extensively in this chapter. At extremely high levels of involvement, it is very likely that the two message appeals will be equally effective. Very highly involved people are likely to read anything they can on the subject, thoroughly process it, and try to understand the message regardless of whether a conclusion is provided. However, it could be that, due to the fact that audience involvement is often highly correlated with whether or not the audience has an extreme initial opinion (Petty, Capioppo, and Schumann 1983), both types of messages will be equally effective but relatively *in*effective at very high levels of involvement.

Again, however, there would be a likely exception to this latter prediction. If people are highly *personally involved* in a situation such as in psychotherapy or a situation in which one's self-esteem is in question (such as a professional colleague pointing out a fault or an error), perhaps only the open-ended message will be even slightly persuasive. When a message is highly involving in a personal way, there is a high probability that people will reject any explicit conclusion that involves an explanation of their own behavior. Just as was pointed out in the third-to-last sentence of the earlier quote of Hadley (1953), people are very likely to need to figure out for themselves the exact reason for the behavior in question. Any explicit conclusion by someone other than the person who is the target of the message is likely to be rejected, either because the explicit conclusion is too personally threatening to one's self-esteem or because the explicit conclusion is not sufficiently correctly and precisely stated that it is easy for the target audience to successfully (in their eyes) at least partially counterargue. Hence, portions of the explicit conclusions that may be accurate and less easily counterargued are dismissed along with the portions that are not stated sufficiently precisely or correctly. Topics high in ego-involvement are likely to be so sensitive that only an open-ended message format has a chance to work.

One last issue about involvement that needs to be briefly discussed is the notion of exactly *when* the involvement exists or occurs. Can somebody make a conclusion from a message and still be characterized as "low in involvement"? If an ad is sufficiently effective to motivate somebody—even an initially *un*involved person—to draw a conclusion for themselves, it may be inappropriate to say that that person is not involved. Clearly, good advertising reaches out and makes people "involved" or at least attentive, even if the topic of the message is not situationally or inherently involving.

## Message Factors

There are many message variables that will influence the effectiveness of an open-ended communication. For example, it seems likely that the more *complex* the message is, the more it may be necessary to draw a conclusion for the audience unless the audience is very heavily involved and is quite intelligent. The *quality of the premise arguments* is likely to be very important. If a conclusion needs to be drawn from weak premise arguments, people may not reach an appropriate (from the advertisers' point of view) conclusion. Of course, similar to the problems of conceptualization of involvement, there are clearly different degrees of "conclusions".

Conclusions could be applied to any belief statement that concludes that "Brand X possesses attribute Y" (Wyer 1974; Wyer, Carlston, and Hartwick 1979). However, I have tried to use the term *conclusion* to denote a situation in which people sum up information, data, or attribute claims and then must make a conclusive decision or choice based on the preceding information. For example, I am using the term conclusion to denote a situation in which somebody has to choose which brand is best or make a decision about which particular position (such as whether to devalue the U.S. dollar or whether the Korean War is a real threat) is to be believed or preferred. Clearly there are many levels of conclusions.

Earlier, there was discussion of the danger of a situation in which an audience exposed to a no-conclusion message might not be able to draw a conclusion or would draw a conclusion inconsistent with the position advocated by the message or that the sponsors of the message would prefer the audience conclude. *Message formats* may be an important determinant of whether open-ended messages result in at least *some* conclusion. For example, a broadcast commercial which leaves the conclusion to the audience may need to leave a sufficient silent pause both to alert the audience that some attention and thinking is necessary and to afford it the temporal opportunity to generate a conclusion (Wright 1974). Other message format variables may also be important. For example, Mitchell and Olson (1981) found that a pictorial message stimulus produced more product attribute inferences than a verbal format. Ads that raise the audience's uncertainty are likely to motivate it to process arguments and to draw a conclusion (Berlyne 1960). One variable that may both heighten uncertainty and suggest that the conclusion may not be given in the message is the use of beginning headlines or endings containing tagline questions (Burnkrant and Howard 1986).

Another important message variable may be manipulations of the *audience's awareness of the importance of fully processing the message content and arriving at a proper conclusion on its own.* In an excellent experiment that essentially tested the hypothesis of this chapter, Kardes (1986) manipulated whether a print advertisement's headline and body copy highlighted the salience of the information about the advertised product (a compact disc player). The headline in the salient personal consequences (high involvement) condition stated, "You Will Probably Own a Compact Disc Player Sooner than You Think. According to Consumer Reports, Some CD Players Are Very Good and Some Are Very Bad." In the nonsalient consequences condition, the ad's headline simply stated "Compact Disc Players." This advertising headline manipulation of involvement resulted in an interaction with the ad copy such that more favorable attitudes for more highly involved subjects resulted from the omission of three explicit conclusions about the attributes of the advertised brand compared to subjects low in involvement, whereas involvement level did not influence audience attitudes when the advertisement included the three explicit conclusions.

*Pretesting* is particularly important for an open-ended message to ascertain the conclusions that the majority of the target segment do, in fact, draw for themselves from the message. In some instances, however, previous surveys may lend great confidence to the sponsor of a message that a particular conclusion will be drawn. I recently saw an example of political advertising that sparked this idea. Like many political campaigns in 1986, the U.S. Senate election campaign in Florida became a series of very uninformative and negative ads that primarily tried to mischaracterize a position of the other candidate and then capitalize on that misinformation. As in most tit-for-tat situations, one candidate appeared to initiate this televised mudslinging, and the other candidate was then drawn into the fray. One commercial for the incumbent Paula Hawkins, who was running against the current governor, Robert Graham, went something like this: "Paula Hawkins voted yes for tougher penalties against people who use and sell drugs. Bob Graham voted no on tougher drug penalties. Bob Graham doesn't want drug pushers to go to jail; Paula Hawkins has shown by her votes that she is against drugs in Florida. *Vote for the candidate whose vote agrees with your views.*"

This Hawkins ad strikes me as a clever, albeit ethically questionable, advertising technique that does not explicitly conclude and tell the voter for whom to vote. Instead, this ad takes a position that the person should vote for whomever they agree with. However, I am sure that surveys in Florida, as well as across the nation, show that most voters are very concerned about drugs and want tougher drug penalties. Therefore, Paula Hawkins, who became infamous for being "out front" on such controversial issues as being against child and drug abuse and for motherhood and apple pie, may have succeeded in having voters exposed to this ad say to themselves, "Well, I am against drugs; I want to vote for the candidate who agrees with my views; and that person is Paula Hawkins." In a more conventional product arena, this message strategy might be quite effective. Fortunately or unfortunately, the ad was not sufficient to re-elect Paula Hawkins. She had used this technique so often in the past and during the 1986 campaign, and newspaper and television editorials and articles had publicized this recurring advertising and public relations tactic sufficiently frequently to alert (and perhaps raise the involvement of) the voters. Hence, the voters may have seen through this technique, formed a "schemer schema" (Wright 1986) for the Paula Hawkins ad, and were not persuaded by the perhaps overly transparent no-conclusion ad. This insight may have led voters to dislike and mistrust Hawkins, the sponsor of the ad, or become more alert (or involved) and more carefully consider and counterargue the premise arguments. Such a boomerang effect may have led voters to at least wonder if Governor Graham were perhaps reasonable or relatively honest, did not want to encourage drug dealers, and had either not voted as characterized by Senator Hawkins or voted against heavier penalties for reasons other than being *for* drug pushers and users.

## Medium and Schedule

The employed communication medium may also influence whether an open-ended message is persuasive. Print media may be more effective than broadcast media for implicit conclusion messages, since premise arguments in print can be processed at the reader's own pace, whereas broadcast media must be processed at a fixed and fast rate (Wright 1974). In addition to perhaps allowing more opportunity to think, print messages may motivate or require such thinking. Print media may also result in more extensive processing of message arguments than broadcast, due to less distraction from nonverbal cues (Chaiken and Eagly 1976; 1983). I recently watched a tape of *Smithsonian World*, a PBS television show. N.C. Wyeth, the famous illustrator of such classic books as *Robin Hood, Kidnapped*, and *Last of the Mohicans*, and father of five accomplished children, including the famous artist Andrew, clearly believed in the power of forceful, explicit conclusions to his creative brood. However, he also strongly believed in the greater potential for thought-provoked, creative conclusions drawn by a reader of books compared to even a great movie. His son Nathaniel cited an example of his famous father's beliefs after the entire family had just exited from the movie *Mutiny on the Bounty* (which they had all thoroughly enjoyed) by quoting his father's reactions and resulting lecture to the family. " 'Turn around now and look at these people coming out of this theater. Did you ever see a duller bunch of faces? Look at those expressions! That's the trouble with movies; they don't leave anything for *this* [points to head]! Your imagination goes to sleep!' Well, he was entirely right, you know. Reading a book, you get so much more out of it because it's not limited by what's on that cellulose" (MacCullough and Grubin 1986).

There has also been much speculation about the relative effects of audio versus video advertisements (see, for example, Ries and Trout 1983; Sawyer 1982; and Worchel, Andreoli, and Eason 1975). There are many adherents of radio advertising because it forces the listener to "visualize" the object of the audio message.

Synergy due to multiple media campaigns can help reduce the variance of this visualization process. For example, I remember my mother commenting to me one weekend when I was home from my undergraduate business school days that when she heard the radio commercial for Doublemint chewing gum that told the listener to "s-t-r-e-t-c-h your coffee break with a piece of Doublemint chewing gum," she could visualize the coffee cup being stretched horizontally because she had seen it in a previous television commercial version of the same advertisement. Admirers of old radio programs wonder if it were more interesting and thought-provoking to listen in to shows such the "The Shadow" because one had to force oneself to imagine what the people looked like and what action was going on and to fill in for oneself the visual portion of the programming or commercials. Perhaps audio-only broadcast commercials, which by definition leave more for consumers to visualize for themselves (Wright 1974) may be more appropriate than telecast ads for open-ended advertising copy which does not draw the conclusion for the listener and aims for a thoughtful conclusion.

As an example of the effects of audio-only versus audio-plus-video, consider the recent controversy about Madonna's latest hit record and video "Papa, Don't Preach."[7] Anti-abortionists argue that the song is a pro-abortion statement. Other people claim that the song is simply an appeal for open communication between parents and their children and a plea for parents to listen in a loving way to the problems of their children. Compared to the audio-only record, the video version of "Papa, Don't Preach" is more likely, I think, to lead to the latter explanation or understanding of the theme of the song. Perhaps it is a good thing that the video helps the audience to make a conclusion that Madonna, the songwriter, or the producer *may* have intended. However, songs, poems, paintings, sculpture, and all other forms of art may have their best potential for impact if the audience is left to draw their own conclusion. This is especially true if the artist has no particular statement in mind or wishes for the audience to choose among several possible explanations. Perhaps the most appropriate and achievable purpose of a song or other art form that involves a particular issue is to get people to *think* about the issue rather than to come to any particular conclusion. It may be that any attitude change regarding highly involving topics can emerge only from careful thought about new information or new values regarding that topic. To the extent that the issue is a very involving one, such as pro-life versus pro-abortion, any message that takes a particular stance is very likely to be very ineffective for the very group that disagrees with the point of view being advocated and, hence, is the likely target of any message with the goal of attitude *change*.

Another medium difference that may affect the effectiveness of open-ended advertisements may be whether the medium is *personal or impersonal*. An impersonal message, especially in a print medium that allows the opportunity to carefully study a message's arguments, that contains an explicit conclusion, particularly on a subject that is highly or even personally involving, may be less persuasive than a personally spoken message. For example, even a series of different print advertisements advocating to a heavy smoker that even light smoking can have very bad health effects might be less effective than one personal sales call with essentially the same arguments but worded in a tailor-made fashion based on evolving feedback.

As a more close to home example, most of us who work within large organizations have experienced the problem, either as a sender or receiver, of an office memo that attempts to come to some very specific conclusions about personally relevant issues. It is a very common experience that such memos either do not work or, in fact, boomerang because the ego-involving message can be refuted at some level by the people who are the target of the message. Unless the author researches an issue very carefully and is an extremely gifted writer, and the memo is written, pretested, and rewritten many times, such memos inevitably fail. I suspect the reason is that ego-involved targets of a written communication are very likely to find some fault with the wording or the explicit or implicit assumptions of the memo. Thus, the recipients of the memo are very likely to be offended by the memo message, reject its relevance or appropriateness, and exhibit no or even negative change in the advocated direction. It is the old case of throwing out the baby with the bath water, in that any weak link in the memo will likely cause rejection of the entire message.

If instead, the potential memo writer talks to the audience person-to-person and takes cues from the person as to how to reformulate his conclusions so that that person will understand and not be so offended that he will reject the advocated point of view, then the message has a chance to succeed. However, again it is probably best to not make explicit conclusions on ego-involving issues but instead to use the indirect, no-explicit-conclusion approach. If people are motivated to understand and improve a situation, then a communication that does not try to force a conclusion on the target audience has at least a chance to succeed. Therefore, there may be a four-way interaction between type of medium, audience involvement, whether an open-ended message is used, and whether the target audience agrees with the message's conclusion (implicit or not). For topics high in involvement, the no-conclusion appeal works best. However, for highly involving situations, it may be even more effective to use a personal medium if a direct conclusion is included in the highly involving message with which the audience initially disagrees strongly. A personally presented message may lead to dyadic, back-and-forth communication that can take advantage of feedback to flexibly adjust stated conclusions to the nature of the other's reaction. Use of feedback to reformulate and restate conclusions so that they are not rejected outright by the audience can lead to perceptions by the audience that the conclusions are its own. Certainly, the use of feedback to help target customers to believe that conclusions congenial to the sales goals are their own ideas is a key principle in training of personal salesmen (Weitz 1981).

Finally, the *schedule* of messages may make a difference. Open-ended, soft-sell advertising is much more likely to benefit from *repetition* than hard-sell, close-ended messages. This is a well-known empirical fact (Sawyer 1977, 1981).

## Summary

This chapter has discussed a hypothesis consistent with both past literature and new empirical results. This hypothesis states that advertising messages that do not make an explicit conclusion but instead leave the conclusion for the audience to decide can be relatively effective in achieving desired attitude change. The likelihood that this type of advertising will be effective is much greater under at least moderate levels of involvement on the part of the audience. It may be that under quite low levels of involvement, the opposite is true and an advertisement must, in William McGuire's words, not only lead the horse to water but also push his head underneath to get him to drink by means of including an explicit conclusion in a message. An explicit conclusion is most likely to be appropriate for a complex message on an unfamiliar topic that the audience is not sufficiently motivated or involved with to carefully process. Possible psychological mechanisms that may underlie this predicted effect were discussed. Finally, other factors in the marketing and advertising and communication situation that are likely to influence whether open-ended advertisements are more effective than close-ended advertisements were listed and expanded upon.

Open-ended message appeals *can* be very effective under some conditions in advertising. However, I am certain that open-ended appeals that do not explicitly draw conclusions for the target of the message can also be extremely effective in other situations that are probably much more important than any advertising campaign. At least, I am positive, after forty-three years of experience in trying to point out conclusions in a very pointed and blunt manner to friends and fellows alike, that such a close-ended explicit conclusion approach often will have no effect or will have a boomerang type of *negative* effect. As a penultimate example, let me refer you to such time-honored axioms involving child raising such as "I'd rather do it myself" and "Experience is the best teacher." All parents have had the experience of trying to tell their children what is best for them. We often try to lecture our children and have them benefit from our own experience so that they will not have to repeat our mistakes. It may very well be that such lectures have a long-term effect in a "sleeper effect" fashion in which the children remember the message long after they either forget the source or at least are chronologically and psychologically mature enough that the source of the advice is irrelevant (see Sawyer and Ward 1979). However, explicit close-ended communication often does not work well at all, at least to my intelligent and increasingly independent young teenage children.

Let me end this chapter with one final example. While revising this chapter one last time, I saw a television commercial for Sony video cameras, which use a different type of videotape than VHS. The ad shows a dramatically lighted courtroom with an attentive audience, judge, and jury listening to a bright, almost arrogant, and brash lawyer with his tie askew. The lawyer is presenting his case about the Sony system versus more conventional systems using VHS. "So the issue is clear, Sony Video-8—the system of the future or VHS-C—the compromise of the past. Now as we've seen, the new Sony Handycam with auto focus and zoom gives you a measurably better picture (superimposed words: 'Compared to the JVC GR-C7 Based on Laboratory Testing'), for superior sound (a very quick glimpse of a bar chart graph showing Sony about four times higher than VHS-C), twice the recording time ('EP mode'), and (as he dramatically demonstrates by dangling a VHS cassette from which the ruined tape unreels in his hand) on Sony video cassettes, your memories are *safe*. On VHS-C, they could be *fleeting* ('only if improperly handled'). I rest my case." (He turns and walks away from the judge's bench to standing applause from the audience in the courtroom.) An announcer closes the commercial by stating, "The Sony Video-8 System. Judge for yourself ('Sony, the one and only')."

I leave it to you readers and the viewers of the Sony commercial to decide whether that commercial will be effective in attaining its communication goals to its target audience at the level of its likely involvement in the buying decision and in gathering information about that purchase in that medium, given the Sony video camera's market position and reputation. I also leave it to you readers to decide whether open-ended messages are best for your advertisements for your products.

## Notes

1. I believe that the IBM "smart desk" commercial only identified IBM with a brief logo at the end or, at the most, also very briefly mentioned "smart desk from IBM" in the first line by the second person. Presumably, IBM with its large market share is willing to leave that brand-name decision to the audience of this commercial and/or to past and future advertisements for IBM. As will be discussed at the end of this chapter, no-conclusion advertisements are likely more "safe" and effective for market leaders than for small market share brands.

2. Most of this research testing headlines or ending slogans with either a question or a statement has included conclusions or, at least, follow-up answers to the conclusions or statements. However, the tested messages that end with a question are analogous to a no-explicit (final)-conclusion message.

3. Or s/he if the person is bisexual. (Dr. Dichter is delightful and is very entertaining and insightful with his Freudian insights. He seems somewhat like the psychiatrist's patient who answered "sex" as a top-of-mind response to various words such as "tree," "ball," and "bicycle" and to all sorts of Rorshach test ink blots. When this patient was asked why he was so fixated on sex and responded as he did to such a variety of stimuli, he responded "Me! *You* are the one who keeps saying all the dirty words and showing me those filthy pictures!")

4. I realize that some of these soft-sell ads have explicit conclusions. However, some of them and many other soft-sell, humorous ads do not include a humorous conclusion.

5. I learned of the Kruglanski theory and empirical results in an excellent working paper by Kardes (1986).

6. A detailed description and discussion of these empirical results is available in Sawyer and Howard (1987).

7. See Baldwin and Mizerski (1985) for a discussion and empirical test of the communication effects of audio-only versus MTV video music.

# 12

# Do Advertising Messages Require Intelligible Content? A Cognitive Response Analysis of Unintelligible Persuasive Messages

*Vernon R. Padgett*
*Timothy C. Brock*

## Introduction: The Missing Volkswagen

In 1959 a series of unusual automobile advertisements began to appear in magazines in the United States. Unlike conventional automobile ads, no effort was made to indicate that ownership conferred a caste mark; no effort was made to convince the reader that superb taste and discernment identified those fortunate few who had the wisdom to purchase the new model. On the other hand, these ads used humor, even made fun of the product they were advertising; they offered a number of facts as part of the ad; and, most unusually, they presupposed some intelligence on the part of the reader. The ads soon became classics in American advertising. According to Daniel Starch, Inc., a sample-interviewing firm that collects page-by-page data on magazine reader "traffic," the Doyle Dane Bernbach Volkswagen ads have consistently been the best read of all auto ads, and some Volkswagen ads have "substantially outscored cover stories in some issues of some magazines" (Rowsome 1970, p. 78).

Some of the ads were remarkably free of content. One featured a single curved line, with the sentence under it: "How much longer can we hand you this line?" (The curve, of course, was the silhouette of the Volkswagen Beetle.) The ultimate in content-free ads in the series, and perhaps in American advertising as well, was a 1961 ad that was simply a blank page, with a sentence at the bottom reading: "We don't have anything to show you in our new models." This prompted a baffled query from the home office in Wolfsburg: "How can you possibly buy all that expensive space and then not do anything with it?" But readership surveys and sales floor comments showed this ad to be quite effective in "driving home the point that Volkswagen did not artifically age its cars as a sales device" (Rowsome 1970, p. 95).

---

Based on portions of an unpublished doctoral dissertation by V.R. Padgett, Ohio State University, 1985.

## Content-free Advertising?

The role of "content-free advertising" has received attention in more formal investigations than that described above: Research on audience involvement in advertising (for example, Leavitt, Greenwald, and Obermiller 1981) suggests that persuasion occurs without message content. People appear to not pay attention to what is advertised, thereby gleaning only a vague generalization about the product. Many argue that content is irrelevant; the issue is to increase name recognition. A politician may say, "I don't care what you say about me, just be sure to spell my name right!"

Name recognition alone, one goal of advertising, is content-free communication: No content regarding the product is transmitted, yet consumers will buy a more familiar product rather than one that is unfamiliar, indicating a more favorable attitude toward the product selected. This implies that attitude change has taken place in the absence of message content.

Consumer research has suggested that people are persuaded by factors such as source attractiveness that appear to rule out message comprehension (Leippe, Greenwald, and Baumgardner 1982). Students were asked to judge the qualities of fictitious consumer products. Ratings of these items spread from non-neutral to formerly neutral products. These researchers note: "Persuasion may occur without high levels of reception or appraisal . . . the recipient may simply learn and accept the message conclusion on the basis of some heuristic cue, such as source attractiveness" (p. 644).

There is little question that message content has occupied a central role in both formal and informal analyses of the persuasion process. There exists, however, a wealth of evidence indicating that people *are* influenced by messages that lack intelligible content. In fact, it is possible to predict that unintelligible messages might be especially persuasive. We will offer support for this claim ranging from informal observation to experimental social psychological research. Each of these suggests that largely or totally unintelligible messages are to some extent persuasive. Taken as a whole, we believe this indicates that largely or totally unintelligible messages play an important, if ignored, role in the process of persuasion.

*Persuasion with Unintelligible Messages: Nonexperimental*
*Evidence Persuasion without Comprehension in Religion*

> On the picturesque Japanese island of Ikitsuki, where the ways of farmers and fishermen die hard, two old men squat before a home altar and chant prayers carefully entrusted to them by their ancestors. The ritual is intense and moving. But something is askew. The rite is partly Buddhist, partly Christian. The language sounds odd, a sort of pidgin Latin. And what do the ancient prayers mean? One of the worshippers admits, "I don't understand a word of this." Neither does anyone else. ("Japan's crypto-Christians," 1982).

Lest we smirk at the Easterners, consider two indigenous phenomena:

1. *Glossolalia.* Glossolalia, or "speaking in tongues," is a common phenomenon in some religious groups. The messages produced by speaking in tongues have been routinely analyzed and shown to be totally without meaningful content (Samarin 1972, p. 88; Williams 1981, chapter 8). Nonetheless, speaking in tongues often has a powerful impact on speaker and listener alike, heightening suggestibility and, presumably, facilitating religious conversion.

2. *Unintelligible language litanies.* Catholic and other religious services in the United States use lengthy passages of Latin or other foreign languages as central parts of their religious ritual, yet these languages are totally incomprehensible to virtually all Americans. There is persuasion in religion—and these communications, although unintelligible, appear to play a role in that persuasion process.

### Persuasion with Ambiguous or Unintelligible Rock Music Lyrics

By the late 1960s, rock music had been singled out as a leading cause of drug use, declining morals, and lack of interest in the Protestant ethic. One anti-rock spokesperson, Art Linkletter, testified before a congressional committee on drug abuse and later singled out top-40 songs as a "complete, total campaign for the fun and thrill of [drug] trips" (Hirsch 1971, p. 375). Many analysts of the popular music scene subscribed to a theory concerning the effect of popular song lyrics that assumed that values expressed in hit songs were clear to a majority of listeners, subscribed to by a large proportion of listeners, and likely to persuade the uncommitted (p. 376).

The message contained in rock-and-roll songs is frequently obscure, and lyrics are treated by the performer as but one of several components of the total sound. Once deciphered, their meaning may remain ambiguous. In a sample of 1,200 Michigan high school students, only 10 to 30 percent were able to write out correctly the "message" allegedly contained in several hit song lyrics. Most teenagers made no reference to drugs, sex, or politics. The coding of "correct interpretations" was based primarily on the explanation given in the popular press. When asked directly if a song's attraction lay in its sound or its meaning, 70 percent responded that they were more attracted by sound. These data suggest that a majority of teenagers fail to perceive the "deviant" messages in a number of hit songs (Hirsch 1971, p. 379). Any persuasion resulting from rock music appears to be a result of messages largely incomprehensible to most listeners.

### Oratory of Adolf Hitler

Even for German-speaking audiences, the oratory of Hitler must have contained persuasive factors beyond message content:

> I spoke on this theme [The Peace Treaties of Brest-Litovsk and Versailles] at meetings of two thousand people, and often I was struck by the glances of three thousand

six hundred hostile eyes. And three hours later I had before me a surging mass full of the holiest indignation and boundless wrath. (Hitler 1926/1971, p. 468)

It is unlikely that audiences concentrated on all the content of a *three-hour* message; it is likely that factors well beyond message content were at play. August Kubizek recounted the following from his adolescent friendship with the sixteen-year-old Hitler:

> Again and again I was filled with astonishment at how fluently he expressed himself, how vividly he managed to convey his feelings, how easily the words flowed from his mouth when he was completely carried away by his own emotions. Not *what* he said impressed me at first, but how he said it. This to me was something new, magnificent. I had never imagined that a man could produce such an effect with mere words. All he wanted from me, however, was one thing—agreement. Nor was it hard for me to agree with him, because I had never given any thought to the many problems which he raised. (Kubizek 1955, p. 14; emphasis in original.)

Adolf Hitler was well aware of the power of the spoken word, and viewed it as far more persuasive than the printed word (1926/1971, p. 469). He anticipated research on one- versus two-sided arguments and conducted research on the social and physical environments in which a persuasive communication is delivered (Hitler 1926/1971, pp. 471, 473, 475, cf. Cantril 1941/1976, pp. 259–261; Doob 1952, pp. 308–309). A common observation among non-German speakers is that a speech by Hitler is moving, powerful, and persuasive—even though none of the words are understood.

## People Have Attitudes toward Nonexistent Stimuli

**Fly Union Airlines.** People will make judgments about airlines which do not exist. "For two years, Allegheny executives smarted with the humiliating knowledge that most air travelers preferred to fly 'USAir,' then nonexistent, rather than the real-life Allegheny" ("Name Game," 1980, p. 13). Some passengers thought USAir was bigger and safer than Allegheny, and a few even said it was better than highly regarded American Airlines. In 1978, Allegheny Airlines found its ratings also lower than that of Union Airlines in a J. Walter Thompson Company consumer poll of airline preferences. Allegheny officials must have been irked further by this, since there is no Union Airlines. (Consumer ratings increased after Allegheny changed its name to USAir.)

**Sex and the History of Psychology.** Students will make judgments about lectures they haven't heard and films they haven't seen. Eighty percent of a thousand students who rated introductory psychology lectures gave higher marks to a lecture on the history of psychology than to three other presentations, even though the lecture had never been delivered (Reynolds 1977). Some of these same students had seen a film on sex and communication; they rated it positively. So did students who had *not* seen the film. About 55 percent of the students who had not seen the film evaluated it anyway, rating it as better than the lecture they didn't hear. Students apparently made an evaluative distinction between the film and the lecture without attending either one. In rating airlines, films, and lectures, people appear willing to evaluate something they haven't seen and cannot have understood.

## Experimental Psychological Research on Unintelligible Persuasion

A variety of psychological research suggests that humans are persuaded under conditions of unintelligibility, for example, anticipatory persuasion (Cialdini and Petty 1981), in which persuasion occurs simply through the anticipation of receiving a communication; and polarization of attitudes, which occurs to the extent one is given time to think about an issue (Tesser 1978). Language development itself may provide a model for the initial impact of unintelligible messages.

**Language Development: Our First Exposure to Unintelligible Messages?** We believe that persuasion with unintelligible messages is not only a ubiquitous feature of the advertising, political, religious, and social environment, but also that our initial social experience involves exposure to unintelligible communications. Infants first hear vocalizations from parents and eventually associate these novel sounds with meanings. Our first exposure to language is thus an exposure to unintelligible messages (Vygotsky 1962).

During their first six months, babies develop an astounding repertoire of vocalizations. Some claim that the repertoire of the babbling baby in the first half-year contains all the sounds of all human languages (Lenneberg 1967; T.G.R. Bower 1977, p. 135). Bower believes it likely that "adults decode the meaning of the baby's utterances by looking at the specific nonverbal behaviors, nonverbal gestures, and so on" that accompany the utterances. The adult "May then utter the correct sound," reinforcing the desired response (1977, p. 143). Bower is offering support here for the peripheral route to persuasion as stated by Petty and Cacioppo (1981): People attend to peripheral cues when the message content is low or absent.

Peter D. Eimas discovered that infants are capable of making fine distinctions between similar sounds. He offered direct evidence that unintelligible messages produce increases in certain responses by exposing one- and four-month old infants to recorded speech sounds (Eimas, Siqueland, Jusczyk, and Vigorito 1971). The babies kept the sound on by sucking on a nipple which contained a switch. At the beginning of a session, the baby could hear a *pa–pa* sound coming from a loudspeaker. "Most subjects responded with interest and sucked vigorously on the nipple to keep the recording playing." They habituated to the sound, and at that point the recording was switched to *ga–ga*. "As soon as the infants heard the new sound, they perked up and their rate of sucking increased significantly."

Similar findings have been offered by Morse (1972) and by Carpenter (1975). Morse reported that infants are able to perceive quite fine distinctions in vocal production at the age of one month; Carpenter found that infants spent significantly more time gazing at their mothers when the mother's voice was broadcast through a loudspeaker than when a stranger's voice was broadcast while the mother made lip movements. And some of the subjects indicated that they were disturbed if their mothers simply stared at them through the porthole without speaking.

Other evidence that unintelligible messages produce predictable responses is offered by Condon and Sander (1974), who found that babies only twelve hours old synchronized head and body movements to "live" voices as well as tape recordings of spoken English and spoken Chinese. These synchronized movements did not seem to be aroused by tape recordings of isolated vowel sounds or tapping noises. Based on this research, one could conclude that newborn babies have a built-in tendency to respond to the human voice—regardless of its intelligibility.

### B.F. Skinner's Verbal Summator: Self-Generated Cognitive Responses to Unintelligible Verbal Stimuli

In 1936, B.F. Skinner published an account of a "verbal summator" or "tautophone" which produced "certain elemental speech-sounds." Skinner viewed this device as "a sort of verbal ink blot" (1936, p. 71). According to his autobiographical *Shaping of a Behaviorist* (1979, pp. 174–176), Skinner's interest in responses to unintelligible messages developed when he was a graduate student. He had put his rats in their boxes and started his programming equipment one sunny Sunday morning. He was still using circuit breakers, and the friction drives under the four disks emitted a rhythmic pulse: "di-*dah*-di-di-*dah*—di-*dah*-di-di-*dah*." Suddenly he heard himself saying "You'll *never* get *out*. You'll *never* get *out*."

Skinner attributed the effect of this rhythmic stimulus to what Sherrington called summation: "An imitative response had joined forces with some latent behavior, which I could attribute to a rather obvious source: I was a prisoner in my laboratory on a lovely day" (1979, p. 174). Skinner had read about organ pipes that played vowel sounds in Sir Richard Paget's *Human Speech* (1930). Unable to duplicate the organ pipes, Skinner mixed stressed and unstressed vowel sounds in various patterns and designed a gadget attached to a portable phonograph which repeated these sounds (see Skinner 1936, pp. 104–107). "Played very quietly, or against a background noise, [the voice patterns] sounded like speech heard through a wall" (1979, p. 175).

Skinner viewed these patterns as "something like auditory ink blots, evoking strong latent verbal behavior" (1979, p. 175), and predicted potential benefit to clinicians: "The 'tautophone' might serve as a kind of auditory Rorschach test, with the advantage that the experimenter could easily control both the level of stimulus complexity and the number of repetitions" (p. 180).

Skinner collected a hundred or more responses an hour simply by having subjects listen to a pattern and state what they heard. Subjects' interpretations were often "significant—in the Freudian sense." For example, "when I showed the apparatus to a psychiatrist and played *I-uh-uh-A-uh,* he said at once, 'Oh, it says, I am a traitor, and I know why. I have just been telling a patient that I can help her and I am not sure I can' " (1979, p. 175). Clinicians using the machine reported that patients produced responses relevant to their personal needs. A man with a marked feeling of inferiority who had studied for the priesthood heard "You're a failure," "A faith hour," "Father O'Connor," and "Each hour of faith" (Shakow and Rosenzweig 1940). In a further application, Skinner reported that the verbal summator proved better than the Rorschach test at screening psychopathic criminals at the Recorder's Court in Detroit (1979, p. 362).

Skinner may have been the first to categorize cognitive elaborations to unintelligible messages. He coded responses as relevant to the external environment, the manner of presentation of the speech stimuli, or body state (1936, pp. 91–93, 100). Another Harvard graduate student, Mary Adah Trussell, compared responses to the verbal summator between psychology students and thirty-two patients in a psychopathic ward. "The groups differed on such things as number of meaningless responses, reference to external stimuli, references to special themes, and so on" (Skinner 1979, p. 362). Further, "W.K. Estes constructed a visual form in which subjects glimpsed meaningless phrases for a fraction of a second" (p. 362). Skinner supplies no further details on this early experimentation on cognitive responses to printed and auditory unintelligible communications.

### Dr. Fox and the Persuasive No-content Lecture: Achievement without Comprehension?

On the basis of evidence suggesting that student evaluations of teachers depend on personality variables and not on educational content, researchers Naftulin, Ware, and Donnelly programmed an actor to "teach charismatically and nonsubstantively on a topic about which he knew nothing" (1973, p. 630). The authors hypothesized that even experienced educators "can be seduced into feeling satisfied that they have learned despite irrelevant, conflicting, and meaningless content conveyed by the lecturer" (p. 630). The authors selected a professional actor "who looked distinguished and sounded authoritative," provided him with the title "Dr. Myron L. Fox, an authority on the application of mathematics to human behavior," dressed him up with a fictitious but impressive vita, and presented him "to a group of highly trained educators." His lecture was derived from a *Scientific American* article on game theory; he was coached to "present this topic and conduct his question-and-answer session with an excessive use of double-talk, neologisms, non sequiturs, and contradictory statements, all interspersed with parenthetical humor and meaningless references to unrelated topics" (pp. 631–632).

The professional educators rated "Dr. Fox" favorably on eight general items, including organization of material, use of examples, arousal of interest, and stimulation of thinking (but not agreement with content). The authors noted that their fifty-five professional educators "obviously failed as 'competent crap detectors,' " were "seduced by the style of Dr. Fox's presentation" (p. 633), and "considering the educational sophistication of the subjects, it is striking that none of them detected the lecture for what it was" (p. 663). The authors concluded: "Student satisfaction with learning may represent little more than the illusion of having learned" (p. 630).

Ware and Williams (1975) criticized the Dr. Fox demonstration by noting that no measure of actual learning was employed. They had the same Dr. Fox present a twenty-minute lecture on "the biochemistry of memory" to a total of 207 students; they replicated the favorable ratings given Dr. Fox's incoherent lecture and in addition measured actual learning. Ware and Williams simultaneously varied amount of content (26, 14 versus 4 substantive teaching points) and speaker "seductiveness," operationally defined as high versus low on a number of speaker-characteristics judged independent of content-coverage: "enthusiasm, humor, friendliness, expressiveness, charisma, and personality" (p. 151).

Ware and Williams reported significant main effects for both content and seductiveness on a 26-item *achievement* test: The higher the content of the lecture, the better the students did on the test. Further, the students who viewed lectures high in seduction did better on the achievement test than students who viewed the lecture designed to be low in seduction. The content by seductiveness interaction was not significant. The researchers concluded: "In terms of total variance accounted for, lecturer seduction appears to be the more important influence on test performance of the two characteristics studied" (p. 154). Contrasting the findings of this experiment to the Naftulin, Ware, and Donnelly (1973) demonstration, Ware and Williams (1975, p. 155) note: "The Doctor Fox Effect appears to be much more than an illusion. Whereas teaching style is a major factor in determining student ratings, it is also a powerful influence on student test performance."

### Anticipated Persuasion: Expectation Produces Attitude Change

Persuasion occurs simply through the anticipation of receiving a communication. These anticipatory opinion changes can be as large as changes resulting from actually receiving a persuasive communication (Cialdini and Petty 1981, p. 217). When people anticipate presenting a position on an issue in public, persuasion occurs in a direction favoring that position (for example, Greenwald 1968b). No shift occurs when people anticipate advocating a position in public but do not have to construct topic-related arguments (Cialdini 1971).

It appears that the anticipation of advocating a position produces persuasion by causing people to consider arguments related to the issue and to "bias their perceptions of the validity of these arguments" (Cialdini and Petty 1981, p. 219). When people expect to receive information that will attempt to change their views on a topic (forewarning), attitude change occurs against the direction advocated (for example, Hass and Grady 1975). In both cases, persuasion occurs with no message content presented.

*Self-Generated Persuasion: Thinking about a Topic*
*Changes Attitudes*

Tesser reported that simply thinking about something often polarizes one's initial feelings about that object (1978, p. 298). Tesser and Conlee (1975) gave subjects an attitude object, and asked them to think about the object for 30, 60, 90, or 180 seconds. Increasing polarization resulted from increases in time given to consider the arguments. Tesser summarized this study as follows: "The results are clear—polarization of attitudes [is] a monotonic function of time spent thinking about the issue" (1978, p. 300). This is another example of attitude change occurring independently of intelligible communications.

*There is No Isomorphic Memory*

Loftus demonstrated that memory is molded by social pressure and by a person's biases and stereotypes (1979; 1980). Memory is unreliable; there is no isomorphic memory. Cognitive response analysis suggests a similar model of persuasion: There is no "true message content," only the perception retained by each individual as unique cognitive responses are created and remembered, anchored to each recipient's biases. The impact of a unintelligible message on a recipient may be like Skinner's (1936) "verbal ink blot": Responses are elicited to the degree that audio stimuli match existing meaningful memories.

*Summary of Literature Reviewed*

The observations and empirical research reviewed suggests that persuasion does occur when message content is largely or completely absent. Persuasion occurs following exposure to unintelligible communications; that is, attitude change occurs without the possibility of comprehension. Further, people appear to generate attitude–object relevant cognitions even when no attitude–object or message exists.

We have examined an unusual but pervasive persuasion phenomenon: attitude change in the apparent absence of message content. Let us turn to one of the oldest areas of inquiry in social psychology, the study of attitude change, to see how existing theory and research explain these unusual persuasion phenomena.

## The Central Role of Message Content in Persuasion Research

The process of persuasion has typically been analyzed in terms of "who says what to whom, how, and with what effect" (Lasswell 1948). The first four parts of this statement refer to the major independent variables in persuasion research: source, message, recipient, and modality. The last part refers to the dependent measure: whether any attitude change has been produced.

Formulations of persuasion vary in the importance of message content, but all attitude-change theories assume that message content has a critical role. For example, one classic treatment of attitude-change theory (Hovland, Janis, and Kelley 1953, p. 12) specifies the research task as the analysis of four factors: (1) the communicator; (2) the stimuli transmitted by the communicator; (3) the audience, and (4) the responses made by the audience to the communication. Two chapters of this classic text were devoted to the second of these four factors: message content.

In another classic monograph, McGuire (1969) suggested several stages in persuasion: (1) attention (does the person hear or see the message?); (2) comprehension (does the person understand the arguments and what changes are expected?); and (3) yielding (does the person go along with the persuasive message?). The central role of message content is also stressed in recent work. A recent text states: "If the message is incomprehensible, or the person has no schema or framework for relating the message to his or her existing beliefs and values, then no processing can occur" (Petty 1981, p. 136). Thus, both classic and current treatments of the persuasion process regard message content as a central part of that persuasion process.

As an example of the acceptance of message comprehension as a necessary condition for "eliciting action," consider the popular text *Social Psychology* (Myers 1983), which includes a figure captioned: "A persuasive message must clear several hurdles" (p. 275). The first hurdle is "Pay attention to the message?" The second is "Comprehend it?" If one attends to a message but does not comprehend it, the message elicits no action.

## The Cognitive Response Approach to Persuasion

A relatively recent theoretical formulation in attitude change research is cognitive response theory (Brock 1967; Greenwald 1968). This approach has become an increasingly viable explanation for a variety of empirical findings and theoretical perspectives (Brock 1981, p. 2). The cognitive response approach to persuasion emphasizes the thoughts that people have while exposed to persuasive messages. When people receive persuasive communications, they attempt to relate the new information to their existing knowledge about the topic. In so doing, the person may consider cognitive material not in the communication itself (Petty, Ostrom, and Brock 1981, p. 13). These additional self-generated cognitions may agree, disagree, or be irrelevant to the communication. To the extent that the communication evokes supportive cognitive responses, the person will tend to agree with the source.

The cognitive response approach differs from approaches such as McGuire's approach (1969) to attitude change. McGuire assigned *learning of message content* a central role in the persuasion process. The cognitive response approach, on the other hand, does not hold that persuasion is dependent on comprehension of the persuasive communication. Indeed, Greenwald suggests that "persuasive communications can induce attitude change without necessarily providing the cognitive content on which the attitude is based" (1968, p. 149). The cognitive response approach postulates that the learning of one's own mental responses intereacts with other variables, such as one's personality and the nature of the situation, to produce persuasion (Perloff and Brock 1980, p. 68).

## The Active Role of the Message Recipient

A central assumption of the cognitive response approach to persuasion is that audiences are active in the persuasion process, providing cognitive material not in the original message. Further, the persistence of persuasion depends on the extent to which one rehearses these self-generated cognitive responses, rather than rehearsing responses based on the communciation such as paraphrases of message points (Petty 1977). It is derivable from this assumption that a message which maximizes self-generated responses will have more long-term effectiveness than a control message. Forcing a recipient of a persuasive message to rely on self-generated cognitive responses therefore may increase the effectiveness of that message. One way to prevent the paraphrasing of message points, and force the recipient to rely on self-generated responses to the message is to present a message that is meaningless or unintelligible—that is, largely or completely content-free.

## How Could an Unintelligible Message be More Persuasive?

As unintelligibility increases, reliance on self-generated responses should increase. A message with gaps may be *more* effective than a control message in which the gapped portions are filled with irrelevant material. This is because less message content is presented in the gapped message, and less message content should force the message recipient to rely more on his or her own cognitive responses, and increased reliance on his or her own cognitive responses produces increased persuasion. It has been shown that people will exert more physical effort to understand a message made partially unintelligible by static when the message is consonant than when the message is dissonant (Brock and Balloun 1967; cf. Kleinhesselink and Edwards 1975). The most extreme case, a message that is entirely unintelligible, or content-free, is interesting because acceptance of such a message does not follow readily from formulations which stress comprehension and understanding. Content-based formulations fail to account for persuasion occurring in the absence of message content. A cognitive response approach, emphasizing one's own responses rather than message-derived responses, can explain these examples. No research, however, has directly examined the problem of persuasion with unintelligible messages by using largely or totally unintelligible messages in an experimental setting.

Experimentally produced persuasion with a largely or totally unintelligible message would present a difficult case for adherents of comprehension-based theories of persuasion. Not only would such research contribute to an understanding of existing examples of persuasion in cases in which message content is partially or totally lacking, but such research would present an extreme test of cognitive response theory. Cognitive response theory assumes richer idiosyncratic cognitive elaboration as message content decreases; a completely content-free or totally unintelligible message should produce the maximum cognitive elaboration and perhaps maximum persistence of persuasion.

### An Analogy with Source Credibility

An analogy can be drawn between the source credibility literature (for example, Hass 1981) and persuasion with messages of varying intelligibility. It is proposed that a highly intelligible communication should be comparable in persuasive effect to a communication originating from a high-credibility source. A less intelligible message may be comparable to a communication originating from a low-credibility source. Both low-intelligible communications and low-credibility communications are pervasive in everyday life.

Few areas of research in social psychology have produced results as consistent as the findings that sources high in expertise or trustworthiness are more persuasive than those low in these qualities (Insko 1967; McGuire 1969). The expertise and trustworthiness of a message source were among the first topics studied by Hovland and his colleagues in their classic research on persuasion (for example, Hovland and Weiss 1951).

More recent research has attempted to determine the variables that interact with source credibility. For example, Sternthal, Dholakia, and Leavitt (1978) reported that a low-credibility source induced greater persuasion than one of high credibility when the issue was one toward which subjects had a positive initial disposition. "Presumably, the less credible source engendered the motivation to generate supporting arguments to bolster advocacy; a highly credible source produced the feeling that the position was already adequately represented, and further bolstering was not needed" (Sternthal, Phillips, and Dholakia 1978). An analogous argument could be offered for messages that vary in intelligibility: An unintelligible message should produce greater persuasion when the subjects have positive initial dispositions, since the lower intelligibility message would tend to motivate people to generate supporting arguments to bolster the less-than-clear message. An intelligible message should be less likely to engender such a bolstering attempt than an unintelligible message, and thus could produce less persuasion.

## Hypotheses

We made four predictions:

1. A substantial portion of people will make evaluative assessments of and offer cognitive responses to unintelligible messages.

2. Increased unintelligibility should produce increased cognitive elaboration, as a function of total number of thoughts: If total thoughts remain constant, more idiosyncratic responses will occur as a function of unintelligibility.

3. Greater credibility increases message acceptance to both unintelligible and intelligible messages.

4. Persons high in Need for Cognition may be more likely to be persuaded by unintelligible messages than people who are low in Need for Cognition.

## The Six Experiments

### Participants and Materials

We tested several hundred undergraduates at Ohio State University and at Marshall University. An experimental booklet contained semantic differential and Likert-type attitude measures identical to those used by Petty, Cacioppo, and Goldman (1981, p. 850). Cognitive response measures were included, identical to those used in Brock (1967). Both sets of dependent measures are described below.

### Apparatus

Students were tested in university language laboratory cubicles designed so that no student could have verbal contact with any other student. Visual contact was limited; students could only see the back of the student sitting directly ahead. A master tape player provided control over the volume delivered to each of the individual consoles through personal headphones. Volume could be adjusted in the individual consoles.

### Procedure

Students heard one message and then the other over headphones. Order was counterbalanced; while half the students heard message 1, the others heard message 2. See figure 12–1 for a schematic of the design in Experiments 1 and 2. The procedure in each experiment went as follows:

> Welcome to Experiment SB6. As some of you already know, the Psycholinguistics Department has contracted out these language facilities and is completing a series of studies on language perception and translation effectiveness. Today you will hear excerpts of position statements delivered recently at the United Nations Conference on Nuclear Arms Limitation. You will help us in our research by giving your honest ratings of these position statements. Your contributions will be submitted to the United Nations' Translator Ministry after the Final Report is prepared by the Department of Linguistics.

| Order 1 | Intro-duc-tion | English-Chinese message (45 sec) | English message (3 min) | Sub-jects complete attitude measures and thought listings | Greek message (3 min) | Subjects complete attitude measures and thought listings again |
|---|---|---|---|---|---|---|
| Order 2 | | | Greek message (3 min) | | English message (3 min) | |

**Figure 12-1. Flow of Events in Experiment I**

One final note. In some cases, we could not supply the simultaneous translations. We regret this, but as it is essential that each of you answer all the questions for this research project, we ask that you *do your best*.

Students first heard a brief English message and then a Greek, or other foreign language or filtered English message (in Order 1). Order of languages was reversed in Order 2. Each message was taped by the same speaker. Following the messages, students read these comments on their booklets:

Because your personal opinion on the position statement you just heard may in-fluence your response to the ratings of the acoustical quality of the message, we need a measure of your own opinion on this issue. Please rate the long statement you just heard on the following scales.

Following these instructions were four nine-point semantic differential scales (good/bad, beneficial/harmful, foolish/wise, and unfavorable/favorable). Preceding both these scales and the instructions was an eleven-point scale anchored by 1—"do not agree at all," and 11—"agree completely." The instructions for this scale were "Please rate your agreement with the message you just heard by making an X somewhere on these scales." Students then responded to several additional scales designed to maintain the cover story: ratings of speaker voice quality, enthusiasm, and general delivery. Next, the experimenter read standard thought-listing instruc-tions to the participants (for example, Cacioppo, Harkins, and Petty 1981).

Finally, students were asked to indicate whether they understood any of the foreign-language message, to guess what language it was in, and to make any other comments they wished. Following this, they were debriefed, their credit slips were signed, and they were thanked and dismissed.

Two judges, blind to the experimental condition, later rated the thoughts that subjects listed as either *speaker relevant, message relevant,* or *irrelevant.* Judges agreed on 86 percent of the statements across experiments. In cases of disagreement between judges, a third judge's opinion was obtained. Manipulations of message length, number of repetitions, and source credibility were added as an additional between-subjects factor in Experiments 3, 4, and 5. See figure 12–2 for the design of Experiment 4.

## Results

Six experiments provided direct evidence that unintelligible messages produce message acceptance, and by implication, persuasion. In Experiment 1, a majority of students provided evaluative ratings and listed cognitive elaborations to a foreign language (Greek) communication which nearly all claimed not to have understood. Experiment 2 replicated the first experiment with a different speaker and extended the effect to a message rendered unintelligible by electronic filtering. In Experiment 3, increased message length did not lead to increased agreement with an unintelligible message, but in Experiment 4 increased repetitions of both intelligible and unintelligible communications produced similar patterns of unfavorable cognitive responses and speaker-relevant cognitive responses, as indicated by tables 12–1 and 12–2. Experiment 5 demonstrated that increased source credibility produced greater agreement to an intelligible message and to an unintelligible message as well (table 12–3). In Experiment 6, unintelligible messages were shown to produce more agreement and cognitive elaborations than a control no-message condition. Further, in every experiment, the number of cognitive elaborations divided by total thoughts listed was greater in response to unintelligible messages than to intelligible messages (table 12–4). To summarize the findings across all experiments:

- Most university students agreed with and listed cognitive responses to a variety of unintelligible communications (every experiment).
- Persuasion processes with unintelligible communications were similar to persuasion processes using intelligible messages (Experiments 4 and 5).
- An unintelligible communication evinced more cognitive responses and more favorable ratings than a nonmessage control (Experiment 6).
- The unintelligible messages produced increased cognitive elaboration as a function of total number of thoughts generated (in each of the first five experiments, a higher proportion of idiosyncratic thoughts were produced in response to the unintelligible message than to the intelligible message. Experiment 6 did not use an intelligible message).

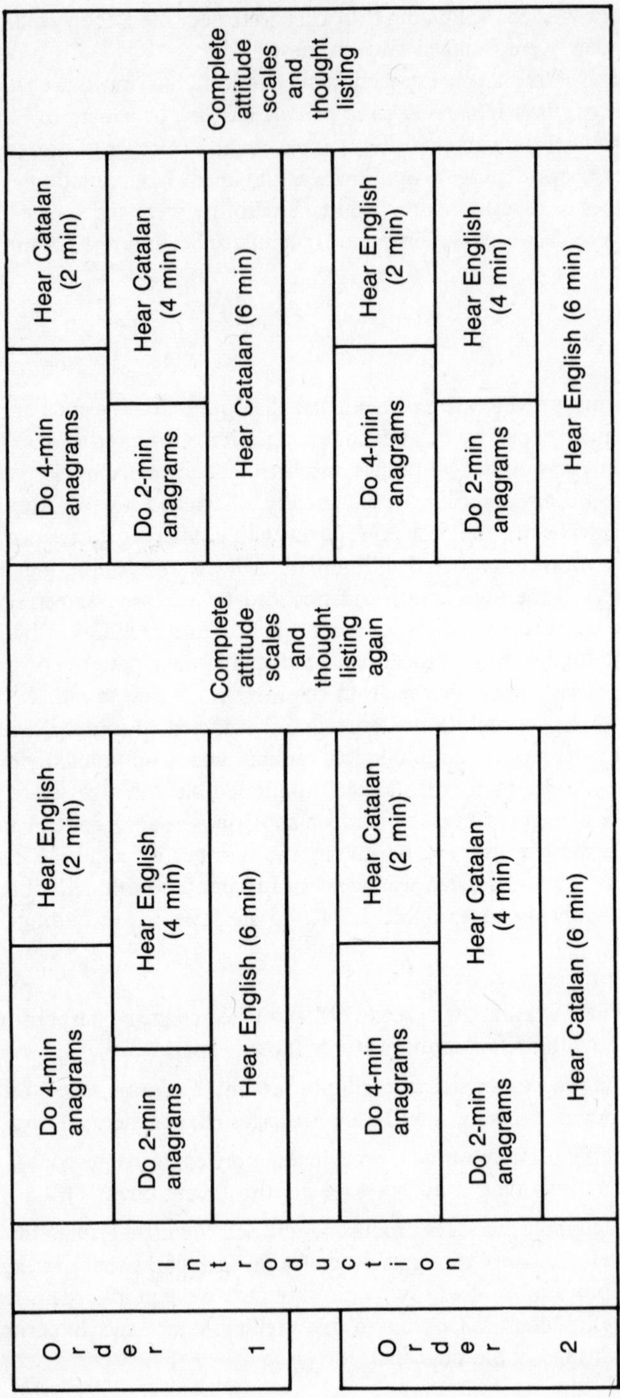


**Figure 12–2. Flow of Events in Experiment IV**

**Table 12-1**
**Descriptive Statistics for Unfavorable Thoughts by Repetition and Intelligibility (English vs. Catalan) in Experiment IV**

| Order 1: English first (n = 21) | | | |
|---|---|---|---|
| Repetition | 1 | 2 | 3 | Marginal |
| English | 1.62 (2.29) | 3.10 (2.74) | 2.33 (1.74) | 2.35[a] 63 |
| Catalan | 1.33 (1.83) | 2.10 (2.10) | 1.48 (2.40) | 1.63[b] 63 |
| Marginal | 1.48[a] 42 | 2.60[a] 42 | 1.90[a] 42 | 1.99 126 |

| Order 2: Catalan first (n = 21) | | | |
|---|---|---|---|
| Repetition | 1 | 2 | 3 | Marginal |
| Catalan | 1.48 (1.60) | 2.14 (1.96) | 1.38 (1.47) | 1.67[a] 63 |
| English | 1.67 (2.08) | 3.05 (1.72) | 2.43 (2.11) | 2.38[b] 63 |
| Marginal | 1.57[a] 42 | 2.60[a] 42 | 1.90[a] 42 | 2.02 126 |

Note: Statistics are presented as Mean/$sd$. Marginal means in any given row or column with different superscript are significantly different by the Newman-Keuls procedure, $p < .05$.

• Students high in Need for Cognition (Cacioppo and Petty 1982) were more persuaded by unintelligible messages than students low in Need for Cognition (Experiments 3 and 4).

These findings were demonstrated in standard laboratory settings with standard experimental social psychological procedures. Dependent measures were summated ratings scales (Likert 1932), semantic differentials (Osgood, Suci, and Tannenbaum 1957) and cognitive response measures based on techniques introduced by Brock (1967) and Greenwald (1968) and used as standard contemporary research tools (for example, Petty, Ostrom, and Brock 1981).

Four different methods of operationalizing unintelligible verbal communications were used. These included Greek (Experiments 1 and 2), Catalan (Experiment 4), Italian (Experiments 5 and 6), and electronically filtered English (Experiment 2). All methods of operationalizing unintelligible speech proved successful as hypothesized (Experiment 3 did not support the hypothesis with Greek as the unintelligible language, but Experiment 1, also with Greek, did support the hypothesis). Different speakers were used: a native Greek in two experiments; a native English speaker for the experiment with the filtered English message; a native Italian and a well-practiced Catalan speaker for two other experiments.

**Table 12-2**
**Analysis of Variance Summary Table on Number of Unfavorable Thoughts Generated in Experiment IV**

| Source of Variance | Sum of Squares | df | F | p |
|---|---|---|---|---|
| Repetition (A) | 49.56 | 2 | 4.31 | .016 |
| linear trend | 5.85 | 1 | 1.02 | ns |
| quadratic trend | 43.71 | 1 | 7.61 | <.01 |
| Order (B) | .06 | 1 | .01 | .92 |
| AB | .13 | 2 | .01 | .99 |
| Subjects/AB | 689.24 | 120 | | |
| Intelligibility (C) | 32.14 | 1 | 12.80 | .0005 |
| AC | 7.14 | 2 | 1.42 | .25 |
| BC | .00 | 1 | .00 | 1.00 |
| ABC | .29 | 2 | .06 | .94 |
| Subjects x C/AB | 301.43 | 120 | | |

**Table 12-3**
**Analysis of Variance Summary Table on Agreement with the Persuasive Message in Experiment V**

| Source of Variance | Sum of Squares | df | F | p |
|---|---|---|---|---|
| Credibility (A) | 113.19 | 1 | 26.57 | .0001 |
| Order (B) | 0.94 | 1 | .22 | .64 |
| AB | 1.57 | 1 | .37 | .55 |
| Subjects/AB | 204.51 | 48 | | |
| Intelligibility (C) | 35.11 | 1 | 16.28 | .0002 |
| AC | .16 | 1 | .07 | .79 |
| BC | 3.65 | 1 | 1.69 | .20 |
| ABC | 4.64 | 1 | 2.15 | .15 |
| Subjects x C/AB | 90.58 | 42 | | |

**Table 12-4**
**Analysis of Variance Summary Table on Idiosyncratic Thoughts in Experiment III**

| Source of Variance | Sum of Squares | df | F | p |
|---|---|---|---|---|
| Length (A) | .19 | 2 | .72 | .49 |
| Order (B) | 2.18 | 1 | 16.97 | .0001 |
| AB | .78 | 2 | 3.01 | .055 |
| Subjects/AB | 10.83 | 84 | | |
| Intelligibility (C) | 1.42 | 1 | 17.68 | .0001 |
| AC | .27 | 2 | 1.65 | .20 |
| BC | .05 | 1 | .60 | .44 |
| ABC | .09 | 2 | .58 | .56 |
| Subjects x C/AB | 6.77 | 84 | | |

## Changes Necessary in Persuasion Theory

These robust findings pose a far-reaching difficulty for all models of persuasion that assume that the understanding, comprehension, and meaning inherent in a communication are *necessary* components of the attitude-change process. The comprehension component was crucial in the influential theories of Hovland, Janis, and Kelley (1953) and McGuire (1969), and comprehension has been assumed in the theoretical formulations of Greenwald (1968b) and Eagly (1974). But a message that is devoid of meaning, such as filtered speech, or (for our subjects) modern Greek, cannot be "understood" or "comprehended" in the sense in which comprehension-based theories use these terms.

Theories that say that comprehension is message-based are the traditional models of social psychology and have served a central role in guiding mainstream research. However, these theories have not been tested under extreme conditions, such as with unintelligible messages, until now. One contemporary formulation, cognitive response theory (Petty, Ostrom, and Brock 1981) could account for many of the present results, although the finding that cognitive elaboration is abetted by unintelligibility appears to undermine a key assumption of routes-to-persuasion theories (for example, Chaiken 1980; Petty and Cacioppo 1981).

The present preferred formulation emphasizes own thoughts (Perloff and Brock 1980). The results showed that a meaningless message could suffice to instigate sufficient own thoughts for confident reporting of differential message acceptance. The locus of meaning, on which acceptance is based, was not anywhere in the message but in the self-originated elaborations of the message recipient.

Implications for advertising include renewed attention to the role of "logical" presentation of product information versus nonverbal, pseudoverbal, or nonrational categories of product information.

# Part V
# Music and Art
# in Advertising

# 13

# Let the Music Play:
# Music as a Nonverbal Element
# in Television Commercials

*Patricia A. Stout*
*John D. Leckenby*

F ew people escape the tug of music at their heartstrings. Advertising practitioners generally agree that music adds energy to the message and stimu-
lates the listener (Reinhard n.d.; Hecker 1984). And yet, the impact of music
on people's response to television commercials has received scant attention by advertising researchers.

Research into the effects of characteristics of television commercial appeals
has a long history in advertising research (Percy 1983). But recent theoretical work
on ad-induced changes in attitude (Mitchell and Olson 1981) has sparked interest
in the importance of the nonverbal characteristics of commercials. The notion
of central and peripheral processing (Petty and Cacioppo 1983) suggests that
peripheral cues, like music, can lead to attitude to the ad and transfer to attitude
to the brand.

In response, advertising researchers are examining more closely the effect of
specific advertising elements upon communication response. Stewart and Furse
(1987) analyzed 1,000 television commercials using over 150 elements, including
verbal and nonverbal variables. Haley (1984) looked at the effect of 17 areas of
nonverbal communication on recall and attitude in 47 commercials.

Since television commercials are delicately orchestrated combinations of sight
and sound, it would be erroneous to suggest that music alone is responsible for
the viewer's response to the ad. However, music is pervasive in commercials,
and its effects are documented in the psychology and music theory literature.
Without a doubt, the power of music to communicate deserves more rigorous
study.

In this paper, we explore the relationship of music and people's response
to advertising. We review previous research in psychology, music theory, and consumer behavior on the effects of music. Research by the authors is presented,
and suggestions are made for future research on the effects of music on advertising response.

## Previous Research

A review of the literature in psychology, music theory, and consumer behavior yields numerous studies investigating the impact of music. However, this research provides little direct insight into the expected effects of music on consumer response to television commercials. Generally, previous studies have focused on the impact of music examined either as a single structural element (like tempo [fast/slow], volume [loud/soft], mode [major/minor] ), or when used only as background. Such simplistic consideration of music necessarily limits the generalizability of the findings to television commercials where music is a complex element, woven into a complicated pattern of sound, movement, and drama. Generally speaking, research studies on music fit into one of two major categories: (1) the effects of music on behavior and (2) the effects of music on affective response, including preference for and emotional suggestiveness of a musical piece.

### Effects of Music on Behavior

Studies in this category examine music as the independent variable associated with various behavioral dependent variables. Two studies look at the effects of the structural elements of volume and tempo on purchasing behavior. Smith and Curnow (1966) found that with loud music, consumers spent less time in the store, although there was no difference in sales or customer satisfaction. Milliman (1982) examined the effects of background music on in-store shopping behavior, finding that music tempo variations significantly affect the pace of in-store traffic flow and sales volume.

Global affect or liking of the music has an impact on product choice behavior. Gorn (1982) found product choice associated with subjects' liking or disliking of background music which accompanied an ad for the product. Subjects avoided choosing the product associated with disliked music. Gorn suggests that through classical conditioning, a product becomes associated with the positive emotions of liked music. When background music was presented, a commercial's emotional appeal appeared to be more influential than product attribute statements in affecting product preference.

The emotional suggestiveness of a piece of music also appears to have an effect on behavior. For example, Biller, Olson, and Breen (1974) found that "sad" music lessened state anxiety of subjects more than did happy music.

### Effects of Music on Affective Response

Research concerning how people feel about music most often examined specific structural elements of music. These studies tend to focus on either (1) a general feeling of global affect or liking of a piece of music or (2) a specific emotional state or mood evoked by the music. Vitz (1966) found that global affect or liking for a piece of music (measured as ratings of pleasantness of a sequence of tones), increases up to a certain point with increasing variation in the sequences of tones, before it decreases. Bradley (1971) found that repetition of a piece of music over time increased preference for the piece. When investigating the emotional suggestiveness of music, Rigg (1940) found that tempo has more influence. The faster tempo tends to make music "happy" (as judged by listeners), and slowing the tempo has the opposite effect of making music "sad."

Quite often the structural elements of major and minor mode are examined for their impact on affective response. Mode is the arrangement of the eight notes or tones of an octave as major or minor. Hevner (1935) suggests that major and minor modes are a more important influence on feelings and moods than tempo or rhythm. Music in a major mode was equated with "happiness," "gaiety," "playfulness," and "sprightliness," whereas music in a minor mode was equated with "sadness," "sentimental yearning," and "tender effects."

In an attempt to look at major/minor mode in combination with visual stimuli, Parrott (1982) exposed subjects to several different paintings previously judged to be "happy" or "sad." This exposure was accompanied by different pieces of music, also previously determined to be "happy" or "sad." He found a conditioned emotional response to music, with the effects of music and painting being additive: "Happy" paintings accompanied by "happy" music achieved a higher "happy" judgment by subjects and a "sad" painting accompanied by "happy" music achieved a lower rating.

Consumer researchers have recently focused on the impact of music upon consumer response to advertising. These studies have examined the impact of music versus no music on both affective and cognitive dependent measures. Park and Young (1986) examined the effects of music on attitude to the ad, the brand, and behavioral intent under different conditions of involvement. With low involvement, music facilitated more favorable brand attitude and behavioral intent among consumers. But if consumers are very cognitively involved, music has a distracting effect (and both brand attitude and behavioral intent are less favorable). When consumers were highly emotionally involved, the effect of music was unclear.

Alpert and Alpert (1986) manipulated the musical structural elements of modality, tempo, dynamics, and rhythm leading to music perceived as happy or sad. These two pieces of music, as well as no music, were presented as background with three different simulated greeting card advertisements. Subjects' moods, perceptions of the card's "mood," and purchase intention were measured. Although results were not clear-cut, music had at least a directional effect on subjects' moods and perceived card "mood." For subjects' moods, happy music generally produced higher "happiness" scores, followed by no music and then sad music. Results were not as clear for perceived card "mood." For purchase intent, cards appearing with sad music were significantly more likely to be selected than cards appearing with happy music.

Stout and Rust (1986) examined the effect of music on emotional and cognitive responses to advertising. They found no significant differences between two commercials (similar except for the use of background music) on recall or the most involving level of emotional response, "experiential." The commercial without music, however, was liked more and elicited more "descriptive" and "empathic" emotional responses. (A detailed explanation of this typology follows below.) It appears that music inhibits generalized affect and the less involving levels of emotional response. This may have occurred because the music used in the commercial was disliked. Haley (1984) found that sometimes nonverbal effects are more likely to be negative than positive.

Thus previous research has focused on two major features of music of particular interest to advertisers: (1) presence or absence of music, and (2) the structural elements of the music, including tempo, volume, mode, and presence of a distinct melody. Advertising practitioners suggest that music can play many roles in advertising (Hecker 1984). Music can create excitement or relaxation, attract attention, and so forth. The effectiveness of music in a commercial depends upon its intended role in the creative execution. This suggests a third important feature of music, the role music plays in the commercial. Previous research (Stewart and Furse 1986) has examined the effects of variables, including the use of a jingle, if the music is readily identified with the brand and the use of lyrics to carry the message, upon advertising recall and persuasion.

To date there has been a paucity of research in advertising examining the relationship between consumer response and the various elements that comprise a musical composition. In the next section we review the findings of research which examines a pool of fifty professionally produced commercials. Although basically descriptive in nature, our intent is to discover some important relationships between music and measures of advertising response. Although the sample size limits the generalizability of the relationships presented, this research provides a foundation for more controlled studies in the future.

## Methodology

### Subjects and Data Collection Procedure

In the research that follows, data were collected by a professional research firm using mall intercepts in several cities across the United States. Completed questionnaires for fifty commercials were provided by 1,498 respondents, 90 percent of whom were female. Each respondent individually viewed only one commercial. Thirty different respondents (except for one commercial with only twenty-eight respondents) provided data for each of the fifty commercials.

An instrument similar to the Viewer Reward Profile (VRP) was used (Schlinger 1979). After viewing the commercial, respondents answered several open-ended questions. Respondents also indicated their degree of agreement with fifty-two statements about the advertising and the product, using a six-point rating scale (where 1 = strongly disagree and 6 = strongly agree). Routine data on product usage and standard demographic information were also collected. Responses to the open-ended questions were analyzed for emotional response. The questions asked were: (1) "Now, I'd like you to tell me what happened to you as you were looking at the commercial. What thoughts or ideas went through your mind, and what feelings did you have?" and (2) "Did anything else come to your mind while looking at the commercial that you would like to mention?"

### Stimulus Objects

Fifty finished, thirty-second television commercials were tested. Commercials were for frequently purchased consumer goods in nine different product categories, including flavored and instant coffees, soft drinks, candy, pudding, muffins, beauty aids, laundry detergent, and a fast-food restaurant. Eleven different brands were represented, with the number of executions per brand ranging from two to ten.

The commercials were created by a major New York advertising agency and tested using the VRP between 1980 and 1984. Eight percent of the commercials had been aired prior to testing and may have been viewed by members of the sample, although this information was not collected.

### Measures

Two main types of measures were taken: (1) commercials were content-coded on several music variables in three broad categories, and (2) viewers' cognitive and emotional responses to the commercials were collected using the VRP.

A review of the above literature guided development of a coding scheme consisting of three broad categories. First, the presence or absence of music was determined. Of the fifty commercials in the sample, ten had no music present and forty had music present. Second, structural elements of the music, including mode, volume, tempo, and a distinct melody were coded. Mode was measured as major, minor, or mixed (when coders could not clearly distinguish between major and minor mode). Volume was measured on a five-point scale from "soft" to "loud." Tempo was measured on a five-point scale from "slow" to "fast." A distinct melody was indicated as present or absent based on the coders' judgment. Third, the complexity of music's use in the commercial included measures of the presence or absence of a jingle, whether or not the lyrics carried the product message, and whether or not the music was readily identifiable with the brand.

The fifty commercials were independently coded by two coders. A third coder resolved disagreements. Although the coders were not music experts, they all had some formal music training.

Measures of three progressively involved levels of intensity of emotional response ("descriptive," "empathic," and "experiential") and brand recall were collected by content-coding each verbatim response. "Descriptive" emotional response indicates the individual's ability to recognize emotions expressed by others. Simple

**Table 13–1**

**VRP Scalar Item Statements with Variable Names**

| Variable Name | Statement |
|---|---|
| 1. DEPENDABLE | I know that the advertised brand is a dependable, reliable one. |
| 2. SOOTHING | The commercial was soothing. |
| 3. ANNOYING | The commercial irritated me—it was annoying. |
| 4. RIGHT IN | I felt as though I was right there in the commercial experiencing the same thing. |
| 5. USEFUL | During the commercial I thought how that product might be useful to me. |
| 6. DISHONEST | What they said about the product was dishonest. |
| 7. DULL | It was dull and boring. |
| 8. ADVANTAGES | The commercial showed me the product has certain advantages. |
| 9. LEARNED | I learned something from the commercial that I didn't know before. |
| 10. POOR TASTE | The commercial was in poor taste. |
| 11. NOT BUY | As I watched, I thought of reasons why I would not buy the product. |
| 12. IRRELEVANT | I don't see how the product has much to do with what was being shown in the commercial. |
| 13. IMPORTANT | The commercial message was important for me. |
| 14. NOT MY NEED | The commercial didn't have anything to do with me or my needs. |
| 15. TIRED | I've seen this commercial so many times—I'm tired of it. |
| 16. WILL BUY | I will definitely buy the brand in the commercial. |
| 17. DIDN'T DEMONSTATE | What they showed didn't demonstrate the claims they were making about the product. |
| 18. LIKE TO TRY | The commercial told about a product I think I'd like to try. |
| 19. LOTS OF FUN | The commercial was lots of fun to watch and listen to. |
| 20. ALL ALIKE | There's no real difference between the product and its competitors. They're all pretty much alike. |
| 21. DISSATISFIED | The commercial reminded me that I'm dissatisfied with what I'm using now and I'm looking for something better. |
| 22. ATTENTION | The characters (or persons) in the commercial capture your attention. |
| 23. NOT LISTEN | I was so busy watching the screen, I didn't listen to the talk. |
| 24. FAVORABLE VIEW | The commercial strengthened my favorable views about the brand. |
| 25. FARFETCHED | It was an unrealistic commercial—very farfetched. |
| 26. SILLY | The commercial was silly. |
| 27. ENTHUSIASM | The enthusiasm of the commercial is catching—it picks you up. |
| 28. EFFORT | It required a lot of effort to follow the commercial. |
| 29. EXAGGERATED | The commercial made exaggerated (and untrue) claims about the product. |
| 30. CLEVER | I thought it was clever and quite entertaining. |
| 31. HOW I FEEL | I felt that the commercial was acting out what I feel like at times. |
| 32. AMUSING | The commercial was amusing. |
| 33. TENDER | The commercial was tender. |
| 34. DISAGREE | I found myself disagreeing with some things in the commercial. |
| 35. NEW IDEA | The commercial gave me a new idea. |
| 36. RIGHT FOR ME | The commercial made me feel the product is right for me. |

*Table 13–1 continued*

| Variable Name | Statement |
| --- | --- |
| 37. DREAMY | The commercial was dreamy. |
| 38. RECOMMEND | That's a good brand, and I wouldn't hesitate recommending it to others |
| 39. PERSONAL | I liked the commercial because it was personal and intimate. |
| 40. PLAYFUL | The commercial was playful. |
| 41. TRY BRAND | The commercial made me think I might try the brand—just to see if it's as good as they say. |
| 42. SAW BEFORE | Saw before |
| 43. EXCITING | Exciting |
| 44. FAMILIAR | Familiar |
| 45. REALISTIC | The commercial was very realistic—that is, true to life. |
| 46. INSULTS | That commercial insults my intelligence. |
| 47. SAMETHING | This kind of commercial has been done so many times—it's the same old thing. |
| 48. TALK DOWN | I felt the commercial talked down to me. |
| 49. COMPLEX | It was too complex. I wasn't sure what was going on. |
| 50. UNIQUE | The commercial was unique. |
| 51. MORE INFORMATION | I would be interested in getting more information about the product. |
| 52. UNDESIRABLE | The commercial described certain specific characteristics that are undesirable to me. |

recognition does not mean that the individual necessarily has experienced any emotion herself, however. "Empathic" and "experiential" emotional response represent two additional levels with which individuals respond to advertising with feelings that might be entirely different from those expressed by the characters in an ad. Empathy is defined as feeling the same emotion a character feels, and indicates the capacity for participating in another's feelings or ideas. Experiential emotional response signifies a depth of feeling occurring as reaction to self-relevant events. Such events can be real or imagined, past or anticipated, depending upon the individual's interpretation of the event in relationship to goals she holds at the time. (Further detail on the emotional response measures can be found in Stout 1985; Stout and Leckenby 1985, forthcoming).

Responses to the fifty-two scalar items provided additional measures on the dependent variables. Table 13–1 presents statements from the VRP and the variable names used here.

The 1,498 verbatim responses to the open-ended questions on the VRP were independently coded by two coders. Ten percent of the total sample was coded by both coders to determine intercoder reliability, with each coder then coding half of the remaining commercial pool. Using the composite reliability coefficient equation (Holsti 1969), intercoder reliability was calculated at .72 for emotional responses and .97 for brand recall. Scalar item data from the VRP was coded by an independent research firm in New York.

# Findings

## Commercials With and Without Music Compared

First, results were obtained on several measures of advertising response, for both commercials with music (n = 40) and commercials without music (n = 10). Proportions were obtained for the three levels of intensity of emotional response: experiential, empathic, and descriptive. Means were obtained on the number of brand mentions and the fifty-two VRP scalar items.

On each of these measures, the commercials with music are compared to the commercials without music, and the significance of the difference between the two groups is tested. The responses for the emotional response levels were either present or absent, which resulted in a sample proportion exhibiting the relevant emotional response. Other measures resulted in a mean response, since those measures were interval or ratio in measurement level.

The appropriate statistical test for comparing the groups on the emotional response measures is a standard normal $z$-test for the comparison of proportions. The appropriate statistical test for the comparison of the groups for the other measures is the between groups $t$-test for the comparison of means.

The results of the data are summarized in table 13–2. Results of the data analysis indicate there was no significant difference (at the .05 level) between the two groups of commercials on any of the three levels of emotional response. There was also no significant difference on brand recall ($p$ = .89). If we are willing to accept a .10 level of significance, purchase intent (measured by the VRP statement, "I will definitely buy the brand in the commercial") was significant ($p$ = .09), with commercials with music scoring higher. Of the fifty-two scalar items, only four were significant at the .05 level: "learned," "tired," "samething," and "talkdown." Respondents felt they learned more from commercials without music. However, they also felt the commercials without music were something they had seen done too many times before, and that the commercial "talked down" to them. Generally, it seems that respondents had a more negative attitude toward the commercials without music.

At a .05 significance level, an analysis of this type would be expected to yield about three variables significant by chance. However, given the similarity of feelings indicated by three of the four significant variables (that is, "tired," "samething," and "talkdown"), it appears that something other than chance is at work here.

## How People Feel about Commercials

A look at the forty commercials with music examined the relationship between the seven structural elements of music and the fifty-two VRP scalar items. The music measures were nominal (present/absent) and interval level data. For this analysis, each measure was classified in a limited number of discrete groups (for example, high and low; fast, moderate, and slow). Mode had the largest number

**Table 13–2**
**Comparison of Mean Responses on VRP Scalar Items, Levels of Emotional Response, and Brand Recall for Commercials with and without Music**

| Variable | With Music (n = 40) | Without Music (n = 10) | Comparison Statistic | Two-tailed Significance |
|---|---|---|---|---|
| | *Means* | | | |
| Learned | 2.7 | 3.2 | $t = 2.43$ | .02 |
| Tired | 2.3 | 2.7 | $t = 2.45$ | .02 |
| Samething | 3.0 | 3.4 | $t = 2.85$ | .01 |
| Talkdown | 2.5 | 2.8 | $t = 2.40$ | .02 |
| Will buy | 4.3 | 3.9 | $t = -1.75$ | .09 |
| Brand recall | .96 | .99 | $t = .14$ | .89 |
| | *Proportions* | | | |
| Experiential emotional response | .37 | .35 | $z = -.56$ | .58 |
| Empathic emotional response | .11 | .07 | $z = -1.10$ | .28 |
| Descriptive emotional response | .11 | .11 | $z = .14$ | .28 |

of significant variables, followed by tempo and melody. For volume, none of the fifty-two items were significant at the .05 level.

For mode, major and mixed mode scored higher on all variables except "not buy," "not my need," "farfetched," and "exaggerates." These four variables tend to indicate a negative evaluation of the ad. The remaining ten variables seem to indicate a more positive evaluation of the ad, seeing it as providing useful, important information about the brand as well as being more on target with the respondent's personal feelings (for example, "how I felt," "right for me," "personal," "realistic"). There is also a greater intent to purchase for ads in major mode. The results of this analysis are presented in table 13–3.

Table 13–4 presents a comparison of the mean responses on the fifty-two VRP items for commercials with slow, moderate, and fast tempo. Eleven statements were significant at the .05 level. Generally, a faster tempo elicited higher mean scores on the more positive scalar items, including "tender" and "advantages." Commercials with slow tempo were rated higher on "not my need," "not listening," "farfetched," "effort," and "insults." Commercials with a moderate tempo scored highest on "dishonest," "tired," "all alike," and "disagree."

In table 13–5, results of a comparison of the fifty-two VRP statement means for commercials with and without a distinct melody are presented. Eight statements are significant at the .05 level. Commercials with a distinct melody scored higher on "dishonest" and "attention" (where the characters in the commercial capture the viewer's attention), indicating that viewers were paying close attention to the commercial message. Commercials without a distinct melody scored higher on "lots of fun," "enthusiasm," "clever," "amusing," "exciting," and "unique." For these

**Table 13-3**
**Comparison of Mean Responses on VRP Scalar Items for Commercials in Major, Minor, or Mixed Mode**

| Variable | Major Mode (n = 9) | Minor Mode (n = 9) | Mixed Mode (n = 22) | Significance (p values) |
|---|---|---|---|---|
| Useful | 4.3 | 3.6 | 4.1 | .02 |
| Not buy | 2.0 | 2.4 | 2.3 | .01 |
| Important | 3.7 | 3.1 | 3.5 | .03 |
| Not my need | 2.5 | 3.2 | 2.8 | .01 |
| Will buy | 4.6 | 4.0 | 4.2 | .04 |
| Favorable views | 4.0 | 3.5 | 4.0 | .01 |
| Farfetched | 2.5 | 3.3 | 2.7 | .04 |
| Exaggerates | 2.0 | 2.5 | 2.2 | .04 |
| How I feel | 3.5 | 3.0 | 3.6 | .05 |
| Tender | 4.0 | 3.1 | 3.9 | .02 |
| Right for me | 4.2 | 3.4 | 3.9 | .01 |
| Personal | 3.8 | 3.0 | 3.7 | .05 |
| Try brand | 4.3 | 3.9 | 4.2 | .03 |
| Realistic | 3.6 | 2.8 | 3.5 | .04 |

ads, viewers found the executions without a distinct melody different from what they were accustomed to seeing.

Commercials were also examined using the role of the music in the execution. The results of these analyses are presented in table 13–6. A comparison of mean responses on the fifty-two VRP items for commercials where music was or was not readily identified with the brand found significant differences ($p < .05$) for ten of the items. When music was identified with the brand, commercials were regarded more positively by respondents (scoring high on "favorable views," "realistic," and "right for me") and were rated as more informative (scoring high

**Table 13-4**
**Comparison of Mean Responses on VRP Scalar Items for Commercials with Slow, Moderate, and Fast Tempo**

| Variable | Slow (n = 22) | Moderate (n = 8) | Fast (n = 10) | Significance (p values) |
|---|---|---|---|---|
| Dishonest | 2.2 | 2.3 | 1.9 | .02 |
| Advantages | 3.9 | 4.1 | 4.4 | .05 |
| Not my need | 3.0 | 2.8 | 2.4 | .01 |
| Tired | 2.2 | 2.6 | 2.2 | .02 |
| All alike | 2.7 | 3.1 | 2.8 | .02 |
| Not listening | 2.9 | 2.7 | 2.6 | .05 |
| Farfetched | 3.0 | 2.8 | 2.3 | .04 |
| Effort | 2.4 | 2.2 | 2.0 | .02 |
| Tender | 3.5 | 3.7 | 4.2 | .05 |
| Disagree | 2.7 | 2.9 | 2.4 | .03 |
| Insults | 2.8 | 2.6 | 2.3 | .05 |

**Table 13–5**
**Comparison of Mean Responses on VRP Scalar Items for Commercials with and without Distinct Melody**

| Variable | With Distinct Melody (n = 19) | Without Distinct Melody (n = 21) | Significance (p values) |
|---|---|---|---|
| Dishonest | 2.2 | 2.0 | .02 |
| Lots of fun | 3.7 | 4.2 | .01 |
| Attention | 4.6 | 4.3 | .04 |
| Enthusiasm | 3.8 | 4.1 | .05 |
| Clever | 3.9 | 4.2 | .04 |
| Amusing | 3.6 | 4.0 | .02 |
| Exciting | 3.3 | 3.7 | .05 |
| Unique | 3.1 | 3.6 | .01 |

on "useful," "important," "new idea," and "more information"). Where the music was not identified with the brand, commercials scored higher on "dishonest," "not my need," and "undesirable."

Fewer of the fifty-two scalar items were found to be significant (at the .05 level) for commercials where the lyrics either did or did not carry the product message. "Useful" and "right for me" had higher mean scores for commercials where the lyrics carried the product message.

Similar results occur when commercials either use or do not use a jingle. Commercials using a jingle scored significantly higher (at the .05 level) for "useful," "important," and "right for me." Thus, for this sample of commercials, when a jingle is used, the lyrics carry the product message, or the music is identified with the brand, commercials are rated more positively on their relevance to the viewer.

*Music and Emotional Response to Advertising*

The literature reviewed above suggests that the effects of music on emotional states or moods has been of particular interest to researchers. This is true for consumer behavior researchers as well (Park and Young 1986; Alpert and Alpert 1986). Operationalizing emotional response on the three levels described above, the relationship between emotional response and nine music variables was examined. (In this analysis, in addition to the seven variables discussed above, two variables, (a) presence/absence of the brand name in the lyrics and (b) whether the lyrics expressed emotion versus product superiority [measured on a five-point scale where 1 = emotion and 5 = product superiority] were considered.) Emotional response was the mean proportion of response elicited by the commercial. VRP scalar item statements were interval level, measured using a six-point scale (1 = strongly disagree and 6 = strongly agree). Data were analyzed using a one-way analysis of variance.

Examination of each of the three levels of emotional response (experiential, empathic, and descriptive) yielded the following results. When the structural

**Table 13-6**
**Comparison of Mean Responses on VRP Scalar Items for Commercials on Three Roles Music Plays**

| Variable | Music Identified With Brand (n = 28) | Music Not Identified With Brand (n = 12) | Significance (p values) |
|---|---|---|---|
| Useful | 4.2 | 3.7 | .01 |
| Dishonest | 2.1 | 2.3 | .02 |
| Important | 3.6 | 3.2 | .05 |
| Not my need | 2.7 | 3.1 | .01 |
| Favorable views | 4.0 | 3.6 | .02 |
| New idea | 3.3 | 2.9 | .03 |
| Right for me | 4.0 | 3.6 | .03 |
| Realistic | 3.5 | 3.0 | .04 |
| More information | 3.7 | 3.4 | .03 |
| Undesirable | 2.3 | 2.6 | .01 |
|  | Lyrics Carry Message (n = 28) | Lyrics Don't Carry Message (n = 12) |  |
| Useful | 4.2 | 3.8 | .03 |
| Right for me | 4.0 | 3.6 | .04 |
|  | With Jingle (n = 30) | Without Jingle (n = 10) |  |
| Useful | 4.2 | 3.7 | .03 |
| Important | 3.6 | 3.2 | .04 |
| Right for me | 4.0 | 3.5 | .02 |

variables were related to the three levels of emotional response, tempo ($p < .01$) and volume ($p < .03$) were significant for descriptive emotional response. Commercials with a slower tempo or a softer volume appear to focus the viewer's attention to "superficial" elements of the commercial (that is, the actions and emotions expressed by the characters in the commercial), inhibiting more involving levels of emotional response. Although not significant, mode ($p < .11$) had the greatest impact upon eliciting empathic emotional response, and the presence of a distinct melody had the greatest impact upon experiential emotional response ($p < .10$). These results are shown in table 13-7.

As shown in table 13-8, an examination of five different roles played by music indicated significant findings only for use of the brand name in the lyrics ($p < .01$) and for lyrics expressing emotion ($p < .03$). Both of these variables were associated with commercials eliciting greater degrees of descriptive emotional response at the .05 level of significance. Thus it seems that the lyrics of the music enable people to describe emotions evoked by the commercial. Interestingly, lyrics expressing emotion was also significant ($p < .03$) for the experiential level of emotional response. Apparently, in some cases emotional lyrics allow viewers only to recognize emotions

**Table 13-7**
**Mean Percentage of Emotional Response for Four Structural Variables of Music**

| Music Variable | | Experiential | Empathic | Descriptive |
|---|---|---|---|---|
| | | *Level of Emotional Response (Mean Percentage)* | | |
| Mode | Major (n = 9) | 36 | 5 | 8 |
| | Minor (n = 9) | 36 | 11 | 12 |
| | Mixed (n = 22) | 39 | 13 | 11 |
| | | (.74) | (.11) | (.63) |
| Tempo | Slow (n = 23) | 39 | 12 | 15 |
| | Moderate (n = 8) | 35 | 6 | 5 |
| | Fast (n = 9) | 37 | 12 | 5 |
| | | (.78) | (.30) | (.01)* |
| Volume | Loud (n = 18) | 36 | 9 | 7 |
| | Soft (n = 22) | 39 | 12 | 14 |
| | | (.53) | (.38) | (.03)* |
| Distinct melody | No (n = 21) | 41 | 10 | 12 |
| | Yes (n = 19) | 34 | 12 | 9 |
| | | (.10) | (.51) | (.35) |

Note: Significance levels in parentheses.
*indicates $p < .05$.

being portrayed by characters in the commercial, but in other cases the emotions expressed in the lyrics actually help evoke very involved levels of emotional response in the viewer.

Although not significant at the .05 level, use of a jingle ($p < .09$) and music readily identified with the brand ($p < .09$) were strongly related to the level of empathic emotional response elicited by the commercials. Not too surprisingly, lyrics carrying the product message was not significant for any of the three levels of emotional response. Although further investigation is warranted, this might be due to the nature of the lyrics, carrying product information rather than emotional appeals.

## Dimensions of Consumers' Response to Commercials

The popularity of the VRP as a copy research instrument has resulted in numerous data analyses for both proprietary and basic research (Schlinger 1979; Cushing and Douglas-Tate 1985). As a result, the VRP has been found to yield relatively stable dimensions representing how consumers feel about advertising. In an attempt to further explore the relationship between music and reponse to advertising, Stout and Leckenby (1986) factor-analyzed the fifty-two scalar items on the VRP. This yielded eight factors (with eigenvalues greater than 1.0) which accounted for

**Table 13-8**
**Mean Percentage of Emotional Response for Five Different Roles of Music**

| Music Variable | | Experiential | Empathic | Descriptive |
|---|---|---|---|---|
| | | \(Level of Emotional Response (Mean Percentage)\) | | |
| Music identified | No (n = 18) | 33 | 7 | 11 |
| with brand | Yes (n = 22) | 40 | 13 | 11 |
| | | (.18) | (.09) | (.86) |
| Lyrics carry | No (n = 12) | 35 | 7 | 10 |
| product message | Yes (n = 28) | 39 | 13 | 11 |
| | | (.38) | (.13) | (.80) |
| Jingle | No (n = 10) | 33 | 6 | 8 |
| | Yes (n = 30) | 40 | 12 | 11 |
| | | (.18) | (.09) | (.46) |
| Lyrics | Much (n = 12) | 45 | 16 | 18 |
| express | Some (n = 7) | 40 | 8 | 7 |
| emotion | Little (n = 8) | 29 | 11 | 6 |
| | | (.03)* | (.27) | (.03)* |
| Brand name | No (n = 18) | 39 | 11 | 16 |
| in lyrics | Yes (n = 22) | 37 | 12 | 7 |
| | | (.55) | (.77) | (.01)* |

Note: Significance levels in parentheses.
*indicates $p < .05$.

59 percent of the variance. These eight factors are similar to the ones emerging from previous factor analyses of VRP items (Schlinger 1979). The eight factors found are called: Irritation, Entertainment, Relevant News, Brand Reinforcement, Empathy, Hard to Follow, Familiarity, and Differentiation. (Factor loadings and a detailed description of the characterization of each dimension can be found in Stout and Leckenby 1986.)

For each of the eight factors, a factor index was computed. First, for the forty commercials, a mean score was obtained for all scalar items loading on a factor. Then that score was divided by the number of statements loading on the factor. The relationship between the eight factor indices was examined for (1) the four structural variables of music and (2) the three different roles music can play in the commercial. The results of these analyses are presented in table 13-9.

When the mode of the music was examined, four factor indices, Irritation, Relevant News, Brand Reinforcement, and Empathy, were significant at the .05 level, making mode the structural variable having the most impact on viewers' ratings of the commercials. Commercials with music in minor mode scored less favorably than major or mixed mode commercials and are rated as more irritating.

**Table 13-9**

**Significant Relationships Found by Stout and Leckenby (1986) for Eight Dimensions of Advertising and Seven Music Variables**

| Music Variable | | Dimensions of Advertising | | | | | | | |
| --- | --- | --- | --- | --- | --- | --- | --- | --- | --- |
| | Irritation | Entertainment | Relevant News | Brand Reinforcement | Empathy | Hard to Follow | Familiarity | Differentiation |
| Structure of Music | | | | | | | | |
| Mode | X | — | X | X | X | — | — | — |
| Tempo | O | — | — | — | — | X | — | — |
| Distinct melody | — | X | — | — | — | — | — | — |
| Volume | — | — | — | — | — | O | — | — |
| Role Music Plays | | | | | | | | |
| Music identified with brand | — | — | X | X | — | — | — | — |
| Jingle | — | — | O | X | — | — | — | — |
| Lyrics carry product message | — | — | — | O | — | — | — | — |

X = p < .05
O = p < .10

Commercials in major and mixed mode were rated higher on Relevant News, Brand Reinforcement, and Empathy. Viewers seem to learn more from, show greater behavioral intent, and have more personal connections with commercials using major and mixed mode. Both tempo ($p < .05$) and volume ($p < .10$) were associated with the commercials scoring higher on being Hard to Follow. Those commercials with a slower tempo or a louder volume were rated as harder to follow. Commercials with slower tempo were also rated as more Irritating. Commercials with no distinct melody rated higher on Entertainment. Apparently, commercials with music not using a distinct melody are viewed as more unique, clever, and arousing.

A look at the various roles music can play in a commercial indicates a definite consensus on the relationship of these variables to consumers' response to the commercials. For all three role variables, commercials were rated as higher on the dimension of Brand Reinforcement. Viewers also indicate a greater intent to recommend, try, and buy the brand. For commercials where the music was identified with the brand or where a jingle was used, commercials were also rated higher in providing Relevant News about the product. Hence, the roles music plays in commercials can have an impact upon the information the consumer receives from a commercial.

## Discussion and Conclusions

In this study, our intent was to examine several music variables that previous research indicated influenced individuals' response to music. A convenience sample of fifty professionally produced commercials, that had been tested using the VRP, was used. Measures of emotional and cognitive responses were taken in an effort to discover the relationship between specific music variables and these responses. The findings of this study can be generalized only to the sample of fifty commercials used. However, we have taken a first step toward isolating features of music beyond the "use of background music" typically studied in advertising research.

Looking at the differences between commercials with and without music, the inclusion of music in the commercials studied had minor effects when the fifty-two VRP items were examined. (Commercials without music were more informative, but purchase intent was higher for commercials with music.) No significant differences between the two groups were found on the three levels of emotional response.

For the forty commercials with music in the sample, commercials with a slow tempo and commercials with a soft volume elicited more descriptive emotional responses. Looking at the different roles music plays in a commercial, when the brand name is in the lyrics and when the lyrics express emotion, greater descriptive emotional response is elicited. Also, when lyrics express emotion, significantly more experiential emotional response is elicited. Other variables, like use of a jingle and use of music identified with the brand, affect the degree of empathic emotional response elicited for a commercial (at a .10 level of significance).

Any evaluative interpretation of the relationship between the fifty-two individual VRP items or the eight factor indices reported on here and the specific music variables should be made in light of the objectives set for music in each commercial. We did not have access to that information. However, certain general relationships resulted for this sample of forty commercials.

Mode was the variable yielding the greatest number of relationships in response to both the fifty-two VRP items and the eight factor indices (including Irritation, Relevant News, Brand Reinforcement, and Empathy). Commercials in major or mixed mode elicited a more positive response to the dependent items. Tempo and a distinct melody also yielded a number of significant differences for several of the fifty-two VRP statements, although each music variable yielded only one significant factor index (Hard to Follow and Entertainment, respectively). Identification of the music with the brand appeared to be the most important role variable for music, yielding significant differences on ten VRP items and two factor indices (Relevant News and Brand Reinforcement).

Music is only one of several nonverbal variables which are interwoven into the tapestry that becomes the finished commercial. But music is a powerful and complex force. Here, only a few of the many roles music can play in advertising have been examined. These findings add to a list of specific music variables warranting study in future large-scale advertising studies, where many commercials are examined, and in more controlled situations.

Future research on music could focus on many different areas. The contribution made by music to brand image or the ability of music to influence the viewer's mood, which might then be associated with the brand, are two areas of concern to advertisers. Also, focus on people's perceptions about what types of music (for example, classical, country and western, rock, and so on) best fit a specific product category or determination of individual preferences for specific types of music based on demographic categories, for example, would also be of interest.

Listening to music is not enough. A great deal more needs to be understood about the elements of music and their effects before we can fully understand how music influences responses to advertising.

# 14

# The Relationship between Music in Advertising and Children's Responses: An Experimental Investigation

*M. Carole Macklin*

**M**usic has long been considered a valuable tool with which the advertiser may enhance the effectiveness of a message. Particularly in the form of a jingle, music is assumed to increase memorability (for example, White 1977; Richards 1979; Sandage, Fryburger, and Rotzoll 1983). The role of music in advertising is important from both an applied and a theoretical perspective.

Commercial practice would suggest that advertisers take advantage of music's potentially valuable role. Kingman (1983) reported that "one in every four or five best commercials in 1982 made use of a jingle or slogan." A *Wall Street Journal* staff reporter (1985) noted the recent proliferation of classic pop and rock music in ads for product categories previously unfamiliar with such use. Staff reporter Alsop (1985) wrote that "companies need more emotional hooks in their ads, such as music, to make their products stand out in people's minds."

In terms of the theoretical perspective of information processing, one can find ready support for music's importance. First, music may serve as an attention-getting device. Without music and subsequent attention, a message may be ignored. Second, music may provide a means for rehearsal. The positive relationship between rehearsal and improved remembering has been well researched (Bettman 1979). As the listener hums a tune or sings a jingle, he or she engages in a rehearsal strategy that results in better memory. Therefore, the intuitively appealing notion that music enhances memorability can be nicely meshed into the information-processing perspective.

However, information-processing theory suggests that there are limitations on our processing capacity. While the early view suggested that a person can handle only one incoming stream at a time (Broadbent 1958), a more recent view still recognizes that capacity is limited (Glass, Holyoak, and Santa 1979). Music may pose a problem in view of these processing limits. While an individual may attend to the music, he or she may become so enraptured by the music that the central message of the advertiser is ignored. Thus, information-processing theory suggests that the type and execution of music can make a difference not only in attention-getting ability but also in allowing for the processing of information intended by the advertiser. To be effective, the music should enhance the central message.

Recent research has clearly indicated that the information-processing perspective does not aptly apply to all advertising situations. While the theory is important to intentional learning situations, its usefulness in incidental ones has proved less helpful. In more recent terminology, research has suggested that much of television viewing may be best described as low involving.

Although consensus on a tight definition of involvement is still lacking in the literature, most researchers would probably agree that involvement refers to importance. When people think that a message is important to them, they attend to it and process it more deeply than when they are disinterested or uninvolved in the message (Greenwald and Leavitt 1984).

The relationship between involvement and consumers' reactions to commercial information has received considerable attention (Krugman 1965; Mitchell 1981; Petty, Cacioppo, and Schumann 1983; Greenwald and Leavitt 1984). If we accept, for the moment, attitude change as occurring through two different mechanisms, the central and the peripheral routes, then the central route can be considered the high-involvement or more cognitive route (Petty, Cacioppo, and Schumann 1983). Thus, the information processing paradigm is useful to the central route. However, the peripheral route centers on low involvement when personal importance is low.

Researchers have recently tried to explain ad-induced changes in attitude in these low-involvement situations. Mitchell and Olson (1981) found that the effects of advertising on brand attitude were mediated by the individual's affective feelings about an ad. What affects a person's feelings about the ad ($A_{ad}$)?

Peripheral cues in persuasive communications are considered key. Haley, Richardson, and Baldwin (1984) offered a typology of seventeen peripheral cues or, as they labeled them, seventeen areas of nonverbal communication. Among them was music. These researchers' initial analyses indicated that music, along with other nonverbal communication, is more likely to work against a commercial than to enhance its effectiveness. They offered the following general explanation: Because people are uninvolved and suspicious of advertising, they are alert to nonverbal cues "that suggest that they can comfortably ignore the commercial" (Haley, Richardson, and Baldwin 1984, p. 15). Thus, music and other nonverbal cues can serve as "distractors," even in the low-involvement route. Thus, the music gets all the attention, much the same as in the more cognitive view of the information-processing perspective.

Recent work suggests that solid conclusions about music's role should not be made prematurely, however. Stewart and Furse (1986) examined how executional variables affected advertising performance. Analyzing over one thousand commercials, their results suggested that a variety of executional devices, such as music, may enhance recall and comprehension. Stewart and Furse argued that, while recall and comprehension appeared to be important mediators of persuasion, they are not the primary functions of advertising. The critical role of advertising in the long run is to persuade. Music, as a possible attention-getting device and memory enhancer, becomes important in a complex fashion, depending on such factors as whether the advertised product is new or established. However, auditory devices appeared to facilitate the important mediators of recall and comprehension.

The role of music is yet to be fully tested or understood by advertisers. Experimental inquiries are scant. Park and Young (1986) reported music as having a facilitative effect on brand attitude for subjects in a low-involvement condition, while music had a distracting effect for those in a cognitive or high-involvement condition. Park and Young (1986) reported that background music interfered with the cognitively involved subjects' information processing, yet enhanced brand attitude for the low-involvement group. Some unexpected results suggested concurrence with Haley et al.'s (1984) assertion that music may distract even in low-involvement situations, however. Park and Young (1986) argued that the attitude toward the ad may contribute to brand-attitude formation when the peripheral cue is integrated into the main concept or theme of the message. Otherwise, music can serve as a distractor, even in the low-involvement situation.

It is apparent that much work remains for us to understand music's role in increasing persuasion. The work to date suggests that, under certain conditions, music may serve as a distractor in both highly involved and less involved subjects. Distraction—or the lack thereof—appears critical. From the information-processing view, music may attract attention, yet become the focus of attention. Likewise, in low-involvement settings, music may also distract if the music is extraneous to the main concept or theme.

It should be noted that the classical conditioning paradigm has been suggested as an explanatory framework to understand the effects of nonverbal stimuli. Gorn (1982) reported evidence for classical conditioning effects of music. However, the nature of the experimental stimuli was such that distraction from the message would not likely have occurred. Moreover, pure classical conditioning, including that in Gorn's study, has been seriously questioned (Allen and Madden 1985). Indeed, strong evidence supporting automatic transfer with humans is scant (Dulany 1974); therefore, classical conditioning explanations for the effects of music may not prove fruitful in the long run for at least two reasons. First, cognitive activity *of some kind* may truly be pertinent in all learning. Second, and perhaps more relevant to the current research, advertising messages are such complex stimuli that providing for simplicity in order to rule out cognitive processing may be virtually impossible. Nonverbal cues such as music are generally complex, in and of themselves, and they may necessarily stimulate some form of cognitive activity. While the theoretical arguments will be avoided in the current study, the author asserts that further research on the classical conditioning paradigm is required to establish that automatic conditioning can occur with such complex phenomenon on human subjects. Indeed, general research on the role of music may help untangle some of these theoretical issues.

The purpose of the current work was to examine empirically the role of music within a particular category of commericals. Young children are the focal subjects. Not only are preschoolers of interest to advertisers, they are also important to musical investigations because of such heavy usage of music to that target audience. Learning about music's role with children may be even more difficult than with adults, however. First, measurement of children persists as a problem. Second, their cognitive complexion is immature. Young children, labeled limited processors, are known to have deficiencies as compared to the adult processor (Flavell 1970). For example, young children have difficulty employing storage and retrieval strategies to enhance learning. Nevertheless, given the importance of music in children's advertising, it is important to ascertain the role of music in learning and persuasion. The current research was theoretically framed from both the information-processing and a less cognitive perspective. The term *less cognitive* is adopted to avoid theoretical debate as to what occurs in a low-involving situation.

Two studies were planned to examine music's impact on behavior, attitudes, and learning. The type of the exposure was planned to be a major difference between the two studies. First, forced exposure was planned in which children's attention would be directed to the television. Second, the test commericals were embedded within a cartoon. Further distractors were introduced to the environment in the second study. This second setting was intended to approximate a more realistic viewing situation. Advertisers are well aware that children divide their visual attention between television viewing and other activities such as playing with toys (Anderson, Alwitt, Lorch, and Levin 1979). The studies will be described separately.

## Study One

### General Description

An experiment using a simple one-way analysis of variance was designed with three levels on one factor—type of music. One condition consisted of a jingle, the second condition consisted of the same message announced with the same instrumental dubbed as background music, and the third condition consisted of just the voice-over; that is, no music. The exposure was forced and occurred in a highly structured setting, a preschool.

### Commercials

Three animatics were produced as test commercials. The form of animatics was chosen for two main reasons. First, production costs are considerably lower for an animatic than for a finished commercial. Second, research on advertising and programming has indicated that children's memory for content is higher for visual than auditory information (Hayes, Chemeski, and Birnbaum 1981; Stoneman and Brody 1983). It was decided that the visual portion should be comparably less distinguished than the auditory one for the test commercials, given the focus on music. Thus, the use of animatics seemed acceptable given the desire to stress the auditory portion.

The author enlisted the help of the composition department of the school of music at her university. With its help, a local audio production house agreed to compose the lyrics and original score for the research project for the nominal fee of $350.00. The production house (Prime Time Productions) was young but well respected in the market area, having produced work for major firms in the region.

The author requested that a jingle be created that could also be announced in the absence of music, without sounding absurd. The tempo requested was upbeat, a lively rock sound versus nursery sound, and that high informational content be included about the product. High informational content was desired for three reasons. First, as Stewart and Furse (1986) reported television commercials, on average, appear to be reasonably informative. Second, one of the purposes of the current study was to examine comprehension; thus, a commercial providing information was necessary. Third, the message was designed not only to reach the child but also his or her parents. The product selected was cereal, a major category of interest to marketers of children's products.

The name *Pop Pops* was selected from a pretest that included two other names. It was found to be highly liked and easy to pronounce among the preschoolers.

Only superficial changes in copy among the versions were made. For example, "Hey, kids" was added to the two announced versions, background music and no music control. It was decided that the copy not only sounded more realistic in terms of a lead-in, but that such an addition did not change the substance of the messages.

*Jingle*
Pop Pops Bang Bang
Strawberry, Orange, and Grape
I wish breakfast came three
   times a day
It tastes great and it's good
   for you
Plenty of minerals and vitamins
   too
Pop Pops Bang Bang
   and it's crunch crunch with
   that fruity taste
Pop Pops your breakfast today
Pop Pops

*Background and Voice-over—No Music*
Hey, Kids
Pop Pops is that strawberry, orange,
   and grape cereal
that makes you wish breakfast came
   three times a day
It tastes great and it's good for you
   because Pop Pops has plenty of
   vitamins and minerals
Yeah, Kids
It's that crunch crunch cereal with
   that fruity taste
Make Pop Pops your breakfast cereal
Pop Pops Yeah

Ten illustrated boards were drawn for the animatic about the cereal. A freelance professional designer (Joel B. Kuhn) drew the illustrations. A "hip" rabbit was portrayed as the product spokesperson. He popped out of a cannon, touted the cereal (for example, juggling cereal bowls), and joined a boy and girl for breakfast. The boy and girl were drawn to look slightly older than the target audience, preschoolers. (Children are generally known to emulate upwards in age, not downwards). The illustrations were videotaped, and then the three audio portions were dubbed to the same video to produce the three versions. Therefore, while the video portions were the same across conditions, the audio portions varied as previously described.

It should be noted that the illustrations were drawn and videotaped as to be in step with the audio information. However, some key attribute information was excluded from the visual portrayals. Specifically, the fruity flavors (strawberry, grape, and orange) were not illustrated and the presence of vitamins was not visually reinforced, nor the crunchy nature of the cereal. The absence of visuals reinforcing these specific features was intentional in view of the audio nature of the test. As previously mentioned, because visual information appears to have a greater impact on children's remembering, a hard audio test was desired. The ten illustrations were, nevertheless, consistent with the overall theme of the message, Pop Pops taste good and are good for you. Indeed, sound effects were intentionally included in the two music versions (for example, popping noise for Pop Pops) to reinforce the central message.

## Subjects

A preschool in a Cincinnati suburb agreed to the children's participation in the project. Parental consent was obtained, and $3.00 was donated to the school for each child's participation. Seventy-five children completed the study. They could best be described as white, middle to upper-middle class children whose mothers worked mainly part-time or not at all (a few mothers did work full-time, and their babysitters brought them to the school for its two-and-a-half-hour sessions). Although the sample was skewed upward socioeconomically, this was not viewed negatively because the children reflect a prime target for cereal makers.

## Procedure

The director of the preschool told the children that they would get "to watch a little television and talk to a lady." Children were individually escorted to a viewing room that was well situated away from the central areas. Each child was asked "to watch a commercial on television." Assignment to a condition was systematically based on room entry. Each child appeared to attend actively. None of the children talked or diverted their eyes away from the television. They sat eye-level to the television at a table, and no items were on the table to offer distraction.

After exposure, each child was asked two questions about a character not included in the commercial, but as a part of a separate study. These two questions were intentionally included for these reasons: (1) children could practice the use of answering boards included in the current study, and (2) the questions served as a distraction task to insure a test of longer-term or deeper memory. The experimenter then said, "Now I want to ask you about what you saw on television." She then proceeded with the questions.

*Measures*

The measures consisted of six categories. First, a child was asked to select a cereal for consumption. Second, a child was questioned about his or her attitude toward the cereal ad ($A_{ad}$); third, free recall of brand name; fourth, attitude toward the brand; fifth, how likely he or she would be to ask Mom to buy the cereal (BI), and, sixth, his or her understanding of brand attributes.

The experimenter first said that she wanted to show the child some cereal boxes, whereupon the experimenter showed three hardwood artist boards that individually illustrated Pop Pops, Honey Nut Cheerios, and Cocoa Puffs. The full-color illustrations were necessary because the portrayal of products had to be similar; thus, boxes of the real products would have stood out as different from the test one. The specific alternative brands, Honey Nut Cheerios and Cocoa Puffs, were selected because they had the highest market shares for children's cereals in the major grocery store serving the test site. A child was asked to *pretend* that he or she could eat cereal at school: "Okay, now let me show you some cereal boxes. . . . If you could pick some cereal right now, which one would you pick?"

$A_{ad}$ was determined by asking each child how much he or she liked the ad and how good he or she thought it was. Two answer boards were constructed to assist the children's responding. The first, illustrated in vertical display, showed large and small circles with smiling to frowning faces. The second board vertically illustrated a four-point, good-to-bad scale. The specific scale points were the following: GOOD, good, bad, and BAD. The size of the circle/box also reinforced the strength of the response. The descriptions were orally provided for each scale point, and the experimeter pointed to each as she provided the descriptions. The child was asked to "point to" his or her response.

The experimenter then asked, "By the way, do you remember the name of the cereal you saw on television?" "Pops" and "Pop" were counted as correct recall along with Pop Pops.

Procedures for determining attitude toward the brand were the same (like and good) as the determination of $A_{ad}$ described above.

BI was determined by the question, "Do you think you'd ask your mom to buy it?" A vertically displayed yes–no scale was used, with the four points of: YES, yes, no, NO. Once again, the size of the box reinforced the intensity of the response.

Finally, visual materials were constructed in order to test memory for brand attributes. For example, each child was asked, "How many times a day did the man say he'd (you'd) like to eat Pop Pops? A horizontal scale was drawn, illustrating a hand counting finger(s) (1 through 5). In addition, numbers were visually and orally provided. If a child pointed to 3, then he or she was counted as correct. The total number of correct responses across the measures (0 to 6) were summed for the analysis of group differences on comprehension.

Two points about the experimental procedures should be stressed. First, children did not have to articulate any answers orally, except for the free recall of the brand name. Nonverbal response measures are important in dealing with young children whose expository skills are often poorly developed (Macklin 1983). Second, the order of questions was planned with a great deal of thought. Brand selection (pretended) was considered a very important measure that was deemed not to contaminate the other measures because the cereal "boxes" were shown without oral articulation of the brand names. The pretest demonstrated what one would guess; that is, because young children cannot read, exposure to an illustration did not assist in the children's articulation of the brand name a few moments later (young children's illiteracy can have its advantages in the design of an experiment). Moreover, the cereal boxes clearly showed the brand characters (the rabbit in the case of Pop Pops) which may increase children's recognition of the product (Rossiter 1980).

*Hypotheses*

In the absence of prior empirical work and clear theoretical reasons to expect differences between the two music conditions, the direction of results depicted in table 14–1 should be considered speculative. Differences were hypothesized between the music conditions and the no-music condition, however.

If we accept the premise that forced exposure roughly equates to a cognitively-oriented or high-involvement manipulation for children, then music would be considered a distractor to processing—not a facilitator. Thus, it was hypothesized that the no-music condition would relate to higher brand selection, higher attitude toward the ad, brand-name free recall, brand attitude, behavioral intent, and aided recall of attributes.

The predictions in table 14–1 in lowercase letters under the columns for the jingle condition and the background music condition are highly tentative because of a lack of a clear basis for prediction. It is asserted that children who are attentively watching will respond most positively to the background music. The basis is that this type of music is less complex than the jingle presentation. Moreover, the music is woven into the central theme by the use of several sound effects. Specifically, the sound effects (for example, popping noises) were left on the background music track to reinforce the brand name, Pop Pops. And the background music was judged to be important to the central message that Pop Pops pops.

**Table 14-1**
**Forced Exposure Predicted Outcomes**

| | Condition | | |
|---|---|---|---|
| *Dependent Measures* | *Jingle* | *Background* | *No Music* |
| Brand selection "pretend" | lowest[a] | lower | HIGHEST |
| Attitude toward the ad | lowest | lower | HIGHEST |
| Brand name recall | lowest | lower | HIGHEST |
| Brand attitude | lowest | lower | HIGHEST |
| Behavioral intent | lowest | lower | HIGHEST |
| Aided recall of attributes | lowest | lower | HIGHEST |

[a]Lower case letters refer to high speculation; the jingle was judged by a panel of graduate students as appealing, but more complex than the background music.

## Results

Table 14-2 indicates no support for the hypotheses based on the premise that the children were cognitively active in attending to the ad. In fact, examination of the means suggests that the background music condition was overall most successful in creating positive attitudes toward the ad and brand, and in affecting attribute recall. No differences among the means were statistically significant, so these directions must be viewed as highly speculative.

The only dependent measure that indicated directional support for the hypotheses was the brand-name recall. More children in the no-music condition recalled

**Table 14-2**
**Table of Results on the Dependent Measures in Forced, Single-Exposure Setting**

| | Condition | | | | |
|---|---|---|---|---|---|
| *Dependent Variables* | *Jingle* Mean or % | *Background* Mean or % | *No Music* Mean or % | *F* | *Sign of F* |
| Brand selection[a] | 36% | 32% | 32% | | |
| Attitude toward the ad[b] | 6.88 | 7.08 | 6.08 | 1.982 | 0.145 |
| Brand name recall[c] | 28% | 20% | 32% | | |
| Brand attitude[d] | 6.52 | 6.80 | 6.04 | 0.907 | 0.408 |
| Behavioral intent[e] | 2.76 | 3.24 | 2.44 | 2.222 | 0.116 |
| Aided recall of attributes[f] | 1.68 | 1.80 | 1.48 | 0.562 | 0.572 |

[a]Percentage who "pretended" to select brand for immediate consumption.
[b]Sum of two 4-point intervally scaled measures: (1) like ad, and (2) how good ad is; range 2 to 8.
[c]Percentage who freely recalled brand name.
[d]Sum of two 4-point intervally scaled measures: (1) like cereal and (2) how good cereal is; range 2 to 8.
[e]Single item measure; range 1 to 4.
[f]Sum of aided recall of content; range 0 to 6.

Pop Pops. The relationship between type of music and free recall of brand name was not statistically insignificant, however:

$$(\chi^2 = .976, \text{n.s.})$$

## Discussion

Given the exploratory nature of the study and the failure to find statistical differences, directional indications from Study One are to be regarded as speculative. Namely, the background music condition seemed better in affecting brand and ad attitudes than the absence of music.

Perhaps the failure to find any statistical differences among the forced-exposure conditions was somewhat surprising, however. Several alternative explanations are offered.

First, the manipulations may have been weak in terms of little difference among stimuli. While this explanation must always be considered, it is argued that the three versions were significantly different auditorily.

Another interpretation of "weak" presents a threat to the importance of music beyond an attention-getting device. It would suggest that different audio tracks will not yield differences in this study, or any other, as long as attention has been captured. A stream of research, mainly on programming, suggests the overwhelming strength of visual aspects (Hayes, Cheneski, and Young 1981; Stoneman and Brody 1983). Music may grab children's attention, but then the visuals take over. As described earlier, this explanation seems more plausible from the information-processing perspective of limited capacity of young children. This explanation would minimize the role of music beyond attention getting.

The possibility of a limited role of music necessitated Study Two, in which the ad was embedded within a cartoon, and other distractors were provided. Anderson, Lorch, Smith, Bradford, and Levin (1981) argued that the watching of television by young children is an active transactional process among the viewer, the television itself, and the television-viewing environment. Therefore, music was observed for its attention-getting ability, and further processing was examined in view of this embedded exposure surrounded with distractors.

A second explanation for a failure to obtain statistical differences rests with the measures themselves. Developing sensitive measures to be used with preschoolers is a notorious problem. The author can only add that she has used similar dependent measures in other projects and obtained statistically significant differences among young children. However, the author recognizes the importance of measure development in dealing with children, and that these measures may have been insensitive in view of the stimuli's similarity.

A third explanation of the statistically homogeneous results stems from the directions indicated by the means. Excluding the brand-name recall measure, the means of the other dependent measures primarily suggested that the background music was most effective. These indications approximated what one would possibly expect from a "low-involved" subject. This is a plausible explanation, given the nature of the procedures. Children are asked to "watch television" and "see a commercial." They were not given any high-involvement instructions typically administered to adult subjects such as "the product will be available soon for sale in Cincinnati." The age of the subject needs special consideration. Four-year-old children can be hesitant, fearful, trusting, outgoing—all during the same session. Not only may deceit be a highly questionable practice with such young children, but also the kinds of instructions most likely to promote "high involvement" may be detrimental to the success of the project due to the subjects' young age. If an experimenter tells a child that he or she is going to "test" the child and that he or she really wants the child to pay attention so the child can answer *correctly*, the child will probably show adverse effects. Namely, the child can become afraid or refuse to participate. Thus, while the author assumed that the forced exposure would roughly equate to a high-involvement exposure, such an assumption may have been false in view of the preschoolers' young age.

Future research should include efforts at creating levels of involvement appropriate for use with children. For example, if a child were told that he or she could sample the product, then he or she may become involved. Truth and sensitivity will be key concerns in constructing involvement manipulations. (Approval by Human Subjects Committees is another consideration.)

The purpose of Study Two, to be described below, was to provide a more natural viewing situation—one in which music's role in attention getting was explicitly considered. This type of exposure is important, if for no other reason than that it gives recognition to more realistic viewing conditions. Television commercials are not viewed in a vacuum.

## Study Two

### General Description

Study Two was conducted to measure effects similar to those examined in Study One, except the ad treatments were embedded twice within a short cartoon. In addition, appealing toys were available in the test room. Lorch, Anderson, and Levin (1979) reported that visual attention to a television in a no-toys group was double that of a toy group (87 percent versus 44 percent). Exposure was *not* forced, but the children were told that they could watch a cartoon and pretend that they were "at home." In addition, three children watched television at a time; thus, Study Two consisted of a group exposure. However, the children were separated for individual testing conducted simultaneously by three female experimenters located in separate rooms.

## Stimuli

The animatics were the same as in Study One. However, each version was embedded around an identical Tom and Jerry cartoon (approximately eight minutes). The particular cartoon was selected because of its short duration and nonviolent theme (Tom and Jerry befriended a baby chick). In addition, the animatic was shown twice within the program segment. No other commercials were included so as not to create undue confusion or strain on the children's potential processing and subsequent ability to respond to questioning.

## Subjects

Arrangements were made with another preschool located approximately five miles from the one used in Study One. The socioeconomic profile was approximately the same as those in Study One. Again, the sample consisted of a suburban, advantaged group of children. The average age was 57 months; 55.6 percent were male, 44.4 percent female; and the children were all white. Parental consent was obtained, and funds were contributed to the school for the children's participation.

## Procedure

General procedures resembled Study One's, but there were some major differences. Children were *not* asked to watch a commercial. They were invited to watch a cartoon because "we want to know if this 'Tom and Jerry' is a good one." Once again, each group of children was systematically assigned to an experimental condition based on its entry to the room.

Another important difference from Study One was the use of group exposure. The preschool teachers selected the groups of three and were asked to do so only in consideration of the classroom's activities. The children were led to a pleasant room at the school that was made to look "homey." Toys were strewn about, carpet squares were scattered, a game table was set up opposite the television. Children were asked to "pretend" that they were at home in their family rooms. "You can watch television, play with the toys, talk with your friends—whatever you want to do is fine just as long as you have a good time!" The three experimenters sat toward the edges of the room on the floor with the children and watched the show. Therefore, conditions were meant to approximate a more natural viewing situation which would also familiarize the children with the experimenters.

After the program, each child was led to a separate room "to tell the lady whether the Tom and Jerry cartoon was a good one." Three female interviewers individually asked the children about the show. These questions served as a practice exercise and as an opportunity for the child to become further familiar with the experimenter before she posed the key questions.

*Measures*

The dependent measures consisted of the following. First, unlike Study One, children's visual attention to the television was measured directly (it will be remembered that children's viewing was forced in Study One and visually appeared to be complete). Three interviewers were assigned to monitor a particular child's viewing during the commercial. The interviewers used sports stopwatches to record visual attention to the television screen during each commercial exposure. The young children appeared oblivious to the experimenters' subtle activity.

In addition, a videocamera was set up behind the television, and the camera recorded the viewing sessions. Once again, no children commented on or even appeared to recognize the camera's inclusion among the barrage of equipment. An independent coder verified the interviewers' measurements included in the analysis of variance to be reported. Originally, the coder's assessments of amount viewed were planned to be the dependent measures. However, due to an occasional technical problem (such as poor lighting at distant camera range), the coding of attention from tapes was difficult with certain subjects. Therefore, the recordings were simply used to check the experimenters' timings.

The structured interviews began after the child answered three questions about the cartoon. Each child was asked how much he or she liked the show, how good he or she thought Tom and Jerry cartoon was, and whether he or she would like to see the show again.

Then the child was reminded that he or she "saw something besides Tom and Jerry. It was called a commercial. Do you remember seeing something besides Tom and Jerry. . . . something to eat that was shown in the commercial? What was it?" If a child responded with "cereal," then he or she was recorded as correctly remembering the product category. Then he or she was asked, "Do you remember anything else about the commercial?" The child's free responses were recorded. These measures were viewed to be critical to the task, although high success was not expected. Preschoolers have been shown to perform poorly in free-recall exposition (see Brown 1972, 1973, 1975). However, the experimenter needed to direct the child's memory to the commercial and to judge whether the child could remember having seen "something besides Tom and Jerry." The experimenters recorded their personal judgment about the child's ability to respond (those indications were surprisingly successful).

Then, the child was asked to "pretend" to select a brand of cereal for immediate consumption. This measure (brand selection) was the same as Study One's.

The child was then immediately asked to recall the brand name. The reader will notice that the order of this free-recall question was changed from Study One. It now preceded questions about attitude toward the commercial. The order was changed for two major reasons. First, Study One indicated that the brand selection measure had little, if no, effect on free recall. Second, it was felt to be important that the child be reminded that the experimenter was concerned with the cereal—not Tom and Jerry. After the child's opportunity to respond freely, he or she was quickly shown the Pop Pops "box" (no articulation of the brand name was provided) and told that he or she would be asked "about the part of the television that talked about the cereal—the commercial."

The next category of questions consisted of those designed to measure attitude toward the ad. The first two *(like* and *good)* were reported in Study One. Five additional measures were used that depicted faces showing the following emotions in relation to the commercial: like, exciting, understanding, fun, and funny. A professional artist (the same one who had illustrated the storyboards) drew four-point ranges of male and female faces depicting each emotion (the "child's" face was the same except that sex was manipulated by the hair and eyebrows). The boys saw the male faces, and the girls saw the female faces. Each subject was asked to think about the commercial and to point to one of the four vertically displayed faces (per emotion) that showed, for example, "how fun you thought the commercial was." These five measures constituted a second effort at measuring feelings toward the ad.

Attitude towards the brand *(like* and *good)* was then queried. The measures were identical to those in Study One's, as was behavioral intent, "Do you think you'd ask your mom to buy it?" Finally, the same measures for memory of brand attributes were posed. It will be remembered that these last measures constituted aided-recall measures through the use of visual materials to assist subjects' responding.

## Hypotheses

Table 14–3 depicts the expected outcomes. The means in the music conditions were expected to exceed, at a statistically significant level, the means in the no-music condition. The background music condition was expected to result in higher means than from the jingle one, although statistical differences were not necessarily

## Table 14–3
## Embedded Exposure Predicted Outcomes

| | Condition | | |
|---|---|---|---|
| *Dependent Measures* | *Jingle* | *Background* | *No Music* |
| Brand selection | lower | highest | lowest |
| Brand name recall | lower | highest | lowest |
| Attitude toward the ad | lower | highest | lowest |
| Brand attitude | lower | highest | lowest |
| Behavioral intent | lower | highest | lowest |
| Aided recall of attributes | lower | highest | lowest |
| Visual attention | lower | highest | lowest |

expected. These outcomes were expected based upon the results from Study One, and from the view that music serves as an attention getting device that allows for processing of the message.

These predictions were consistent with information-processing theory. Children's attention must be gained, particularly when competing alternatives are offered. In addition, given speculation and early findings about nonverbal effects (Haley, Richardson, and Baldwin 1984), one would expect a positive effect of music on brand and ad attitudes because the music in the test stimuli is both central and interwoven into the entire message. The jingle is more complex, however.

## Results

Table 14–4 presents a summary of results from Study Two. Perhaps the most remarkable finding was the failure to find statistical differences among the conditions—except on visual attention paid to the ads. Let us look at the attention

**Table 14-4**
**Table of Results on the Dependent Measures in Embedded, Double-Exposure Setting**

|  | Condition | | | | |
|---|---|---|---|---|---|
| *Dependent Variables* | *Jingle mean or %* | *Background Mean or %* | *No Music Mean or %* | *F* | *Sign of F* |
| Brand selection[a] | 23.8% | 23.8% | 23.8% | | |
| Brand name recall[b] | 9.5% | 38.1% | 28.6% | | |
| Attitude toward the ad[c] | | | | | |
| 1. 2-item (r = 0.75) | 5.74 | 6.15 | 6.25 | 0.316 | 0.731 |
| 2. 5-item (α = 0.79) | 15.21 | 15.70 | 17.00 | 1.952 | 0.323 |
| Brand attitude[d] | 5.89 | 5.90 | 6.20 | 0.099 | 0.905 |
| Behavioral intent[e] | 2.53 | 2.75 | 2.62 | 0.126 | 0.882 |
| Aided recall of attributes[f] | 1.84 | 1.35 | 1.52 | 1.489 | 0.234 |
| Visual Attention[g] | | | | | |
| 1. Individual | 39.55% | 64.19% | 72.62% | 7.893 | 0.001 |
| 2. Group | 37.79% | 63.51% | 72.61% | 15.283 | 0.000 |

[a]Percentage who "pretended" to select brand for immediate consumption.
[b]Percentage who freely recalled brand name.
[c](1) Sum of two 4-point intervally scaled measures:
    (1) like ad, and (2) how good ad is; range 2 to 8.
 (2) Sum of five, sex-based 4-point intervally-scalled faces:
    (1) like, (2) exciting, (3) understand, (4) fun, (5) funny; range 5 to 20.
[d]Sum of two 4-point intervally scaled measures:
    (1) like cereal and (2) how good cereal is; range 2 to 8.
[e]Single item measure of how likely child would request Mom to buy Pop Pops; range 1 to 4.
[f]Sum of aided recall of content; range 0 to 6.
[g] (1) Percentage of individual attention to ads across two exposures;
    (2) Percentage of group attention to ads across two exposures.

findings first. (This analysis was based on the timed observations conducted during the sessions.)

The hypothesized assist of music in gaining visual attention was not supported. Table 14-4 indicates that the jingle resulted in a marked decrease in individual attention. Tukey's test indicated that the attention paid during the jingle was significantly lower than background and no-music conditions, where statistical differences between the latter conditions did not emerge. Also, as one would expect given that the experiment was designed to induce group interaction, group attention demonstrated the same pattern (individual and group attention were correlated, Pearson r = .81., sign . < 0.000). Thus, contrary to expectation, the jingle resulted in less visual attention, while the no-music voice-over performed better than expected. A discussion of plausible explanations will be presented later in this chapter.

The reader will further observe on table 14-4 the failure of statistical differences to emerge on the other measures. The use of music did not result in increased brand selection, brand-name recall, attitudes toward the ad or the brand, behavioral intent, or aided recall of attributes.

The pattern of results, which must be considered as speculative in view of an absence of statistical differences, can be compared to those from Study One previously depicted on table 14-2. Overall, the embedded exposure resulted in fewer children "pretending" to select Pop Pops. Results from both the embedded and forced exposures indicated that the use of music did not enhance selection in either setting.

Nor was brand name recall statistically significant:

$$(\chi^2 = 0.10, \text{ df } = 2, \text{ sign } = 0.99).$$

The speculative pattern from Study One was not repeated in Study Two, however. In Study One, the background condition resulted in the lowest brand name recall (20 percent), while the jingle performed in the middle (28 percent). However, during the embedded exposure of Study Two, the background music resulted in the best recall (38.1 percent), with the jingle resulting in the poorest recall (9.5 percent).

Unlike Study One, attitude toward the ads was most favorable in the no-music condition. A review of table 14-2 reminds the reader that the background music condition was the highest in Study One.

Likewise, attitude towards the brand indicated the same reversal from Study One to Study Two. While the brand was rated most favorably in the background music condition of Study One, the voice-over, no-music condition was the highest in Study Two.

Only the dependent measure of behavioral intent gave similar indications as to the superiority of the background music condition. Both Study One (3.24 on a 4-point scale) and Study Two (2.75 on a 4-point scale) indicated that this condition was the best in affecting the request made to mother. Again, none of these differences was statistically significant and, therefore, these indications must be considered as speculative.

The reader will notice that, overall, the ratings from Study Two were lower than those from Study One. This overall indication matches intuition that the forced exposure in Study One would inflate ratings by subjects. This also suggests that the forced exposure was more involving than the embedded one.

Finally, the generally poor recall of attributes was repeated with Study Two. The background music condition did not appear superior, however, as indicated in Study One.

To summarize, forced exposure (Study One) and embedded exposure (Study Two) indicated that the use of music did not improve pretended selection, attitudes, or memory for a fictitious cereal, Pop Pops, in either situation. The results were not statistically significant. However, the use of a jingle in an embedded exposure did result in statistically lower visual attention directed to the commercial.

## Discussion and Future Directions

Typically, music has been considered as an enhancement to advertising effectiveness. Results from the current project suggest that this commonly accepted view needs cautious consideration. Music did not enhance outcomes typically desired by advertisers. Plausible explanations for a failure to find musical assistance for preschoolers' performance will be briefly described in the order of measures, type of messages, type of music, nature of setting, and repeated exposures over time.

First, the measures used may simply have been too insensitive to capture effects. The pattern of results offered some support for this interpretation. The jingle-embedded condition resulted in less visual attention to the television during its airing. This statistical difference suggested that music can indeed serve as a distraction. In the current instance, the jingle may have been overtaxing of children's processing capacities. Support for this interpretation comes from Anderson, Lorch, Field, and Sanders (1981), who reported that a major determinant of young children's visual attention to a television program was the degree to which they were able to comprehend it. (It should be noted that Anderson and his colleagues' work has focused on children's programming.)

Alternatively, because the jingle closely resembled the sound of current children's advertising, it may have served as a cue that the children could take a "break" from Tom and Jerry. After all, the children were told that they would be asked if the cartoon "was a good one." This explanation is plausible (Haley et al. 1984) and is worth examining in a commercial context.

Moreover, equating visual attention to full attention perhaps constitutes an unwarranted assumption. Of course, a precondition for learning is exposure. But, given exposure, children may auditorily attend without visually attending to the television. First, we have all observed that some people listen to music by shutting their eyes. However, in Study Two, children appeared to have actually increased their activities with more playing and/or talking when the jingle played. Thus, the extent to which visual attention equates to audio attention is impossible to determine in this instance. Indeed, the author does not know of any unobtrusive measures of auditory attention. Moreover, it can be argued that strictly visual attention may be relatively unimportant given the research question regarding the impact of music. Auditory attention is vital. Indeed, aren't we really more interested in music's impact on behavior?

A second, major concern or explanation for the experimental results stems from the type of message used. A review of the words in the animatics suggests high information content with scant use of repetition. (This message was intentionally selected by the experimenter because (1) it offered appropriate interest in testing and (2) it represented the dual message directed to "mother.") A different type of message, for example, high repetition/low content, may have produced differences due to music.

Third, the type of music, in regard to tempo, instrumentation, rhythm, intensity, and so forth, can create differences. We know that music is "emotional" and that it creates feelings, thoughts, and so forth that may be difficult to measure with pencil and paper. The current music employed an electronic synthesizer and was intended to relay a rock, upbeat sound. As such, the jingle may have "hyped" the children into activity that was fun. Indeed, if exposures had been repeated, then the "fun" may have been associated in some fashion and over time with Pop Pops. (A brief discussion of repetition will be forthcoming.) On the other hand, the fast tempo may have impeded comprehension. Wakshlag, Reitz, and Zillmann (1982) reported that rhythmic, fast-tempo background music significantly reduced visual attention and information acquisition to an educational program.

Moreover, context effects need consideration. If children are accustomed to hearing music, then a "serious" commercial absent of music may appear novel. Once again, the long-term impact is difficult to determine based upon a short, experimental situation.

Fourth, the type of setting needs consideration. While Study One (forced, single exposure) was designed to be different from Study Two (embedded, double exposure), the actual exposures may have been very similar to one another. Even the four-year-old child may reason "school is school." He or she may think along the following lines: "Gee, these ladies are here to show me something on television—I'd better watch even if I don't want to—I don't want them to tell my teacher I was bad."

The author argues that we as advertising researchers *really* need to enter children's homes to assess advertising's impact. Only in truly natural environments can we be confident that our results represent reality. Recent work by Anderson, Field, Collins, Lorch, and Nathan (1985) showed that visual attention to the television averaged 67 percent, but that the percent visual attention to television was uncorrelated with time spent with television. That is, "heavy" viewers in terms of time may not be heavy processors because children do other things while the television is on. However, in a more practical mode, the author recognizes that while home entry may be our goal, our actual task may be to better represent the natural viewing situation in the structured setting.

Fifth, the failure to include prolonged, over-time exposures may best explain a failure to establish effects. Can one or two exposures for cereal really affect attitudes and/or behavior? Especially if we assume that the child is *not* as sensitive to a testing effect as the adult, then brief exposures cannot be expected to produce large effects. Thus, contrary to some of my prior discussion, this latter point suggests that the failure to find statistical differences reflects the real impact. That is, minimal exposure(s) produced nil effects in terms of differences. Further, it can be argued that preschoolers constitute a subject pool too unsophisticated to fake results for an experimenter. However, as in real life, multiple exposures may have produced differences in responses to music.

Therefore, as with any project failing to produce statistical differences, one can only speculate as to whether such a failure represents truth or whether the design precluded accurate assessment. This author suspects that the current outcome may actually reflect both sources. First, one- and two-exposures are probably not enough to reflect subtle differences in execution in either the lab or real life. Second, Studies One and Two may both have appeared contrived, even to the child. It is the author's opinion that we adults tend to underestimate the child's awareness of our desires. The child may have figured out that he or she had better watch television because, otherwise, the experimenter would not bother coming to his or her school. Thus, a failure to find execution differences probably reflects a blend of truth (that is, small effects) and experimental artifacts.

It is suggested that advertising researchers try to design more naturalistic settings or actually devise means to enter children's homes. Perhaps we have to engage mothers as test experimenters exposing children to commercials on home VCRs. Certainly, embedded commercials viewed at home would better resemble actual advertising with repeated exposures and divided viewing. The author still suspects that, in the long run, music makes a difference with children. Given the experimental findings (that is, lack of findings), the type of music and the conditions of exposure must be carefully considered. If the failure to find differences were repeated with more exposures, then music's value would be questioned. However, the particulars of the music used must always be considered. We must carefully weigh the nature of the music (tempo, pace, and so on), the experimental setting, and the measures used to detect music's impact.

Perhaps this last item, measures used, constitutes the biggest challenge to future research. While we can create music and manipulate the experimental conditions in terms of setting, we still have to devise "emotional" measures appropriate for use with preschoolers. We must think creatively, be cognizant of young children's illiteracy, but continue to work on pencil-and-paper measures. The use of brand choice measures is urged. The author argues that ultimately the advertiser cares whether music favorably impacts brand choice. It becomes apparent that deciphering music's role in advertising to children presents an arduous, multifaceted task for us as researchers.

# 15
# Surrealism as Nonverbal Communication in Advertisements: A Social Adaptation Theory Perspective

*Lynn R. Kahle*
*Pamela M. Homer*

S urrealistic art techniques, outgrowths of the early twentieth-century artistic movement, are often evident in contemporary advertisements. Surrealistic artists stress the subconscious or nonrational significance of imagery by exploitation of chance effects, unexpected juxtapositions, and unorderly connections. Although these nonverbal (or sometimes verbal) methods are quite widely used, research concerning their effectiveness and persuasive capacities is virtually non-existent. Research on surrealism in advertising is needed in order to understand whether and how these techniques influence consumers. We believe that social adaptation theory provides a useful framework for understanding surrealism and guiding such research.

## The Basic Theory

Social adaptation theory has been developed primarily to account for attitude change and advertising effectiveness (Kahle 1984; Kahle and Homer 1985). It has, however, been applied to a variety of other areas, such as attitude-behavior consistency (Wittenbraker, Gibbs, and Kahle 1983), personality effects (Kahle, Kulka, and Klingel 1980), values (Kahle 1986; Kahle, Beatty, and Homer, in press; Kahle and Timmer 1983), adolescent growth (Eisert and Kahle 1982), life span development (Timmer and Kahle 1983), and prejudice (Piner and Kahle 1984). As a neo-Piagetian account of cognition and other aspects of knowledge, its potential range of applications includes topics as diverse as infant development and epistemology (Eisert and Kahle 1986). The present chapter will emphasize how social adaptation relates to the effectiveness of surrealism as a nonverbal aspect of advertisements.

At the heart of any theory of consumer behavior is the central mechanism through which change occurs. The two building blocks of change in social adaptation theory are assimilation and accommodation. When someone encounters new information, that information can be assimilated into existing mental schemata (singular = schema) without altering the schemata, or it can lead to accommodation (revision) of the schemata. Assimilation is the fusion of a new object to an already-established schema. Accommodation is the most direct sense in which the environment acts on the individual's cognitive structure. An unexpected or surreal stimulus will likely foster adaptation because it will not fit into any established schema. In many cases, assimilation and accommodation occur simultaneously. Their joint action is known as adaptation. Adaptation is the fundamental goal of information processing, as well as of many other human activities. People seek to establish equilibrium with the environment through adaptation. When a person transforms the environment or is transformed by the environment to promote more effective interchanges between the person and the environment, this phenomenon is known as equilibration through adaptation.

To provide an example of these functions, consider the person who believes that Fords are good cars. As new information, such as from advertisements, is encountered, that information will be assimilated if it fits or is made to fit into the schema about Fords. As long as that schema fosters effective interchanges between the person and the environment (for example, a family Ford provides adequate transportation), positive new information will be primarily assimilated, even if at times that information does not fit into the schema neatly. For example, if Joe claims that Fords have bad transmissions, that information may be interpreted as a personality flaw of Joe (negativism) rather than as a mechanical flaw of Fords. Some accommodation will also take place as the schema becomes more complex. The view may develop that Fords are good cars in spite of (or except for) fuel system problems. As long as a state of equilibrium exists between the external environment and that schema, it will be resistant to major change. If that system should inhibit adaptation and effective interchanges with the environment (for example, the Ford has a mechanical problem that ruins the family vacation), then the schema would be ripe for a phase of extensive accommodation, for reequilibration.

A complementary function to adaptation is organization. It is the tendency to systematize processes into coordinated, coherent systems. It is the mechanism through which internal representations of the external environment are related to one another. Thus, both the person and the situation or environment influence the person. An advertising stimulus will have a unique impact on an individual, depending upon that person's previous experience and knowledge about the world. But at the same time, that impact is not entirely random or arbitrary. Even if the external world is interpreted only through current schemata unique to the individual, schemata reflecting poor equilibration with the environment will change more readily than schemata that closely approximate the environment or something correlated with the environment because of their inhibition of adaptation. To continue with our Ford example, if a person knows from experience that Fords have good electrical systems and good air-conditioning systems, organization may push the individual to believe that the cooling system on Fords is superior to the cooling system on other cars, in spite of the lack of direct experience with particularly impressive success stories about Ford cooling systems.

Attitudes are schemata, stored as preferences, that provide abstract accounts of adaptation. Each experience with an attitudinal object, such as a product, will influence the attitudinal schema, whether through assimilation, accommodation, or organization. For example, suppose a person has an attitudinal schema, "I like Smucker's strawberry jam." This schema summarizes previous experiences with Smucker's strawberry jam. It is a much more efficient method of information summarization than the recall of every single experience with strawberry jam. Presumably such a schema would develop from a history of positive experiences with the jam. For a person with hundreds of experiences with Smucker's strawberry jam, this schema would be a well-honed abstraction and therefore resistant to change if all of the evidence had fit the schema well. High-involvement products probably are conducive to more elaborate schemata. People probably also spend a greater amount of time seeking and processing information relevant to high-involvement products (Kahle and Homer 1985).

Attitudes change when the equilibrium described in the attitudinal schema demonstrably fails. When one state of equilibrium proves to be inadequate, accommodation or organization will likely push the attitude toward a more complex schema that better fosters adaptation to the environment, expecially the social environment. Many of the most significant changes in attitudes result from shifting social equilibrium, as when a person moves to a new job or a new social context. For example, if one takes a new job at double the former salary working for an otherwise wonderful boss who hates Fords, a long-standing love of Fords may be suppressed or revised as a part of adapting to the new environment.

Kahle and Homer (1985) proposed that social adaptation theory could account for nonverbal information processing in an advertising context. They examined how people respond to magazine advertising by manipulating the physical attractiveness of celebrity sources, likability of celebrity sources, and participant product involvement in a simulated print advertisement for Edge disposable razors. Celebrities with extreme ratings on physical attractiveness and likability were selected for inclusion in the simulated advertisements, based on a preliminary survey of respondents from the same subject population as the participants in the actual experiment. Kahle and Homer reasoned that for products such as disposable razors, for which consumer interest is relatively low, subjects would not examine information from an advertisement very long. Any information conveyed in the advertisement would probably be observed within the first second or two of observing the advertisement. Thus, the adaptive significance of the celebrity's image relative to the function of the advertised product would be crucial in determining the effectiveness of the advertisement. More specifically, they predictd that, because razors are used more to enhance physical attractiveness than to enhance likability, the endorsement of physically attractive celebrities would facilitate attitude change and advertisement effectiveness more than the endorsement of likable celebrities. The results were consistent with this prediction. Only advertisements that included attractive celebrities were associated with optimal levels of favorable attitudes toward the product.

These results conflict with the interpretation of results of research conducted by Petty, Cacioppo, and Schumann (1984) on the Elaboration Likelihood Model (ELM). In the ELM, peripheral and central information are processed in a qualitatively different manner, whereas in social adaptation theory the difference between highly adaptive versus modestly adaptive information is merely a difference in quantity of processing, not a difference in quality of processing. This study failed to find the ELM-predicted effect for involvement, but this result did not contradict social adaptation theory predictions. That is, the message information was processed under both low and high involvement.

## Surrealism

Surrealism is a form of art, developed primarily in the twentieth century, in which artists attempt to represent and interpret the phenomena of dreams and similar experiences. Surrealistic artists stress the subconscious or nonrational significance of imagery by exploitation of chance effects, unexpected juxtapositions, and unorderly connections. By juxtaposing unrelated objects, they reveal unexpected affinities between different objects. The unexpected combinations represented a vision suddenly free of the stereotyped mental habits considered to belong to those artists trapped by their own talent, virtuosity, and little aesthetic specialties (Gablik 1970). "The object was to free artists from the normal association of pictorial ideas and from all accepted means of expression, in order that they might create according to the irrational dictates of their subconscious mind and vision" (Murray and Murray 1965, p. 194). As expressed by Salvador Dali, "My whole ambition on the pictorial plane consists in materializing with the greatest imperialistic rage for precision images of concrete irrationality . . . images not explicable nor reducible by systems of logical intuition or by rational mechanisms" (1935, p. 12). Surrealists seek dialectically to deny opposites, such as waking and dreams, reason and irrationality, seriousness and humor, or good and evil.

Surrealist constructions appear to take shape primarily in an intermediary position between consciousness and the dream world. Common sense denounces the surreal, dreamlike vision that nevertheless possesses psychological truth. Many surrealists seek to fuse the waking and dreaming mental images, as when Gablik (1970) maintains that the understanding of surrealism begins with a recognition that dreams translate waking life and that waking life translates dreams.

Surrealists achieve maximum impact and a crisis of the object through a variety of nonverbal mechanisms:

1. *Isolation* occurs when an object once situated outside its own field is freed of its expected role.

2. The mechanism of *modification* requires the artist to change some aspect of the object so that a property not normally associated with the object is introduced or some property normally associated with the object is withdrawn.

3. Two familiar objects are combined to produce a "bewildering one" in *hybridization.*

4. A change in scale, position, or substance creates *incongruity.*

5. *Paradox* uses intellectual antitheses.

6. *Conceptual bipolarity* uses interpenetrating images in which two situations are observed from a single viewpoint, thus modifying spatio-temperal experiences. Other mechanisms include:

7. *Provocation of accidental encounters* and

8. *double images.*

It is not surprising that advertisers would also seek to create unique, unexpected, and dreamlike images for use in promotions, because advertisers often try to gain consumers' attention, to fuel their fantasies, and to encourage them to view a product in a new way. Advertisers have even been called dream merchants, implying a link between dreams and advertisements. Recent advances uniting video technology and computer technology now permit advertisers to create surrealistic broadcast advertisements more easily.

## Relationship between Surrealism and Social Adaptation Theory

Social adaptation theory predicts that employing surrealistic techniques should draw attention to the inadequacy of the existing schemata, because the information will be perceived as novel, unexpected, and out of context. It will not fit existing schemata, thus stimulating accommodation. In contrast, if communications prime audiences with cues facilitating expectations of typical, product-relevant verbal information, assimilation will abound. The most effective information processing occurs when assimilation and accommodation are in balance; therefore, a combination of accommodative surrealism and assimilatory priming ought to optimize advertising effectiveness, we hypothesize.

### Experiment One

We tested this hypothesis (Homer and Kahle 1986) in a laboratory experiment on processing of information from magazine advertisements. The surrealistic ad in this study depicted athletic young people interacting socially in a full cocktail glass, and the remaining subjects were exposed to a nonsurreal ad depicting a winter mountain scene. Both ads promoted the consumption of the same brand of liquor. We found that priming improved recall of verbal information in the advertisement, and that the surreal ad reduced the amount of incorrect recall. Most importantly, purchase intentions were greatest when priming and surrealism both were present. We interpreted these findings as confirming of our hypotheses.

### Experiment Two

In the second experiment (Homer 1986), a sample of 190 upperclass business college students read a booklet containing five print advertisements, one of which was manipulated to contain a surreal, novel, or non-novel ad. Involvement and message strength also were manipulated. Results were supportive of social adaptation theory, which suggests that new information is integrated into existing schemata through assimilation and accommodation. Affect toward the ad was greatest when a surreal ad contained strong message arguments under high involvement. High involvement facilitates relatively greater elaboration of both message arguments and visual cues. Strong arguments are consistent with the high-involvement condition and are incorporated into existing schemata through the activation of assimilation and accommodation processes. Deep processing and accommodation are necessary due to the novel and unexpected nature of surreal designs. This magnified level of processing acted to increase the persuasive capacity. This study provided evidence that both peripheral (that is, surreal designs) and central information (that is, message arguments) were processed under high and low involvement—contrary to ELM predictions. Results also failed to conform to the rationale of social judgment theory applied to this context.

## Surrealism and Subliminal Advertising

The dreamlike nature of surrealistic ads may stimulate subconscious responses in much the same manner as some early proponents of subliminal advertising thought that it would work. Subliminal advertisements have not proven effective (Moore 1982), in part because stimulus intensity is too weak, and this same feature has created widespread distrust of subliminal advertisements. Surreal advertisements, in contrast, have adequate stimulus intensity and sufficient visibility that the distrust of subliminal ads is overcome, and perhaps these surreal ads are more effective as well. Their novelty certainly should augment information processing, and some types of surreal advertisements may influence subconscious processes as well.

## Surrealism and the Matchup Hypothesis

Our first study on social adaptation theory and the processing of nonverbal information (Kahle and Homer 1986) suggested that the matchup between celebrity, target market, and message is an important link in the quest for advertising effectiveness. For example, Karl Malden has an image as an actor who portrays streetwise cops and honest priests. This image matches well with a desirable image for American Express, and his endorsements have therefore been effective. We anticipate that the same type of matchup will foster increased effectiveness in surrealistic advertisements. For example, the surreal elements of an ad ought to match with the message being conveyed, even if it is nonsensical visually. For example, a picture of ears on the product in an advertisement for stereos may increase the effectiveness of the ad because good stereos sound good to ears. A picture of sheep in that ad may not have the same effectiveness.

## Conclusions

Social adaptation theory implies that the nonverbal material in surrealistic advertisements provides an important part of the impetus for optimal processing of information in advertisements. Two experiments have supported this prediction. This discussion suggests that surrealism research has implications for the subliminal advertising controversy and for the matchup hypothesis. We hope that our efforts will stimulate further investigation into this important topic of surrealism.

# Part VI
# Conclusion

# 16

# The Future of Research on Nonverbal Communication in Advertising

*David W. Stewart*
*Sidney Hecker*

Systematic research on nonverbal communication is only about twenty years old (Patterson 1982b), and rather little of that research has occurred in advertising settings. The previous chapters in this book represent a first step toward advancing knowledge in the field. The fourteen contributed chapters cover a wide spectrum of issues, methodologies, approaches, and problems associated with the study of nonverbal communication in advertising. Some deal with nonverbal communication, broadly defined, while others deal with very specific aspects of the broader phenomenon. Theoretical orientations in the chapters range from the psychoanalytic to learning paradigms to cognitive information processing approaches to the holistic view of impression formation. The breadth and diversity of approaches represented in these chapters reflect the multidimensionality and complexity of nonverbal communication and the relative recency of attention to it by researchers in the behavioral sciences and advertising. Such diversity, while perhaps frustrating for some readers, is nonetheless healthy, since it provides a means for obtaining a deep and rich description of the phenomenon. Multiple approaches also serve to keep researchers honest by establishing broad boundaries for the phenomenon. Broad boundaries make it difficult to borrow ready-made theories more suitable for explaining other phenomena and thereby prematurely limit empirical investigation, a problem that has plagued advertising research all too frequently in the past. Despite the differences in perspective among the chapters in this book, there are some clear and rather significant common elements. In this, the concluding chapter, we will review these common elements and attempt to place the current chapters within the larger stream of research on nonverbal communication in advertising. In so doing, we hope to point the way for future research on nonverbal elements in advertising.

The contributed chapters in this book appear to make a number of important points about nonverbal communication. All point to the importance of nonverbal communication in the formation of beliefs, impressions, and attitudes about products.

Further, a number of themes appear to cut across these contributions. Among the points that appear again and again are the following:

1. Nonverbal communication is more difficult to define than verbal communication, and this makes operationalization of nonverbal cues all the more critical.

2. Nonverbal communication may be more important than (dominant), less important than, or complementary to verbal communication depending on the situation and context. Thus it is important to know the situation in which communication takes place.

3. Nonverbal communication may be more subtle and context-dependent than verbal communication. The meaning and influence of nonverbal cues are mediated by situational and contextual factors to a far greater extent than are verbal cues.

4. Nonverbal communication is more closely linked to affective and global evaluative responses than is verbal communication.

5. Traditional measures of response to communication are not adequate for capturing responses to nonverbal communications. Other measures are required in addition to, or instead of, more traditional measures.

6. Nonverbal communication influences recipients in a number of different ways: it may carry information in its own right; it may supplement or modify verbal information; or it may serve as a means for controlling the rate and type of communication; that is, it may serve a regulatory function.

These common themes also have implications for the advertising practitioner. They suggest a need for great care in the selection of nonverbal stimuli for use in advertising executions, and a need for testing nonverbal elements to determine whether they do, in fact, evoke the intended response from the target audience. Traditional approaches to copytesting (measures of recall, comprehension, and belief-based attitude change) tend, however, to emphasize the verbal content of advertising. This suggests that in testing nonverbal communication, new approaches to copytesting may be required. For both the researcher and the practitioner, these chapters suggest that the influence of nonverbal communication is a fertile ground for further work, and much work remains to be done.

Each of the themes found among the chapters in this book on advertising have found expression in the literatures of other disciplines as well. It is useful, then, to consider each of these themes in some detail, a task to which we now turn.

## Defining Nonverbal Communication

We noted in the introductory chapter that not one of the contributed chapters in this book makes an effort to offer a general definition of nonverbal communication.

Rather, each author defines by example. This is not atypical, however, in the broader literature on nonverbal communication. Virtually anything other than words, including, as we have seen, the way words are used, has the potential to be a nonverbal cue. This does not mean, however, that every nonverbal stimulus is a nonverbal element in communication. Communication requires something more than a stimulus. Communication implies a socially shared signal system (a code), an encoder who makes something public via that code, and a decoder who responds systematically to that code (Harper, Wiens, and Matarazzo 1978). Verbal communications are relatively easy to identify. The encoder is identified by an unambiguous action, speech or writing; that a code is present is clear, since words are spoken or written; and it is usually possible to readily identify the decoder who is the target of the communication. Things become much more complicated with nonverbal communication. There are many nonverbal signs or behaviors that are not communication. A nonverbal sign implies only that a decoder has made an inference about behavior or attached significance to behavior; nothing is implied about the encoding end of the process.

A substantial amount of the literature on nonverbal communication has focused on the differentiation of nonverbal communication from signs. From the perspective of a marketer or advertiser, this distinction is particularly significant. It is one thing to observe that consumers make inferences about particular nonverbal stimuli. It is quite another to try to design a marketing communications program that makes use of nonverbal cues that are intended to communicate a particular message, evoke a feeling, or otherwise convey information. In this latter case, the marketer must understand what a particular nonverbal stimulus means for a given consumer in advance of the consumer being exposed to the stimulus. This implies the need for a nonverbal language (a coding system). Such a system has not been worked out for much that could be considered nonverbal communication, and for good reason.

The number of nonverbal signs is legion. Consideration of only those signs that are clearly within the definition of communication does not do much to make the task of enumerating signs easier. Researchers in the area of nonverbal communication have attempted to develop various classification systems for nonverbal communication. Among the more frequently identified classes are:

1. Paralinguistic phenomena (how something is said) and the temporal characteristics of language
2. Facial expression
3. Body movements (kinesics)
4. Gestures
5. Spacing or proxemics
6. Eye movements

7. Touch

8. Pictures (pictics or vidistics)

9. Symbolic artifacts (such as the gavel given a new presiding officer of an organization)

Each of these broad classes contains numerous elements which may, in turn, differ with respect to a number of dimensions. The complexity of these systems is well illustrated in a paper by Mehrabian (1969) who identified twelve dimensions of posture (body position) alone! The development of a dictionary of nonverbal language would obviously be a Herculean task.

Further, such a nonverbal language is of necessity far more complex than a verbal language, because nonverbal stimuli often interact in subtle ways, and meanings are often defined by context or situation in ways that are not present for verbal communications. This, of course, brings us to two additional themes struck by the contributors to this book, the situational and contextual basis of the meaning of much nonverbal communication.

## The Contextual Nature of Nonverbal Communication

Consider the following scene: "She lay before him. He looked into her face and moved toward it. She closed her eyes, opened her lips. . . ." This is not the opening of a pornographic novel; it is a description of the interaction between a dentist and his patient. The situation and the context in which a nonverbal sign occur radically alter the meaning of the sign. It is apparent from much of the research on nonverbal communication that the meaning of a nonverbal cue cannot be understood outside of context. This poses problems that are not present in the analysis of verbal communication. While it is certainly clear that the meanings of some words change with context, such changes tend, on the whole, to be subtle. Most words (verbal codes) have a meaning apart from context. This is often not the case for nonverbal codes.

The situation specificity of the meaning of nonverbal signs and behaviors greatly complicates the development of a nonverbal language that can be useful to the marketing practitioner. The potential meanings of an already large number of nonverbal cues is multiplied manyfold by this situation specificity. Dealing with such complexity is a major problem confronting researchers in the field, and there is no one methodology that provides a definitive solution. Researchers in the behavioral and social sciences have used a variety of approaches, however, and each appears to offer promise for expanding knowledge about nonverbal communication.

In a selective review of the literature on nonverbal communication, Patterson (1982b) identified several approaches for examining nonverbal communication:

1. Descriptive approaches
2. Role or situational approaches
3. Ecological approaches
4. Functional approaches
5. Experimental approaches.

These approaches are not mutually exclusive, of course, but they do represent somewhat different perspectives on the problem. We will briefly consider each approach in turn.

## Descriptive Approaches

Much of the research on nonverbal communication over the past twenty years has been descriptive and has tended to concentrate on a single, or at most a few, nonverbal elements (Knapp 1978). Such research has frequently taken the form of descriptions of events in various social interactions such as greeting behaviors, courtship, and so forth. Generally, one type of nonverbal behavior will serve as the focus of such research, for example, distance, touching, or facial expression. An example of one stream of such research is Ekman's work on facial expressions (Ekman and Friesen 1975, Ekman and Friesen 1976, and Ekman and Taussig 1969). This stream of research has sought with considerable success to develop reliable codes for facial expressions that convey various emotional responses. This work has been extended to include descriptions of cross-cultural similarities and differences. The emphasis of this program of research and others like it is a thorough description of one mode of nonverbal communication.

## Role and Ecological Approaches

Other research programs have examined nonverbal communication from somewhat different perspectives. Goffman (1959, 1961, 1963, 1967, 1970) has been more concerned with the role of nonverbal communications in role relationships. In this approach, descriptive analysis focuses on social behavior. The individual or actor is de-emphasized; the situation and social structure, or "frame" in Goffman's terminology, is the unit of analysis. The emphasis of this approach is the way in which nonverbal elements regulate social interactions. Goffman incorporates dramaturgical analysis in his approach as a means for understanding how nonverbal cues serve to create greater meaning than words alone. A somewhat similar approach is Barker's ecological psychology (Barker 1968). Barker is also concerned with understanding interaction of situational factors and nonverbal elements, but his emphasis is not understanding social roles but rather understanding the impact of environment on behavior. Both Goffman and Barker place much emphasis on description of behavior, including nonverbal communication in naturalistic settings as opposed to laboratory settings, in order to assure a minimum of reaction to researchers.

## Functional Approaches

In more recent years, there has been an increasing concern for discovering the "function" of nonverbal communication. Just as Goffman suggested that nonverbal cues may facilitate role relationships, so have others suggested other purposes. The functional approach to the study of nonverbal communication has arisen with the recognition that nonverbal communication is purposive. The central tenet of this approach is that nonverbal communication cannot be understood without an understanding of its function. The same nonverbal sign may serve very different functions, so meaning can only be attributed in the context of purpose. Patterson (1982b) identifies a number of classes of functions for nonverbal communication: providing information, as in a gesture or nod of agreement; regulating interaction, such as through a decrease in the loudness of one's voice or termination of a gesture; expressing intimacy, as in the physical distance established between individuals or the time spent gazing at another; and social control, as in a look of disapproval. Purpose cannot readily be discovered by observation alone, so this approach must rely on techniques such as introspection, role playing, and self-reports to supplement pure observations.

## Experimental Approaches

Although observation would appear to be a rather straightforward approach to the study of nonverbal communications, it is not as simple as might be imagined at first brush. Knapp (1978) suggests that in order to understand the full meaning of nonverbal cues offered by one individual, the researcher must include (1) all simultaneous and proximal behaviors of the individual, (2) any concomitant verbal behavior, (3) the setting in which the cues are offered, (4) the physical characteristics of all interactants, and (5) the verbal and nonverbal behavior of all other persons. This is difficult to accomplish even with the aid of cameras and video recorders. Research on the use of cameras suggests that how an event is filmed, the lack of the total context and potentially some interactants, and the intrusiveness of the camera itself may influence the interpretation of signs, the nonverbal signs emitted, or both (Ekman and Taussig 1969). Further, regardless of the method of observation, there are problems associated with determining the appropriate unit of analysis and the optimal level of precision in categorizing behavior (Ekman and Friesen 1968). For example, a touch is not just a touch. There are many different types of touch, and each type may be interpreted differently depending on where the touching takes place (the setting), and the place touched. Frequency of recording is also a problem, since anything short of continuous recording is likely to result in the loss of some potentially important information.

All of the approaches that rely on naturalistic observation for studying nonverbal communication suffer from an inability to make statements of causality. While this may not be necessary for certain types of inquiry, statements of causality are required in order to make use of nonverbal communication in such applications as the design of advertising campaigns. Statements of causality can only be identified by means of experimentation, and a number of researchers have sought to use experimental approachs for extending the understanding of nonverbal communication. Early experimental studies tended to concentrate on a single nonverbal cue and its influence on some dependent variable. More recent research has tended to be more complex. Further, there has been a growing appreciation for the fact that laboratory studies and the results they produce are context-bound and may have little to say about how nonverbal communication actually influences behavior in natural settings. These problems have led researchers in the field to suggest that rigorously designed experiments be carried out in realistic settings (Argyle 1972). This may be accomplished in a number of ways: (1) through field experiments on unsuspecting subjects, (2) through laboratory experiments that replicate real-life situations, and (3) through role-played laboratory experiments. Several of the chapters in this collection, notably Macklin's study of children's response to music in advertisements, take this approach. There are, however, relatively few such examples to cite. This has led Siegman and Feldstein (1978) to criticize much of the experimental work on nonverbal communication for being too artificial. Stewart and Furse (1986) and Stewart (1987a,b) have criticized much of advertising research for failing to provide realistic tests of advertising effects. Research on the influence of nonverbal cues in advertising is even more likely to suffer from criticisms of artificiality if it is not carried out with stimuli and in settings that closely approximate actual advertising.

The artificiality of much of the experimental work on nonverbal communication grows from several sources. First, much experimental work has had difficulty in dealing with the interaction among multiple *dependent* variables. While interactions among independent variables are commonly hypothesized and reported, the problem of interacting dependent variables has received scant attention. The Relevance–Accessibility Model proposed by Baker and Lutz in this book provides one example of the complexity that may arise when dependent variables interact. A more distal outcome, such as purchase, may be influenced by factors both proximal and distal to an advertisement. The final outcome is not simply the result of the advertising message, but also a function of responses set in motion by the message and a variety of situational and individual difference variables. This type of problem leads rather naturally to a discussion of issues involved in measuring responses to nonverbal communications.

## Measuring Response to Nonverbal Communication

There is something strangely incongruous about measuring response to a nonverbal stimulus by means of verbal instruments. This book uses over 150,000 words to discuss nonverbal communication. The problem with nonverbal communication, which a number of the contributors to this book point out, is that we don't know enough about how to measure it. The meaning of nonverbal communication is frequently better portrayed than explained, and understanding is often less important than feeling. This is not to suggest that nonverbal stimuli do not elicit verbal or cognitive responses, but it does raise the question of whether verbal response measures are adequate for fully capturing the effect of nonverbal communication. Research cited throughout this book seems to suggest that nonverbal stimuli often elicit responses that respondents do not consciously recognize. Many nonverbal stimuli elicit affective responses and evoke unconscious value systems. There is a need for measures that complement traditional verbal responses. Such measures may well include projective techniques that have not seen wide-scale use in marketing research for over twenty years. The profile of emotional responses presented by Holbrook and Batra is one step in this direction, but even their measure is essentially verbal, one in which respondents are asked to label what they feel. This is still a long distance from the type of research on advertising that dominated academic journals for a long period. The idea that affective responses may exist independent of cognitive responses, and may, at least in some circumstances, dominate cognition is a relatively new idea among contemporary advertising researchers.

The measurement of affective responses has been the focus of numerous other publications (see as one example Tybout and Cafferata 1987), and we will not dwell on it here. Affect is but one type of response that may occur as a result of exposure to nonverbal cues. Cognitions may also occur, although Padgett and Brock demonstate that such responses may have nothing to do with the content of the message itself. Behavioral responses may also occur, and have seldom been the focus of research on advertising.

One problem with much of the theorizing about advertising is that theory often suggests specific measures for observation. This may prematurely stifle the discovery of interesting phenomena that are not addressed by particular theories or paradigms. It appears to be particularly important for the understanding of the influence of nonverbal communication to encourage the use of a wide range of measures and the reporting of simple empirical facts even in the absence of a particular theory of nonverbal communication. Inasmuch as empirical facts are the raw materials for theory building, it would seem wise to build an inventory of such facts. This is not to suggest that theory building should not proceed simultaneously. Indeed, theory building has already begun in other disciplines, and it is to those theories that we now turn.

# A Theoretical Foundation for the Study of Nonverbal Communication

While the problems presented by nonverbal communication are serious, and no fully satisfactory solutions for these problems exist, marketing researchers may find comfort in the substantial theoretical work that has been completed in other disciplines. At least four theories of nonverbal communication have been proposed. Birdwhistell (1970) offered a classification and model of body motion that was designed to offer a nonverbal body code that parallels language structure. This theory appears to have been particularly useful for cases where body motion is closely tied to the verbal stream (Harrison 1973). Ekman and Friesen (1968, 1969) examined the origin, usage, and coding of nonverbal behaviors, and distinguish five key classes: (1) emblems, intentional communicative signs that have widely shared meanings, the most direct counterpart of verbal symbols; (2) illustrators, actions that accompany verbal behavior; (3) regulators, actions that help manage the flow of conversation; (4) affect displays, behaviors that reveal or portray feelings; and (5) adaptors, behaviors that began as useful manipulations of the self, objects, or others but that may now have additional informative value. Mehrabian (1970, 1971, 1972a,b), in contrast to the two previous theories, has sought to develop a dimensional system of nonverbal communication. He has sought to define a nonverbal counterpart to Osgood, Suci, and Tannenbaum's (1957) dimensions of verbal symbols. While verbal signs can be located in a semantic space defined by evaluation, potency, and activity, Mehrabian suggests that nonverbal behaviors reveal a communicator's stance on liking, potency, and responsiveness. The fourth theorist, Patterson (1982a), has taken yet another approach to nonverbal communication by focusing on the functions served by nonverbal communication. His work was briefly described earlier in this chapter.

Although each of these theories approaches the study of nonverbal communication from a somewhat different perspective, there are significant similarities between the several approaches. All four theoretical approaches share some important methodological characteristics. First, all place considerable emphasis on the use of observational techniques. The emphasis is on what the communicator does and how the receiver responds. While observation is not unknown in marketing and advertising research, it has, at least until very recently, been secondary to verbal self-report measures. Second, these approaches place significant emphasis on the study of the communication stimuli, as well as the response to those stimuli. This is in marked contrast to much of the recent research on marketing communications, which has tended to emphasize response to the near exclusion of the stimulus. Stewart (1987) has offered a rationale for placing greater emphasis on the stimulus side of the marketing communications equation. Among the reasons for examining stimuli is the need to assure that receivers are actually responding to the hypothesized stimulus event, rather than some other aspect of the communications stimulus or situation. The need for such assurance appears to be particularly critical for the student of nonverbal communication because of the subtleties and nuances that exist in such communication. Stewart and Furse (1986) provide an illustration of a stimulus-based research program applied to the advertising domain, which includes consideration of the influence of nonverbal stimuli.

Finally, these theories all emphasize the need to understand the complementary roles of verbal and nonverbal communication. The role of one form of communication cannot be understood apart from the other. Marketing and advertising researchers have long sought to understand the influence of verbal communication without adequate attention to nonverbal factors. This approach appears destined to reveal an incomplete, if not misleading, understanding of communication.

Much of the theoretical work on nonverbal communication in other disciplines is rather primitive relative to what is typically considered theory in the fields of marketing and advertising. The theories of nonverbal communication are largely concerned with classification, and place little emphasis on causal mechanisms at this point in their development. These are attempts to build theory from the ground up, based on an empirical foundation, and with emphasis on capturing the phenomenon in its natural complexity. This is in stark contrast to the borrowing of theories designed to explain another phenomenon that has characterized much of the prior work on marketing and advertising. Since the meaning of nonverbal communication exists only within context, simplicity is not a virtue in building a theory, since the phenomenon itself may disappear as simplification occurs. This will, no doubt, make theory building slow and frustrating, but at the same time will make it a rich and exciting endeavor.

## Summary

It appears clear that the role of nonverbal communication is an important element in the behavior of consumers. There is even some evidence to suggest that it may be more important than verbal communication. Certainly it is not less important. Unfortunately, the study of nonverbal communication presents methodological problems that are not found in the study of verbal communications. These difficulties may be one reason for the relatively little research on nonveral communication in advertising and marketing. Research is more difficult and time-consuming, and understanding of the phenomenon appears to come in smaller pieces. Yet, a firm foundation for future research has already been established. The chapters in this book represent a rich source of ideas and problems for future research. The course of future research is difficult to predict, though it is likely to continue to be multidimensional, with no single paradigm, approach, or methodology dominant. This means that there will be a need for integration of diverse perspectives as well as a continuing need for basic research. There is much to be done and much to be learned.

# References

Aaker, David A., and Donald E. Bruzzone (1981), "Viewer Perceptions of Prime-Time Television Advertising," *Journal of Advertising Research*, 21 (October), 15–23.

Aaker, David A., Douglas M. Stayman, and Michael R. Hagerty (1986), "Warmth in Advertising: Measurement, Impact and Sequence Effects," *Journal of Consumer Research*, 12 (March), 365–381.

Aaker, David A., and John G. Myers (1975), *Advertising Management* (Englewood Cliffs, N.J.: Prentice–Hall).

Abelson, R.P., and D.E. Kanouse (1968), "Subjective Acceptance of Verbal Generalization," in S. Feldman (ed.), *Cognitive Consistency: Motivational Antecedents and Behavior Consequent* (New York: Academic Press).

Alba, Joseph W., and J. Wesley Hutchinson (1987), "Dimensions of Consumer Expertise," *Journal of Consumer Research*, 14 (March), 411–454.

Alba, Joseph W., and Lynn Hasher (1983), "Is Memory Schematic?" *Psychological Bulletin*, 93 (March), 203–231.

Alba, Joseph W., and Howard Mamorstein (1987), "The Effects of Frequency Knowledge on Consumer Decision Making," *Journal of Consumer Research* (forthcoming).

Alesandrini, K.L. (1983), "Strategies that Influence Memory for Advertising Communications," in R.J. Harris (ed.), *Information Processing Research in Advertising* (Hillsdale, N.J.: Lawrence Erlbaum), 65–82.

Alesandrini, K.L., Kathryn Lutz, and Anees A. Sheikh (1983), "Research on Imagery: Implications for Advertising," in A.A. Sheikh (ed.), *Imagery: Current Theory, Research, and Application* (New York: Wiley), 535–556.

Allen, C.T., and T.J. Madden (1985), "A Closer Look at Classical Conditioning," *Journal of Consumer Research*, 12, 301–315.

Alpert, Judy I., and Mark I. Alpert (1986), "The Effects of Music in Advertising on Mood and Purchase Intentions," Working Paper 85/86-5-4, Department of Marketing Administration, University of Texas at Austin, May.

Alsop, R. (1985), "Ad Agencies Jazz Up Jingles By Playing on 1960s Nostalgia," *The Wall Street Journal* (April 18), 31.

Anderson, D.R., E.P. Lorch, D.E. Field, and J. Sanders (1981), "The Effects of TV Program Comprehensibility on Preschool Children's Visual Attention to Television," *Child Development*, 52: 151–157.

Anderson, D.R., D.E. Field, P.A. Collins, E.P. Lorch, and J.G. Nathan (1985), "Estimates of Young Children's Time with Television: A Methodological Comparison of Parent Reports with Time-Lapse Video Home Observation," *Child Development*, 56, 1345–1357.

Anderson, D.R., E.P. Lorch, R. Smith, R. Bradford, and S.R. Levin (1981), "Effects of Peer Presence on Preschool Children's Television-Viewing Behavior," *Developmental Psychology*, 17 (4), 446–453.

Anderson, J.R. (1983), "A Spreading Activation Theory of Memory," *Journal of Verbal Learning and Verbal Behavior*, 22 (June), 261–295.

Anderson, J.R., and Gordon Bower (1980), *Human Associative Memory* (Hillsdale, N.J.: Erlbaum).

Anderson, J.R., and L.M. Reder (1979), "An Elaborative Processing Explanation of Depth of Processing," in L.S. Cermak and F.I.M. Craig (eds.), *Levels of Processing in Human Memory* (Hillsdale, N.J.: Erlbaum).

Anderson, N.H. (1972), "Looking for Configurality in Clinical Judgment," *Psychological Bulletin*, 78, 93–102.

Anderson, N.H. (1974), "Cognitive Algebra: Integration Theory Applied to Social Attribution," in L. Berkowitz (ed.), *Advances in Experimental Social Psychology*, Vol. 7 (New York: Academic Press).

Anderson, N.H. (1981), *Foundations of Information Integration Theory* (New York: Academic Press).

Anderson, N.H. (1982), *Methods of Information Integration Theory* (New York: Academic Press).

Anderson, N.H., and A.A. Barrios (1961), "Primacy Effects in Personality Impression Formation," *Journal of Personality and Social Psychology*, 63, 346–350.

Anderson, N.H., and C.I. Hovland (1957), "The Representation of Order Effects in Communication Research," in Hovland et al. (eds.), *The Order of Presentation in Persuasion* (New Haven: Yale University Press), 158–169.

Anderson, N.H., and S. Hubert (1963), "Effects of Concomitant Verbal Recall on Order Effects in Personality Impression Formation," *Journal of Verbal Learning and Verbal Behavior*, 2, 379–391.

Archer, D., and R.M. Akert (1984), "Problems of Context and Criterion in Nonverbal Communication: A New Look at the Accuracy Issue," in M. Cook (ed), *Issues in Person Perception* (London: Methuen).

Arnold, Magda B. (1960), *Emotion and Personality* (New York: Columbia University Press).

Argyle, Michael (1972), "Non-verbal Communication in Human Interaction," in R.A. Hinde (ed.), *Nonverbal Communication* (Cambridge: University Press).

Asch, S.E. (1946), "Forming Impressions of Personality," *Journal of Abnormal and Social Psychology*, 41, 258–290.

Asseal, H. (1987), *Consumer Behavior and Marketing Action* (Boston: Kent Publishing).

Avery, R.D., and J.E. Campion (1984), "Person Perception in the Employment Interview," in M. Cook (ed.), *Issues in Person Perception* (London: Methuen), 202–241.

Baker, William E. (1985), "Advertising Generated Brand Evaluation: A Memory Based Information Processing Perspective," Master's Thesis: University of Florida.

Baker, William, J. Wesley Hutchinson, Danny Moore, and Prakash Nedungadi (1986), "Brand Familiarity and Advertising: Effects on the Evoked Set and Brand Preference." In Richard J. Lutz (ed.), *Advances in Consumer Research* (Provo, Utah: Association for Consumer Research), 637–642.

Baldwin, Lori, and Richard Mizerski (1985), "An Experimental Investigation Concerning the Comparative Influence of MTV and Radio on Consumer Market Responses to New Music," in Elizabeth C. Hirschman and Morris B. Holbrook (eds.), *Advances in Consumer Research*, 12, 476–481.

Bargh, John A. (1984), "Automatic and Conscious Processing of Social Information," in Robert S. Wyer, Jr., and Thomas K. Srull (eds.), *Handbook of Social Cognition*, Volume 3 (Hillsdale, N.J.: Erlbaum).

Barker, Roger C. (1968), *Ecological Psychology: Concepts and Methods for Studying the Environment of Human Behavior* (Stanford, Cal.: Stanford University Press).

Batra, Rajeev (1984), " 'Low Involvement' Message Reception—Processes and Advertising Implications," unpublished doctoral dissertation, Stanford University.

Batra, Rajeev, and Michael L. Ray (1982), "Advertising Situations: The Implications of Differential Involvement and Accompanying Affect Responses," in Richard J. Harris (ed.), *Information Processing Research in Advertising* (Hillsdale, N.J.: Erlbaum).

Batra, Rajeev, and Michael L. Ray (1986), "Affective Responses Mediating Acceptance of Advertising," *Journal of Consumer Research*, 13 (September), 234–249.

Batra, Rajeev, and Michael L. Ray (1986), "Situational Effects of Advertising Repetition: The Moderating Influence of Motivation, Ability, and Opportunity," *Journal of Consumer Research*, 12 (March), 432–445.

Batra, Rajeev, and Michael L. Ray (1985), "How Advertising Works at Contact." in Linda F. Alwitt and Andrew A. Mitchell (eds.), *Psychological Processes and Advertising Effects: Theory, Research, and Application* (Hillsdale, N.J.: Erlbaum), 13–43.

Bauer, Raymond A., and Stephen A. Greyser (1968), *Advertising in America: The Consumer View*, (Boston, Mass.: Division of Research, Graduate School of Business Administration, Harvard University).

Beattie, A.E., and A.A. Mitchell (1985), "The Relationship Between Advertising Recall and Persuasion: An Experimental Investigation," in L.F. Alwitt and A.A. Mitchell (eds.), *Psychological Processes and Advertising Effects: Theory, Research and Applications* (Hillsdale, N.J.: Erlbaum), 129–155.

Beatty, Sharon E., Lynn R. Kahle, Pamela M. Homer, and Shekhar Misra (1985), "Alternative Measurement Approaches to Consumer Values: The List of Values and the Rokeach Value Survey," *Psychology and Marketing*, 2 (3), 181–200.

Begg, I., and A. Paivio (1969), "Concreteness and Imagery in Sentence Meaning," *Journal of Verbal Learning and Verbal Behavior*, 8, 821–827.

Belch, George E., and Richard J. Lutz (1982), "A Multiple Exposure Study of the Effects of Comparative and Noncomparative Television Commercials on Cognitive Response, Recall, and Message Acceptance," Cambridge, Mass: Marketing Science Institute, Working Paper No. 82-107, September.

Berlyne, D.E. (1970), "Novelty, Complexity, and Hedonic Value," *Perception and Psychophysics*, 8, 279–285.

Berlyne, Daniel E. (1960), *Conflict, Arousal and Curiosity* (New York: McGraw-Hill).

Bettman, James R. (1979), *An Information Processing Theory of Consumer Choice* (Reading, Mass.: Addison-Wesley).

Biehal, Gabriel, and Dipankar Chakravarti (1986), "Consumers' Use of Memory and External Information in Choice: Macro and Micro Perspectives," *Journal of Consumer Research*, 12 (March), 383–405.

Bierley, Calvin, Francis K. McSweeney, and Renee Vannieuwkerk (1985), "Classical Conditioning or Preferences for Stimuli," *Journal of Consumer Research*, 12 (December), 316–323.

Bierley, C., F.K. McSweeney, and R. Vannieuwkerk (1985), "Classical Conditioning of Preferences For Stimuli," *Journal of Consumer Research*, 12, 316–323.

Biller, Jack D., Peggy J. Olson, and Thomas Breen (1974), "The Effect of 'Happy' Versus 'Sad' Music and Participation Anxiety," *Journal of Music Therapy*, 11 (Summer), 68–73.

Birdwhistell, Ray L. (1970), *Kinesics and Context* (Philadelphia: University of Pennsylvania Press).

Blaney, P.H. (1986), "Affect and Memory: A Review," *Psychological Bulletin*, 99, 229–246.

Block, J. (1957), "Studies in the Phenomenology of Emotions," *Journal of Abnormal and Social Psychology*, 54, 358–363.

Bower, G.H. (1972), *Cognition in Learning Memory* (New York: Wiley).

Bower, Gordon H. (1981), "Mood and Memory," *American Psychologist*, 36, 129–148.

Bower, G.H. and P.R. Cohen (1982), "Emotional Influences in Memory and Thinking," in M.S. Clark and S.T. Fiske (eds.), *Affect and Cognition* (Hillsdale, N.J.: Erlbaum).

Bower, G.H., S.G. Gilligan, and K.P. Monteiero (1981), "Selectivity of Learning Caused by Affective States," *Journal of Experimental Psychology: General*, 110, 451–73.

Bower, G.H. and J.D. Mayer (1985), "Failure to Replicate Mood-Dependent Retrieval," *Bulletin of the Psychonomic Society*, 23, 39–42.

Bower, T.G.R. (1977), *A Primer of Infant Development* (San Francisco: Freeman).

Bradley, I.L. (1971), "Repetition as a Factor in the Development of Musical Preferences," *Journal of Research in Music Education*, 19, 295–298.

Brehm, Jack W. (1966), *A Theory of Psychological Reactance* (New York: Academic Press).

Brien, M. (1979), *Consumer Involvement in Health Care Evaluation and Decision Making*, Unpublished Ph.D dissertation, Kansas State University.

Brien, M., N. Haverfield, and J. Shantean (1983), "How Lamaze-Prepared Expectant Parents Select Obstetricians," *Research in Nursing and Health*, 6, 143–150.

Britton, B.K. (1980), "Use of Cognitive Capacity in Reading: Effects of Processing Information From Text For Immediate Recall and Retention," *Journal of Reading Behavior*, 7, 129–137.

Britton, B.K., R. Zieglar, and R. Westbrook (1980), "Use of Cognitive Capacity in Reading Easy and Difficult Text: Two Tests of an Allocation of Attention Hypothesis," *Journal of Reading Behavior*, 7, 23–28.

Britton, B.K., R.D. Westbrook, and T.S. Holdredge (1978), "Reading and Cognitive Capacity Usage: Effects of Text Difficulty," *Journal of Experimental Psychology: Human Learning and Performance*, 4, 582–591.

Britton, B.K. and A. Tesser (1982), "Effects of Prior Knowledge on Use of Cognitive Capacity in Three Complex Cognitive Tasks," *Journal of Verbal Learning and Verbal Behavior*, 21, 421–436.

Britton, B.K., T.S. Holdredge, C. Curry, and R.D. Westbrook (1979), "Use of Cognitive Capacity in Reading Identical Text with Different Amounts of Discourse Level Meaning," *Journal of Experimental Psychology: Human Learning and Memory*, 5, 262–270.

Britton, B.K., A.C. Graesser, S.M. Glynn, T. Hamilton, and M. Penland (1983), "Use of Cognitive Capacity in Reading: Effects of Some Content Features of Text," *Discourse Processes*, 6, 39–57.

Britton, B.K., S.M. Glynn, B.J.E. Meyer, and M.J. Penland (1982), "Effects of Text Structure on Use of Cognitive Capacity During Reading," *Journal of Educational Psychology*, 74, 51–61.

Broadbent, D.E. (1958), *Perceptions and Communication* (London: Pergamon Press).

Brock, T. (1967), "Communication Discrepancy and Intent To Persuade As Determinants of Counterargument Production," *Journal of Experimental Social Psychology*, 3, 296–309.

Brock, T. (1981), "Historical and Methodological Perspectives in the Analysis of Cognitive Responses: An Introduction," in R. Petty, T. Ostrom, and T. Brock (eds.), *Cognitive Responses in Persuasion* (Hillsdale, N.J.: Erlbaum), 1–3.

Brock, Timothy C., and Stuart M. Albert (1970), "Familiarity, Utility, and Supportiveness as Determinants of Information Receptivity," *Journal of Personality and Social Psychology*, 14 (4), 292–301.

Brock, T., and J. Balloun (1967), "Behavioral Receptivity to Dissonant Information," *Journal of Personality and Social Psychology*, 6, 413–428.

Brock, T.C., and Lee A. Becker (1965), "Ineffectiveness of 'Overheard' Counterpropaganda," *Journal of Personality and Social Psychology*, 2, 654–660.

Brown, A.L. (1972), "Context and Recency Cues in the Recognition Memory of Children," *American Journal of Mental Deficiency*, 77, 54–58.

Brown, A.L. (1973), "Judgments of Recency for Long Sequences of Pictures: The Absence of a Development Trend," *Journal of Experimental Child Psychology*, 15, 473–480.

Brown, A.L. (1975), "Recognition, Reconstruction, and Recall of Narrative Sequences by Preoperational Children," *Child Development*, 46, 156–66.

Burnkrant, Robert E., and Alan G. Sawyer (1983), "Effects of Involvement and Message Content on Information Processing Intensity," in Richard J. Harris (ed.), *Information Processing Reserarch in Advertising* (Hillsdale, N.J.: Erlbaum).

Burnkrant, Robert E., and Daniel J. Howard (1986), "Effects of the Use of Introductory Rhetorical Questions Versus Statements of Information Processing," *Journal of Personality and Social Psychology*, 5, (forthcoming).

Butzin, C.A., and N.H. Anderson (1973). "Functional Measurement of Children's Judgments," *Child Development*, 44, 529–537.

Cacioppo, John T., and Richard E. Petty (1982), "The Need for Cognition," *Journal of Personality and Social Psychology*, 42 (January), 116–131.

Cacioppo, J., S. Harkins, and R. Petty (1981), "The Nature of Attitudes and Cognitive Responses and Their Relationships to Behavior," in R. Petty, T. Ostrom, and T. Brock (eds.), *Cognitive Responses in Persuasion* (Hillsdale, N.J.: Erlbaum), 31–54.

Cantril, H. (1976), *Psychology of Social Movements* (New York: Krieger) (originally published 1941).

Carlston, Donald E. (1980), "Events, Inferences, and Impression Formation," in Reid Hastie, Thomas M. Ostrom, Ebbe B. Ebbesen, Robert S. Wyer, David L. Hamilton, and Donald E. Carlston (eds.), *Person Memory: The Cognitive Basis of Social Perception* (Hillsdale, N.J.: Erlbaum), 89–119.

Carpenter, G. (1975), "Mother's Face and the Newborn," in R. Lewin (ed.), *Child Alive* (London: Temple Smith).

Chaiken, Shelly (1980), "Heuristic Versus Systematic Information Processing and the Use of Source Versus Message Cues in Persuasion," *Journal of Personality and Social Psychology*, 39 (November), 752–766.

Chaiken, Shelly, and Alice H. Eagly (1976), "Communication Modality as a Determinant of Message Persuasiveness and Message Comprehensibility," *Journal of Personality and Social Psychology*, 34, 606–614.

Chance, Paul (1975), "Ads Without Answers Make the Brain Itch," *Psychology Today*, 9 (November), 78.

Chapanis, N.P., and A. Chapanis (1964), "Cognitive Dissonance: Five Years Later," *Psychological Bulletin*, 61, 1–22.

Childers, T.L., and M.J. Houston (1984), "Conditions for a Picture-Superiority Effect on Consumer Memory," *Journal of Consumer Research*, 11, 643–654.

Cialdini, Robert (1971), "Attitudinal Advocacy in the Verbal Conditioner," *Journal of Personality and Social Psychology*, 17, 350–358.

Cialdini, Robert (1984), *Influence: The New Psychology of Modern Persuasion* (New York: Morrow).

Cialdini, Robert, and R. Petty (1981), "Anticipatory Opinion Effects," in R. Petty, T. Ostrom, and T. Brock (eds.), *Cognitive Responses in Persuasion* (Hillsdale, N.J.: Erlbaum), 217–235.

Cialdini, Robert, Richard E. Petty, and John T. Cacioppo (1981), "Attitude and Attitude Change," in *Annual Review of Psychology*, 32, 357–404.

Clark, Margaret S. (1982), "A Role for Arousal in Explaining the Link between Feeling States, Judgments and Behavior," in M.S. Clark and S.T. Fiske (eds.), *Affect and Cognition* (Hillsdale, N.J.: Erlbaum).

Clark, Margaret S., and Alice M. Isen (1982), "Toward Understanding the Relationship Between Feeling States and Social Behavior," in A.M. Hastorf and A.M. Isen (eds.), *Cognitive Social Psychology* (New York, N.Y.: Elsevier), 73–108.

Clee, Mona A., and Robert A. Wicklund (1980), "Consumer Behavior and Psychological Reactance," *Journal of Consumer Research*, 6 (March), 389–405.

Clore, Gerald, and Andrew Ortony (1983), "The Cognitive Causes of Emotion," paper presented at the Nags Head Conference on Emotion, Stress and Conflict, Nags Head, North Carolina, June.

Cohen, A.R. (1959), "Communication Discrepancy and Attitude Change: A Dissonance Theory Approach," *Journal of Personality*, 27, 386–396.

Cohen, Joel B. (1982), "Involvement: Separating the State From Its Causes and Effects," Working Paper No. 33, University of Florida.

Cohen, Joel B. (1983), "Involvement and You: 1000 Great Ideas," *Advances in Consumer Research*, vol. 10, 325–328.

Cole, C.A., G. Gaeth, and S.N. Singh (1986), "Measuring Prior Knowledge," in R.J. Lutz (ed.), *Advances in Consumer Research*, vol. XIII, (Provo, Utah: Association for Consumer Research).

Condon, W.S. and L. Sander (1974), "Neonate Movement is Synchronized With Adult Speech: Interactional Participation and Language Acquisition," *Science*, 183, 99–101.

Conrad, C. (1974), "Context Effects in Sentence Comprehension—A Study of the Subjective Lexicon," *Memory and Cognitions*, 2, 130–138.

Cook, M. (1984), *Issues in Person Perception* (London: Methuen).

Cooper, Eunice, and Helen Dinerman (1951), "Analysis of the Film 'Don't Be A Sucker,' A Study of Communication," *Public Opinion Quarterly*, 15 (Summer), 243–264.

Crano, W.D. (1977), "Primacy Versus Recency in Retention of Information and Opinion Change," *Journal of Social Psychology*, 101, 87–96.

Cushing, Peter, and Melody Douglas-Tate (1985), "The Effect of People/Product Relationships on Advertising Processing," in Linda F. Alwitt and Andrew A. Mitchell (eds.), *Psychological Processes and Advertising Effects* (Hillsdale, N.J.: Erlbaum).

Dali, Salvadore (1935), *La Conquete de L'irrationel* (Paris: Editions Surrealists).

Davitz, Joel R. (1969), *The Language of Emotion* (New York: Academic Press).

Degrott, A.D. (1965), *Thought and Choice In Chess* (The Hague: Mouton).

de Rivera, Joseph (1977), *A Structural Theory of the Emotions* (New York: International Universities Press).

de Saussure, F. (1916), *Cours de Linguistique Generale.* Translated (1959) as *Course in General Linguistics* by W. Baskin (New York: McGraw-Hill).

Dichter, Ernest (1960), *The Strategy of Desire* (New York: Doubleday).

Dichter, Ernest (1986), "Testing Nonverbal Communications," paper presented at Fifth Annual Advertising and Consumer Psychology Conference, New York City, May 15, 1986.

Doob, L. (1952), *Social Psychology* (New York: Wiley).

Domzal, T.J., and L.S. Unger (1985), "Judgments of Verbal Versus Pictorial Presentations of a Product with Functional And Aesthetic Features," in E.C. Hirschman and M.B. Holbrook (eds.), *Advances in Consumer Research,* vol. 12 (Provo, Utah: Association for Consumer Research), 268-272.

Druckman, Daniel, Richard M. Rozelle, and James C. Baxter (1982), *Nonverbal Communication, Survey, Theory, and Research* (Beverly Hills, Cal.: Sage Publications).

Dulany, D.E. (1974), "On the Support of Cognitive Theory in Opposition to Behavior Theory: A Methodological Problem," in W.B. Weimer and D.S. Palermo (eds.), *Cognition and the Symbolic Processes* (Hillsdale, N.J.: Erlbaum).

Dutta, S., and R.N. Kanungo (1972), "Retention of Affective Material: Effects of Intensity of Affect on Retrieval," *Journal of Personality and Social Psychology,* 23, 64-80.

Eagly, A. (1974), "Comprehensibility of Persuasive Arguments as a Determinant of Opinion Change," *Journal of Personality and Social Psychology,* 29, 758-773.

Edell, J.A., and R. Staelin (1983), "The Information Processing of Pictures in Print Advertisements," *Journal of Consumer Research,* 10, 45-60.

Edell, J.A., and M.C. Burke (1984), "The Moderating Effect of Attitude Toward an Ad On Ad Effectiveness Under Different Processing Conditions," in T.C. Kinnear (ed.), *Advances in Consumer Behavior,* vol. II (Provo, Utah: Association for Consumer Research), 644-649.

Edinger, Joyce A., and Miles L. Patterson (1983), "Nonverbal Involvement and Social Control," *Psychological Bulletin,* 93 (January), 30-56.

Eimas, P., E. Siqueland, P. Jusczyk, and J. Vigorito (1971), "Speech Perception in Infants," *Science,* 171, 303-306.

Eisert, Debra C., and Lynn R. Kahle (1986), "The Development of Social Attributions: An Integration of Probability and Logic," *Human Development,* 29, 61-81.

Eisert, Debra C., and Lynn R. Kahle (1982), "Self-evaluation and Social Comparison of Physical and Role Change during Adolescence: A Longitudinal Analysis," *Child Development,* 53 (Winter), 98-104.

Ekman, Paul, and W.V. Friesen (1968), "Nonverbal Behavior in Psychotherapy Research," in John M. Shlien (ed.), *Research in Psychotherapy* (Washington, D.C.: American Psychological Association).

Ekman, Paul, and W.V. Friesen (1969), "The Repertoire of Nonverbal Behavior: Categories, Origins, Usage, and Coding," *Semiotica,* 1, 49-98.

Ekman, Paul, and W.V. Friesen (1975), *Unmasking the Face* (Englewood Cliffs, N.J.: Prentice-Hall).

Ekman, Paul, and W.V. Friesen (1976), "Measuring Facial Movement," *Environmental Psychology and Nonverbal Behavior,* 1, 56-75.

Ekman, P., Wallace V. Friesen, and Phoebe Ellsworth (1982), "What Emotion Categories or Dimensions Can Observers Judge from Facial Behavior? in Paul Ekman (ed.)., *Emotion in the Human Face* (Cambridge: Cambridge University Press), 39-55.

Ekman, P. and T.J. Taussig (1969), "VIDR-R and SCAN: Tools and Methods in the Analysis of Facial Expression and Body Movement," in G. Gerbner, O. Holsti, K. Krippendorff, W. Paisley, and P. Stone (eds.), *Content Analysis* (New York: Wiley).

Elwork, A., B. Sales, and J. Alfini (1977), "In Ignorance of the Law or In Light of It?" *Law and Human Behavior*, 1(2), 163–189.

Engle, J.G., R.D. Blackwell, and P.W. Miniard (1986), *Consumer Behavior* (5th ed.) (Chicago: Dryden Press).

Ettenson, R., J.L. Krogstad, and J. Shanteau (1984), "Context and Experience in Auditors' Materiality Judgments," *Auditing: A Journal of Practice & Theory*, 4, 54–73.

Fazio, Russel H. (1986), "How Do Attitudes Guide Behavior," in R.M. Sorrentino and E.T. Higgins (eds.), *The Handbook of Motivation and Cognition: Foundations of Social Behavior* (New York: Guilford Press), 204–243.

Fazio, Russel, H., and Mark P. Zanna (1981), "Direct Experience and Attitude–Behavior Consistency," in Leonard Berkowitz (ed), *Advances in Experimental Social Psychology* (New York: Academic Press), 161–202.

Festinger, Leon, and Nathaniel Maccoby (1964), "On Resistance to Persuasive Communications," *Journal of Abnormal and Social Psychology*, 46, 92–100.

Fine, Bernard J. (1957), "Conclusion-Drawing, Communicator Credibility, and Anxiety as Factors in Opinion Change," *Journal of Abnormal and Social Psychology*, 54 (May), 369–374.

Firestone, I.J. (1977), "Reconciling Verbal and Nonverbal Models of Dyadic Communication," *Environmental Psychology and Nonverbal Communication*, 2, 30–44.

Fishbein, Martin (1963), "An Investigation of the Relationship Between Beliefs About an Object and the Attitude Toward that Object," *Human Relations*, 16, 233–240.

Fishbein, Martin (1967), "A Consideration of Beliefs and Their Role in Attitude Measurement," in M. Fishbein (ed.), *Readings in Attitude Theory and Measurement* (New York: Wiley).

Fiske, Susan (1982), "Schema-Triggered Affect: Applications to Social Perception," in M.S. Clark and S.T. Fiske (eds.), *Affect and Cognition* (Hillsdale, N.J.: Erlbaum).

Fitch, E. (1985), "Ad Music Composer Humming A Happy Tune," *Advertising Age*, (February 28), 38.

Flavell, J. (1970), "Developmental Studies of Mediated Memory," in H.W. Reese and L.P. Lippsitt (eds.), *Advances in Child Development and Behavior* (New York: Academic Press).

Forester, K.I., and L.A. Ryder (1971), "Perceiving the Structure and Meaning of Sentences," *Journal of Verbal Learning and Verbal Behavior*, 10, 285–296.

Foxall, G.R. (1980), *Consumer Behavior: A Practical Guide* (New York: Wiley).

Friestad, M., and E. Thorson (1985), "The Role of Emotion in Memory for Television Commercials," Paper presented at the annual meeting of the International Communication Association, Honolulu, Hawaii, May.

Frijda, Nico H. (1970), "Emotions and Recognition of Emotion," in Magda Arnold (ed.), *Feelings and Emotions: The Loyola Symposium* (New York: Academic Press), 241–250.

Gablik, Suzi (1970), *Magritte* (Greenwich, Conn.: New York Graphic Society).

Gaeth, G.J. (1984), *The Influence of Irrelevant Information in Judgment Processes: Assessment, Reduction, and a Model*, unpublished PhD. dissertation, Kansas State University.

Gaeth, G.J., and J. Shanteau (1984), "Reducing the Influence of Irrelevant Information on Experienced Decision Makers," *Organizational Behavior and Human Performance*, 33, 263–282.

Galizio, M., and C. Hendrick (1972), "Effect of Musical Accompaniment on Attitude: The Guitar as a Prop for Persuasion," *Journal of Applied Social Psychology*, 2, 350–359.

Gardner, David (1971), "Is There a Generalized Price–Quality Relationship?" *Journal of Marketing Research*, 8, 241–243.

Gardner, M.P. (1985), "Does Attitude Toward the Ad Effect Brand Attitude Under a Brand Evaluation Set?" *Journal of Marketing Research*, 22 (May), 192–198.

Gardner, M.P., and M.J. Houston (1986), "The Effects of Verbal and Visual Components on Retail Communications," *Journal of Retailing*, 62, 64–78.

Gardner, M.P., A.A. Mitchell, and J.E. Russo (1985), "Low Involvement Strategies for Processing Advertisements," *Journal of Advertising*, 14, 4–12.

Gentry, J.W., and J. Shanteau (1979), "Revision of Consumer Intention Models: Two Models," *OMEGA: International Journal of Management Science*, 7, 241–247.

Glass, A.L., K.J. Holyoak, and J.L. Santa (1979), *Cognition* (Reading, Mass.: Addison-Wesley).

Goffman, E. (1963, *Behavior in Public Places* (New York: Free Press).

Goffman, E. (1959), *The Presentation of Self in Everyday Life* (Garden City, N.Y.: Anchor).

Goffman, E. (1961), *Encounters* (New York: Bobbs–Merrill).

Goffman, E. (1967), *Interaction Ritual* (Garden City, N.Y.: Anchor).

Goffman, E. (1970), *Relations in Public* (New York: Harper Colophon).

Goffman, E. (1974), *Frame Analysis* (New York: Harper and Row).

Goldman-Eisler, F., and M. Cohen (1971), "Symmetry of Clauses and the Psychological Significance of Left Branching," *Language and Speech*, 14, 109–114.

Gorn, Gerald J., (1982), "The Effects of Music in Advertising on Choice Behavior: A Classical Conditioning Approach," *Journal of Marketing*, 46 (Winter), 94–101.

Gough, P.B. (1965), "Grammatical Transformation and Speed of Understanding," *Journal of Verbal Learning and Verbal Behavior*, 4, 107–111.

Green, P.E. (1962), "Bayesian Decision Theory in Advertising," *Journal of Advertising Research*, 2, 33–41.

Greenwald, A. (1968a), "Cognitive Learning, Cognitive Response to Persuasion, and Attitude Change," in A. Greenwald, T. Brock, and T. Ostrom (eds.) *Psychological Foundations of Attitudes* (New York: Academic Press), 147–170.

Greenwald, A. (1968b), "On Defining Attitude and Attitude Theory," in A. Greenwald, T. Brock, and T. Ostrom (eds.), *Psychological Foundations of Attitudes* (New York: Academic Press), 361–388.

Greenwald, Anthony G., and Clark Leavitt (1984), "Audience Involvement in Advertising: Four Levels," *Journal of Consumer Research*, 11 (June), 581–592.

Grossman, L., and M. Eagle (1970), "Synonymity, Antonymity, and Association in False Recognition Response," *Journal of Experimental Psychology*, 83, 244–248.

Gwynne, P., and C. Panati (1977), "Eye Opener," *Newsweek*, June 6.

Hadley, Howard D. (1953), "Applied Psychology in Action: The Non-Directive Approach in Advertising Appeals," *Journal of Applied Psychology*, 32, 496–98.

Haley, R.I., J. Richardson, and B.M. Baldwin (1984), "The Effects of Nonverbal Communications in Television Advertising," *Journal of Advertising Research*, 24 (4), 11–18.

Hamilton, H.W., and J. Deese (1971), "Comprehensibility and Subject Verb Relation in Complex Centers," *Journal of Verbal Learning and Verbal Behavior*, 10, 163–170.

Harper, Robert G., Arthur N. Wiens, and Joseph D. Matarazzo (1978), *Nonverbal Communication: The State of the Art* (New York: Wiley).

Harrison, Albert A. (1977), "Mere Exposure," in Leonard Berkowitz (ed.), *Advances in Experimental Social Psychology* (New York: Academic Press).

Harrison, Randall P. (1973), "Nonverbal Communicatin," in Ithiel De Sola Pool and Wilber Schramm (eds.), *Handbook of Communication* (New York: Rand McNally).

Hasher, L., K.C. Rose, R.T. Zaelis, H. Sanft, and B. Dorin (1985), "Mood, Recall, and Selectivity Effects in Normal College Students," *Journal of Experimental Psychology: General*, 114, 104–118.

Hass, R. (1981), "Effects of Source Characteristics on Cognitive Responses and Persuasion," in R. Petty, T. Ostrom, and T. Brock (eds.), *Cognitive Responses in Persuasion* (Hillsdale, N.J.: Erlbaum), 141–172.

Hass, R., and K. Grady (1975), "Temporal Delay, Type of Forewarning and Resistance to Influence," *Journal of Experimental Social Psychology*, 11, 459–469.

Hastings, N.A., and J.B. Peacock (1975), *Statistical Distributions* (New York: Halsted Press).

Hausknecht, D.R., and D.L. Moore (1985), "The Effects of Time Compressed Advertising on Brand Attitude Judgments," in Richard J. Lutz (ed.), *Advances in Consumer Research, Vol. XII* (Provo, Utah: Association for Consumer Research).

Hayes, D.S., B. Chemelski, and D.W. Young (1981), "Young Children's Incidental and Intentional Retention of Televised Events," *Developmental Psychology*, 17, 230–232.

Hecker, Sidney (1984), "Music For Advertising Effect," *Psychology & Marketing*, 1 (Fall/Winter), 3–8.

Heimbach, James T., and Jacob Jacoby (1972), "The Zeigarnik Effect in Advertising," in M. Venkatesan (ed.), *Proceedings, Third Annual Conference* (Chicago: Association for Consumer Research), 746–757.

Hendrick, C., and A.F. Costantini (1970), "Effects of Varying Trait Inconsistency and Response Requirements on the Primacy Effect in Impression Formation," *Journal of Personality and Social Psychology*, 15, 158–164.

Hevner, Kate (1935), "The Affective Character of the Major and Minor Modes in Music," *American Journal of Psychology*, 47, 246–268.

Hinde, R.A. (1972), *Non-verbal Communication* (Cambridge, England: Cambridge University Press).

Hirsch, P. (1971), "Sociological Approaches to the Pop Music Phenomenon," *American Behavioral Scientist*, 14, 377–381.

Hitler, A. (1971), *Mein Kampf* (Boston: Houghton Mifflin) (originally published 1926).

Hjelmsler, L. (1953), "Prolegomena to a Theory of Language" (translated by F.J. Whitfield), *International Journal of American Linguistics*, Memoir 7.

Hock, Stephen J. (1984), "Availability and Interference in Predictive Judgments," *Journal of Experimental Psychology: Learning, Memory, and Cognition*, 10 (October), 649–662.

Holbrook, Morris B. (1978), "Beyond Attitude Structure: Toward the Information Determinants of Attitude," *Journal of Marketing Research*, 15 (November), 545–556.

Holbrook, Morris B. (1986), "Emotion in the Consumption Experience: Toward a New Model of the Human Consumer," in Robert A. Peterson, Wayne D. Hoyer, and William R. Wilson (eds.), *The Role of Affect in Consumer Behavior: Emerging Theories and Applications* (Lexington, Mass. D.C. Heath and Company).

Holbrook, Morris B., and Donald R. Lehmann (1980), "Form Versus Content in Predicting Starch Scores," *Journal of Advertising Research*, 20 (4), 53–62.

Holbrook, M.B., and W.L. Moore (1981), "Feature Interactions in Consumer Judgments of Verbal Versus Pictorial Presentations," *Journal of Consumer Research*, 8, 103–113.

Holbrook, Morris B., and John O'Shaughnessy (1984), "The Role of Emotion in Advertising," *Psychology & Marketing*, 1 (2), 45–64.

Holbrook, Morris B., and Richard A. Westwood (1986), "The Role of Emotion in Advertising Revisited: Testing a Typology of Emotional Responses," in Pat Cafferata and Alice M. Tybout (eds.), *Advertising and Consumer Psychology* (Lexington, Mass.: Lexington Books).

Holmes, J.M. (1973), "Order of Main and Subordinate Clauses in Sentence Perception," *Journal of Verbal Learning and Verbal Behavior*, 12, 185–293.

Holsti, O.R. (1969), *Content Analysis for the Social Sciences and Humanities* (Cambridge, Mass.: Addison–Wesley).

Holyoak, K. (1974), "The Role of Imagery in the Evaluation of Sentences: Imagery or Semantic Relatedness?" *Journal of Verbal Learning and Verbal Behavior*, 13, 163–166.

Homer, Pamela M. (1986), *Surrealism in Advertising: A Test of Alternative Explanations*, unpublished doctoral dissertation, University of Oregon.

Homer, Pamela M., and Lynn R. Kahle (1986), "A Social Adaptation Explanation of the Effects of Surrealism on Advertising," *Journal of Advertising*, 15, 50–60.

Houston, M.J., and M. Rothschild (1978), "Conceptual and Methodological Perspectives in Involvement," in S. Jains (ed), *Research Frontiers in Marketing: Dialogues and Directions* (Chicago: American Marketing Association), 184–187.

Hovland, C., I. Janis, and H. Kelly (1953), *Communication and Persuasion* (New Haven: Yale University Press).

Hovland, Carl I., and Wallace Mandell (1952), "An Experimental Comparison of Conclusion-Drawing by the Communicator and by the Audience," *Journal of Abnormal and Social Psychology*, 47 (July), 581–588.

Hovland, C., and W. Weiss (1951), "The Influence of Source Credibility on Communication Effectiveness," *Public Opinion Quarterly*, 15, 635–650.

Hutchinson, J.W., and D.L. Moore (1984), "Issues Surrounding the Examination of Delay Effects in Advertising," in T.C. Kinnear (ed.), *Advances in Consumer Research*, vol. 11 (Ann Arbor: Association for Consumer Research), 650–655.

Ibok, E. (1985), *Cognitive Structures and Processes in Recall of Different Types of TV Programs*, doctoral dissertation, School of Journalism and Mass Communication, University of Wisconsin-Madison, September.

Imada, A.S., and M.D. Hakel (1977), "Influence of Nonverbal Communication and Rater Proximity on Impressions and Decisions in Simulated Employment Interviews," *Journal of Applied Psychology*, 62, 295–300.

Insko, C. (1967), *Theories of Attitude Change* (New York: Appleton–Century–Crofts).

Isen, A.M. (1984), "Toward Understanding the Role of Affect in Cognition," in R.S. Wyer, Jr., and T.K. Srull (eds.), *Handbook of Social Cognition*, vol. 3 (Hillsdale, N.J.: Erlbaum).

Isen, A.M., M. Clark, T.E. Shalker, and L. Karp (1978), "Affect Accessibility of Material in Memory and Behavior: A Cognitive Loop?" *Journal of Personality and Social Psychology*, 36, 1–12.

Izard, Carroll (1977), *Human Emotions* (New York: Plenum Press).

Jacoby, J. (1978), "Consumer Research: A State of the Art Review," *Journal of Marketing*, 42, 87–96.

Janis, I.L., D. Kaye, and P. Kirscher (1965), "Facilitating Effects of 'Eating While Reading' on Responsiveness to Persuasive Communications," *Journal of Personality and Social Psychology*, 11, 181–186.

"Japan's Crypto-Christians," (1982, January 11), *Time*, p. 71.

Johnson, E., and A. Tversky (1983), "Affect, Generalization, and the Perception of Risk," *Journal of Personality and Social Psychology*, 45, 20–31.

Jorgensen, C.C., and W. Kintsch (1973), "The Role of Imagery in the Evaluation of Sentences," *Cognitive Psychology*, 4, 110–116.

Kahle, Lynn R. (1984), *Attitudes and Social Adaptation: A Person-Situation Interaction Approach* (Oxford, Eng.: Pergamon).

Kahle, Lynn R. (1986), "The Nine Nations of North America and the Value Basis of Geographic Segmentation," *Journal of Marketing*, 50 (April), 37–47.

Kahle, Lynn R., Sharon E. Beatty, and Pamela M. Homer (1986), "Alternative Measurement Approaches to Consumer Values: The List of Values (LOV) and Values and Life Styles (VALS)," *Journal of Consumer Research*, 13 (December), 405–409.

Kahle, Lynn R., and Pamela M. Homer (1985), "Physical Attractiveness of the Celebrity Endorser: A Social Adaptation Perspective," *Journal of Consumer Research*, 11 (March), 964–971.

Kahle, Lynn R., David M. Klingel, and Richard A. Kulka (1981), "A Longitudinal Study of Adolescent Attitude–Behavior Consistency," *Public Opinion Quarterly*, 45 (Fall), 402–414.

Kahle, Lynn R., Richard A. Kulka, and David M. Klingel (1980), "Low Adolescent Self-Esteem Leads to Multiple Interpersonal Problems: A Test of Social Adaptation Theory," *Journal of Personality and Social Psychology*, 39 (September), 496–502.

Kahle, Lynn R., and Susan Goff Timmer (1983), "A Theory and a Method for Studying Values," in Lynn R. Kahle (ed.), *Social Values and Social Change: Adaptation to Life in America* (New York: Praeger).

Kanouse, D.E. (1972), "Verbs as Implicit Quantifiers," *Journal of Verbal Learning and Verbal Behavior*, 11, 1141–1147.

Kapferer, Jean-Noel, and Gilles Laurent (1985), "Consumer Involvement Profiles: A New Practical Approach to Consumer Involvement," *Journal of Advertising Research*, 25 (December), 48–55.

Kaplan, M.F., and G.D. Kemmerick (1974), "Juror Judgment as Information Integration: Combining Evidential and Non-Evidential Information," *Journal of Personality and Social Psychology*, 30, 493–499.

Kardes, Frank R. (1986), "Spontaneous Inference Processes in Advertising: The Effects of Conclusion Omission and Salience of Consequences on Attitudes and Memory," Massachusetts Institute of Technology Working Paper No. 1832-86 (November).

Kardes, Frank R., and Alan G. Sawyer (1983), "Effects of Involvement and Message Content on Information Processing Intensity," in Richard Harris (ed.), *Information Processing Research In Advertising* (Hillsdale, N.J.: Erlbaum).

Kausler, D.H., and A.V. Settle (1973), "Associate Relatedness vs. Synonymity in the False Recognition Effect," *Bulletin of the Psychonomic Society*, 2, 129–131.

Kerr, B. (1973), "Processing Demands During Mental Operations," *Memory & Cognition*, 1 (4), 401–412.

Key, Mary Ritchie (1982), *Nonverbal Communication Today: Current Research* (New York: Mouton Publishers).

Kingman, M. (1983), "And Now, A Few Words That Sell," *Advertising Age* (October 23), M-26.

Kirmani, Amna, and Peter L. Wright (1986), "Consumer Inferences About Advertising Costs and Product Quality," Working Paper, Stanford University.

Kisielius, Jolita, and Brian Sternthal (1984), "Detecting and Explaining Vividness Effects in Attitudinal Judgments," *Journal of Marketing Research,* 21 (February), 54–64.

Kisielius, Jolita, and Brian Sternthal (1986), "Examining the Vividness Controversy: An Availability-Valence Interpretation," *Journal of Consumer Research,* 12 (March), 418–431.

Kleinhesselink, R.R., and R.E. Edwards (1975), "Seeking and Avoiding Belief Discrepant Information as a Function of Its Perceived Refutability," *Journal of Personality and Social Psychology,* 31, 787–790.

Knapp, Mark L. (1978), *Nonverbal Communication in Human Interaction* (New York: Holt, Rinehart and Winston).

Kroeber-Riel, Werner (1979), "Activation Research: Psychological Approaches in Consumer Research," *Journal of Consumer Research,* 5 (March), 240–250.

Kroeber-Riel, Werner (1984), "Emotional Product Differentiation by Classical Conditioning," in Morris E. Holbrook and Barbara Hirschman (eds.), *Advances in Consumer Research,* vol. 11 (Ann Arbor, Mich.: Association for Consumer Research), 538–543.

Kruglanski, Arie W., and Icek Ajzen (1983), "Bias and Error in Human Judgments," *European Journal of Social Psychology,* 13, 1–44.

Kruglanski, Arie W., and Tallie Freund (1983), "The Freezing and Unfreezing of Lay-Inferences: Effects on Impression Primacy, Ethnic Stereotyping, and Numerical Anchoring," *Journal of Experimental Social Psychology,* 19 (September), 448–468.

Kruglanski, Arie W. (1980), "Lay Epistemological Process and Contents: Another Look at Attribution Theory," *Psychological Review,* 87 (January), 70–87.

Krugman, Herbert E. (1965), "The Impact of Television Advertising: Learning Without Involvement," *Public Opinion Quarterly,* 29, 349–356.

Krugman, Herbert E. (1966–1967), "The Measurement of Advertising Involvement," *Public Opinion Quarterly,* 30 (Winter), 583–596.

Kubizek, A. (1955), *The Young Hitler I Knew* (Cambridge, Mass.: Riverside).

Laffal, J. (1973), *A Concept Dictionary of English* (Essex, Conn.: Gallery Press).

Lampel, A.K., and N.H. Anderson (1968), "Combining Visual and Verbal Information in an Impression-Formation Task," *Journal of Personality and Social Psychology,* 9, 1–6.

Lasswell, Harold D. (1948), "The Structure and Function of Communication in Society," in L. Bryson (ed.) (New York: Harper).

Laurent, Gilles, and Jean-Noel Kapferer (1985), "Measuring Consumer Involvement Profiles," *Journal of Marketing Research,* XXII, 41–53.

Lautman, M.R., and L. Percy (1984), "Cognitive and Affective Responses in Attribute-Based Versus End-Benefit Oriented Advertising," in T.C. Kinnear (ed.), *Advances in Consumer Research,* vol. XI (Provo, Utah: Association for Consumer Research).

Lavidge, R.J., and G.A. Steiner (1961), "A Model for Predictive Measurement of Advertising Effectivness," *Journal of Marketing,* 25, 59–62.

Lynch, J.G. (1985), "Uniqueness Issues in the Decompositional Modeling of Multiattribute Overall Evaluations: An Information Integration Perspective," *Journal of Marketing Research,* 22, 1–19.

Lynn, M., S. Shavitt and T. Ostrom (1985), "Effects of Pictures on The Organization and Recall of Social Information," *Journal of Personality and Social Psychology,* 49, 1160–1168.

Leavitt, Clark, A. Greenwald, and C. Obermiller (1981), "What is Low Involvement Low In?" in K. Monroe (ed.), *Advances in Consumer Research,* vol. 3, (Ann Arbor: ACR).

Leavitt, Clark, C. Waddell, and William D. Wells (1970), "Improving Day-After Recall Techniques," *Journal of Advertising Research,* 10, 13–17.

Leippe, M., A. Greenwald, and M. Baumgardner (1982), "Delayed Persuasion as a Consequence of Associative Interference: A Context Confusion Effect," *Personality and Social Psychology Bulletin*, 8, 644–650.

Lenneberg, E.H. (1967), *Biological Foundations of Language* (New York: Wiley).

Levy, Sidney J. (1959), "Symbols for Sale," *Harvard Business Review* (July–August), 117–124.

Lichtenstein, Meryl, and Thomas K. Srull (1985), "Conceptual and Methodological Issues in Examining the Relationship Between Consumer Memory and Judgments," in Linda F. Alwitt and Andrew A. Mitchell (eds.), *Psychological Processes and Advertising Effects: Theory, Research and Application* (Hillsdale, N.J.: Erlbaum), 113–128.

Likert, R. (1932), "A Technique for the Measurement of Attitudes," *Archives of Psychology*, 140, 1–55 (whole).

Lincoln, Yvonna S., and Egon G. Guba (1985), *Naturalistic Inquiry* (Beverly Hills: Sage Publications).

Linder, Darwyn E., J. Cooper, and R.A. Wicklund (1968), "Pre-Exposure Persuasion as a Result of Commitment to Pre-Exposure Effort," *Journal of Experimental Social Psychology*, 4, 470–482.

Linder, Darwyn E., and Stephen Worchel (1970), "Opinion Change as a Result of Effortfully Drawing a Counterattitudinal Conclusion," *Journal of Experimental Social Psychology*, 6 (October), 432–448.

Lingle, John H., and Thomas M. Ostrom (1979), "Retrieval Selectivity in Memory-Based Impression Judgments," *Journal of Personality and Social Psychology*, 37, 180–194.

Loftus, E. (1979), *Eyewitness Testimony* (Cambridge, Mass.: Harvard University Press).

Loftus, E. (1980), *Memory: Surprising New Insights Into How We Remember and Why We Forget* (Reading, Mass.: Addison–Wesley).

Lorch, E.P., D.R. Anderson, and S.R. Levin (1979), "The Relationship Between Visual Attention and Children's Comprehension of Television," *Child Development*, 50, 722–727.

Louviere, J.L., and G.J. Gaeth (1987), "Decomposing the Determinants of Retail Facility Choice Using the Method of Hierarchical Information Integration: A Supermarket Illustration," *Journal of Retailing*, 63, forthcoming.

Lutz, K.A., and R.J. Lutz (1977), "Effects of Interactive Imagery on Learning: Applications to Advertising," *Journal of Applied Psychology*, 62, 493–498.

Lutz, Richard J. (1975), "Changing Brand Attitudes Through Modification of Cognitive Structure," *Journal of Consumer Research*, 1 (March), 49–57.

Lutz, Richard J. (1977), "An Experimental Investigation of Causal Relations Among Cognitions, Affect, and Behavioral Intention," *Journal of Consumer Research*, 3 (March), 197–207.

Lutz, Richard J. (1985), "Affective and Cognitive Antecedents of Attitude Toward the Ad: A Conceptual Framework," in Linda F. Alwitt and Andrew A. Mitchell (eds.), *Psychological Processes and Advertising Effects: Theory, Research, and Application* (Hillsdale, N.J.: Erlbaum).

Lutz, Richard J., Scott B. MacKenzie, and George E. Belch (1983), "Attitude Toward the Ad as a Mediator of Advertising Effectiveness: Determinants and Consequences," in Richard P. Bagozzi and Alice M. Tybout (eds.), *Advances in Consumer Research*, vol. 10 (Ann Arbor: Association for Consumer Research).

Lutz, Richard J., and John L. Swasy (1977), "Integrating Cognitive Structure and Cognitive Response Approaches to Monitoring Communicatoin Effects," in William D. Perrault (ed.), *Advances in Consumer Research*, vol. 4 (Atlanta, Ga.: Association for Consumer Research), 363–371.

Lynch, J.G. (1985), "Uniqueness Issues in the Decompositional Modelling of Multiattribute Overall Evaluations: An Information Integration Perspective," *Journal of Marketing Research*, 22, 1–19.

Meadowcroft, J., and B. Reeves (1985), "Children's Attention to Television: The Influence of Story Schema Development on Allocation of Cognitive Capacity and Memory," paper presented to the Speech Communication Association, Denver.

Mehrabian, Albert (1970), "A Semantic Space for Nonverbal Behavior," *Journal of Consulting and Clinical Psychology*, 35, 248–257.

Mehrabian, Albert (1971), *Silent Messages* (Belmont, Cal.: Wadsworth).

Mehrabian, Albert (1972a), "Nonverbal Communication," in James K. Cole (ed.), *Nebraska Symposium on Motivation*, vol. 19 (Lincoln, Neb.: University of Nebraska Press).

Mehrabian, Albert (1972b), *Nonverbal Communication* (Chicago: Aldine–Atherton).

Mehrabian, Albert (1980), *Basic Dimensions for a General Psychological Theory* (Cambridge, Mass.: Oelgesschlager, Gunn & Hain).

Mehrabian, Albert, and James A. Russell (1974), *An Approach to Environmental Psychology* (Cambridge: The MIT Press).

MacCullough, David, and David Grubin (1986), "The Wyeths: A Father and His Family," *Smithsonian World* (Washington, D.C.: Greater Washington Educational Telecommunications Association, Inc., and the Smithsonian Institution).

MacKenzie, S.B., and R.J. Lutz (1982), "Monitoring Advertising Effectiveness: A Structural Equation Analysis of the Mediating Role of Attitude Toward the Ad," Working Paper Series, Center for Marketing Studies, University of California, Los Angeles, Paper No. 117.

MacKenzie, Scott B., Richard J. Lutz, and George R. Belch (1986), "The Role of Attitude Toward the Ad as a Mediator of Advertising Effectiveness," A Test of Competing Explanations," *Journal of Marketing Research*, 23 (May), 130–143.

Macklin, M.C. (1983), "Do Children Understand TV Ads?" *Journal of Advertising Research*, 23 (1), 63–69.

McEwen, W.J., and C. Leavitt (1976), "A Way to Describe TV Commercials," *Journal of Advertising Research*, 16, 35–39.

McGovern, T.V. (1976), "The Making of a Job Interviewee: The Effect of Nonverbal Behavior on an Interviewer's Evaluation During Selection Interview (doctoral dissertation, Southern Illinois University), Dissertation Abstracts International, 1977, 37, 4740B–4741B (University Microfilms No. 77–6239).

McGuire, William J. (1960), "A Syllogistic Analysis of Cognitive Relationships," in Carol I. Hovland and Milton J. Rosenberg (eds.), *Attitude Organization and Change: An Analysis of Consistency Among Attitude Components* (New Haven and London, Conn.: Yale University Press).

McGuire, William J. (1969), "The Nature of Attitudes and Attitude Change," in Gardner Lindzey and Elliot Aronson (eds.), *The Handbook of Social Psychology*, vol. 3 (Reading, MA: Addison–Wesley), 136–314.

McGuire, William J., and Demetrius Papageorgis (1962), "Effectiveness of Forewarning in Developing Resistance to Persuasion," *Public Opinion Quarterly*, 26, 24–34.

McHugo, Gregory J., Craig A. Smith, and John T. Lanzetta (1982), "The Structure of Self-Reports of Emotional Responses to Film Segments," *Motivation and Emotion*, 6 (4), 365–384.

McQuire, William (1978), "An Information Processing Model of Advertising Effectiveness," in H.L. Davis and A.J. Silk (eds.), *Behavioral and Management Science in Marketing* (New York: Ronald Press).

McSweeney, Frances K., and Calvin Bierley (1984), "Recent Developments in Classical Conditioning," *Journal of Consumer Research,* 11 (September), 619–631.

Miller, G.A., and S. Isand (1964), "Free Recall of Self-Embedded English Sentences," *Information and Control,* 7, 292–303.

Miller, Ronald E. (1982), "Using Background Music to Affect the Behavior of Supermarket Shoppers," *Journal of Marketing,* 46 (Summer), 86–91.

Mills, Jonathan, and Eliot Aronson (1965), "Opinion Change as a Function of Communicator's Attractiveness and Desire to Influence," *Journal of Personality and Social Psychology,* 1, 173–177.

Mills, Jonathan, and J.M. Jellison (1967), "Effect on Opinion Change of How Desirable the Communication is to the Audience the Communicator Addressed," *Journal of Personality and Social Psychology,* 6, 98–101.

Miniard, Paul W., and Joel B. Cohen, "Isolating Attitudinal and Normative Influences in Behavioral Intention Models," *Journal of Marketing Research,* 16 (February), 102–110.

Mitchell, A.A. (1981), "The Dimensions of Advertising Involvement," in K.B. Monroe (ed.), *Advances in Consumer Research* (Arlington, Va.: Association for Consumer Research).

Mitchell, A.A. (1983), "The Effects of Visual and Emotional Advertising: An Information-Processing Approach," in L. Percy and A.G. Woodside (eds.), *Advertising and Consumer Psychology* (Lexington, Mass.: Lexington Books), 197–217.

Mitchell, A.A. (1983), "Cognitive Processes Initiated by Exposure to Advertising," in R.J. Harris (ed.), *Information Processing Research in Advertising* (Hillside, N.J.: Erlbaum), 13–42.

Mitchell, A.A. (1986a), "Some Issues Surrounding Research on the Effects of 'Feeling' Advertisements," in R. Lutz (ed.), *Advances in Consumer Research,* vol. 13 (Ann Arbor: Association for Consumer Research).

Mitchell, A.A. (1986b), "The Effect of Verbal and Visual Components of Advertisements on Brand Attitudes and Attitude Toward the Ad," *Journal of Consumer Research,* 13, 12–24.

Mitchell, Andrew A., and Jerry C. Olson (1981), "Are Product Attribute Beliefs the Only Mediator of Advertising Effects on Brand Attitude?" *Journal of Marketing Research,* 18 (August), 318–332.

Moore, Danny L., and J. Wesley Hutchinson (1983), "The Effects of Ad Affect on Advertising Effectiveness," in R.P. Bagozzi and A.M. Tybout (eds.), *Advances in Consumer Research,* vol. 10 (Ann Arbor, Mich.: Association for Consumer Research), 526–31.

Moore, Danny L., and J. Wesley Hutchinson (1985), "The Influence of Affective Reaction to Advertising: Direct and Indirect Mechanisms of Attitude change," in L. Alwitt and A.A. Mitchell (eds.), *Psychological Processes and Advertising Effects: Theory, Research, and Application* (Hillsdale, N.J.: Erlbaum).

Moore, Timothy, E. (1982), "Subliminal Advertising: What You See Is What You Get," *Journal of Marketing,* 46 (Spring), 38–47.

Morse, P.A. (1972), "The Discrimination of Speech and Nonspeech Stimuli in Early Infancy," *Journal of Experimental Child Psychology,* 14, 477–492.

Monroe, Kent (1973), "Buyers' Subjective Perceptions of Price," *Journal of Marketing Research,* 10, 70–80.

Muhlbacher, Hans (1986), "An Involvement Model of Advertising Information Acquisition and Processing Motivation," Unpublished working paper, University of Innsbruck, Austria.

Myers, D.G. (1983), *Social Psychology* (New York: McGraw-Hill).

Naftulin, D., J. Ware, and F. Donnelly (1973), "The Doctor Fox Lecture: A Paradigm of Educational Seduction," *Journal of Medical Education,* 48, 630–635.

Nagy, G.F. (1975), *Female Dating Strategies as a Function of Physical Attractiveness and Other Social Characteristics of Males,* unpublished Master's thesis, Kansas State University.

Nagy, G.F. (1981), *How Are Personnel Selection Decisions Made? An Analysis of Decision Strategies In a Simulated Personnel Selection,* unpublished doctoral dissertation, Kansas State University.

"Name Game" (1980, 7 July), *The Wall Street Journal,* p. 13.

Nelson, Phillip (1974), "Advertising as Information," *The Journal of Political Economy,* 82 (4), 729–754.

Nida, E.A. (1964), *Toward a Science of Translating* (London: Brill).

Nord, Walter R., and J. Paul Peter (1980), "A Behavior Modification Perspective on Marketing," *Journal of Marketing,* 44 (Spring), 36–47.

Nowlis, V. (1965), "Research with the Mood Adjective Check List," in S.S. Thompkins and C.E. Izard (eds.), *Affect, Cognition and Personality: Empirical Studies* (New York: Springer Publishing Company), 352–389.

Nunnally, Jim C. (1967), *Psychometric Theory* (New York: McGraw-Hill).

Obermiller, Carl (1985), "Varieties of Mere Exposure: The Effects of Processing Style and Repetition on Affective Response," *Journal of Consumer Research,* 12 (June), 17–30.

Olney, T.J., Morris B. Holbrook, and Rajeev Batra (1986), "The Effects of Advertising Content and Emotional Responses on Viewing Time," work in progress.

Osgood, Charles E., George J. Suci, and Percy H. Tannenbaum (1957), *The Measurement of Meaning* (Urbana: University of Illinois Press).

Osgood, Charles E. (1966), "Dimensionality of the Semantic Space for Communication Via Facial Expressions," *Scandinavian Journal of Psychology,* 7, 1–30.

Padgett, V. (1985), *Persuasion With Unintelligible Messages: A Cognitive Response Analysis,* doctoral dissertation, Ohio State University.

Paget, R. (1930), *Human Speech* (London: Kegan Paul), 360.

Paivio, A. (1971), *Imagery and Verbal Processes* (New York: Holt, Rinehart and Winston).

Paivio, A., J.D. Yuille, and S.A. Madigan (1968), "Concreteness, Imagery, and Meaningfulness Values for 925 Nouns," *Journal of Experimental Psychology: Monograph Supplement,* 76 (3, p. 2).

Palmer, F.R. (1976), *Semantics: A New Outline* (Cambridge: Cambridge University Press).

Panksepp, Jaak (1982), "Toward a General Psychobiological Theory of Emotions," *The Behavioral and Brain Sciences,* 5, 407–467.

Park, C.W., and S. Mark Young (1986), "Consumer Response to Television Commercials: The Impact of Involvement and Background Music on Brand Attitude Formation," *Journal of Marketing Research,* 23 (February), 11–24.

Parrott, A.C. (1982), "Effects of Paintings and Music, Both Alone and In Combination, On Emotional Judgments," *Perceptual and Motor Skills,* 54, 634–641.

Patterson, Miles L. (1982a), "A Sequential Functional Model of Nonverbal Exchange," *Psychological Review* 89 (May), 231–249.

Patterson, Miles L. (1982b), "Personality and Nonverbal Involvement: A Functional Analysis," in William Ickes and Eric S. Knowles (eds.), *Personality, Roles, and Social Behavior* (New York: Springer–Verlag), 141–164.

Percy, L. (1981), "Psycholinguistics: Some Simple Rules for Do-It-Yourself Ad Testing," *Proceedings of the 3rd Business Research Conference* (New York: Advertising Research Foundation).

Percy, Larry (1982), "Psycholinguistic Guidelines for Advertising Copy," in A.A. Mitchell (ed.), *Advances in Consumer Research:* vol. IX (Ann Arbor: Association for Consumer Research).

Percy, Larry (1983), "A Review of the Effect of Specific Advertising Elements Upon Overall Communication Responses," in James H. Leigh and Claude R. Martin, Jr. (eds.), *Current Issues and Research in Advertising* (Ann Arbor: University of Michigan Press).

Percy, L., and J.R. Rossiter (1983), "Mediating Effects of Visual and Verbal Elements in Print Advertising Upon Belief, Attitude, and Intention Responses," in L. Percy and A.G. Woodside (eds.), *Advertising and Consumer Psychology* (Lexington, Mass.: Lexington Books), 171–196.

Perloff, R., and T. Brock (1980), ". . . And Thinking Makes It So: Cognitive Responses to Persuasion," in M. Roloff and G. Miller (eds.), *Persuasion: New Directions In Theory and Research* (Beverly Hills: Sage), 67–99.

Petty, Richard E. (1977), *A Cognitive Response Analysis of the Temporal Persistence of Attitude Changes Induced by Persuasive Communications*, doctoral dissertation, Ohio State University.

Petty, Richard E. (1981), "The Role of Cognitive Responses In Attitude Change Processes," in R. Petty, T. Ostrom and T. Brock (eds.), *Cognitive Responses in Persuasion* (Hillsdale, N.J.: Erlbaum), 135–139.

Petty, Richard E., and John T. Cacioppo (1979), "Issue Involvement Can Increase or Decrease Persuasion by Enhancing Message-Relevant Cognitive Response," *Journal of Personality and Social Psychology*, 37. 1915–1926.

Petty, Richard E., and John T. Cacioppo (1981), *Attitudes and Persuasion: Classic and Contemporary Approaches* (Dubuque, Iowa: William C. Brown).

Petty, Richard E., and John T. Cacioppo (1983), "Central and Peripheral Routes to Persuasion: Application to Advertising," in Larry Percy and Arch Woodside (eds.), *Advertising and Consumer Psychology* (Lexington, Mass.: Lexington Books), 3–23.

Petty, Richard, E., J. Cacioppo, and R. Goldman (1981), "Personal Involvement As A Determinant of Argument-Based Persuasion," *Journal of Personality and Social Psychology*, 41, 847–855.

Petty, Richard E., John T. Cacioppo, and Martin Heesacker (1981), "The Use of Rhetorical Questions in Persuasion: A Cognitive Response Analysis," *Journal of Personality and Social Psychology*, 49 (March), 432–440.

Petty, Richard E., John T. Cacioppo, and David Schumann (1983), "Central and Peripheral Routes to Advertising Effectiveness: The Moderating Role of Involvement," *Journal of Consumer Research*, 10 (September), 135–146.

Petty, R., T. Ostrom, and T. Brock (1981), "Historical Foundations of the Cognitive Response Approach to Attitudes and Persuasion," in R. Petty, T. Ostrom and T. Brock (eds.), *Cognitive Responses in Persuasion* (Hillsdale, N.J.: Erlbaum), 5–29.

Piner, Kelly E., and Lynn R. Kahle (1984), "Adapting to the Stigmatizing Label of Mental Illness: Foregone but not Forgotten," *Journal of Personality and Social Psychology*, 47 (October), 805–811.

Pirolli, Peter L., and John R. Anderson (1985), "The Role of Practice in Fact Retrieval," *Journal of Experimental Psychology: Learning, Memory, and Cognition*, 11, 136–153.

Plutchik, R. (1962), *The Emotions: Facts, Theories and a New Model* (New York: Random House).

Plutchik, R. (1980), *Emotion: A Psychoevolutionary Synthesis* (New York: Harper & Row).

Posner, M.I. and C.R. Snyder (1975), "Attention and Cognitive Control," in R.L. Solso (ed.), *Information Processing and Cognition: The Loyola Symposium* (Hillsdale, N.J.: Erlbaum).

Preston, I.L. (1968), "Relationships Among Emotional, Intellectual, and Rational Appeals in Advertising," *Speech Monographs*, 35 (4), 504–511.

Preston, Ivan L. (1970), "A Reinterpretation of the Meaning of Involvement in Krugman's Models of Advertising Communication," *Journalism Quarterly*, 47, 287–295.

Pribram, Karl H. (1980), "The Biology of Emotions and Other Feelings," in Robert Plutchik and Henry Kellerman (eds.), *Emotion: Theory, Research, and Experience* (vol. 1: *Theories of Emotion*) (New York: Academic Press), 245–269.

Rapoport, Amos (1982), *The Meaning of the Built Environment, A Nonverbal Communication Approach* (Beverly Hills, Cal.: Sage Publications).

Ray, Michael L. (1978), "The Present and Potential Linkages Between the Microtheoretical Notions of Behavioral Science and the Problems of Advertising: A Proposal for a Research System," in Harry Davis and Alvin Silk (eds.), *The Behavioral and Management Sciences in Marketing* (New York: Wiley).

Ray, M.L., and R. Batra (1983), "Emotion and Persuasion in Advertising: What We Do and Don't Know About Affect," in R.P. Bagozzi and A.M. Tybout (eds.), *Advances in Consumer Research*, vol. 10 (Ann Arbor: Associates for Consumer Research).

Ray, Michael L., and Alan G. Sawyer (1971a), "Behavioral Measurement for Marketing Models: Estimating the Repetition Function for Advertising Media Models," *Management Science*, 19 (December), 73–89.

Ray, Michael L., and Alan G. Sawyer (1971b), "Repetition in Media Models: A Laboratory Technique," *Journal of Marketing Research*, 8 (February), 20–29.

Ray, Michael L., Alan G. Sawyer, Michael Rothschild, Roger Heeler, Edward Strong, and Jerome Reed (1973), "Marketing Communication and the Hierarchy-of-Effects," in P. Clarke (ed.), New Models for Mass Communication Research, *Sage Annual Review of Communication Research*, vol. II (Beverly Hills: Sage), 147–176.

Reeves, Byron, E. Thorson, and J. Schleuder (in press), "Attention to Television: Psychological Theories and Chronometric Measures," in Jennings Bryant and Dolf Zillman (eds.), *Perspectives on Media Effects* (Hillsdale, N.J.: Erlbaum).

Reinhard, Keith L. (n.d.), "I Believe in Music, " Needham, Harper and Steers, Inc, Chicago.

Reis, Al, and Jack Trout (1983), "The Eye vs. the Ear," *Advertising Age* (March 14), M-27.

Reyes, Robert M., William C. Thompson, and Gordon H. Bower (1980), "Judgmental Biases Resulting from Differing Availabilities of Arguments," *Journal of Personality and Social Psychology*, 39, 2–12.

Reynolds, D. (1977), "Students Who Haven't Seen a Film on Sexuality and Communication Prefer It to a Lecture on the History of Psychology They Haven't Heard," *Teaching of Psychology*, 4, 82–83.

Richards, N. (1979), "The Myth of Memorability in Commercial Music," *Advertising Age* (July 23), S-23, 24.

Rigg, Melvin G. (1940), "Speed as a Determiner of Musical Mood," *Journal of Experimental Psychology*, 27, 566–571.

Riskey, D.R. (1979), "Verbal Memory Processes in Impression Formation," *Journal of Experimental Psychology: Human Learning and Memory*, 5, 271–281.

Robertson, Thomas S. (1976), "Low Commitment Consumer Behavior," *Journal of Advertising Research*, 16, 19–24.

Roper Organization (1987), *The Public Pulse*, 2 (1), January.

Rosenberg, M.J. (1956), "Cognitive Structure and Attitudinal Affect," *Journal of Abnormal and Social Psychology*, 53, 367–372.

Rossiter, J.R. (1980), "Source Effects and Self-Concept Appeals in Children's Television Advertising," in R.P. Adler, G.S. Lesser, L.K. Meringoff, T.S. Robertson, J.R. Rossiter, and S. Ward (eds.), *The Effects of Television Advertising on Children* (Lexington, Mass.: Lexington Books).

Rossiter, J.R., and L. Percy (1978), "Visual Imaging Ability as a Mediator of Advertising Response," in H.K. Hunt (ed.), *Advances in Consumer Research*, vol. 5 (Ann Arbor: Association for Consumer Research), 621–629.

Rossiter, J.R., and L. Percy (1980), "Attitude Change Through Visual Imagery in Advertising," *Journal of Advertising*, 9 (2), 10–16.

Rossiter, J.R., and L. Percy (1983), "Visual Communication in Advertising," in R.J. Harris (ed.), *Information Processing Research in Advertising* (Hillsdale, N.J.: Erlbaum), 83–125.

Rowsome, F. (1970), *Think Small: The Story of Those Volkswagen Ads* (Brattleboro, Vermont: Stephen Greene).

Ryan, Michael J., and E.H. Bonfield (1975), "The Fishbein Extended Model and Consumer Behavior," *Journal of Consumer Research*, 2 (September), 118–136.

Runyon, K.E. (1984), *Advertising*, 2nd ed. (Columbus, Ohio: Merrill).

Russell, James A. (1980), "A Circumplex Model of Affect," *Journal of Personality and Social Psychology*, 39 (6), 1161–1178.

Samarin, W. (1972), *Tongues of Men and Angels: The Religious Language of Pentecostalism* (New York: Macmillan).

Sandage, C.H., V. Fryburger, and K. Rotzoll (1983), *Advertising Theory and Practice*, Eleventh ed. (Homewood, Ill.: Richard D. Irwin, Inc.).

Sawyer, Alan G. (1973), "The Effects of Repetition of Refutational and Supportive Advertising Appeals," *Journal of Marketing Research*, 10 (February), 23–33.

Sawyer, Alan G. (1977), "Repetition and Affect: Recent Empirical and Theoretical Development," in Arch G. Woodside, Jagdish W. Sheth, and Peter D. Bennett (eds.), *Foundations of Consumer and Industrial Buying Behavior* (New York: American Elsevier), 229–242.

Sawyer, Alan G. (1981), "Repetition, Cognitive Response, and Persuasion," in Richard E. Petty, Thomas M. Ostrom, and Timothy C. Brock (eds.), *Cognitive Responses to Persuasion* (Hillsdale, N.J.: Erlbaum), 237–262.

Sawyer, Alan G. (1982), "Problems in Estimating Qualitative Inter-Media Comparisons," in John Keon (ed.), *Market Measurement and Analysis, Volume III* (New York: The Institute of Management Sciences), 78–91.

Sawyer, Alan G., and Daniel Howard (1987), "Communication Effects of Advertisements with Explicit or Implicit Conclusions to Audiences of Low and Moderate Involvement," Working Paper Series, Center for Consumer Research, University of Florida.

Sawyer, Alan G., and Scott Ward (1979), "Carry-Over Effects in Advertising," *Research in Marketing*, 2, 259–314.

Schlinger, Mary Jane (1979), "A Profile of Response to Commercials," *Journal of Advertising Research*, 19 (2), 37–46.

Schmitt, N. (1976), "Social and Situational Determinants of Interview Decisions: Implications for the Employment Interview," *Personnel Psychology*, 29, 79–101.

Settle, Robert B., and Linda L. Golden (1974), "Attribution Theory and Advertiser Credibility," *The Journal of Marketing Research*, 11, 181–185.

Shakow, D., and S. Rosenzweig (1940), "The Use of the Tautophone as an Auditory Apperceptive Test for the Study of Personality," *Character and Personality*, 8, 216–226.

Shanteau, J. (1974), "Component Processes in Risky Decision Making," *Journal of Experimental Psychology*, 103, 680–691.

Shanteau, J. (1975), "Information Integration Analysis of Risky Decision Making," in M.F. Kaplan and S. Schwartz (eds.), *Human Judgment and Decision Processes* (New York: Academic Press), 109–137.

Shanteau, J. (1983), "Cognitive Psychology Looks at Advertising: Commentary on a Hobbit's Adventure," in R.J. Harris (ed.), *Information Processing Research in Advertising* (Hillsdale, N.J.: Erlbaum), 153–166.

Shanteau, J. (1984), "Some Unasked Questions About the Psychology of Expert Decision Makers," in M.E. El-Hawary (ed.), *Proceedings of the IEEE Conference on Systems, Man, and Cybernetics* (New York: IEEE).

Shanteau, J. (1985), "Application of Information Integration Theory to Methodology of Theory Development," Paper presented at American Psychological Association meeting, Los Angeles.

Shanteau, J. (1987a), "Psychological Characteristics of Expert Decision Makers," in J. Mumpower (ed.), *Expert Judgment and Expert Systems*, (Berlin: Springer–Verlag).

Shanteau, J. (1987b), "Consumer Integration Theory: The Five Processes of Information Integration in Consumer Judgment," unpublished manuscript, Kansas State University.

Shanteau, J., and G.F. Nagy (1976), "Decisions Made About Other People: A Human Judgment Analysis of Dating Choice," in J.S. Carroll and J.W. Payne (eds.), *Cognition and Social Behavior* (Hillsdale, N.J.: Erlbaum).

Shanteau, J., and G.F. Nagy (1979), "Probability of Acceptance in Dating Choice," *Journal of Personality and Social Psychology*, 37, 522–533.

Shanteau, J., and G.F. Nagy (1984), "Information Integration In Person Perception: Theory and Application," in M. Cook (ed.), *Issues in Person Perception* (London: Methuen), 48–86.

Shanteau, J., and C.H. Ptacek (1978), "Situation Determinants of Consumer Decision Making," in C. Leavitt (ed.), *Consumer Psychology Proceedings*, vol. 2 (Columbus, Ohio: APA Division 23).

Shanteau, J., and C.H. Ptacek (1983), "Role and Implications of Averaging Processes in Advertising," in L. Percy and A.G. Woodside (eds.), *Advertising and Consumer Psychology* (Lexington, Mass.: Lexington Books), 149–167.

Shanteau, J., and C.M. Troutman (1975), "Commentary on Bettman, Capon, and Lutz," *Journal of Consumer Research*, 1, 16–18.

Shanteau, J., C.M. Troutman, and C.H. Ptacek (1977), "Averaging Processes in Consumer Decision-Making," *Great Plains-Rocky Mountain Geographical Journal*, 6, 86–99.

Sheehan, P. (1970), "The Relation of Visual Imagery to True-False Judgment of Simple Sentences," unpublished master's thesis, University of Western Ontario.

Sheikh, Anees A. (1983), *Imagery: Current Theory, Research and Application* (New York: Wiley).

Shepard, R.N. (1967), "Recognition Memory for Words, Sentences, and Pictures," *Journal of Verbal Learning and Verbal Behavior*, 6, 156–163.

Sherif, M., and H. Cantril (1947), *The Psychology of Ego-Involvement* (New York: Wiley)

Sherif, M., and H. Cantril (1961), *Social Judgment: Assimilation and Contrast Effects in Communication on Attitude Change* (New Haven: Yale University Press).

Shimp, Terrence A. (1981), "Attitude Toward the Ad as a Mediator of Consumer Brand Choice," *Journal of Advertising*, 10 (2), 9–15.

Shimp, Terrence A., and J. Thomas Yokum (1982), "Advertising Inputs and Psychophysical Judgments in Vending-Machine Retailing," *Journal of Retailing*, 58 (Spring), 95–113.

Siegman, A.W., and S. Feldstein (1978), *Nonverbal Behavior and Communication* (Hillsdale, N.J.: Erlbaum).

Silk, Alvin J., and Terry G. Vavra (1974), "The Influence of Advertising's Affective Qualities on Consumer Response," in G. David Hughes and Michael L. Ray (eds.), *Buyer/Consumer Imformation Processing* (Chapel Hill: University of North Carolina Press), 157–186.

Skinner, B.F. (1936), "The Verbal Summator and a Method for the Study of Latent Speech," *Journal of Psychology*, 2, 71–107.

Skinner, B.F. (1979), *The Shaping of a Behaviorist* (New York: Knopf).

Slobin, D.I. (1966), "Grammatical Transformation and Sentence Comprehension in Childhood and Adulthood," *Journal of Verbal Learning and Verbal Behavior*, 5, 219–227.

Slobin, D.I. (1971), *Psycholinguistics* (Glenview, Ill.: Scott, Foresman and Company).

Slovic, P., and S. Lichtenstein (1971), "Comparison of Bayesian and Regression Approaches to The Study of Information Processing in Judgment," *Organizational Behavior and Human Performance*, 6, 649–744.

Smith, Robert E., and William R. Swinyard (1982), "Information Response Models: An Integrated Approach," *Journal of Marketing*, 46 (Winter), 81–93.

Smith, Robert E., and William R. Swinyard (1983), "Attitude–Behavior Consistency: The Impact of Product Trial Versus Advertising," *Journal of Marketing Research*, 20, 257–267.

Smith, Patricia Cane, and Ross Curnow (1966), "Arousal Hypotheses and the Effects of Music on Purchasing Behavior," *Journal of Applied Psychology*, 50 (3), 255–256.

Solomon, Robert C. (1976), *The Passions: The Myth and Nature of Human Emotion* (Garden City, N.Y.: Anchor Press).

Spreen, O., and R.W. Schultz (1966), "Parameters of Abstraction, Meaningfulness, and Pronounceability for 319 Nouns," *Journal of Verbal Learning and Verbal Behavior*, 5, 459–468.

Srull, T.K. (1983), "Affect and Memory: The Impact of Affective Reactions in Advertising on the Representation of Product Information in Memory," *Advances in Consumer Research*, 10, 520–525.

Srull, T.K. (1984), "Effects of Subjective Affect States on Memory and Judgment," in T. Kinnear (ed.), *Advances in Consumer Research*, vol. 11 (Ann Arbor: Associates for Consumer Research).

Starch, Daniel (1966) "How does the Shape of Ads Affect Readership?" *Media/Scope*, 10, 83–85.

Sternthal, Brian, Ruby Dholakia, and Clark Leavitt (1978), "The Persuasive Effect of Source Credibility: Tests of Cognitive Response," *Journal of Consumer Research*, 4 (March), 252–260.

Sternthal, Brian, L. Phillips, and R. Dholakia (1978), "The Persuasive Effect of Source Credibility: A Situational Analysis," *Public Opinion Quarterly*, 42, 285–314.

Stewart, David W. (1987a). "Perspectives on Measuring Advertising Stimuli," in Joel G. Saegert (ed.), *Proceedings of the Division of Consumer Psychology*.

Stewart, David W. (1987b), "Toward Ecological Inquiry in Marketing," in Russell Belk and Gerald Zaltman (eds.), *Proceedings of the 1987 Winter Educators' Conference of the American Marketing Association* (Chicago: American Marketing Association).

Stewart, David W., and David H. Furse (1986), *Effective Television Advertising* (Lexington, Mass.: Lexington Books).

Stoneman, Z., and G.H. Brody (1983), "Immediate and Long-Term Recognition and Generalization of Advertised Products as a Function of Age and Presentation Mode," *Developmental Psychology*, 19 (1), 56–61.

Stotland, Ezra, Daniel Katz, and Martin Patchen (1959), "The Reduction of Prejudice Through the Arousal of Self-Insight," *Journal of Personality*, 27, 507–531.

Stout, Patricia A. (1985), *Emotional Response to Advertising*, unpublished dissertation, University of Illinois at Urbana-Champaign.

Stout, P., and J.D. Leckenby (1984), "The Rediscovery of Emotional Research in Copy Research," in Donald R. Glover (ed.), *Proceedings of the American Adademy of Advertising* (Lincoln, Nebraska: D.R. Glover, School of Journalism, University of Nebraska-Lincoln), R37–R41.

Stout, Patricia A., and John D. Leckenby (1985), "The Pendulum Swings—A Return to Emotion in Copy Research," in Nancy Stephens (ed.), *Proceedings of the 1985 Convention of the American Academy of Advertising*, (Tempe, Arizona: Arizona State University), 39–43.

Stout, Patricia A., and John D. Leckenby (1986a), "Relating the Role and Structure of Music to Advertising Response," unpublished working paper, Department of Advertising, University of Texas at Austin, June.

Stout, Patricia A., and John D. Leckenby (1986b), "Measuring Emotional Response to Advertising," *Journal of Advertising*, 15 (4), 35–42.

Stout, Patricia A., and Roland T. Rust (1986), "The Effect of Music on Emotional Response to Advertising," in Ernest Larkin (ed.), *Proceedings of the 1986 Convention of the American Academy of Advertising* (Normoa, Okla.: University of Oklahoma), R82–R84.

Swasy, John L., and James M. Munch (1985), "Examining the Target of Receiver Elaborations: Rhetorical Question Effects on Source Processing and Persuasion," *Journal of Consumer Research*, 11 (March), 877–886.

Taylor, E., and C. Thompson (1982), "Stalking the Elusive 'Vividness' Effect," *Psychological Bulletin*, 89, 155–181.

Taylor, S.E., and S.T. Fiske (1978), "Salience, Attention, and Attribution: Top of Head Phenomena," in L. Berkowitz (ed.), *Advances in Experimental Social Psychology*, vol. 11 (Academic Press: New York).

Teasdale, J.D., and S.J. Fogerty (1979), "Differential Effects of Induced Mood on Retrieval of Pleasant and Unpleasant Events," *Journal of Abnormal Psychology*, 88, 248–257.

Tesser, A. (1978), "Self-Generated Attitude Change," *Advances in Experimental Social Psychology*, 11, 289–338.

Tesser, A., and M. Conlee (1975), "Some Effects of Time and Thought on Attitude Polarization," *Journal of Personality and Social Psychology*, 31, 262–270.

Thistlethwaite, Donald L., Henry de Haan, and Joseph Kamentzky (1955), "The Effects of 'Directive' and 'Nondirective' Communication Procedures on Attitudes," *Journal of Abnormal and Social Psychology*, 51 (July), 107–113.

Thorndike, E.L., and I. Lorge (1944), *The Teacher's Word Book of 30,000 Words* (New York: Bureau of Publications, Teachers College).

Thorson, Esther, and Marian Friestad (in press), "The Effects of Emotion on Episodic Memory for TV Commercials," in Alice Tybout and Pat Cafferata (eds.), *Advertising and Consumer Psychology* (Lexington, Mass.: Lexington Books).

Thorson, Esther, B. Reeves, and J. Schleuder (1985), "Message Complexity and Attention to Television," *Communication Research*, 12 (4), 427–454.

Timmer, Susan Goff, and Lynn R. Kahle (1983), "Birthright Demographic Correlates of Values," in Lynn R. Kahle (ed.), *Social Values and Social Change: Adaptation to Life in America* (New York: Praeger).

Toglia, M.P., and W.F. Battig (1978), *Handbook of Semantic Word Norms* (Hillsdale, N.J.: Erlbaum).

Tomkins, Silvan S. (1980), "Affect as Amplification: Some Modifications in Theory," in Robert Plutchik and Henry Kellerman (eds.), *Emotion: Theory, Research and Experience* (New York: Academic Press).

Toy, Daniel R. (1982), "Monitoring Communication Effects: A Cognitive Structure/Cognitive Response Approach," *Journal of Consumer Research*, 9 (June), 66–76.

Troutman, C.M. (1977), *Processes in Husband-Wife Decision-Making on Health Care Factors*, unpublished Ph.D. dissertation, Kansas State University.

Troutman C.M., and J. Santeau (1976), "Do Consumers Evaluate Products By Adding or Averaging Attribute Information?" *Journal of Consumer Research*, 3, 101–106.

Tsal, Y. (1985a), "Effects of Verbal and Visual Information on Brand Attributes," in E.C. Hirschman and M.B. Holbrook (eds.), *Advances in Consumer Research*, vol. 12 (Provo, Utah: Association for Consumer Research), 265–267.

Tsal, Y. (1985b), "On The Relationship Between Cognitive and Affective Processes: A Critique of Zajonc and Markus," *Journal of Consumer Research*, 12, 358–362.

Tulving, Endel (1972), "Episodic and Semantic Memory," in Endel Tulving and W. Donaldson (eds.), *Organization of Memory* (New York: Academic Press), 381–403.

Tversky, A. (1972), "Elimination by Aspects: A Theory of Choice," *Psychological Review*, 79, 281–299.

Tversky, A., and D. Kahnemann (1973), "Availability: A Heuristic for Judging Frequency and Probability," *Cognitive Psychology*, 5, 207–232.

Tybout, Alice, and Pat Cafferata (1987), *Perspectives on the Affective and Cognitive Effects of Advertising* (Lexington, Mass.: Lexington Books).

Tyler, Sherman W., Paul T. Hertel, Marvin C. McCallum, and Henry C. Ellis (1979), "Cognitive Effort and Memory," *Journal of Experimental Psychology: Human Learning and Memory*, 5 (November), 607–617.

Ullmann, S. (1962), *Semantics: An Introduction to the Study of Meaning* (Oxford: Basil Blackwell).

Vitz, Paul C. (1966), "Affect as a Function of Stimulus Variation," *Journal of Experimental Psychology*, 71 (1), 74–79.

Vygotsky, L. (1962), *Thought and Language* (Cambridge: MIT Press).

Wakshlag, J.J., R.J. Reitz, and D. Zillmann (1982), "Selective Exposure to and Acquisition of Information From Educational Television Programs as a Function of Appeal and Tempo of Background Music," *Journal of Educational Psychology*, 74 (5), 666–677.

Walster, Elaine, and Leon Festinger (1962), "The Effectiveness of 'Overheard' Persuasive Communications," *Journal of Abnormal and Social Psychology*, 65, 395–402.

Ware, J., and R. Williams (1975), "The Dr. Fox Effect: A Study of Lecturer Effectiveness and Ratings of Instruction," *Journal of Medical Education*, 50, 149–156.

Washburn, P.V., and M.D. Hakel (1973), "Visual Cues and Verbal Content as Influences on Impressions After Simulated Employment Interviews," *Journal of Applied Psychology*, 58, 137–140.

Wason, P.C. (1965), "The Contexts of Plausible Denial," *Journal of Verbal Learning and Verbal Behavior*, 4, 7–11.

Wearing, A.J. (1973), "The Recall of Sentences of Varying Length," *Australian Journal of Psychology*, 25, 155–161.

Weiss, D.J., and N.H. Anderson (1969), "Subjective Averaging of Length with Serial Presentation," *Journal of Experimental Psychology*, 82, 52–63.

Weitz, Barton A. (1981), "Effectiveness in Sales Interactions: A Contingency Framework," *Journal of Marketing*, 45 (Winter), 85–103.

Weitz, S. (1974), "Body Movements and Gestures," in S. Weitz (Ed.), *Nonverbal Communication: Readings With Commentary* (New York: Oxford University Press), 127–133.

Wells, William D. (1964), "EQ, Son of EQ, and the Reaction Profile," *Journal of Marketing*, 28 (4), 45–52.

Wells, William D., Clark Levitt, and Maureen McConville (1971), "A Reaction Profile for TV Commercials," *Journal of Advertising Research*, 11 (December), 11–17.

Wheatley, John J., Richard G. Walton, and John S.Y. Chiu (1982), "The Influence of Prior Product Experience, Price, and Brand Name on Quality Perception," in W. Perrault (ed.), *Advances in Consumer Research*, vol. 4 (Ann Arbor: Association for Consumer Research), 72–77.

White, H. (1977), "Whether You Spend a Little Or a Lot, Music Can Color Commercials," *Advertising Age* (December 5), 55.

Wickens, C.D. (1980), "The Structure of Attentional Resources," in R.S. Nickerson (ed.), *Attention and Performance VIII* (Hillsdale, N.J.: Erlbaum).

Wiener, M., S. Devoe, S. Rubinow, and J. Geller (1972), "Nonverbal Behavior and Nonverbal Communication," *Psychological Review*, 79, 185–214.

Wiener, M., and A. Mehrabian (1968), *Language Within Language: Immediacy, a Channel in Verbal Communication* (New York: Appleton–Century–Crofts).

Wilkie, William, and Edgar A. Pessemier (1973), "Issues in Marketing's Use of Multi-Attribute Attitude Models," *Journal of Marketing Research*, 10 (November), 428–441.

Williams, C. (1981), *Tongues of the Spirit: A Study of Pentecostal Gloosolalia and Related Phenomena* (Cardiff: University of Wales).

Williams, R.L. (1979), "Imagery and Linguistic Factors Affecting the Solution of Linear Syllogisms," *Journal of Psycholinguistic Research*, 8, 123–140.

Wittenbraker, John, Brenda Lynn Gibbs, and Lynn R. Kahle (1983), "Seat Belt Attitudes, Habits, and Behaviors: An Adaptive Amendment to the Fishbein Model," *Journal of Applied Social Psychology*, 13, 406–421.

Wong, R. (1973), *A Theory for Integration of Two Source-Adjective Combinations in a Personality Impression Formation Task, unpublished senior honors thesis, University of California, San Diego.*

Worchel, Stephen, Virgina Andreoli, and Joe Eason (1975), "Is the Medium the Message? A Study of the Effects of Media, Communicator, and Message Characteristics on Attitude Change," *Journal of Applied Social Psychology,* 5 (April–June), 157–172.

Wright, Peter L. (1973), "The Cognitive Responses Mediating Acceptance of Advertising," *Journal of Marketing Reserach,* 10 (February), 53–62.

Wright, Peter L. (1974), "Analyzing Media Effects on Advertising Responses," *Public Opinion Quarterly,* 38 (Summer), 192–205.

Wright, Peter L. (1975), "Consumer Choice Strategies: Simplifying Versus Optimizing," *Journal of Marketing Research,* 12, 60–67.

Wright, Peter L. (1980), "Message-Evoked Thoughts: Persuasion Research Using Thought Verbalizations," *Journal of Consumer Research,* 7 (September), 151–175.

Wright, Peter L. (1986), "Schemer Schema: Consumers' Intuitive Theories About Marketers' Influence Tactics," in Richard Lutz (ed.), *Advances in Consumer Research,* vol. 13, 1–3.

Wright, Peter, and Peter Rip (1980), "Product Class Advertising Effects on First Time Buyers' Decision Strategies," *Journal of Consumer Research,* 7 (September), 176–188.

Wyer, Robert S., Jr. (1974), *Cognitive Organization and Change: An Information Processing Approach* (Hillsdale, N.J.: Erlbaum).

Wyer, Robert S., Donald E. Carlston, and Jon Hartwick (1979), "The Role of Syllogistic Reasoning in Inferences Based Upon New and Old Information," in Robert S. Wyer, Jr., and Donald E. Carlston, *Social Cognition, Inference, and Attribution* (Hillsdale, N.J.: Erlbaum), 221–274.

Wicklund, R.A., J. Cooper, and Darwyn E. Linder (1967), "Effects of Expected Effort on Attitude Change Prior to Exposure," *Journal of Experimental Social Psychology,* 3, 416–428.

Young, D.M., and E.G. Beier (1977), "The Role of Applicant Nonverbal Communication in the Employment Interview," *Journal of Employment Counseling,* 14, 154–165.

Yuille, J.C., and A. Paivio (1969), "Abstractness and Recall of Connected Discourse," *Journal of Experimental Psychology,* 82, 467–471.

Zaichowsky, J.L. (1985), "Measuring the Involvement Construct," *Journal of Consumer Research,* 12, 341–352.

Zajonc, R.B. (1968), "Attitudinal Effects of Mere Exposure," *Journal of Personality and Social Psychology Monograph Supplement,* 9 (2), part 2.

Zajonc, R.B. (1980), "Feeling and Thinking Preferences Need No Inferences," *American Psychologist,* 35 (February), 151–175.

Zajonc, R.., and Hazel Marcus (1982), "Affective and Cognitive Factors in Preferences," *Journal of Consumer Research,* 9 (September), 123–131.

Zajonc, R.B., and Hazel Marcus (1985), "Must All Affect Be Mediated by Cognition?" *Journal of Consumer Research,* 12, 363–364.

Zielske, Hubert (1982), "Does Day-After Recall Penalize 'Feeling' Ads?" *Journal of Advertising Research,* 22 (1), 19–22.

Zeigarnik, B. (1927), "Uber das Behalten von Erledigten und Unerledigten Handlungen," *Psychologische Forschungen,* 9, 1–85.

# About the Contributors

**William E. Baker** is Vice-President of Marketing Services at Eric Ericson Advertising in Nashville, Tennessee. He received his Ph.D. in marketing from the University of Florida.

**Rajeev Batra** is associate professor of marketing at Columbia University's Graduate School of Business. He received an MBA from the Indian Institute of Management, an M.S. (advertising) from the University of Illinois, and his Ph.D. from the Stanford Business School. From 1977 to 1979 he was a Brand Manager with Chesebrough-Pond's in India. His research interests include emotional advertising, budgeting and frequency issues, and the attitudinal effects of advertising. His recent publications have appeared in *Journal of Consumer Research, Psychological Processes and Advertising Effects*, and *The Role of Affect in Consumer Behavior*.

**Timothy C. Brock** (Ph.D., Yale, 1960) is professor of psychology at Ohio State University. Beginning with collaboration with Carl Hovland on *Order of Presentation in Persuasion*, Brock has published extensively about the formation, reinforcement, and endurance of beliefs and attitudes about consumer topics ranging from college tuition to preferences for toys, foods, paints, cigarettes, and drugs. His seminal contributions to consumer psychology include the demonstration of the effects of salesperson-consumer similarity on purchasing behavior (instore paint department field experiments) and the important role of cognitive responses in determining acceptance of persuasive messages. The quest underlying 150 articles, chapters, and refereed presentations has been better basic understanding on belief formation and change. Other books include *Psychological Foundations of Attitudes* (with Greenwald and Ostrom), *Cognitive Responses in Persuasion* (with Petty and Ostrom), *Interdisciplinary Research and Doctoral Training* (with L. Comitas), and *Psychology of Persuasion* (in preparation).

**Ernest Dichter** has had a long and distinguished career in marketing. He pioneered motivation research in marketing and is recognized as one of the founding fathers of modern consumer research. He has authored numerous books, including the

*Handbook of Consumer Motivation.* Dr. Dichter's work has influenced several generations of academic and professional marketers. His research has also led to some very memorable advertising concepts, including the slogan, "put a tiger in your tank" for Esso.

**Julie A. Edell** is associate professor of business administration at the Fuqua School of Business at Duke University, where she has taught since receiving her Ph.D. in marketing from Carnegie-Mellon University. Her current research interests concern the affective reactions of consumers to advertising and the various elements of advertising that elicit these reactions. She currently serves on the Editorial Board of *Psychology and Marketing.* Her research has appeared in the *Journal of Consumer Research* and *Advances in Consumer Research.*

**Morris B. Holbrook** is a professor on the faculty of the Graduate School of Business at Columbia University. Professor Holbrook earned his B.A. at Harvard College in English in 1965. He earned an MBA and a Ph.D. in business administration at Columbia University, in 1967 and 1975, respectively. Recently, his work has focused on the consumption experience, with emphasis on its aesthetic and playful components.

**Pamela M. Homer** is an assistant professor in the Department of Advertising at the University of Texas. She completed her doctoral degree in marketing at the University of Oregon.

**Lynn R. Kahle** is an associate professor of marketing at the University of Oregon. He is the author of numerous papers in both psychology and marketing journals. His recent work has focused on the role of values in consumer behavior.

**John D. Leckenby** has held the Everett D. Collier Centennial Chair in Communication in the Department of Advertising in the College of Communication at The University of Texas at Austin since 1985. Prior to that time he was professor and director of graduate studies in the Department of Advertising and research professor in the Institute of Communications Research at the University of Illinois at Urbana-Champaign, where he had been since 1974. He was a Visiting Scholar in the Graduate School of Business and Institute for Communication Research at Stanford University in 1984–85. He has been a Visiting Professor at Young & Rubicam, New York. His research interests are in the areas of copy research and media model research. He is the author of an advertising management text and has published in *Journal of Marketing Research, Journal of Advertising Research, Journal of Advertising, Journalism Quarterly, Journal of Broadcasting,* and several other academic journals.

**Donald Lowry** is associated with Communication Companies International (CCI) of Irvine, California, a consulting organization specializing in the development of interpersonal communication and enhancement of self-esteem.

**Richard J. Lutz** is professor of marketing at the University of Florida. He received his B.S., M.S., and Ph.D. degrees in Marketing from the University of Illinois-Urbana. He was at UCLA for nine years before joining the University of Florida in 1982. Dr. Lutz's primary research interests have been in the area of attitude changes in an advertising context. He has authored over 50 articles and has edited two books. He is currently President-Elect of the Association for Consumer Research and Editor of the *Journal of Consumer Research*.

**M. Carole Macklin** is an associate professor of marketing at the University of Cincinnati. Dr. Macklin received her B.A. in political science and B.S. in education (1969) from The Ohio State University, her MBA (1974) from the University of West Florida, and her Ph.D. (1981) in marketing from Ohio State. Her interests include consumer behavior and advertising, with particular emphasis on advertising directed to children. Dr. Macklin's previous work on advertising effects and methodology has appeared in such journals as *The Journal of Consumer Research, Journal of Advertising Research, Journal of Advertising, Psychological Reports,* and *Journal of Consumer Affairs*.

**Andrew A. Mitchell** is the Patricia Ellison Professor of Marketing in the Faculty of Management at the University of Toronto. He received his Ph.D. from the University of California, Berkeley. His articles have appeared in numerous journals, including *Management Science, Journal of Consumer Research, Journal of Marketing Research,* and the *International Journal of Man Machines Studies*. His current research interests include the effects of mood in an advertising context, identification of moderators of the attitude-behavior relationship, attitude change processes, the measurement of the content and structure of knowledge within a domain, and the development of knowledge-based decision support systems.

**Vernon R. Padgett** is assistant professor of psychology at Marshall University. His interests include applications of social cognition research and factors influencing persuasion.

**Thomas J. Page, Jr.** is assistant professor of marketing at Michigan State University. He received his Ph.D. in marketing from Ohio State in 1983. His research interests include attitude-behavior relationships, information processing, and structural equation modeling. His work has appeared in the *Journal of Marketing Research* and numerous AMA and ACR proceedings. His teaching interests include marketing research and consumer behavior. In addition, he has served as a consultant to numerous research agencies.

**Larry Percy** is Vice President and Director of Corporate Research for HBM/ Creamer in Pittsburgh. He also holds an adjunct faculty appointment in the department of marketing at the University of Pittsburgh. He is co-author (with John

Rossiter) of *Advertising and Promotion Management* and a frequent contributor to the marketing and advertising literature.

**Alan G. Sawyer** is Professor of Marketing and Chair of the Department of Marketing at the University of Florida, which he joined in 1984. He had previously taught at The Ohio State University, University of Massachusetts, and the State University of New York at Buffalo. His Ph.D. is from Stanford University. His research and publications have focused on research methodology and the communication effects of advertising and promotion. Dr. Sawyer is a member of the editorial review boards of the *Journal of Consumer Research, Journal of Marketing,* and *Journal of Marketing Research.*

**James Shanteau,** professor of psychology, received his Ph.D. from the University of California, San Diego, in 1970. Since joining the faculty at Kansas State University, he has held visiting appointments at the University of Michigan, University of Oregon, University of Colorado, and Cornell University. He is recognized for his research on the analysis and training of decision makers. He has over 80 publications in journals, books, chapters, and monographs, including co-authorship of a widely cited 1981 book, *Concepts in Judgment and Decision Research.* He has served on the editorial boards for six scientific journals, including *Organizational Behavior and Human Decision Processes* and *Psychology and Marketing.*

**Patricia A. Stout** is assistant professor of advertising at the University of Texas at Austin. Her Ph.D. in communication is from the University of Illinois at Urbana-Champaign. Her research interests include copy research, emotional response to television advertising, and nonverbal features of advertising. Her work has appeared in the *Journal of Advertising, Psychology & Marketing,* and in a variety of conference proceedings.

**Esther Thorson** is associate professor of journalism and mass communication at the University of Wisconsin-Madison. She holds a Ph.D. in psychology from the University of Minnesota. Her research focuses on how people process television and television commercials, including such topics as emotional influences, overtime processes, program context effects, and physiological responses.

# About the Editors

**Sidney Hecker** is currently Associate Research Director at Young & Rubicam. He joined Young & Rubicam in 1966 after successful experience with SSC&B, *The New York Times* and Gallup and Robinson Research. Current responsibilities include evaluation of advertising research methods, design of new methods, and custom applications for specific client needs.

Dr. Hecker holds a B.S. and an MBA, both from New York University. He majored in marketing, with considerable work in psychology and economic theory. He has taught marketing and advertising at N.Y.U., East Carolina College, and C.U.N.Y. He conducted original work on the theory of subliminal projection while teaching at N.Y.U. His publications include articles on marketing and advertising research and the psychology of hobby activities, as well as a book of photographs. He has spoken at numerous industry conferences, and was Chair of the Advertising Research Foundation Conference on Copy Research, May, 1985, and Co-Chair of the APA Nonverbal Communications Conference in 1986.

**David W. Stewart,** Ph.D. is a member of the marketing faculty at the University of Southern California. Prior to moving to Southern California, he was associate dean and associate professor of marketing at the Owen Graduate School of Management, Vanderbilt University. Dr. Stewart is a past president of the Division of Consumer Psychology and a fellow of the American Psychological Association. He has authored or co-authored four books, *Secondary Research: Sources and Methods* (Sage), *Effective Television Advertising: A Study of 1000 Commercials* (Lexington), *Consumer Behavior and the Practice of Marketing* (Merrill), and *Nonverbal Communication in Advertising* (Lexington). His publications have appeared in the *Journal of Marketing Research, Journal of Marketing, Journal of Consumer Research, Journal of Advertising, Journal of Advertising Research, Academy of Management Journal, Journal of Applied Psychology, Psychology and Marketing,* and *Current Issues and Research in Advertising,* among others. Professor Stewart serves on the editorial boards of the *Journal of Marketing Research, Current Issues and Research in Advertising,* and *Journal of Consumer Marketing.* He is an associate editor of *Psychology and Marketing* and a member of the policy board of the *Journal of Consumer Research.* His research has examined a wide range of issues including advertising effectiveness, consumer information search and decision making, and marketing strategy.

Dr. Stewart received his Ph.D. in psychology from Baylor University. He is a member of Phi Kappa Phi National honorary, Beta Gamma Sigma business honorary, and Alpha Iota Delta decision sciences honorary. He has been honored for innovation in teaching by the Decision Sciences Institute. His experience includes work as a manager of research for a major advertising agency and consulting projects for a wide range of organizations.